A Survivor's Practical Travel Guide to Parish Councils

by

Jean Lowe

A Survivor's Practical Travel Guide to Parish Councils

a Frome Watch series

Volume one

First published as an Ebook 2014
First published as a paper book 2015

A catalogue record for this book is available from the British Library

First published in Great Britain in 2015 by Earthscape Publishing

Published by Earthscape Publishing
Alexandra Road, Frome, Somerset BA11 1LX

Websites:
www.earthscape.co.uk (http://www.earthscape.co.uk)
www.fromewatch.co.uk (http://www.fromewatch.co.uk)

Ebook ISBN 978 0 9929988 0 6
Paper book ISBN 978 0 9929988 1 3

Acknowledgements

My thanks go to all whose comments and knowledge, editing and proof reading have helped to create this chronicle, you know who you are.
But a special mention to James E, Michael E, Tim B and Gerald Q.

FROME HORTICULTURAL SOCIETY DISPLAY AT FROME CHEESE SHOW

A Survivor's Practical Travel Guide to Parish Councils
a FROME WATCH series

The Introduction:
An informative even entertaining look at what goes on.
Why a guide?

Frome:
A Profile: odd and interesting facts about this vibrant market town

The Beginnings:
The back story and a bit of history, how we got to be where we are today and what Frome did

The People:
A lot about Councillors, the organisations they sit on, and those they help fund

The Power:
Allotments, what you can expect "them" to do, what you can do, and a round–up of Planning, the Parish Poll and the annual Parish meeting

The Money:
Who has got it and where it goes

The Processes and the Support:
How it works, what to look out for, the Parish Clerk

The Politics:
Government ideas and legislation, Best Value and Quality Councils, creating and disbanding Parishes, Parties who's who

The Accountability:
How we know what goes on, Freedom of Information Act, Frome's minuted highlights

The Involvement:
Having a go yourself

The Known Unknowns:
6, Frome Short Stories: Tourism, Land Purchases
The Bailey Bridge, The Cheese and Grain, Twinning, Shopping, Shops and Supermarkets

Town Walk:
Every guide book has one; a map and town trail

Thematic Index

The Contents

A VIEW ACROSS FROME FROM WHATCOMBE FIELDS TO CLEY HILL

1 - THE INTRODUCTION

"Quis custodiet ipsos custodes"
Juvenal 1st/2nd Century BC
"Who will protect us from our protectors?"

An informative, relevant, up-to-date even entertaining look at what goes on.
So why a travel guide?

A Travel Guide?

Everyone needs a helping hand when visiting a country for the first time, there are phrases to learn, customs to get used to, mysterious rituals to watch and etiquette to understand.

Every village, hamlet and town across England is organised into a patchwork of Parishes, raising millions of pounds annually (£299 million in 2007-08) from their surrounding communities and run by one of the country's biggest groups of volunteers, Parish Councillors. Whilst they sign up for four years, little is known about what they do. These ordinary people become embroiled in the detailed day to day concerns of Parish life, they are the heart of their Parish Councils. Islands of individuality, unique in local government; this is their story.

The Survivor's Practical Travel Guide to Parish Councils is the story of the complex tapestry of people, groups and organisations of a modest West Country market town whose Parish Council spends, perhaps unexpectedly, close on £l million annually. Chronicling the ambitions of the people and the Councillors of Frome (pronounced Froom). Their failures, successes and near misses.

The Guide follows the events and the decisions Councillors juggled with, against a background of changing government rules, Planning regulations and disquiet over high spending. It could be any Parish.

Delving into the forgotten stories of the past and those that lie behind more recent often sparse news reports. Looking in-depth at events in Frome over roughly a one four year electoral cycle (2007-11).

Included are the effects of decisions by Councillors in the local government tiers above Frome as well as national government's radical changes. Relevant and up-to-date with the latest 2012 to 2014 legislative (for Councillors) and Planning changes which has revolutionised the decision making landscape.

All Parishes are made up of the people who live in them, their clubs and societies, workplaces, homes and shops. All of whom increasingly expect to have a greater say and control over what happens in their Parish. The balance of power has begun to tilt away from the institutions of old, and the lone posses of Councillors who grappled with them. The assumption that involvement ends with the ballot box is changing.

Nationally, as Parishes up and down the country begin to flex their collective muscles. It has become increasingly important for everyone to know where and with whom the power lies and essential to know how to use it.

Accessible, ambitious and a self-help guide. The Survivor's Practical Travel Guide to Parish Councils should, as any good guide: inform, educate, entertain and intrigue.

Practical Tips and Ideas for everyone seen through the townspeople of this small quintessential market town, exploring:

- The unseen world of Parish Councils;
- The twists and turns of life in Frome;
- The dos and don'ts of being a Councillor;
- How "the system" came about, and how it works in practice;
- Understanding and tackling it;
- The ins and out of Planning;
- The money, who spends it;
- Behind the scenes, looking at the labyrinthine workings of local government and how national government fits in;
- Joining in being an activist, being a Councillor, creating a new Parish Council;
- And a general all round useful reference guide.

A Datafile, to dip into and explore. Each section has a list of books and web addresses for further research.

With over 10,000 Parishes in England (Wales has a similar system of Community Councils) the range and size, the traditions, the personalities of people and places varies enormously. Indeed there is something quintessentially English and slightly eccentric about many of them. Their minutes can be masterpieces of understatement, shielding unspoken and hidden undercurrents, yet still capturing the unique flavour of each place, as each Parish interprets its needs, and works out its own solutions.

Who does what
Governmental care and day to day local government administration is provided by District, Unitary, or County Councils and the Metropolitan Boroughs. In Frome, this is provided by Mendip District Council and Somerset County Council. The District Council has distinct set of responsibilities, differing from Somerset County Council's which provides a policy framework as well as having a separate set of responsibilities. The newer Unitary Authorities will combine District and County responsibilities. Despite claims of partnership, any that does take place between the various governmental tiers is often haphazard and sporadic.

A working definition of a Parish Council
A Parish Council provides a framework for community interaction mirroring the area it serves. Establishing policies and actions through its Councillors resulting from consultation with the community and showing direct, demonstrable benefits. Parish Councils are perhaps at their best when responding with small scale targeted support to the detailed needs of identifiable, usually self-identified, groups within the community. They also provide some, albeit it can appear limited, representation for their area to the higher or principal tiers of local government. Parish Councils are the stewards of their Parish, raising money from all the households in their area to provide specified services; spending money prudently, lawfully, and without risk, whilst achieving Best Value.

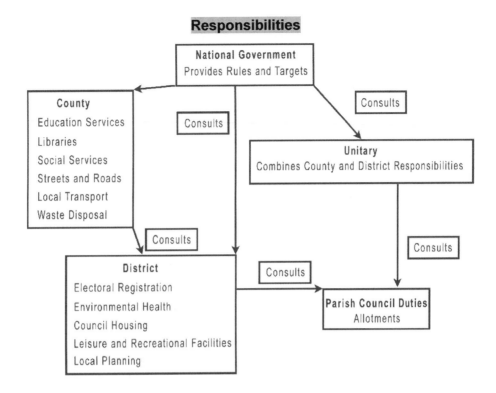

Responsibilities

National Government
Provides Rules and Targets

County
Education Services
Libraries
Social Services
Streets and Roads
Local Transport
Waste Disposal

Consults

Consults

Unitary
Combines County and District Responsibilities

Consults

District
Electoral Registration
Environmental Health
Council Housing
Leisure and Recreational Facilities
Local Planning

Consults

Consults

Parish Council Duties
Allotments

Information for the Guide was gleaned from Town, District and County Council minutes, statements and reports, government websites, the organisations involved, going to Council meetings, talking to those involved, both local and national newspapers and specialist books.

Whilst information has been researched and cross checked, as far as possible, it is general information only and should not be seen as legal or other form of advice. Readers should not rely on this information to make (or refrain from making) any decisions. Always do your own research on top or obtain independent professional advice to ensure it is right for your own specific circumstances. The Datafile is for information only and does not constitute endorsement. Readers should be aware that legislation, particularly legislative guidance notes, interpretations, policies, protocols, procedures and processes as well as websites can change alarmingly quickly. Certainly the 2010 Coalition Government in their first year made almost daily announcements of major policy changes and reverses. Readers should therefore make their own enquiries before embarking upon any course of action.

Key
To make it easier to follow:
- The main text gives a general explanation;
- Grey boxes give specific points of information;
- Sections titled "Frome Watch" look at the happenings in Frome;
- A "Datafile" suggests websites or books for further reading and research;
- Photographs of Frome are scattered throughout;
- An Index at the end.

THE MARKET PLACE FROME

2 - FROME - A PROFILE

Odd and interesting facts about this vibrant market town

Frome is a West Country market town of great charm, with a wealth of beautiful old buildings of warm yellow /grey limestone with a mediaeval centre off steep winding streets; Cheap Street with its open stream running down the centre and cobbled Catherine Hill. Frome nestles in a river valley of the same name in the top right-hand corner of Somerset.

A sociable, unpretentious and friendly town with a determined spirit, a strong sense of community, and with an enormous number and range of organisations and societies. A town always ready to give time and money to a good cause, a town comfortable with itself; a town in which warm spring Sunday mornings bring the sound of church bells and light aircraft lazily looping the loop. Hot summer afternoons are enveloped and enfolded in a miasma of country smells with an added piquancy from the town centre abattoir. Crisp autumns are of carnival and shows, and winter of craft fayres and concerts with the impish delights of Christmas decoration disasters.

It has grown, doubling in size over the last 30 years as incomers, particularly from London, have settled on its leafy banks, many choosing Frome over its more expensive neighbour the City of Bath, or the more urbanised Trowbridge.

With Celtic and Anglo Saxon roots, Frome dates itself from the founding of a church mission on the river by St Aldhelm in AD 685. Mentioned in the Doomsday Book in 1086 the town developed a thriving agricultural market and a cloth industry which grew from the 1300's, prospering, to become one of the most important wool towns in the West of England.

Frome was larger at one point than the nearby Cathedral cities of Bath, or Salisbury in Wiltshire. Competition from the woollen towns of northern England started a decline in the 1800s, with the last woollen mill closing in 1965.

With its more recent large scale industries of brass and iron foundries, breweries, cloth and carpet makers, printing, and chemicals, having faded away it has become a town of small individual enterprises.

Its history has left Frome with more listed buildings than any other town in Somerset (369) including at Grade 1 the Wesleyan Rook Lane Chapel dating from 1707, and the Blue House, almshouses for residents of the Parish built in 1726 (one of 2,000 nationally). The many merchant houses in the town are reminders of the rich history of the West of England's cloth industry and sit cheek by jowl with the humbler cottages of their workers.

Unusually the town bridge is one of only three bridges in the country which has shops and homes on it (the others are Pulteney Bridge in the City of Bath and High Bridge in Lincoln). The town has one of the country's best examples of industrial housing dating from the 1600's in the Trinity area, where narrow streets of terraced houses are built to a grid plan.

Frome largely escaped insensitive post war redevelopment of its historic areas due to lack of money, the vigilance of the newly formed Civic Society - started in the mid 1970's, and the Frome Historic Buildings Trust saving and restoring streets of cottages as well as individual buildings. Despite this, fine buildings were destroyed to become car parks or for road widening.

Since the 1980's older buildings have been increasingly enthusiastically and sympathetically restored. The tree lined housing estates built in the middle of the 20th century have by its end, been superseded by new cramped terraced housing, with small back gardens and no green public open space, reminiscent in many ways of the homes which were demolished 40 years earlier, but with an added emphasis on the car. Streets are dominated by cars lining roads and pavements.

The largest and perhaps the quirkiest of five Mendip towns, it is internationally renowned for its thriving arts, music and crafts community with an annual Frome Festival and a range of arty events in pubs, halls, churches and gardens throughout the year.

There are a number of art galleries, many professional craftspeople work in individual workshops with specialities ranging from designer jewellery and textiles to musical instrument makers and artist blacksmiths.

It is a centre for a myriad of alternative health therapies including acupuncture, homoeopathy and shiatsu. Frome hosts an annual national Town Crier Competition and every September a Carnival of illuminated floats, starting off the West Country Carnival season.

Always with non-conformist tendencies, Frome was said to have had a chapel or a public house for every week of the year. Certainly in 1885 there were 57 public houses listed-18 remain (2011). It is notable now for small specialist shops in the town centre with the larger national chains warehoused on the perimeter.

The town unusually supports two theatres, an outdoor theatre, an independent cinema which uniquely allows beer in the auditorium and two concert cum community venues. It has a Symphony Orchestra, a community radio station, - Frome FM, which can be listened to over the internet and has recently gained a permanent broadcast frequency and a Museum focusing on industrial history which has an extensive research facility.

The street markets continue twice a week Wednesdays and Saturdays, with a weekly livestock, produce and chattel market just outside the town in the hamlet of Standerwick. The annual Cheese Show in September, an agricultural show originally centred around cheeses (there are around 1,000 on display) now hosts regional livestock judging competitions, alongside rural based trade stands, marquees of specialist local foods and crafts With the traditional flower and dog shows and arenas for horse and pony competitions.

Frome has a semi-professional football team (Frome Town) founded in 1904 now in the Evo-stick League Southern League, a Rugby Club over 100 years old with the Frome Cricket Club founded in 1906, playing in the West of England Premier League Somerset division, plus two bowling clubs and two golf courses nearby.

...Frome Watch...

Famous sons of Frome celebrated in 2009:

Benjamin Baker, dates 1840-1907. Born in Keyford Frome (where the fire station is now), he became the Engineer of the Forth Road Bridge in Scotland. Using his new cantilever design it was the longest bridge in Europe at 1.5 miles (2.5 km). A celebratory exhibition showed the design and construction. The bridge built in 7 years, by around 5,000 men was opened in 1890 by the then Prince of Wales.

Jenson Button, born 1980 in Frome. He becoming the Formula One World Champion Racing Driver of 2009 and was given the Freedom of the Town in 2010. Unfortunately, this does not give any particular right or quaint customs unlike the nearby City of Wells or Glastonbury where sheep can be driven down the High Street! He was given a framed scroll. But with an eye to celebration and the tourist pound the new town centre footbridge was named Jenson Button Bridge; there is also a Jenson Road on the out of town industrial estate.

Frome Facts

Population - the 2001 census recorded 24,510 persons or 10,198 households.
Registered voters - 20,450 in April 2010.
Frome is the fourth largest town in Somerset and the largest in Mendip.

The Five Mendip Towns in size order:
- Frome
- Shepton Mallet featured in the 2010 BBC series on the evolution of shops "Turn Back Time."
- Glastonbury of international Festival fame,
- Wells England's smallest cathedral city, and
- Street officially a village,
- with 62 Parishes of villages and hamlets making up Mendip District Council

The 5 District Councils of:
- Mendip,
- Sedgemoor,
- South Somerset,
- Taunton Deane, and
- West Somerset

make up the County of Somerset.

Frome is in the parliamentary constituency of Somerton and Frome and in the South West England European Parliamentary constituency.

Frome was also home to (during 2007-2011):
- A new, much campaigned for hospital (opened 2009) new health centre/health park (started 2011)
- Seven First or Primary schools
- Two Middle schools for ages 9 to 13
- A Secondary school for ages 13 to 18 with media arts status
- Two proposed free schools (2011) a Steiner school for 620 children and Frome Free School for 160 children.

- A Further Education Centre (county run)
- Frome Further Education, a not for profit company (2011)
- 10 churches/chapels/meeting rooms
- A Performing Arts Academy
- A municipal Leisure Centre
- A Library
- Tourist Information Centre, now part of Town Council from 2010
- A railway station on the Bristol to Weymouth line, only remaining Through Train Shed designed by the railway engineer Isambard Kingdom Brunel 1850
- A Fire station and volunteer brigade
- A section of the National Cycle Route No 24
- A Millennium Green
- A gas lit Valentine Lamp, with celebrations every Valentine's Day
- An annual Well Dressing ceremony
- An annual Cobble Wobble for 200 Cyclists aged from10 to 60 years
- A Bailey bridge, one of three of its type, demolished (2010)
- A Farmers Market, monthly on a Saturday
- A Country Market, - formally WI - weekly on a Thursday
- The Catherine Hill Artisans Market, monthly on summer Sundays
- The Frome Lottery
- A travelling fair in September and 3-4 times a year
- A circus in the autumn and spring
- A Gypsy camp of 28 pitches
- A Talking Newspaper
- Two weekly local Newspapers (one closed May 2011)
- One fortnightly local paper
- The De La Beche geological unconformity at Vallis Vale
- The "Frome Hoard" 52,500 Roman coins (2010)
- The Vallis Vegetable Box scheme (suspended 2011)
- Frome Town Youth Band
- Keyford and The Mount Community Gardens
- A vinyl record shop (one of around 269 in the country)
- An independent book shop (one of around 1,200 in the country)
- A tobacconist shop
- A launderette
- An auction house - auctions twice monthly
- Three sub-post offices
- Two Car share schemes
- Two film clubs
- A Credit Union
- Rodden Nature Reserve
- Otters on the river
- Four areas for industry and commerce
- An Adult Training Centre (FETE)

- 3 Eastern European Big Issue sellers replacing the 3 or 4 Gypsy lucky white heather sellers
- Occasional street musicians and regular ones
- The Griffin Brewery one of 1,009 small breweries nationally (2012)
- An occasional beggar and a regular beggar
- The Bastion /Alcove Garden
- Burne-Jones stained glass church windows in Trinity Church
- A cemetery and a Dissenters cemetery
- A Police Station, a Magistrates Court (closed 2011) and a Police Post
- Frome TV via the internet
- Thursday half day closing (for independent shops)
- and a Transition Town with a Slow Food movement group and a Food Frome research group

Frome Town Council Budgets

Year	Budget
1976/1977	£9,941.94 (roughly £46,000 to-day)
1990/1991	£148,256 (roughly £240,000 to-day)
2000/2001	£399,978 (roughly £543,000 to-day)
2005/2006	£588,592
April 2006 to 2007	£627,836
April 2007 to 2008	£800,000
April 2008 to 2009	£827,390
April 2009 to 2010	£800,561
April 2010 to 2011	£914,879

Frome has always been a high spending Council. Budgets originally centred on the concerns of parks and hanging baskets, of Councillor Twinning trips, and the annual grant giving. Later more ambitious councils added staff and as the budget climbed, a layer of unexpected sophistication developed with a determination to be an economic powerhouse, and a business in its own right.

Datafile

The Book of Frome by Michael McGarvie published by Barracuda Books 1980
The Making of Frome by Peter Belamy published by Frome Society for Local Study 1985
Portrait of Frome, published by Mendip District Council Dec 2008
English Heritage, www.englishheritage.org.uk
National Archives,www.nationalarchives.org.uk
Measuring Worth, www.measuringworth.org.uk
Bank of England, www.bankofengland.org.uk
Somerset Intelligence Network, www.sine.org.uk

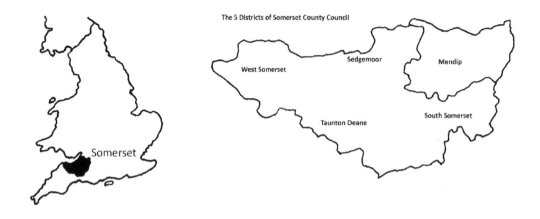

The 5 Districts of Somerset County Council

West Somerset

Sedgemoor

Mendip

Taunton Deane

South Somerset

Somerset Towns

The Bristol Channel and Coast

Weston-super-Mare

Bath

Mendip Hills

Radstock

Trowbridge

Wells

FROME

•Shepton Mallet

Exmoor National Park

Somerset Levels

Glastonbury

Quantock Hills

Street

The County of Wiltshire

Somerton

Taunton

Yeovil

The County of Devon

The County of Dorset

3 - BEGINNINGS - A History

The back story and a bit of history, how we got to be where we are today and what Frome did

The Parish Council system developed from the mediaeval period, with our present system of local government to a greater extent the result of a flurry of nineteenth century reforms.

In Saxon times Frome headed the largest and wealthiest Hundred (administrative area) in Somerset, with two substantial Charter markets. The town's listing in the Domesday Survey of 1086 underlines its importance. In the Middle Ages, local government was limited to law and order which was shared between the Manor and the Hundred Courts. But, with the breakdown of the manorial courts system in Tudor times, the government looked for another structure.

From the reign of Elizabeth I the Parish Vestry had had responsibility for the care of the poor and aged, and the maintenance of roads within its area. The Church, with its system of Parishes was an ideal organisational base, and the only nationwide organisation with literate people in authority. Everyone had to be a member of their local church and attend regularly; the church levied tithes - a tenth of the produce from land and stock usually in-kind.

The whole body of parishioners met to vote money for church purposes and to elect at least one of the churchwardens. It was the ideal structure to deal with local matters. Meeting in the only building which could hold everyone, the church, were the Officers of the Vestry; the Church Warden, Constables, Parish Clerk, Waywardens and from 1601, the Overseer of the Poor. These men were elected yearly.

Parliament gave the Vestry duties to look after the poor in 1536, to register baptisms, marriages and later burials in 1538. The responsibility for maintaining the highways within their Parish boundaries came in 1555. In 1601 Parishes were allowed to levy a Rate (a property tax) to fund the Parish. This would have applied to only the few wealthy households in any Parish.

The Officers of the Vestry were:
- The Church Warden, who was responsible for pest control, the upkeep of the church and later for collecting the Rate;
- The Constables, up to six in any village maintained order and kept the stocks and the lockup,
- The Parish Clerk, the only paid officer who had to be over 20 years of age, kept the minutes and the accounts so had to be competent at reading, writing and even singing – as he may also have led the singing in church;
- Finally, the two Waywardens or Surveyor of Highways who made sure the roads were maintained and repaired. All householders were obliged to provide initially, four days labour (later increased to six days) each year with local farmers providing horses and carts;
- Later the Overseers of the Poor, who dealt with unmarried mothers, absconding parents, issued paupers badges and found the poor work.

These posts were unpaid despite carrying considerable duties and those elected were compelled to serve, albeit sometimes reluctantly. They were overseen by the Justices of the Peace meeting in Quarter Sessions. They could order Parishes and Parish officers to carry out their duties and acted as an appeal court against decisions made by the Parish or its officers.

With the growth of towns, changing agricultural practices (including the Inclosures of Common Land), increasing industrialisation and long wars with France, by the 19th Century Parishes were finding it difficult to cope with the social and financial burdens. Many built poorhouses where the sick and aged poor could be accommodated, others, such as Frome, provided workhouses where poor people could be employed as well as helped. Small payments called "outdoor relief" (for those not in the poor houses) were also given, raised by the Parish Rate.

In Frome there was an alarming increase from a constant of around £1,971 (roughly £190,000 in today's value) to £3,125 (roughly £250,000 today) in the first two years of the Napoleonic Wars from 1793-95 despite Frome supplying the fine black broadcloth for British soldier's uniforms for which it was famed. Even in 1882, 5,000 townspeople including children worked in the woollen cloth industry, this was around half the town.

The Poor Laws of 1834 enabled Parishes to group into Unions to build the new purpose built Workhouses to a national template, and use the later Highways Act of 1862 to provide road building and maintenance. Despite attempts to get the Frome poor to emigrate to Canada in the early 1830s and the building of a new Workhouse, the poor rate had, by 1836, risen to £11,723, (roughly £1 million today) a colossal burden on the very few ratepayers but also pointing to the extent of their wealth.

The Frome Union was overseen by a Board of Guardians including the Justices of the Peace for the area and other members elected by local ratepayers in each Union, the higher paying ratepayers having more votes. Outdoor relief was administered by the Union under much stricter controls, and tests of need were applied. They provided education for children and Parliament later extended their role to include the Registration of Births, Marriages and Deaths. The Unions organised: the periodic censuses, Vaccination, the Assessment and Valuation of property, School Attendance (in areas where there was no other organising authority, such as a borough, existed), and Infant Life Protection.

The Frome Guardians met initially in the Magistrates room in Justice Lane before leasing offices, on the corner of Bath Street and Palmer Street until 1890 paying Lord Bath £35 per year. With the lease ending the Union bought land "Behind Town" from the Marquess of Bath and commissioned a Renaissance palace with a sweeping staircase from architects Anderson and Halliday. Joseph Bird, a builder from Radstock, undertook the building which beginning in June 1890 finished the following year. Local stone from a nearby quarry in The Butts was used for the walls and Bath freestone for the ornament.

It was the first purpose built offices in Frome. The Public Offices today, on present day Christchurch Street West, are occupied by the County Council.

With no public supply of pure water, with only the most primitive sanitation and without any planned means of sewage disposal, epidemics of cholera led to the passing of the Public Health Act of 1848.

The Act encouraged (but did not enforce) the setting up of local Boards of Health. The Boards which levied rates, were elected by ratepayers who also got more votes the more they paid (up to 6 votes).

The Frome Local Board set up in 1865 had as its chairman for ten years, Alderman Flatman who is commemorated in a clock above the Public Offices which the Local Board shared with the Guardians. He also donated an ornamental fountain in nearby Victoria Park in celebration of the Queen's Jubilee (said to be stored in one of the sheds). In the thirty years of its existence the Board established waterworks, a sewerage scheme, the Cottage Hospital in Castle Street for infectious diseases, and a recreation ground.

The Public Health Act of 1875, created compulsory local sanitary districts, based on the Poor Law Unions. They were responsible for, amongst other things, sewerage, water supplies, scavenging that is household waste collection, the control of nuisances, treatment of infectious diseases, and the provision of allotments.

The Local Boards were transformed into Urban or Rural District Councils in the Local Government Act of 1894. Locally, the surrounding Parishes were grouped into a Rural District Council which included Selwood, a large part of the old Parish of Frome, with Frome itself becoming the Urban District Council.

The elections for Council places were held on 15th December 1894, the Act gave one vote to all who were entitled to vote at parliamentary elections (very few) and the civil functions of the Parish Vestries were given to the new Parish Councils. Women were entitled to vote in Parish Council elections under the Municipal Franchise Act 1869. This gave voting rights (in local elections) to women ratepayers who could also become Poor Law Guardians.

The new Frome Urban District Council (UDC) had 15 seats which were contested by 28 candidates. However, 13 of the old Local Board were elected to the new body, many whose names still resonate in the town today gaining the number of votes today's Councillors would be proud of : Charles Bailey - wine and spirit merchant topped the poll with 739 votes followed by J.W Singer - metal worker with 624. Others elected: Joseph Tanner, Edward Trotman and Benjamin Butcher - gentlemen, E.G Ames - solicitor, James Bartholomew - hairdresser, Henry and Samuel Rawlings - manufacturers, John Hodder - retired builder, Joseph Chapman - marble worker, and auctioneers Charles Cooper and Thomas Harding. The newcomers were Frederick Weeks – printer, and Joseph Heath - carpenter.

The new Council had the wide scope of the Local Board and powers which gave it remarkable autonomy including: a waterworks engineer, a surveyor, a sanitary inspector, an accountant, a rent collector and a medical officer of health. All to oversee a population of 11,057 as recorded in the census of 1901 (it is around 28,000 today).

Under the UDC the town was gifted many of its gems, built as the result of public subscription, which the Council was then given to maintain. The Victoria Park created in 1887, the Victoria Baths off Rook Lane one of the first public swimming baths in the country to be raised by public subscription in 1899. The Council later added more recreational areas around the town and was given the Mary Bailey Playing Field in 1930.

The Memorial Hall (on Christchurch Street West) later theatre was built by subscription for the fallen of the Great War came under Frome UDC control to which it later added the Assembly Rooms before its own demise.

The Market Hall which had been originally built by the Frome Market Company in 1874, was taken over by Frome UDC in 1946 who moved its community usage to a replacement wooden hall in 1964, this once stood next to the present day library in the Market Yard Car Park.

...Frome Watch...
What was provided

Frome Urban District Council provided: town sewers and sewerage works, council housing, toilets, allotments, planning and building control, parks, markets, public health, abattoirs, finance and legal services, democratic representation, highways, cemeteries, refuse-collection and disposal.

Considerable public housing was started initially after World War One on Nunney Road and Summerhill with 143 built, gaining apace after World War Two with the conversion of dilapidated properties at the top of Trinity Street. A further 275 new houses were built with plans for another 250 made. The Council also maintained the roads, demolishing and widening at North Parade, Badcox, Gorehedge, Butts Hill and Rodden Road.

It later drew up plans to provide a radical inner ring road cutting through the historic centre providing an additional river crossing and finally the pedestrianisation of the Market Place - still being considered today, with the demolition of much of Frome's historic heart in favour of four new 1960's shopping malls. With no money to fund these schemes, they were narrowly avoided and later abandoned.

Frome Urban District Council purchased North Hill House (a fine Georgian mansion) and 7.3 acres of land for £5,750 (roughly £124,000 today, not even the present day price of a two bedroom house) for Council Offices in 1955. It had been the home of the Le Gros Family. Philip Le Gros, a clothier who had become a partner in Thompson's Silk and Crepe Mills in Merchants Barton – it is craft and arts workshops today. The family had given North Parade Gardens, later renamed "Murrhardt Gardens", (after Frome's German twin town) to the town in 1953 under the Theodora Le Gros Open Space Trust.

...Frome Watch...
Local Wages - 1970

* The Victoria Swimming Bath attendant earned £14.2s (roughly £185 today) for a 40 hour week, but with summer overtime, it rose to £19 (roughly £250)
* Shepton Mallet Prison offered £948 - £1,292 per annum (roughly £12,500 - £17,000 today) plus free accommodation.
* Farm workers asked for a raise from £13.3d (roughly £170 today) for a 43 hour week to £18 (roughly £236 today) for 40 hours

Eighty years later in 1972 it all came to a shuddering halt when local government was again reorganised (Local Government Act 1972) to create larger administrative areas that the government of the day decided were more efficient and economic without being less democratic.

The town however lost all of its power and autonomy to both the newly created Mendip District Council and Somerset County Council.

The Urban District of Frome was joined with the Boroughs of Wells and Glastonbury, the Urban Districts of Street and Shepton Mallet and the Rural Districts of Frome, Shepton Mallet and Wells to form the Mendip District Council. This was one of the five Districts into which the new and now smaller County of Somerset was divided; it lost the City of Bath to the newly created Wansdyke.

From 1st April 1974 the Urban District Council (UDC) ceased to exist and was replaced by a Successor Parish Council becoming Frome Town Council with a newly created title of Mayor for the Chairman of the Council. With little power it would exist to act as a voice for the opinions and aspirations of Frome. Disquiet had been voiced during the January 1974 UDC meeting by Councillor H.M. Scott, *"one of the chief arguments in favour of the reorganisation was that it would bring local government nearer to its grass roots, instead it is being taken further away from the people and the interests of Frome are being absorbed into a larger area and Frome people's control diminishing."*

Overall, there was surprisingly little discussion reported in the local newspaper, and although the Council felt unease about losing control of buildings and land, its opposition was muted. Councillor H.M. Scott spoke again of the passing out of Frome's control of every item of her heritage and added, *"The senior officers will build up a big Empire. There is no doubt about that. It is on the way already. There are a number of obvious things which ought not to pass out of the control of Frome people,"* unfortunately he does not say what these were. The general mood was conciliatory the Council would wait and see, and hope that perhaps it could retain some control over the amenity land and act as an agent for the new authority.

From a workforce of 32, the new Town Council would only employ the current Parish Clerk, Mr T.A.Towndrow and only part-time. The Somerset Standard newspaper reported Mr Towndrow's disgruntled comments, *"even Street Town Council are employing a Clerk full time on £2,000 per year"* (roughly £17,000 today).

Frome was represented on the new Mendip District Council by seven Councillors and the Town Council kept the same 15 members who were on the Urban District Council until elections in 1976. The Town Clerk rented an office in the Public Offices on Christchurch Street West which also housed the Frome Rural District Council.

North Hill House was given to Mendip District Council who used it until 1985 when it was sold to Mendip Dairy Crest, cheese processors, for their company headquarters. North Hill House is currently a private school. This loss resulted in feelings of bitter resentment and accusations of town assets "stolen". An anger which still persists today as successive Councils including the 2007-11 Council perhaps hoping to regain lost prestige continue in the perennial hunt for new offices.

...Frome Watch...

Notable Frome MP's:

- Liberal and social reformer Thomas Hughes 1868-74 wrote several novels including "Tom Brown's School Days", based on his and his brothers experiences at Rugby School.
- Mary "Maybird" Tate Conservative MP 1935-45 and an equal pay for women campaigner, raced 166 pigeons of the Radstock Fellowship Homing Society from Birmingham to Radstock in a light aircraft, the Foxhound II, setting down on Frome's edge of town airstrip -The Gypsy Lane Flying Ground.

The Flying Ground was later used as a secret airfield in World War II enabling the Chiefs of Staff to plan the D Day Landings. She covered the 92 miles in 62 minutes before driving to end the race at Radstock, the fastest pigeon took 3 hours and 27 minutes.

Frome was, and is, the largest town in Mendip; however the new headquarters for the new District Council were built at Shepton Mallet which is geographically central. Frome today still feels sidelined, ignored, and undervalued with its problems unheard and unnoticed as the District focuses on its "prettier" sister towns. Curiously, District Council jobs are not advertised in Frome local papers nor are many Public notices or information announcements such as auditing inspection dates or District Councillors allowances and expenses, so the feeling of antipathy is in part justified.

Somerton

Somerton shot to fame (October 2009) when 12 of Somerton Town Council's 15 members resigned after their decisions were heavily criticised in an internet blog "Muck & Brass".

This can be seen in a wider context; Frome had a proud parliamentary tradition and was a parliamentary borough from 1832 to 1885 returning mainly Liberal MPs, before being absorbed into the Wells constituency. Frome reappears in 1983 to be part of the new Parliamentary constituency of Somerton and Frome - an awkwardly shaped area and looking not unlike a boot. Somerton in the west of the constituency is a small market town of around 8,000 inhabitants. There is no contact, economic or social ties between the two towns and it appears an arbitrary pairing, made seemingly more unfair when Frome as the larger town takes second place in the constituency title!

Frome Town Council in the 1980's leased St John's Church cottage next to St John's Church renting out the lower rooms to the Citizens Advice Bureau. However, something grander was wanted than two small rooms. A 20% hike in the precept for 1988 would in part go to fund new offices and pay for a full time Town Clerk as the town budgeted for £135,000 (roughly £307,000 today).

The present day Palmer Street offices had previously been a shop - Walwin Gentleman's Outfitters and was bought in 1991 for the sum of £75,000. The Town Council took out loans from the Public Works Loan Board for £65,000 over 15 years at £8,500 per annum. It was estimated at the time that there would be £30,000 worth of repairs to do.

The move was controversial as the Council employed only one part-time office staff besides the Town Clerk providing similar provision for the town up to 2011. However the Council itself felt it was a bargain as the shop was initially on the market for £100,000 though local opinion thought even the final price of £75,000 (roughly £137,000 today) was steep.

A Town Meeting solely about the purchase met in the January of 1991 and asked the Town Council to look into alternatives beginning with the Memorial Hall. The Council at the time was heavily involved in paying off a loan to Mendip District Council on behalf of the Hall. The Meeting pointed out pedestrian access was a problem, with steps into the former shop off a narrow footpath and parking an ongoing difficulty in narrow Palmer Street. At one time the Council produced its own parking exemption badges for Councillors to get round the problem, "allowing" parking on the yellow lines. Again the purchase cost and the cost of ongoing maintenance was considered prohibitive.

The loss of a town centre shop, the Meeting said would undermine trade in the town. Despite the voted resolutions of the Meeting asking the Council to reconsider, it went ahead. The Council arguing that the flat above the shop and the rental of some of the surplus office space mitigated the overall cost.

With the loan paid off, the Town Council has investigated various options to relocate, citing pedestrian access and parking as a problem and a proposed increase to around 8 office staff. It recently precepted £167,000 into an Earmarked Reserve and looked for a more central location; buildings considered have included the Zion Chapel, offices in King Street and it was rumoured, the Police Station.

The last ten years has brought rafts of local government legislation, some of which has tweaked what Parish Councils can do, but for the most part their powers are still based on the 1972 Local Government Act.

Downhead – a Parish Meeting

A scattered hamlet, off the beaten track a few miles from Frome once part of the Portland Estate, with its unique house numbering system. (The houses of the whole Estate were numbered consecutively from No1 Portland Place reaching the 900s at Downhead). With just a church and a telephone box as its public facilities - the Parish bought the building which was the Old Bakehouse turning it into a bus shelter for school children waiting for school buses. It shares a common modern problem with other small villages with many houses to rent or as holiday cottages there are few people to take up issues. The Parish Meetings, which still take place in the church, revolve around commenting on planning applications, organising village events with the modest precept of around £600 used to take care of the churchyard and to provide salt for the roads. Speeding traffic, loose dogs and grass verges are intermittent problems. There are around 50 electors.

Parish Meetings

Not all Parishes have a large enough population to form a Council so they hold Parish Meetings at least twice a year, or as the need arises. They have the same powers as a Parish Council. A Chairman and Clerk are elected at the annual meeting of electors which takes place between the 1st March and the 1st June. Meetings cannot begin earlier than 6 o'clock in the evening or take place on licensed premises. Any Parish property such as bus shelters, village greens, allotments are held by the Parish trustees: the Meeting chairman and some-one appointed by the District Council. The Meeting publication scheme will give information on who's who, budgets and spending, minutes, strategies and priorities.

Smallest Parish Council?

One of the smallest Parish councils in England is Erringden near Hebden Bridge, covering just 50 or so houses and about 190 inhabitants.

Previously Parishes with 200 or less electors could form Parish Meetings. This has been reduced to 150 for new Parishes by The Local Government and Public Involvement in Health Act 2007. Existing Parish Councils of 150 or less electors will continue. For Parishes which have between 151 and 999 electors, the Principal Council (District or Unitary) can decide whether to create a Parish Council or a Parish Meeting. With over 1,000 electors there is a duty to create a Parish Council.

Datafile
English Heritage Extensive Urban Survey, Clare Gathercole,
www.somerset.gov.uk/archives
The Book of Frome by Michael McGarvie published by Barracuda Books 1980
The Making of Frome by Peter Belamy published by Frome Local History Study Group
1985

FROME TOWN BRIDGE with shops

4 - PEOPLE - Councillors

"You can fool some of the people all of the time, and all of the people some of the time, but you cannot fool all of the people all of the time," Abraham Lincoln.

A lot about Councillors, the organisations they sit on and those they help with funding.

Councillors have traditionally been seen as male and elderly. Television and film has characterised them into a set of clichés: the bluff old colonel, the buffoon, the strident female - probably a spinster, the wheeler dealer - probably a builder, the harassed neurotic mother, and the bully, all in turn pompous and self-aggrandising.

Some criticisms do hit home. Somerton, Frome's sister constituency town was surprised by the mass resignation of 12 of its Councillors (October 2009) the result of criticism on the internet blog site "Muck & Brass". Somerton's 15 member Parish Council needed a quorum of 5, meaning the remaining Councillors were unable to make decisions.

South Somerset District Council, the controlling authority appointed 6 District Councillors, based on the political balance, to act as temporary Town Councillors, so that any urgent decisions could be made. Major decisions such as setting the Budget and commenting on Planning applications were deferred until the new Council was in place (about a couple of months). 20 people came forward when the 12 vacancies for permanent Councillors were advertised. The election took place (January 2010) during some of the worst snows in Somerset for 30 years, special buses were laid on to ferry voters to the polls. The turnout was a creditable 38%.

A police investigation centred around allegations of fraud over the Town Council's sale of land at Etsome Terrace, the purchase of a warehouse and its conversion into a community hall (2008/09) at Somerton Business Park. 3 Councillors and the Town Clerk were arrested, released on bail and later released without charge. The Audit Commissions Public Interest Report (Feb 2012) highlighted "significant failings... demonstrating an abuse of public funds", and "failure to follow proper procedures may have resulted in unlawful expenditure", including:

- not getting the best price for Etsome Terrace,
- buying a business unit and converting it into a hall not knowing if it was needed in terms of size, type and location,
- paying more than it needed for the hall,
- failure to budget and monitor costs and an inability to explain the doubling in expenditure,
- holding informal unminuted meetings so not all Councillors could be aware of all the facts.
- proper Declarations of Interest were not made by two Councillors.

The 2½ year inquiry cost around £60,000. Somerton has since tightened its procedures.

The Auditor also recommended training for Councillors and the Town Clerk.

Parish Councillors see themselves as volunteers albeit they stood for election, there are no qualifications, no particular knowledge is needed and there is no need to be a supporter of a political party.

Anyone can stand for election.
Whilst it is usually unpaid, unlike Councillors in the higher tiers of local government where there is a basic allowance - which has become increasingly generous with time, expenses can still be claimed.

Most Councillors when asked why they wanted to become involved with their Parish Council, say it is because they *"want to make a difference"* or *"to put something back"*, and are heart-warmingly idealistic, hoping to use skills honed in other areas of life. Many have a strong sense of place and see themselves as fiercely independent, championing the causes of their home turf and that of the ordinary person. Holding out against the juggernaut of the state, righting the wrongs of the higher tiers of local government bureaucracies and trouncing developers. However, for some Councillors, there is an element of feudalism and listening to the electorate is undertaken with a deep sense of dispensing largesse. The days in office may be full of heady self-importance but when they have left, their trace rarely lingers let alone leaving anything that can be glamorised as a legacy. For others, election confers wisdom and any further electoral consultation is seen as unnecessary. Some are fiercely defensive, with the electorate caricatured as an ungrateful and difficult child, with any challenge unwelcome and spoken of as a vexatious interruption inevitably creating a lack of transparency compounded by a dismissive attitude. Others are quietly collaborative, inventive and simply get on with it. The public at large looks upon being a Councillor as simply applying common sense and often have surprisingly high expectations in their abilities to tackle any problem and get instant results - a view often held by Councillors themselves. Many are in fact handling issues, decisions and budgets with very little knowledge or experience.

For those wanting to be involved in their local community being a Councillor is the ideal opportunity, particularly for the retired. There is still a bit of kudos in some quarters and there is a delight in being *"in the know"*, the excitement of spending other people's money, knowing that what you think or say effects the lives of others and there is nothing they can do about it. The public may not share in any of these beliefs and if anything have become increasingly cynical about the effectiveness and motives of Councillors; this may be reflected in the low voter turnout at local elections.

As in any walk of life, Councillors vary in temperament and ability. Not all have strong political views, or views which align with any political party. Many do hold to the general view that Parish Councils should be collaborative, consensual and community builders but in practice Councillors can also be, bigoted, spiteful, meddlesome and combative, gleefully pillorying fellow Councillors ideas.

Rather bafflingly, Parish Councillors are considered with some disdain by fellow Councillors in the higher tiers of local government (Unitary, District or County), even though some may also sit on them or have progressed up from Parish level.

...Frome Watch...

Ambitious Councillors

Many take it further. Ex-Mendip District Councillor, ex-Frome Town Councillor and ex-Mayor Jim Knight became a Member of Parliament (MP) for Dorset South in 2001 and 2005 (after failing in 1997). He was later a junior minister, then a Minister of State in the Brown Labour Government before losing his seat in 2010 and becoming Lord Weymouth. Frome optician David Heath became the MP for Somerton and Frome in 1997, 2001, 2005, and 2010 after previously being a Somerset County Councillor and Leader. A Liberal Democrat in the 2010 Coalition government, he became the Deputy Leader of the House of Commons, later agricultural minister.

Twice ex-Mayor and Frome and Mendip District Councillor Bob Ashford stood twice as a Labour Party parliamentary candidate for Somerton and Frome in 1992 and 1997. Frome Mayor (2009/10) and ex-Conservative and latterly Liberal Democrat Councillor Damon Hooton stood in the 2010 election as a Liberal Democrat parliamentary candidate for Swindon South. Frome Town Councillor and Deputy Mayor (2010-11) David Oakensen stood as the Labour parliamentary Candidate for Somerton and Frome in 2010. More recently, in the House of Commons, only one MP was also a Parish Councillor. David Drew the MP for Stroud lost his seat in 2010 and had been a Stonehouse Parish Councillor for over 20 years.

The Government has tried to remedy the antipathy it felt the higher tiers of local government showed to their Parishes, by encouraging the Quality Council Scheme for Parish Councils. Hoping that dealing with a certified Parish Council would encourage District, County and Unitary authorities to work more collaboratively and share some of the decision making. Parish Councillors have found the higher tiers frustrating and obstructive particularly when it has become part of an ingrained culture which affects officers, who do the day to day administration, as well as Councillors. Parishes also hoped the move from a three tier to a two tier system with the introduction of Unitary authorities would be the opportunity to takeover some responsibilities of the defunct District Councils. Unitary authorities were not necessarily of the same opinion.

Little is known of the general views of Parish Councillors. However, the Local Government Association publishes a biennial national census of local authority Councillors, surveying Councillors in the tier above Parish level and making a comparison with ten years ago.

The 2008 survey discovered:
- Over two thirds were male, the remaining third of women was barely higher than it was ten years previously;
- The average age had increased from just over 55 to nearly 59;
- Over 96% were white;
- Over half held a position of special responsibility within their authority and over half received an additional payment for this work on top of the basic allowance;
- 88% considered themselves effective or very effective; however this was a slight drop on the previous 2006 survey;
- Again, around 88% said they were Councillors because of a desire to serve the community;
- A remarkable 22 hours was reported to be spent on Council and/or political work each week;
- Over 60% thought key services such as health and police should be more accountable to them;
- 40% thought Councillors should have a devolved personal budget to spend on local amenities or initiatives (Somerset County Councillors had £10,000 per year until budgetary cuts abolished the grant);
- Over half would stand again at the end of their term of office and over 80% would recommend standing to a friend.

A survey of the opinions of all 17 Frome Parish Councillors undertaken in 2010 resulted in only three replies (see Accountability).

After an election, all Councillors are automatically on the Full or main Council Committee. In small Parishes there may be only the one Council Committee. In larger Parishes, Councillors can put themselves forward for more than one of the main Committees; some will be unique to the Parish or may be more general such as Planning, finance, or playing fields. The Full or main Council has - by law - to meet four times a year; (twice if it is a Parish Meeting) many will meet monthly. Some Parishes have a separate Planning Committee so that the Parish does not fail to discuss and report back on Planning issues within the 21 day time-frame that the local Planning authority works to, others just miss the deadline some Parishes do request a time extension. Temporary working parties and subcommittees may be created as and when necessary when a smaller number of people are needed to tackle a single issue. These groups report to the Committee that spawned them. However, Councillors often find enthusiasm taking the place of discernment and it is all too easy to give an issue its own Committee or working group. This can take up a huge amount of time and create vast amounts of paperwork out of all proportion to what can be or will be achieved. Such enthusiasms should always be treated with caution.

If there is a dominant political party, their voting choices for a Committee will be carried, as they will have - when the appointments are voted on – a majority. On an unpopular Committee or where numbers need to be made up, occurring: when Councillors who also sit on higher tiers have little time to spare; or if a particular specialisation is needed; or an unexpectedly elected Councillor with no plans to take an active part has to be replaced, other Councillors may be allotted, even to a Committee of their choice. The dominant party in all cases will try to ensure it has a majority.

Compared to Councillors in the higher tiers of local government, a Parish Councillor is said (Government statistics) to spend about 3 hours a week on Council work. This will include attending meetings, reading agendas, briefing documents and minutes of meetings plus responding to approaches from parishioners. The Mayor as a representative of the whole community will be invited to attend functions and events, such as opening fêtes, giving presentations, occasionally meeting with representatives of other Government bodies and campaigning organisations. The chairman of the various Committees which includes the Mayor, who is chairman of the whole Council, will spend time approving minutes before they are circulated and adding agenda items to a basic agenda plus progress chasing Committee decisions via the Parish Clerk who co-ordinates between any staff, other organisations and Councillors.

It can come as a surprise to new Councillors that there are additional opportunities for volunteering, in many cases they will be expected to do so, and sit on the management Committees of other organisations - the whimsically named Outside Bodies. These can be Parish Trusts, public institutions such as schools, other local authority Committees, local charities or community groups, many of whom may have a long association with the Parish Council, often receiving regular grant funding. These appointments can be divided up on a personal preference basis, though the dominant party will probably wish to cherry pick. For a Councillor dropped into a situation with no previous knowledge, it can be a very steep learning curve making it difficult to judge what value they bring. The time commitment involved will vary greatly between organisations and of course what Councillors are prepared to do.

These appointments are notionally for a year but many enthusiastically continue even when not appointed by the Council or even a Councillor. Alternatively the Council can appoint a person who is not a Councillor but who they think is appropriate to fill a vacancy and represent the Parish. Outside Bodies accept whoever they are given. Councils should monitor attendance and ask for a regular report or a review of activities and a Councillor should declare a disclosable non-pecuniary interest if a matter concerning the Outside Body becomes a Parish Council agenda item e.g. grant funding or Planning applications, but many forget.

What to expect from your Councillor

The excitement of winning an election and hopefully well and truly trouncing the opposition will for many Councillors mark the end of public involvement, as they sink quietly into oblivion with the door closed firmly for the next four years onto a very private cloistered world from which an occasional edict is issued. For others it will be a steep learning curve grappling with unexpected processes and responsibilities with the expectation to represent the views of the whole electorate, not just those who voted, both in Council, to outside organisations and to the higher tiers of local government.

Because there are few things a Parish Council cannot do especially as its spending is not capped unlike the higher tiers, individual Councillors should have a firm grasp of the background and full sweep of what their Parish does, including its leases, assets, Parish plans, design statements, contracts and internal arrangements such as standing orders and financial regulations.

There is a lot a proactive Councillor can do:

- Go to meetings - there is in fact a legal obligation to attend. Turn up on time and not leave early, or if it is unavoidable warn the Chairman beforehand. Late arrivals and early departures should be minuted.
- Meetings are formal events not social occasions and Councillors should address each other and officers in a formal manner, especially for the watching audience who will not know who they are;
- Study the agendas and read past minutes;
- Take part in discussions - some Councillors go their full 4 years without saying anything, questions should be asked on behalf of the Parish and replies made to queries raised in Public Forum. Questions should be asked of organisations making presentations and not be treated as entertainment;
- Report back in writing on outside meetings and conferences;
- Keep speeches short and to the point; don't be unpleasant about other Councillors or the public and no political point scoring;
- Challenge assumptions and ask questions don't just accept what others say, progress chase issues and responses;
- Ask Councillors from the higher tiers to meetings to explain what decisions are being made and what the effect is locally and note it in the minutes;
- Check facts, do research, consult widely, and ask for information in writing so it can be referred to;
- Check the minutes actually say something and any resolutions are properly made in meetings and formally noted;
- Check the Parish Publication Scheme is in place and up to date.

- Keep up to date the Declaration of Interests and read other Councillors Declarations to know where their expertise and interests lie;
- Understand when disclosable pecuniary interests and non-pecuniary interests should be declared and understand the importance and role of the Code of Conduct;
- Ask for views on important issues to be minuted and have minuted and named votes;
- Vote on proposals clearly, only abstaining, if genuinely no view is held or if undecided (but not too often);
- Have an overview of the finances, become part of the Councillor review group which periodically checks spending areas;
- Understand what is being budgeted for and check regularly spending details rather than looking at the overall total or rough percentages (statements commenting that 30% of the Budget has been spent helps no-one);
- As Planning is a big part of Parish affairs local knowledge is vital. Councillors should: visit the application sites, practice looking at and understanding plans; listen to the views of both the applicant and the objectors - personal feelings about a Planning applicant are not relevant.
- Suggest, know and monitor Section106 or Community Infrastructure Levy agreements (generally monetary contributions made to the Parish resulting from development).
- Make sure design and landscaping details of Planning permissions are adhered to.
- Make a Parish Plan/Design Statement/Neighbourhood Plan which applicants wanting Planning permission can follow;
- Substitute for each other at Committee meetings (at the higher tiers this is not always possible as certain Committees such as the Regulation Committee where specific training in the current legislation is needed or Cabinet Councillors who have non-transferable delegated powers);
- Read out statements of opinion from absent Councillors (due to illness, work or holidays).

There is certain ambiguity between Councillor and electorate but successful Councillors will represent the views of the whole electorate, not just make personal decisions, but in order to do so they need to be well informed about their Parish. The literature suggests a number of ways: surveys or questionnaires for simple issues; whilst long term policies can be set out in Parish plans and design statements developing opinions using their associated forums and workshops; an annual "state of the nation" review; or a Parish Poll for controversial issues. Creating a "listening" Council which can show what firm support it has for its actions and budget plans. However, whilst time consuming, cumbersome and unlikely to be undertaken very frequently public opinion can be used to: support requests to the higher tiers of local government, help decide whether to provide or support a local service either by offering funding, office space or staff time, by sharing direct control of a community organisation, or by teaming up with a neighbouring Parish.

However, Councillors can find it difficult to distinguish between the things it would be nice or fun to do and the things a Parish Council should do. The principle of Best Value which matches spending to the benefit for local people has to be at the back of every Councillor's mind. At the end of the day Council decisions are group decisions aiming to provide constructive solutions on a common ground.

Where else can Councillors stand?

Some prospective Councillors may be persuaded to stand for the higher Council tiers: District and County (in the three tier system) or Unitary (in the newer combined two tiered), as well as, or perhaps instead of for their local Parish Council. Elections often take place at the same time. District, Unitary and County Councillors represent a larger population than Parish Councillors, there will be a greater time commitment as issues and bureaucracies are more complex and meetings may be in the daytime as well as evening.

District Councils

District Councils collect monies on behalf of all three tiers of local government through the Council Tax and can provide: Economic Regeneration, Business Support and Licensing, Planning Policy and Development Control, Housing Advice, Street/Pavement Cleansing and Landscape Services, Recycling and Waste Collection, Pest Control, Dog Wardens, Town Markets, Car Parks, Swimming Pool and Leisure Facilities, Public and Environmental Protection, Benefits and Non Domestic Rates.

County Councils

County Councils provide: Health Care and Community Services, Education and Library Services, Culture and Heritage Services , Public Transport, Traffic Regulation, Highways and Pavements, Police, Fire and Ambulance Services, Emergency Planning, Rights of Way, Regulation and Development of Minerals and Waste Management.

... Frome Watch...

Recent Frome elections

Councillors face election or re-election every four years. In the 2007 elections out of the possible 17 Councillors, 16 were elected, with the remaining Councillor co-opted. A co-opted Councillor can be a candidate who failed to be elected, a person who had expressed an interest, a friend of the leading group or someone who has a specialisation and is invited to join, the co-optee should in law be appointed by the whole Council.

In Frome, past vacancies have been advertised in the local paper and those keen to be Councillors have supported their nomination by a presentation at one of the Full Town Council meetings. In this instance the decision was made not to advertise the vacancy, two of the political parties put forward their nominee who wrote a short letter by way of application outlining their enthusiasm for Frome. The dominant party's nominee was co-opted.

The 2007 election results show seven women elected and the newly signed Councillors Declarations of Interest showed 9 were retired and 2 were shop keepers. Few had any involvement in other organisations and these were mainly national charities, one or two added the clubs they were later appointed to. Indeed few admitted to being sponsored by the political party under whose banner they stood. Twinning was ignored and gifts and hospitality only noted by one Councillor.

A surprising eight of the eleven possible Frome District Councillors were also Frome Town Councillors and one Parish Councillor was also a County Councillor and therefore sat on all three authorities. As County meetings are day time this turns being a Councillor into a full time job.

Besides Full Council the 3 main Committees in the 2007-11 election cycle were: Policy, Finance and Economic Development, Planning, and Recreation and Properties. A number of sub-Committees grew up: Civic, Christmas Spectacular, Grants, and Personnel, with smaller task forces dealing with single issues such as new premises. At one time meetings would have commenced with prayers. This ended in Frome in the 1990's although still continues today at Full Council at Mendip District Council.

Frome Councillors have also had the opportunity to sit on community organisations (the wittily named Outside Bodies), in 2007/08 there were 22 (described in Chapter 7). Council Committee meetings in common with other Parishes are in the evening starting around 7.00pm lasting between one and two hours. Planning, with greater Councillor discussion and public input started at the inconveniently early time of 6.30pm. Townspeople wanting to voice an opinion at meetings and working find this especially difficult and themselves, annoyingly, accused of apathy.

With such a range of Committees and sub-committees meetings can seem frequent, totaling around 35 per year plus 16 for Planning, though for individual Councillors the commitment varied wildly between 3 and 40 hours a year each.

Frome contributes 11 Councillors from its 6 Parish Wards to the total of 47 representatives on Mendip District Council (2007/8); 8 were also Parish Councillors rising to 9 in 2009. Frome is also divided into 2 County Council Electoral Wards Frome North and Frome South, plus Frome Selwood – a largely rural area encircling Frome like a ring doughnut; each contributes 1 Councillor to the 58 representatives on Somerset County Council. In 2007/08 only 1 County Councillor was also a Frome Parish Councillor this changed to all 3 after the 2009 elections.

Prayers

Bideford Town Council was taken to the High Court by an atheist ex-Councillor who felt *"disadvantaged and embarrassed"* when Christian prayers were said at the start of Council meetings. The National Secular Society acting for the Councillor suggested prayers were an unlawful practice when part of the meeting's agenda and brought religion into a "secular environment"; breaching articles 9 and 14 of the European Convention on Human Rights - Councillors with no religion were being indirectly discriminated against without justification. Bideford Council had twice voted against change. Nationally it was thought half of Councils start meetings with prayers. Bideford lost in the High Court (Feb 2012). But the Church, shocked at what it saw as an attack and the gradual marginalisation of the country's Christian values launched a protest. The Government rallying to this outrage brought forward the "general Power of Competence"; an element of the Localism Act 2011 allowing Parishes, for the first time, to be able to do anything individuals can do unless specifically prohibited by law.
Bideford was thus saved from appealing to the Supreme Court.

The Mayor

The title of Mayor has been widely adopted by the chairman of larger Parish Councils since the Local Government Act of 1972 which reorganised the roles and responsibilities and (to a degree), the nature and extent of public representation in local government. Previously it had been the Boroughs with Charters granting them a Mayor, many of these with their Corporations (the other Councillors) kept the full regalia of "Councillors in State"- a black tricorn hat and heavy red robe often trimmed in white ermine or with a lacy shirt bib. These are worn at Full Council and ceremonial civic occasions adding colour, pomp and ceremony. Most Mayors have a chain of office.

...Frome Watch...

Wells and Glastonbury

Frome's sister towns of Wells and Glastonbury both wear the full regalia. Wells in the main for church and cathedral services particularly Remembrance Sunday and Carol Services. Whilst at Glastonbury regalia is worn for the annual Glastonbury Pilgrimage Procession of Witnesses and Abbey service, the Cutting of the Holy Thorn, and Remembrance Sunday.

The Councillor voted in as Chairman of the Parish Council takes on the role of Mayor at the Annual Town Council Meeting both titles running concurrently. The Deputy Chairman becomes the Deputy Mayor and as with Council meetings will deputise for the Mayor at events where there is a timetabling difficulty or may be jointly invited to events with the Mayor.

The roles of Mayor and Deputy Mayor are purely ceremonial but are taken on with much pride with wives or partners often included in invitations and many have their own more modest chains of office. Most Mayors enjoy the experience which lasts the one year and will be thereafter be introduced as the ex-Mayor in often quite reverential tones.

The Mayor is invited by organisations, clubs, charities and individuals from within the Parish to celebrate: birthdays, sponsorship, funding successes and sporting achievements, to congratulate winners of competitions, to open new buildings, schools and hospital events, to attend fêtes and shows and to launch appeals, visiting the sick and the elderly in retirement homes particularly at Christmas and acting as the town's representative at civic and religious occasions such as the annual Remembrance Sunday parade. Neighbouring towns and Mayors issue invitations throughout the year to their charitable events such as gala dinners or music festivals. Although invited, the Mayor may pay for the ticket for himself and any accompanying partner out of the mayoral allowance. These events are explained as *"cementing friendships"* and *"as gestures of goodwill"* between towns, and oddly, in an unexplained way, are seen as promoting the economic viability of a town. But as one Mayor was quoted as saying when refusing an invitation to a neighbouring town's gala dinner, *"it is not as though they are going to invade if I don't go."*

Generally a few words of welcome or congratulations are all that is needed with the occasional short speech or biblical reading in church. Most Mayors will spend time talking to organisers, chatting to those they meet, enjoying a cup of tea and perhaps buying small gifts at fête stalls. The local newspaper is often there to record the event and this may be the only time the public are aware of any Parish Council activity.

Certainly, at one time the publicity of the Mayor opening a fête would have brought the townspeople in crowds to watch. This is less likely today, when many people are unclear what the Mayor does, or even why he wears a chain of office. In this less deferential age it is certainly less valued.

Organisations who do ask perhaps gain a sense of recognition, or want to do something out of the ordinary to mark an achievement or see the invitation as a means of ensuring publicity or continued Parish funding.

Other Committee chairmen are rarely asked.

..... **Frome Watch....**

Frome Mayors

The Mayor is given an annual allowance £1,200 (2008/09) - which co-opted Mayors cannot receive and travel expenses to help with the costs involved, as the number of events can easily top 100 and inevitably occur at weekends and particularly in the weeks before Christmas. Recently in recognition of the year of office each past Mayor received a badge. There is a specially commissioned framed photograph kept as a town record in the Town Office.

Whilst there is no regalia, this is confined to the Town Crier - who supplies his own scarlet great coat and black tricorn hat, there is a Mayoral chain on a velvet collar which is worn on ceremonial occasions. The centre piece is the enamelled Town Coat Of Arms on a medallion with the motto "Time Trieth Troth" and on the links of the chain are engraved the names of all previous Mayors. The Deputy Mayor has a similar but less ostentatious chain of office and there are ceremonial chains for their partners to wear as well.

In more recent years the Mayor has chosen local charities to support, either donating part of the annual allowance or accepting donations towards it. The Town Office organised fundraising events usually by invitation only to the Mayors from the surrounding towns in the region or local businessmen.

The 2010 Mayor's Charity Dinner and Auction with other fundraising raised around £2,000 for the two chosen local charities. The Mayor's Ceilidh the fundraising centrepiece of the following year raised £1,800. At the reinstated Annual Civic Church Service, the Mayor presented the Civic Awards, nominated by friends and colleagues, to townspeople who have made special contributions over many years to the life of the town.

The Mayors have approached gleaning the towns views in different ways with: monthly "Meet the Mayor", a Saturday stall in a chilly corner of the shopping precinct, previous administrations had experimented with this from the warmth of the library, but abandoned it when most issues turned out to be litter and dog fouling; a Mayoral blog which never quite got off the ground; but the Frome Mayor Facebook page (2010/11) was a surprise success.

The Mayor and Deputy Mayor have honorary membership of the Twinning Association; this voluntary group began in the mid 1970's organising visits to French Château Gontier and later German Murrhardt. On the annual summer visits the Mayor is invited to represent Frome exchanging gifts to cement goodwill and signing charters. With the Twinning of a third town from Poland (2009) the focus moved away from purely social occasions to somewhat unspecified education and commercial objectives. The Town Council absorbed much of the Twinning Associations responsibilities assuming more direct control.

Over time some Mayoral events have disappeared such as the Mayor's Ball and the Mayor's Fête in Victoria Park.

Chairman of the Council and other Chairmen

The Mayor, who is also the Chairman of the Council, presides over the meetings of Full Council and is the coordinating Chairman of the other Committee Chairmen and may lead prayers at the start of Council meetings. In common with the Mayor, the Chairmen of the Council's Committees are a point of contact for the public to raise issues with; to address at meetings or when writing letters to the Council.

Committee Chairmen make public statements on behalf of the Council. Indeed they will be tremendously flattered if groups and societies ask to make a presentation on their activities, alternatively a Chairman may invite speakers. Full Council meetings should be the highlight of the Council calendar, a "master of the universe" moment, where the delights and hard work of all the other Committees are laid out for all to see.

The Chairman of the Council, in consultation, will set the Full Council agendas based on a template allowing all Committees and sub-committees an equal chance to be heard. Indeed Committees should expect to provide written reports updating current topics. Items should be prioritised according to their importance which includes answers to questions and progress reports on decisions made at previous meetings. The Chairman should progress chase as necessary and not just hope things will happen. Although rare it is considered bad practice to combine Parish Chairman and Parish Clerk roles as impartiality is compromised.

Chairmanship- How to Do it

Chairing a Committee - if done well - looks effortless, if done badly; meetings are chaotic, appear unfair and produce limitless amounts of bad feeling. Many go into chairing ill prepared assuming they can make it up on the spot, and become heavily reliant on the Committee secretary to get them by often inadvertently handing over control of the meeting. Chairing requires a high level of commitment.

There are some fundamental points to be borne in mind:

Preparation
The Chairman of a Committee can be easily spotted at a meeting as the one shuffling papers and in deep conversation with the Parish or Committee Clerk. He or she will have arrived early to check the practical details of the venue having read the background papers thoroughly (even if the members haven't) and will have an understanding and some knowledge of the issues and topics under discussion, having earmarked areas of contention or areas which need discussion. The Chairman should, as should all Councillors, know the meeting procedures and Standing Orders - these are rules specific to each Parish Council, and regulate what can and can-not be done.

Balance
The Chairman strikes a difficult balance between getting the business on the agenda carried out efficiently, whilst enabling everyone to get involved and encouraging all members to take part ensuring that there are real discussions.

Councillors and public alike become irritated if a meeting rambles on and runs over time. They will be equally annoyed if they are not given the opportunity to speak and get their point across, and exasperated when discussions cannot be followed because of lack of explanation or there is a confusing use of jargon - whilst everyone else appears or pretends to know what is under discussion. It is only when a vote is about to be taken that it becomes obvious how few did understood and so discussions may need to be restarted. Perhaps even worse is to hear Councillors whispering to one another after a vote asking what the issue was about or a Councillor realising he/she voted the "wrong way".

Many Councillors are enthusiastic to become the Chairman and are reluctant to give up the role particularly if the opposition party can be blocked from this position of control. Many Councillors feel that being the Chairman strongly influences decisions, perhaps through the control of the agenda or by having the last word. The Chairman may, in a summing up, modestly express a viewpoint or a reservation, hopefully increasing the level of credibility and respect in which the Chairman is held. It is not the Chairman's role to; bully the public or Councillors, or use their position to insist on their own viewpoint or to dictate resolutions but to hit a consensus.

Impartiality

The Chairman's personality and attitudes set the tone and mood of meetings and can affect the way issues are discussed. The Chairman should not mumble into the Committee papers, or whisper to the Committee Clerk, but should look around at the other Committee members and any members of the public not forgetting to welcome and thank them for coming at the beginning of the meeting. It is a politeness to ensure that members of the public do at least have an agenda to follow and jargon should be explained for the benefit of all. A Chairman will also need to deal with people outside the meeting when Councillors and public may wish to have further discussions. Overall, being seen to be fair will make meetings enjoyable and productive.

The Chairman should be impartial and not impose a viewpoint. This will come as a shock to many Committee Chairmen who see chairmanship as an opportunity to dominate, railroad, and bully the members to their viewpoint. The Chairman can formally step aside if particularly passionate about an agenda item and wishes to strongly influence the decision, letting the Deputy Chairman take control of the meeting during the discussion.

Keeping Order

The Chairman keeps order at meetings, these are formal occasions, and the agenda should be conducted in such a way that ensures members are professional in their approach; this can include language and dress. Although the times when everyone wore their "Sunday best" has probably passed although it still persists in the higher tiers of local government. Councillors, who turn up in beach wear and address each other by first names, including the secretariat (and indeed vice versa) do affect the quality of discussion and decisions, giving a very poor impression to any watching audience undermining credibility. Indeed as many an audience can report - everyone had a nice chat, some half-hearted decisions were nearly made but were shelved with vague calls for more information or the setting up of a working group which, not meeting for months, effectively postpones any possible action indefinitely, but everyone goes home very pleased with themselves.

Control

A Chairman will be precise and concise, effective and decisive, speak clearly and listen attentively, making notes on the main points or have the Committee Clerk do so. The Chairman will summarise the points to be voted on whilst keeping in mind the time but not so as to stifle discussion.

If some members are still discussing the previous item, not noticing that things have moved on, then that is the fault of the Chairman.

A Chairman will tactfully prevent discussions wandering and prevent those who have nothing new to add from constantly repeating previous speakers, something that happens all too easily and wastes huge amounts of time. The Chairman will not allow personal attacks on fellow Councillors or members of the public. The Chairman, Councillors and the public should consider reporting any incidents to their local Standards Committee.

Ego boosting performances from members should be curtailed so no one personality or group dominates the meeting. Equally, members holding and expressing a contrary opinion is not a sign of insurrection and does not have to be ruthlessly put down.

A Chairman will understand how to table motions and how amendments are made. Making sure the wording of a resolution is exact for the Committee minutes, and will not assume everyone has been following what has been said. It is disconcerting again to realise that some members have not been aware that a resolution had been passed, or were not even sure on what they were voting. Voting should be clear to fellow Councillors and the public with a raising of hands rather than a desultory nod of the head. The Chairman also considers requests on serious issues for a named vote where individual Councillors are asked for their decision in turn and the response noted. In voting, the Chairman traditionally has the casting vote to break any deadlock; it is considered good practice to maintain the status-quo that there is no change.

Finally meetings should start and finish on time.

Things to Remember
Successful chairmanship is a learned skill that can be practiced and perfected to provide opportunities for everyone to be heard, to give appropriate rulings and protect the minority whilst abiding by the majority decisions. Much is common sense and in doing so the Chairman will have avoided:

- taking sides,
- becoming a dominating participant in the discussion,
- manipulating the group towards a personal agenda,
- criticising the values and ideas of other members,
- forcing own ideas on the group,
- saying too much and
- making decisions for the members without asking them for agreement.

Datafile
The Coat of Arms and Regalia, Frome Town Council Leaflet
National Census of Local Authority Councillors in England 2008 at www.lga.gov.uk.
Muck&brass.blogspot.com.

FROME MUSEUM

5 - PEOPLE - Councillor Conduct

Councillors have not always been highly regarded and for the most part there were few rules that governed their behaviour and certainly not at Parish level.

In 1997, Lord Nolan produced the Nolan Report, into the Standards of Conduct in Local Government, changing what he described as a confusing tangle into a simple clear code of the seven general principles which still underpin Councillor conduct today. These are both common sense and aspirational.

The Seven Principles of Public Life
Councillors should show:

- Selflessness, by only serving the public interest not in order to gain financial or material benefits for themselves, family or friends or to advantage or disadvantage anyone;
- Integrity, by avoiding obligations to individuals or organisations who would influence their decisions;
- Objectivity, by basing decisions on merit including: making appointments, awarding contracts, or recommending individuals for rewards or benefits;
- Accountability, by enabling actions and decisions to be open to public scrutiny;
- Openness, by giving reasons about how and why decisions are made and actions taken, only limiting information if there is a wider public interest;
- Honesty, by declaring any private interests that could influence decisions and always aiming to protect the public interest and;
- Leadership, by example and by promoting and supporting the 7 Principles.

This heralded a new era of rules, expectations of behaviour, increasingly complex guidance and a Standards Board for England to enforce them. Set up in 2000 it oversaw the then Model Code of Conduct. All elected, appointed, co-opted and independent members of local authorities, including Parish Councils, fire, police and the national park authorities, were covered by the Code.

The Board held the central register of all suspended and disqualified Councillors and monitored and gave advice to local Standard Committees investigating complaints or passing on allegations of misconduct to the Adjudication Panel which could suspend Councillors for a up to one year or disqualify for up to 5 years.

Complaints ranged from: conspiracies over local authority appointments, leaking information to the press, abusive comments to the public or presumed unfairness or bias when deciding an issue – frequently Planning decisions. An apology or disqualification for a year was the most common outcome of a complaint with the Councillor's constituents transferred to the care of a fellow Councillor.

The Coalition Government decided this top heavy bureaucratic approach, damaged local government's reputation, encouraging petty or politically motivated complaints and swept it away in the Localism Act (2011).

Now it would be local solutions for local problems. Completing earlier moves towards local accountability with the development of local Standards Committees, a mixture of Councillors including Parish and independent (people of note outside the Council) members taking an investigative role. The rules, the Government emphasised, covers current Councillors but not their private lives.

Under Localism, the Standard Committees are able to ignore trivial, vexatious, malicious or politically motivated complaints. The new regime will try to solve problems, initially by discussion between the two parties after some initial sieving by the Monitoring Officer who may start an investigation and with advice available to both sides from the newly appointed advisory "Independent Person". Only if necessary going before the Standards Committee/Hearing Panel, where both sides present evidence and witnesses in public. There are few sanctions the Monitoring Officer can impose (and can only recommend to Parish Councils): removal from Committees and outside bodies or limited Council contact (that is barred entry to Council offices). Councillors can no longer be suspended. The Localism Act has effectively swept away any sanctions on Parish Councillors, forgetting with the introduction of the Community Infrastructure Levy some Parishes will be controlling £1,000s.

The Code of Conduct
All Councils can now write their own Code, these may now vary enormously with some putting the new rules of Disclosable Pecuniary Interests on top of the old complex personal and prejudicial format.

Many will tweak and elaborate the previous Model Code which stated:
* No bullying,
* No discrimination,
* No intimidation of those investigating misconduct,
* No compromising staff impartiality and neutrality,

Neither should Councillors:
* Damage the role of Councillor or the local authority by poor conduct,
* Use their position for their own on someone else's advantage or disadvantage,
* Misuse the authorities resources including for political party purposes,
* Take part in discussions or decisions or even influencing decisions where a Councillor's own interests such as listed in disclosable pecuniary interests are present,

And Councillors should:
* Register and name the source of gifts or hospitality received over the value of £25,
* Treat everyone with respect,
* Keep confidences,
* Let the public have the information they are entitled to,
* Register financial and other interests,
* Report registered interests (pecuniary and non-pecuniary) at meetings.

Top complaints:
* Poor conduct which brings disgrace to the position of Councillor or its authority.
* Not treating others with respect,

- Using or attempting to use the role of Councillor improperly. Giving or obtaining an advantage or disadvantage for themselves or others.

Personal and prejudicial interests
"Personal": Are those listed on the public Register of Interests, or by association. An all-encompassing phrase, where an item under discussion affects the well-being or financial position of a Councillor or family member or close associate more than it affects the majority of other people within the ward or electoral division of the authority's area.

"Prejudicial": Personal issues become prejudicial if, those interests are so significant that a reasonable member of the public with knowledge of all the facts would think the decisions or the judgement of the public interest made by a Councillor was affected and they were therefore no longer impartial.

With the abolition of the Standards Board the Government hoped to return to a previous time when misconduct for personal gain is brought before the criminal courts.

Now failing to register, or disclose, or give misleading information about an Interest or by benefiting from involvement in any Council work is a criminal offence. This becomes a police responsibility with fines of up to £5,000 and a ban on being a Councillor for up to 5 years. The Government hopes this will be a greater deterrent to town hall corruption than the old Standards Board regime where a Councillor could simply be asked to apologise or be suspended.

Accusations of bias, or predisposition and not being open minded over any discussions or a decision has haunted Councillors. Many voted into office on the back of a cause found they were unable to express their views directly, or able to openly champion local causes such as opposing Planning developments or higher car parking charges resulting in convoluted expressions of opinion. Much to the frustration of the people they represented, Councillors could find themselves barred from the decision making process and prevented from speaking or voting in meetings. Indeed the old Standards Board guidance even discouraged Councillors from car sharing when travelling to Planning meetings to avoid "the appearance of bias" and the possibility of complaints to their local Standards Committee.

Now local codes can enshrine freedom of speech and not be used to silence Councillors or prevent whistle-blowing on misconduct. Councillors can now speak out, hope to influence and campaign freely either supporting the public view or their own whilst (of course) being prepared to listen to counter arguments and evidence avoiding any challenge of bias. It is up to a Councillor's own integrity with hopefully guidance written into their Code of Conduct which will help Councillors decide how relevant disclosable non-pecuniary interests are.

The previously confusing system of personal and prejudicial interests and their inevitable overlap, the Government says, is abolished.

The Register of Interests
Vital to avoid conflicts of interest especially on issues such as Planning applications or when financially benefiting from the issuing of council contracts is the oversight of pecuniary interests.

These are business interests - employment, trade profession, contracts plus any associated companies, and wider financial interests - trust funds, investments, land and property and are logged using the Register of Interests. Balancing electoral accountability against personal privacy the Register now includes details of a Councillor's spouse or civil partner and includes couples living as such.

Each authority can also add additional rules so Registers need to be read in conjunction with each authority's Code of Conduct. The Registers will now be published on both the higher tiers of local government and Parish websites with Parish Registers also available at District or Unitary offices or on their websites. The Register is completed by all elected, appointed and co-opted members, 28 days are allowed for the initial listing and to update any changes.

Most are still poorly filled in, most still do not admit belonging to the political party under whose banner they stood, membership of other organisations are frequently not included and gifts forgotten. Perhaps more concerning is the fact rather too many Parish Councillors do not fill them in at all! And it goes unnoticed and unremarked.

With so much of the current political emphasis on integrity and transparency, the shock of discovering not all Councillors fill in their Register of Interests is now obvious with on-line publication as is the fact that the higher tiers of local government do not necessarily monitor or take steps to correct discrepancies.

All, the (newly named) Disclosable Pecuniary Interests, should be listed and described for both Councillors and their partners:
- Any employment carried out for gain with the name of the organisation or business;
- Payments or financial benefits to off-set expenses paid whilst carrying out Councillor duties or sponsorship for election expenses, including from trade unions in the previous 12 months;
- Council contracts (for the relevant authority);
- Land owned if in the relevant authority's area, this includes Councillor's homes;
- Licenses for land or property (from the relevant local authority) including homes and allotments;
- Council tenancies as an individual or if there is a connection to a company that is a tenant (in the relevant authority area);
- Shareholdings, naming the company if it is based within the relevant authority area when the value is over £25,000 or 1/100th of the issued share capital.

Councillors should also list organisations they have any involvement with:
- Organisations the Council itself appointed Councillors to;
- Public organisations such as: other Councils, health authorities, school governorships;
- Local or national charities, mutual and provident societies or bodies of a charitable nature;
- Policy and public opinion forming groups such as trade unions, professional bodies, and political parties;
- Gifts and hospitality whilst in the role of Councillor, with the date, the name of donor, a description of what was received and the reason, where the value is £25 and above.

Councillors who fear intimidation or violence can have some details withheld.

If a Councillor's Disclosable Pecuniary Interests relate to anything discussed at a meeting they are unable to take part, discuss, vote or speak and should leave the room if their Councillor Code of Conduct says so or at the very least think about it, or if the Code is not specific, in the light of the 7 Principles of Public Life. There are exceptions to the non-participation rule but Councillors must apply in writing to their Monitoring Officer, these include: too many Councillors would be missing from a meeting making it unquorate; the political balance would be upset; to participate would be in the general interests of the locality; or it could be just thought to be appropriate!

… Frome Watch…

The Frome Register

Frome's Standards authority is Mendip District Council; Somerset County Council has its own. Each has 8 members made up of Councillors and locally appointed worthies. Both Committees pay an allowance (described Chapter 6).

Overall the Frome Register of Interests revealed: 8 out of the 17 Councillors were probably not employed it was difficult to tell, two ran shops and one was employed by their own political party and whilst two sets of two Councillors were partners (in a marital sense) this would not be obvious from the Register; There was a light smattering of outside interests mainly national charities, perhaps surprisingly few, and few links to any Frome organisations; only one or two mentioned their appointments to local groups or charities - even when appointed by the various Council tiers. There was an unexpected amount of uncertainty over who had sponsored them, most seemingly not understanding the question, again only one or two mentioned the political party they belonged to; Twinning hospitality was mentioned only once and no gifts were noted despite Twinning's high profile in Councillor life. Most appeared not to understand the Register's questions frequently putting the answers in the wrong sections. Few Councillors updated their Register after the first confused attempt.

What appear to be rigorous questions revealed little, giving no insight into those elected in the May 2007 election. A comparison of Registers across District and County of the same Councillors showed marked inconsistencies, where answers would be expected to be identical. Indeed the same Councillors at District level looked far more interesting and it seems odd that anomalies are not corrected. For those looking for a supporter of an issue or for what Declarations of Interests to expect at meetings the Register was of little value.

Councillor Investigation

A "*somewhat unusual complaint*" for the Standards Committee investigator was a "protest" by a Frome Parish and District Councillor intervening in a neighbour dispute.

The Councillor's sympathies had been roused by one neighbour over the ownership and demolition of a stone wall which allowed access to the complainant's neighbouring parcel of land where a house was being built. The Councillor arrived at the fenced and padlocked site entrance and wearing his steel helmet settled down on a picnic chair with a flask of coffee to picket. Quickly arrested for a breach of the peace he was whisked off to the police station where after a couple of hours he was released without charge. But returning to the "protest" site to collect his car he was photographed by the press wearing the steel helmet and carrying a Canadian Flag. Later the same day he visited and chatted with the complainant- a librarian, at her place of work.

The complaint pivoted on the Councillor's lack of respect and offensive behaviour by appearing in public in "military regalia" and referring to the development as a "wartime invasion", combined with a lack of courtesy - demonstrated by not enquiring into the complainant's side of the issue and by visiting her workplace without introduction or explanation. She believed her personal and professional reputation could be damaged by comments in the press.

Mendip District Council's Standards Committee decided that the Councillor had not treated the complainant with respect and suspended him for 2 months, ordering a written apology. The Councillor allowance was also suspended. However, the Councillor's subsequent appeal was successful although by then he had already been reinstated. Curiously, the published report was redacted with the principals' names and addresses occasionally blanked out whilst remaining in the rest of the text allowing the reader a pleasant half hour of fun filling in the blanks. The whole process took 18 months and cost £4,260.84p

COCKEY LAMP

6 - PEOPLE - Allowances

Councillors (although voluntary) have been able to claim increasingly generous allowances when elected to the higher tiers of local government to offset the time in or preparing for, Council meetings, meeting with outside organisations and associated duties. The Basic Allowance is paid regardless of the number of Committees appointed to or number of meetings attended. Councillors may take on additional roles such as Leader of the Council, Deputy Leader, or Portfolio Holder – in charge of a specific set of responsibilities. They are voted into these roles by their fellow Councillors and a Special Responsibility Allowance is paid for the extra work this entails.

The political party with the largest number of Councillors elected usually becomes the ruling party and each Committee can reflect this political balance, the largest grouping is able to chair the Committees and lead the Council. Perhaps unexpectedly the leaders of political opposition groups are also given an allowance as are the co-opted members who make up the Standards Committee overseeing the Code of Conduct.

Allowances are subject to income tax. All authorities offer carer's, travel and subsistence allowances.

Parish Level

Although at Parish level a basic annual allowance can be paid to all Councillors and there may be an annual vote on it, it is unlikely that any Parish does pay one. They would be set by the District or Unitary authorities Parish Remuneration Panel. The Chairman of the Council or Mayor may be paid an allowance in recognition of the extra time spent on additional duties. However, there is no allowance for appointed or co-opted Councillors. Many Parishes offer a carers allowance enabling Councillors with children or adult dependents to pay for a "babysitter" or a carer so they can go to meetings. Travel allowances (train, car or bicycle) and subsistence allowances for meals out may be offered to all Councillors going to meetings, on training courses, for Twinning responsibilities, conferences or events on behalf of the Council both inside and outside the Parish.

...Frome Watch...

Frome, Mendip and Somerset Allowances

Councillors on the Policy, Finance and Economic Committee (P&F) had always voted annually against Councillor allowances. However, Somerset was expected to change from a County to a Unitary authority under Government reorganisation (2007) abolishing the District Councils.

The Town Council gleefully expected to take-over guessed at District responsibilities and earnest discussions at P&F decided on a full set of allowances with additional sums for Committee Chairmen along current District Council lines when the change took place. Councillors worried whether it was too soon for the Parish Remuneration Board to set the amounts. The Government (against all expectations) kept Somerset as a County with its Districts whilst unexpectedly turning neighbouring Wiltshire into a Unitary authority.

The Mayoral allowance (£1,052 in 2007 rising to £1,200 by 2011) offsets the cost of attending civic engagements (around 100 a year). Some past Mayors have either not claimed or have donated their allowance to a local charity. All Town Councillors could claim a £50 annual stationery allowance to off-set the cost of printing the minutes, agendas and briefing documents e-mailed to them.

In the past, car parking badges were issued enabling Councillors to park on the double yellow lines outside the Town Council Office on Palmer Street and avoid a parking ticket. The carers, travel and subsistence allowances are rarely taken up, except when involved with Twinning duties abroad. Councillors are provided with an e-mail address. The allowances paid to individual Councillors are not published.

Mendip District Council Allowances

8 Frome Parish Councillors were elected District Councillors rising to 9 (June 2009).
The Mendip Basic Allowance is the lowest in the area.

From April 2009/10	
Basic Allowance of £3,605, plus if a:	
Leader of the Council	£10,000
Deputy Leader of the Council	£4,000
Portfolio Holder or Committee Chairman	£4,000
Planning Committee Chairman	£4,000
East Mendip Community Partnership Chairman	£2,000
Standards Committee Chairman	£2,700

Travel allowances were set at 40p per mile for cars with all other transport at cost. Frome is 12 miles distant from its sister town Shepton Mallet. A set amount for meals could be claimed if meetings were more than 3 miles from home and the time away longer than 4 hours. The carers' allowances were rarely claimed.

The District provides an e-mail address and a laptop computer if needed with Blackberries for the Council Leader and Planning Chairman.

A table of the total allowances paid (as lump sums) to each District Councillor including the members of the Standards Committee was published annually in April or May as a Public Notice in the local free paper, The Fosseway Magazine - which covered most of the District before its demise.

Somerset County Council Allowances

One Frome Parish Councillor was also a County Councillor (and combined this with a role as a District Councillor) rising to 3 after the 2009 elections.

Interestingly, the Somerset County Council basic allowance was based on the wages for white collar jobs in the South West discounted for the voluntary nature of some of the work multiplied by 132 days per year (approximately 2.5 days a week) which was the average amount of time Councillors were assumed to spend on Council business.

Again there are additional payments for Councillors taking on special responsibilities such as Committee Chairman. All Chairmen are not necessarily paid at the same rate as the complexity and the number of meetings varied. A travel allowance of 40p per mile for cars with separate amounts for shared car travel, bicycle and train journeys. Frome is 48 miles distant from County's Taunton headquarters. There is a set meal allowance when away from home, at meetings, for longer than 4 hours with hotels at cost. A carers allowance provides for child care or professional care for elderly, sick or dependent relatives.

A Computer laptop, printer and e-mail address can be provided, with Blackberries for high profile Councillors such as Cabinet Members.

The previous year's Councillor Allowances are published on County's website but not in the local papers.

From April 2010/11	
Basic Allowance	£9,880 plus if a:
Leader	£39,520
Deputy Leader	£27,688
Committee Chairman varied from	£11,856 - £18,772
Standards Committee	£11,856

Other Authorities
Each authority sets its own rates.

The adjacent District of South Somerset announced a 25% pay rise for the year 2008-09 increasing allowances to:

Basic Allowance	£5,434, plus if a:
Leader of the Council	£14,004
Deputy Leader	£8,400
Portfolio Holders	£7,000

Each District Councillor represents around 2,500 people and the Leader of the Council estimated each Councillor spent 19 hours a week on Council issues.

Bath and North East Somerset – one of the first Unitary authorities in the country, paid a Basic Allowance of £7,700 in 2010/11.

Its neighbour, the Wiltshire Unitary Authority paid a Basic Allowance of £10,638 plus an additional technology allowance of £250.

Member of Parliament (MP) Allowances
MP's Allowances have been included for the sake of completeness, partly because so many Frome Councillors have become prospective parliamentary candidates illustrating that the ambition to be an MP is within the grasp of all Parish Councillors, and partly because of the expenses scandal furore caused by revelations in a national newspaper.
The Daily Telegraph published the surprising, previously secret, expenses details of a large number of MP's (2009). Initially dismissed as a few rotten apples and not indicative of the majority of MP's, the scale of the revelations forced the Government to reconsider and investigate reform.

MP Allowances
In 2007/08 MP's allowances came to £93 million, £5 million more than the previous year.

Members of Parliament receive both a salary and a set of allowances to run an office in their constituency, pay for travel and offset the cost of being in London dealing with constituency and parliamentary work.

A regular salary of £400 was first introduced in 1911 and by April 1st 2009 had risen to £64,766. Over time a number of allowances had been added, and it was these and their administration that caused huge controversy and extensive national press coverage with calls to limit the scope of allowances and provide a greater explanation of what the payments had been made for - many claims had not been backed by receipts.

The MP's accused of misuse claimed they were acting within the rules which were set out in the Green Book, although certain allowances, such as the £400 per month food allowance was not listed. Some resigned and many decided not to stand for re-election in 2010, whilst others said they would repay claims. The range of claims was extraordinary from: cleaning a moat, buying a duck house for a pond, buying dog food, hiring adult videos, buying iPods, or flat screen TVs, claiming the second homes allowance whilst staying with relatives, claiming for mortgages which did not exist, changing the nomination of a second home in order to avoid paying Capital Gains Tax.

Parliamentary Allowances outlined in the Green Book in 2008:

Described in the press as the second homes allowance, the Additional Costs Allowance (ACA)/ Personal Additional Accommodation Expenditure (PAAE), reimbursed the cost of living away from the main home (generally in the constituency) enabling MPs to work in Parliament by paying for a hotel room or renting, or paying a mortgage on a flat. It included items on the "John Lewis List" which listed generously priced furnishings such as: carpets, fridges, chairs, dry cleaning, etc. The ACA was not paid to MPs with constituencies in Inner London. The maximum was £24,006.

- MPs with Inner London constituencies could choose the London Supplement/London Costs Allowance at £2,916; it rose to £7,500 in April 2009. Outer London MPs could choose this or the ACA.
- Office running costs such as: rents rates, equipment, supplies etc up to a maximum of £22,193.
- Staffing costs paid for by the Commons finance department and equal to 3.5 full time staff. The proposed ban on MPs employing their spouse or other relatives was shelved, but now (2010) MPs have to declare any relatives employed. A maximum of £100,205 plus pensions at 10% of salary. Temporary staff can also be employed for security or to help a constituent in exceptional cases.
- Stationery to a maximum of £7,000 and postage for constituency correspondence is centrally provided.
- IT equipment i.e. computers, laptops, printers etc. centrally provided and maintained at around £5,000.
- Allowances for constituency newsletters, websites, surveys of views, direct mailing etc generally getting to know or informing constituents but not for party political, fundraising or election campaigning. A maximum of £10,400.
- Travel by air/train (cost) or bike (20p/mile) or car (40p/mile) from the constituency or home to the House of Commons at Westminster. Plus a limited number of journeys by spouse and children (30) and staff (24) including 3 trips to the European Union.

...Frome Watch...

The Constituency of Somerton and Frome

An awkwardly shaped constituency, with Frome in the north as the major town with an industrial past and a natural tendency to look economically to the nearby west Wiltshire towns and the City of Bath. Somerton in the south is a rural market town the third of the size of Frome. Most of the constituency's population live in small villages and hamlets scattered in between and to the south of Somerton.

David Heath MP Somerton and Frome	
Claimed Allowances, for April 2007 to March 2008	
• Cost of staying away from main home, mortgage and council tax	£23,002
• Office running costs	£20,429
• Staffing costs	£84,508
• Centrally purchased stationery	£907
• Postage costs	£2,260
• Centrally provided IT equipment	£1,265
• Communications allowance	£6,905
• Travel:	
• Road travel	£5,744
• Rail travel	£615
• Miscellaneous	£8
• Spouse travel	£603-7 times
• Family travel	£0
• Employee travel	£567-15 times
Total	**£146,813**

There were two end of career allowances:

- The Winding-up Allowance which met the cost of completing outstanding parliamentary and constituency work, undertaken by or on behalf of a former Member on their death, defeat or retirement to a maximum of £40,799.

- The Resettlement Grant which helped with the costs of adjusting to a "non-parliamentary life" paid when a MP ceased to be an MP at a General Election. The amount was based on age and length of service and varied between 50% and 100% of the annual salary being paid to a Member of Parliament at the time, and could have been as much as £64,000.

Changes

Since the furore over allowances more details have been made public, some of the receipts themselves have been scanned and published, however, with much blanked out or redacted, much was still unclear. It was promised (March 2010) that future published receipts would retain more information.

Sir Thomas Legge published a report in February 2010 which audited claims under the second homes allowance back to 2004 and as a consequence asked 390 MP's to return £1.3 million of over-payments, three MP's and one member of the House of Lords were investigated for fraud. Perhaps surprisingly the MP's were given legal aid to fight their cases. Meanwhile, the main inquiry under Sir Christopher Kelly issued a raft of proposals; these in turn were discussed by the Independent Parliamentary Standards Authority under Sir Ian Kennedy and the adopted proposals becoming law in time for the new government in May 2010 bringing in a revised set of parliamentary allowances.

In the end (March 2010) the reforms proposed the seemingly obvious but, they were hailed as ending 300 years of MP independence and a clean break with the past.

The reforms included: no claim without a receipt, no cleaning or gardening claims, only one family member to be employed (this was kept in after intense lobbying by MPs, only 250 employ a family member), no second home for MP's who live within 20 miles or one commuting hour of London, all others to be allowed enough to claim rent of up to £1,450 per month equal to a one bedroom flat - so no more mortgages, no first class rail fare, the resettlement grant to be abolished, office costs allowance to be reduced, but extra help for MP's with children; all to be overseen by a newly created compliance officer.

Datafile
www.telegraph.co.uk
www.parliament.uk
www.theyworkforyou.com
www.measuringworth.com

THE YELLOW CHAIR

7 - PEOPLE - Committee Watching in Frome

"A Committee consists of a number of important people who singly cannot make a decision and collectively decide there is no decision to be made." Anon.

"By their fruit ye shall know them." Matthew 7

Frome's Budget for the electoral cycle April 2007-11 was around £3.4 million.

Everyone can and should go to a Parish Council meeting. This is the opportunity to see the personalities behind the names, see how the claims made in the election literature (if any) match up in practice and if and how political party differences show themselves. But, most importantly, it is an opportunity to see how decisions are made, what evidence is used to back them and how this is worked into a budgetary plan. It is this group of people who, for a set period of four years, will spend often unexpectedly large sums of money as they see fit.

As with any group of people some Councillors like to expound, others say little, whilst others just seem embarrassed. Many mumble and it is clearly a skill to put across views in a clear, precise and cogent manner. The level of debate (if any) can be disappointing and is all too frequently limited to statements rather than constructed arguments. Although meetings are formal, often stilted events occasionally some humour does breaks through.

...Frome Watch...
Wells and Glastonbury Parish Incomes
Frome's sister Mendip towns of Wells and Glastonbury, had both previously been Boroughs, and had retained impressive civic buildings after the 1972 reorganisation. In Wells, a Town Hall, a Market Hall, shops, and a cemetery. In Glastonbury a Town Hall, car parking, shops and a cemetery. Generating an income for Wells of around £152,000 and for Glastonbury of around £190,000.

Committees generate a language of their own and can become bogged down in jargon. For Parishes with few strategic decisions an uncomplicated approach really works otherwise arguments can become convoluted and Kafkaesque particularly in Planning Committees. The audience's presence is either regarded with suspicion or as an opportunity to give a performance.

This can reach epidemic proportions, particularly at Full Council, when Councillor after Councillor repeats the same point over and over again despite the attempts of an often despairing Chairman to curb them. It can also be frustrating for the audience when poor, wrong or misinformation is used to back up a decision especially as audience intervention is not allowed.

Going armed with an agenda will make any meeting easier to follow; an enthusiastic Clerk will supply one. Reading the previous minutes will give, (hopefully) some continuity making the experience understandable and even enjoyable.

...Frome Watch...

Where to meet?

Frome held the smaller Committee meetings and working parties in the reception area of its Palmer Street Council Offices, a narrow street tricky for parking whilst the space inside the building is intimate. Previously Full Council and Planning Committee meetings had been held in the town centre public Library, light and airy with room for a sizable audience, but accessed through the loading bay at the rear of the building, not immediately obvious and more than a little off-putting.

The smaller Parishes will usually combine all their business in one general meeting of which there have to be at least four a year whereas the larger Parishes such as Frome assign areas of responsibility to specific Committees. These will meet at intervals throughout the year with perhaps a break during the August peak holiday period.

Where they meet

After the reorganisation of local government in 1972 some larger Parishes kept their Town Halls with the smaller Parishes meeting in the local community hall or school, meetings must not be held in private homes. Quirkily meetings cannot be held where alcohol is being sold, such as the pub, perhaps going back to a time when there was a danger of the Poor Rate being drunk by the Officers of the Vestry. Meeting rooms are free of charge if paid for from the Council Tax, such as a school (with a small charge for heating, lighting and cleaning).

When they meet

Parish Council meetings are generally on set weekday evenings whilst higher tiered authorities may also meet on weekday afternoons, but any day of the week can be chosen. Start times can be varied but 7.00pm is the most popular with meetings lasting around only a couple of hours - useful as after which concentrations often lapse and minds wander. Earlier start times of 6.30pm or even 6.00pm can make audience participation and Councillor involvement difficult, conflicting with work, travel or family commitments. Many Councils add estimated timings for each agenda item a useful guide for possible late arrivals but it can give the impression of rushing through items and not giving Councillor views a thorough airing on heavy weight issues, such as the annual Budget.

Joining In

Every Committee meeting is an open meeting and before each formal meeting there is a Public Forum. A 10 to 15 minute slot put aside for comments, presentations, statements or questions from the audience. This is the public's only opportunity to express any views. Every Parish has one or two stalwarts who regularly question and generally try to bring the Council to account. They are looked upon with a mixture of exasperation, dread and fondness.

Comments are limited to three minutes per person, or even per subject if a group of people wish to speak. A practice which has spread from the time allowed for representations at the higher tiers of local government Planning Boards. This puts a considerable strain on those speaking to explain sometimes quite complex, emotive issues, particularly if inexperienced at public speaking.

Comments and views need to be clear, precise and concise, reading from written notes and some practice beforehand always helps.

Speakers can be unkindly cut off when their time is up, even told to shut-up, making it an unpleasant experience for all creating an air of bad grace and offhand dismissal. Although used rarely, a Committee can ask the views of an acknowledged expert in the audience by suspending Standing Orders.

...Frome Watch...

Standing Orders

Oddly, Frome's Standing Orders do not allow for a reply or discussion from Councillors, when the townspeople ask questions. Although this could be easily solved by suspending Standing Orders for an interval whilst a debate or explanation takes place. The lack of willingness to do this has caused much bad feeling.

Presentations, given by organisations, often with the ubiquitous PowerPoint, are allowed more time. The questions, views or discussions resulting may not be recorded so the reading of the subsequent minutes will not betray what has happened. Without minuting there is no continuity or opportunity for the development of a discussion and other people with views or knowledge are unable to add to it.

Whilst public comments are made at the beginning of a meeting on a forth-coming agenda item, it can be a long wait for the subsequent Council discussion hoping the points raised have been fully absorbed. These encounters can feel frustrating, pointless and unproductive often leaving the audience with the distinct impression that the Committee is, "just going through the motions." If the press are present they may be persuaded to take up a Public Forum viewpoint. However, it is prudent to write your own press statement for the reporter on the night or send it in to the newspaper editor rather than leaving matters to chance. Any media interest may be short lived and may not highlight the points that seem most pertinent to those embroiled in a subject.

Hopefully, Councillors will give a positive response to queries, but speakers should press for comments or a specific action and insist on a written response with a named Councillor in order to pursue an issue in the future. Otherwise vague assurances will be forgotten and feedback non-existent - perhaps inevitable when Committee meetings are several months apart. It may be worth persuading Councillors to include a subject as a regular agenda item to keep a particular issue alive.

A Council can only formally exclude both the public and the press from specific agenda items if there are sensitive issues to be discussed such as, legal, contractual or difficult personnel matters. But, this has been used to be secretive for its own sake or to hide embarrassments. Exclusion will be flagged up on the agenda in advance and if there is an audience, these items may be moved to the end of the meeting so the public do not have to leave and re-enter the meeting, particularly important if they have to stand outside in the cold and rain.

Which Committee

Smaller Parishes still operate mixed agendas discussing items as they arise, only Planning applications, playing fields and community halls generally having a permanent place.

...Frome Watch...

Frome Town Council (2007-11) is a general illustration of how a larger Parish can organise itself.

Frome with its Full Council, for all Councillors to attend, delegates powers to 3 permanent Standing Committees (operating independently of the rest of the Council): Planning, Recreation and Properties (R&P) and Policy, Finance and Economic (P&F), each with a handful of decision making Councillors. P&F spawned 3 sub-committees: Christmas Spectacular, Grants and Personnel. Although the numerous Working Parties, such as Civic Matters (latter up-graded to a sub-committee) and the Task and Finish Groups (2008), were not open meetings. Most Working Parties reported to P&F (see Accountability).

Full Council

Full Council was the most interesting and lively of all the Committees. Councillors watched presentations (looked upon as something of a treat) from across a range of local organisations and groups including: commercial companies and voluntary groups, national and local charities, the police and local schools, with occasionally officers or Councillors from either County or District Councils. Giving updates on progress, announcing initiatives, making heartfelt pleas for money, or thank-yous for grants. Occasionally small groups of children put on musical performances and with a cup of tea in a proper cup and a gypsy cream biscuit in prospect, thoughtfully made by a voluntary group of elder ladies of the town, it made for a very pleasant evening. Of all the Committees Full Council and Planning were the most likely Committee to have an audience, though sparse, with 3 or 4 people at most, these stalwarts, had put in many years of service. Although with the downgrading of Full Council (meetings became short and uneventful) they moved their allegiance to Planning. The press too were more likely to attend if forewarned of an interesting news item, and could sometimes be seen in a quiet corner enjoying a sandwich, a can of Coke and generally joshing with Councillors.

All Councillors are expected to attend and as it is the only time all Councillors meet together there is often an air of guarded hostility. There is little socialising by the whole Council either before or after meetings, although those in political groupings may meet between Committee meetings to devise strategies. The new regular secret meetings of the political group leaders (Liberal Democrat, Conservative and Labour) outside the Committee framework, plus the one Independent Councillor who went as the representative of her individual "party", went unreported and unminuted. It was, it was suggested, intended to smooth the running of the official meetings.

In the past, meetings started with prayers led by the Mayor, and met monthly to ratify the minutes and question the decisions of the Standing Committees. The Council's income and expenditure statement were tabled and discussed in detail and any expenditure cheques signed. But by the 2007-11 electoral cycle Full Council was reduced to a rump of 4 or 5 meetings a year. This has sadly also become the norm in other large Parishes.

The power and the responsibility for taking decisions had been delegated to the Standing Committees. There were occasional short verbal updates on the minutes previously circulated however, any questions were quickly quashed with debate limited to statements of opposition. Councillors were told Standing Committee's decision could not be challenged. Councillors with opposing views became concerned they would be locked out of sitting on Committees altogether if they became "too difficult".

The statements of accounts were seen at P&F and cheques signed in office, making the criteria for Councillors to be jointly and severally responsible for the workings of the Council impossible to achieve. Effectively reducing responsibility from 17 to a handful of Councillors, inevitably from the ruling party, causing many to feel ignored.

As a result, the Full Council became less pivotal, unable to carry out a rigorous scrutinising role, merely a body to be reported to, with little heat or debate. The possibility and the uncertainty that Full Council could upend any Committee decision, as in the past, had been lost.

Now with little bite; Full Council set the precept, taking recommendations from P&F, set some principle policies and processes such as Standing Orders and dealt with some of the larger legal matters such as borrowing money and Bye Laws. Councillors on Outside Bodies occasionally reported to it. Standing Committee Chairman could request Full Council to take forward and implement its recommendations if it was not meeting for several months. Controversial issues would be sent from other Committees when a whole Council comment was needed, such as the perennial problem of District Council car parking charges. The Policy, Finance and Economic Committee was now where the power rested.

The Annual Meeting of the Council

This Full Council meeting takes place in May and is 1 of the 4 statutory meetings, not to be confused with the Annual Parish Meeting (which is for the electorate).

The meeting elects the Chairman, Deputy Chairman and appoints Standing Committee members (the list is drawn up by the ruling party); sub-committees are appointed by their controlling Committee. The Annual Meeting allows the previous year's Mayor to step down and for the appointment of a new Mayor and Deputy Mayor to take place. The outgoing Mayor gives a speech of thanks and summarises the year just past, with the incoming Mayor expressing continued hope. Mayoral chains are adjusted and photographs taken watched by proud family members.

In the past there was the Annual Inspection of Deeds, where all Councillors had the opportunity to examine the deeds, leases and trust documents of buildings, land and other responsibilities held on behalf of the town to see that they were present and correct. Interesting in themselves they were also a useful reminder of Councillor accountability but now had been abandoned as unnecessary.

Councillors were also appointed or reappointed as observers on town organisations management teams (Outside Bodies). A list of the Meeting dates for all Committees for the whole year circulated and set to avoid clashes with District Council meetings particularly important where Planning is concerned.

Now very brief, the 2009 meeting took just 20 minutes (a record it was said) and was followed by a buffet reception. All sense of gravitas lost.

Planning

Controversial and unpredictable, Planning meets the most frequently of all Committees, at three weekly intervals, making approximately 16 meetings a year, enabling comments on Planning applications to be sent to the Planning authority within the 21 days allowed.

Two of the 7 (2008-2010) strong Planning Committee were also part of the Mendip District Planning Board (which itself increased its Frome representation from 2 to 6 over the 4 years) giving Frome an extremely strong voice. However, the then Planning rules meant whilst they could listen to the diverse opinions and objections to a Planning application they could not form an opinion. Indeed at the start of meetings Councillors recited a mantra explaining in detail that any comments or support given would not necessarily be their final opinion. Balancing on a fine line, so as not to prejudice any discussion at the Planning authority's Planning Board, where decisions made are based on the evidence presented to the Board at its meeting. However, it was still possible for Councillors to act as an advocate for the town over wider controversial matters.

This messily awkward situation was swept away by the Localism Act 2011 allowing Councillors free rein to voice opinions.

The Parish Council is one of a set of statutory consultees on Planning applications. The Committee discusses all applications received by Mendip District Council for development within the Parish. As in most Parishes, most applications are for small scale changes: conservatories, and house extensions, including Listed Building Consent or Conservation Area Consent, and tree pruning if protected by a Tree Preservation Order.

Popular with the public particularly with neighbours most affected by proposals, the townspeople have just three minutes to voice an opinion. Disappointingly, their views are not necessarily repeated by Councillors in their comments to the Planning authority which are tersely written and summarised in a strangulated faux Planning language. Over the four years the Committee's tone changed from a chirpy *"approve subject to neighbours and the tree officer (?),"* to a pompous *"proceed to a decision,"* or if objecting, the generalised *"detrimental to visual amenities,"* or the even vaguer *"overdevelopment."* No suggestions were made for affordable housing, or for cash to help provide play parks, open space, community halls, allotments, or general town improvements.

Busy and varied, the Planning authority can ask for opinions on: the licensing of premises, market licenses, local footpaths - closures and re-routes, street names, street lighting and street furniture, car park charges - always controversial with local objections always overruled, CCTV coverage, and announcements of road closures within the Parish, either for repairs or for festivals and street celebrations. Parishes can create new byelaws such as the alcohol exemption zone in force in Frome town centre.

The Committee's budget provided dog poo, litter and grit bins, bus shelters and street lights. It is this Committee which deals with the small niggles of life: overgrown hedges - writing to the owners, "A" frames blocking pavements – writing to County Highways often and for years; and listening to local complaints on dog poo - sympathetic comments. Frome has an official reporting and monitoring agreement with County for loose manhole covers and potholes.

The Committee has delegated authority and only matters of a high local impact will be taken to Full Council for discussion, where it is felt more publicity or the full wrath of the Council is needed, such as the annual proposals for car parking charge increases.

The Civic Society, part of the Frome Group for Local Study, has for many years commented on all applications presented to the Committee. Composed of local historians and retired architects, their written comments are read out as each application is discussed. There was a suggestion to give the group a seat on the Committee but this was voted down.

Policy and Finance and Economic (P&F)

An executive Committee with delegated authority operating independently, it effectively runs the Council giving limited verbal updates to Full Council. It ran 3, later 4, sub-committees: Grants, Christmas Spectacular, Personnel and Civic Matters plus a large range of working parties and Task and Finish Groups, with membership mainly drawn from within the Committee of 7 Councillors. For such a major Committee it met infrequently between 4 and 6 times a year.

Running the Parish Budget (around £3.4 million over 4 years) it oversaw spending, income, auditing arrangements and general housekeeping. It set the annual Budget taking suggestions from all Committees in October/November of each year for the forthcoming Parish financial year (1st April to 31st March). The proposed Budgets were agreed in the following January at Full Council setting the precept for the coming year.

The District Council incorporates the Parish precept into the Council Tax.

P&F decided the town's major projects: Twinning, funding and extending the original social purpose of the group adding economic ambitions by adding a 4th town in Poland; the pursuit of new offices – a long held ambition; additional land ownership; the takeover of Tourist Information; lease negotiation and the proposed takeover of the *Cheese & Grain*.

The Grants sub–committee

Always a generous town, 5 Councillors met twice a year initially distributing £65,000 to local groups - £46,000 under three year funding plans and £20,000 in small generally one-off amounts. Over the four years of the electoral cycle the amount given slipped although the overall Budget doubled.

Christmas Spectacular sub-committee

The only Committee to use outside expertise, originally with 2 Councillors and 5 volunteers. It met irregularly to discuss: the evening's entertainments, the towns Christmas decorations, the switching on of the Christmas Lights and the Mayors Christmas Card competition before being abandoned.

Frome's Festive Fortnight was first run by the Chamber of Commerce in 1956, festooning the Market Place, Cheap Street and Catherine Hill with long lazy loops of coloured bulbs, a Christmas tree for choirs of carol singers to congregate round and a festive window display competition *"to delight resident and visitor alike."* Later at the end of 1990's and with some Town Council money, the Extravaganza was launched. Headed up by shopkeepers from the Chamber of Commerce it introduced a new idea, Late Night Christmas Shopping on the last Friday in November when most of the townspeople had been paid keeping the Christmas spend within the town.

The first evenings had historic themes with shop keepers, Councillors and customers dressing up in Elizabethan or Victorian costumes. Families wandered from shop to shop sampling food and drink, banks and estate agents kept open house with mince pies and mulled wine, art galleries held late night exhibitions, music and circus performers entertained in the streets alongside children's fairground rides, Father Christmas was in his grotto and local charity stalls held raffles and tombolas in windy shopping precincts.

The highlight of the evening was the switching on of the Christmas lights, by the Mayor and the Carnival Queen accompanied by a choir next to the Christmas tree. The tree, always controversial: either by taking up *"valuable parking spaces,"* leaning at a precarious angle - as the occasional car driver collided with it, having too few light bulbs - reportedly only 6 one year, or decorated on only one side, or indeed as in one year to the scrunch of broken glass as the lights were run over by the Mayor as he stopped his car to see how the tree decorating was progressing - the resulting altercation hitting the news headlines locally and nationally.

Until in its final years, as a health and safety culture swept through the Council, crash barriers heaped against it resulting in a marooned, sad and forlorn tree. So by 2009, in the Christmas tree's old spot, a replacement decoration, looking remarkably like a rotary washing line, split public opinion, the dismissed tree's anarchic years now behind it.

The Extravaganza night was equally eventful as the lights: either failed to switch on at all, or blacked out the whole of the town centre several years running - an extension lead run from a local bank overloaded, a laser display was rumoured to be a torch from an upstairs window; and last but not least there was one year the police unexpectedly released riot gas on the crowd. Fireworks were later introduced and became a regular feature despite initial complaints of noise which included a letter from the owner of a traumatised goldfish.

The lights originally organised by the Frome Chamber of Commerce, and put up and taken down by the town's volunteer fire brigade, hoped to keep people shopping in Frome or attract customers from neighbouring towns when competition between neighbouring town's Christmas lights was fierce. The Town Council eventually leased the lights (6 stars arcing across the main street) and the 40 odd strong Chamber contribute around £600-700 each year to their cost.

In 2008 this was all swept away with the, (by now renamed) Spectacular taking place on a Sunday afternoon in the Market Yard's dark, bleak and puddly car park. The link with local shopping lost especially as the new stalls market and arts and craft fair took place the following week. But by 2010 there was a small and now free "ice" rink, a reindeer to pet, music, fairground rides and a fantastic firework display. The Mayor's speech, was given from the balcony of the George Hotel to a packed Market Place of carol singing crowds, heralding the switching on of the town centre Christmas lights by the winner of the Mayor's Christmas Card competition (in previous years the carnival queen and retinue of princesses added a touch of glamour) lowering a plunger as simultaneously a man perched at the top of a ladder plugged them in (what could go wrong).

Personnel sub–committee

A perhaps unexpected Committee for a Parish Council, the 5 Councillors met 4 or 5 times over the 4 years dealing with employment issues such as pay and conditions but primarily staff recruitment. The Town employing 16 staff with the absorption of the Tourist Information Office and recently taking on 2 apprentices.

The Town buys in contract staff for: cleaning the 2 toilet blocks, tree maintenance, grass cutting, floral beds, personnel and accountancy advice and internal auditors on a regular basis. Other services such as building surveyors and architects are bought in by the relevant Committee. Staffing has grown as roles have been broken into specialisations; a critical mass having been reached which requires less decision making from Councillors as the bureaucracy becomes self-perpetuating. Meetings have moved away from the Town Clerk minuting meetings to a minute taker and at least one extra staff member in an advisory role. Indeed one Councillor remarked that Councillors were in danger of being outnumbered by staff at meetings.

Civic Matters

Initially a Working Party, eventually becoming a sub-committee of P&F. It revived the Civic Community Awards, made to townspeople who had made outstanding contributions to the life of the town nominated by colleagues and friends. In its first year (July 2008) the 7 Awards of paperweights were presented at the revived annual Civic Church Service with a reception for invited guests and dignitaries from the surrounding towns. The local newspapers snapped up the idea, running their own community awards, overshadowing the Council's own with lots of categories and a sheaf of contenders voted for by readers.

Councillors, realising they had nothing to remember their year as Mayor by now had medals struck and included all past Majors since the post's inception in 1974. These were presented at a special ceremony. Thereafter a medal is given annually as each Mayor steps down from office.

Councillors discussed becoming a robed Council, with the ceremonial black tricorn hat and long red ermine or lace trimmed robes as in the nearby historic ex-Borough Councils of Wells and Glastonbury where this tradition is maintained today. It was however, thought not to be in-keeping with the character of Frome.

Working Parties

These were various single issue research and discussion groups which were generally set up by P&F but also by R&P reporting to their founding Committee.

They may or may not have met (see also Accountability).

Task and Finish Groups

Set up by Policy and Finance in 2008 as a result of the Council's "away day" – which also produced the 2 ½ year Strategic Plan - where Councillors discussed and decided on the main areas of concern within the town. 5 areas were identified and members of P&F appointed to the groups, they were expected to report back within a few months, but faded away.

Recreation and Properties (R&P)

This is the main focus of the Town's spending, yet the 7 Councillors met just 4-5 times a year. Overseeing Victoria Park, Mary Bailey Playing Field, the floral hanging baskets, Rodden Meadow and the maintenance of the town allotments, the town offices, the Cheese & Grain community hall, and the District Council toilets, employing 6 staff adding an apprentice gardener in 2011 from the original 2 gardeners in the 1980s.

It spent a controversial annual budget of around £200,000 in 2007/08, on Victoria Park whereas Frome's sister town of Shepton Mallet ran its similarly sized Collett Park as a Trust for around £50,000, The Committee has bought in additional contractors for tree maintenance, flower bed construction and floral basket watering, toilet maintenance and building work. Most of Frome's green spaces are looked after by the District Council which charges a Special Rate Precept as a part of every household's Council Tax.

On the south side of the town lie two of the town's gems:

The first, Victoria Park, surrounded by fine Victorian villas on what is still considered to be the two most desirable streets in the older part of the town, was funded by public subscription in 1887 to celebrate Queen Victoria's Diamond Jubilee and handed to the Frome Urban District Council to maintain. The large grassed area of about 6 acres was designed as a pleasure garden to stroll round with fine specimen trees planted (there is a Council leaflet describing them).

On a sweltering July summers day the Prime Minister of New South Wales Australia, the Hon JST McGowen with the Lord Lieutenant of Somerset, the Marquess of Bath (from nearby Longleat House) planted two oak trees to commemorate the coronation of King George V in 1911, watched by over half the town's population (2,000 school children and 5,000 townspeople).

Resounding cheers were raised as both men dispensed with top hat and frock coat to do the planting and as an exchange of flags with Mantraville in New South Wales was made and hoisted onto the flag-staff, *"for the love of country, pride of Empire and loyalty to the Crown."* Frome's unexpected Australian connection, was James Mantra, (giving his name to a suburb of Sydney) a native of Frome who spearheaded the colonisation of Australia, *"to people an uninhabited continent."* The plaque commemorating this intense moment of patriotism still lies beneath one of the trees.

The modest ornamental fountain (another gift by Alderman Flatman) and the public drinking fountain have long since disappeared (but may be still in pieces in a store room) but the Park still has the one remaining set of impressive iron gates on Weymouth Road. The thatched bandstand topped with a weather vane is unique and hosted free brass band concerts on summer Sunday afternoons; the Town underwriting the bands' travel costs. Though little advertised, it was a quintessentially English pleasure. The summer months are also a time of fêtes, toddler group picnics and local school events. Previous years have seen music concerts, jazz concerts and theatrical plays. The Park hosts the Frome Town Crier competition with around 24 national entrants with the season ending with the Children's Carnival competition before the evening Carnival procession through the town in late-September.

The three tennis courts, the modest putting green, boule court, and with 1 of the 6 bowling rinks hired out, along with the equipment, contributes a small annual income of about £1,000. Frome Park Bowls Club (one of two bowls clubs in the town) started in the Park in 1931 and in recent years has run and maintained, in lieu of rent, the bowling green, with its spectacular flower beds alongside the "pavilion". The Town contributes a £1,000 annually to the cost and replaced the original charming black wooden verandah'd club house with its hand-made terracotta tiled roof in 2000 with an unassuming shed.

The long held and agonised over ambition to bring back the café (Gazzards popular in the 1950's) was realised in 2009 with the conversion and leasing of the original tea house latterly a Park shelter for the summer months. Costed out at a surprising £45,000 it may bring in an income of around £3,000 in future years.

The second, the 4 acre Mary Bailey Playing Field given to the Town (Urban District Council) in 1930 by Miss Mary Bailey and was home to the Red Triangle Hut (its shape still emerges from the grass in dry summers) a popular dance venue which played to a packed house when it showed the film of Elizabeth II's Coronation. Later passing to the National Playing Fields Association (renamed Fields in Trust (FIT)) it is now managed by the Town Council. Local graffiti artists have painted a mural alongside the footpath between the two parks.

The Committee planned spend of £150,000 on new children's play equipment, replacing the 1999 equipment, part-funded (£10,000) by the now defunct Somerset Aggregate Levy Fund and was the only time grants had been successfully applied for.

A large grassy field for ball games, it has the towns only skate board/BMX cycle area, the second skate board park next to the Cheese & Grain, in the Market Yard was closed when Mendip District Council decided not to fund the safety checks or any repairs. A play wall with a basketball ring was funded by FIT.

Riverside Rodden Meadow at the end of Willow Vale is part of a large area of green fields which reach into the heart of the town centre from Wallbridge, bounded to the north by the Millennium Green on the steep valley side and crossed by the Colliers Way, part of the Sustrans national cycle network. Bought at auction in 1990's for £20,000 (Mendip District Council retained, until recently, ownership of the river's edge causing some conflict of management), the 6 acres of rough grazing creates a large wildlife area (badgers frequently raided the nearby back gardens from their sett in the Meadow) used mainly by dog walkers.

The Somerset Wildlife Trust's yearlong species survey suggested the additional planting of native wildflower species, complementing, the additional native shrub and tree species planted by the local Lyn Young Trust, at present the grass is taken off once a year to increase the diversity of flowering plants. Local charity, Friends of the River Frome regularly clean-up the riverbanks through the town and have paid for information boards for the Meadow. They are a practical point of contact for all the river's landowners. Over the years there have been other suggested uses for the Meadow such as camping but these have never been taken up.

In common with most towns, Frome has renamed various floral areas after its Twin towns: North Hill House Gardens given to the town by Miss Theodora le Gros is now renamed Murrhardt Gardens after the German twin town, a revamped Château Gontier Walk in the town centre for the French town and with the addition of the Polish town of Rabka, a small Rock Garden in a corner of Victoria Park.

The Town has been a regular runner-up in its Britain in Bloom category, the competition is the highlight of many a Parish Council year. Originally entered by Frome in Bloom, who organise their own town-wide competition which contributes to the national scheme. The town also competes with the other four Mendip towns for Mendip in Bloom. The Park nursery grows on plants from plugs and over-winters exotics such as daturas, and abutilons. 14,000 bedding plants are grown for Victoria Park, the three entrance signs to the town, Murrhardt Gardens and tubs and planters in the town centre including the 40 hanging baskets.

Merchants Barton, the last of the District Council toilet blocks which was due for closure until the Town took over the cleaning and maintenance. Councillors stressed it was an important community service until it too closed them in 2011, even stripping the toilets of their hanging baskets. The 1997 Labour Government had worried about toilet closures nationwide and offered grants of £1,000 to shops so people could use their toilets – the Council thought it a good idea but there were no takers. The District built a replacement town centre block or "Beacon" toilets and were triumphant when it won (2011) the 5 star national Loo of the Year for the 4th year running.

The Town's 109 allotments are run and managed by the Frome Allotment Association and nominally overseen by R&P.

Over the years and somewhat puzzlingly, R&P has undertaken the tree work and tidying up of Zion Path – a short gloomy footpath, although a Somerset County Council responsibility. This raises the issue of double taxation which goes unanswered. However, it does act as a paid agent for the County, cleaning road signs, and notifying road problems and with some pavement weed spraying (now ended) bringing in an income of around £4,000.

A flurry of activity undertaken in secret in the last six months of the electoral cycle brought unexpected areas of land for the Town: Château Gontier Walk, the footpath and woodlands area from the Cheese & Grain to Welshmill.
The Welshmill Adventure Playground - previously the leat off the river feeding a Mill (long demolished) and at one time containing an original quarry shunting engine, an unlikely feature today and Weylands (a boggy grassy riverside kick-about area) - 2 of the 15 areas the District Council list as play areas, again whether the problem of double taxation had been investigated is not minuted. Attempts to buy car parking next to the Cheese & Grain, at Badcox and by the Market Cross was momentarily thwarted by Mendip District asking the Town what they wanted to do with it and, with local elections looming, time ran out.

Datafile
National Playing Fields Association now Fields in Trust, www.npfa.co.uk
Sustrans, www.sustrans.org.uk
Friends of the Somerset River Frome, www.friendsoftheriverfrome.org.uk

CHEAP STREET FROME

8 – PEOPLE - Growing a Community - Outside Bodies

Frome, as in any Parish, has groups of enthusiasts organising, running and funding an impressive range of societies, clubs, organisations and groups, occasionally helped by money from the town. These groups often referred to by Councils as "Outside Bodies", are a surprise for new Councillors who find there is an assumption they will be part of one of these management teams. Appointments are made annually for a year at a time at the May Annual Meeting of the Town Council. With no previous knowledge and faced with an unexpected responsibility it can make contributing a daunting task. Expected to attend regularly and take part in discussions, a Councillor is an observer when it comes to decision making and voting - although not all Councillors realise this. With District and County Committees and school governorships there is an active voting role.

There can be competition between Councillors to sit on the more prestigious organisations with an additional opportunity for political point scoring, as each appointment is proposed and seconded. Some Councillors have an enthusiasm to be on everything, equally there are organisations no one wants to be on.

Organisations to, may decide not continue appointing Councillors; The Blue House, an almshouse for the retired of Frome Parish, now appoints trustees rather than asking for Councillors from the surrounding Parishes. However, once appointed Councillors tend to stay with their choice in the following years, and often continue in membership when no longer a Councillor. The amount of time involved will vary and will depend on the level of commitment each wishes to put in. Councillors are expected to report regularly to Full Council but rarely do.

In (2007/08) 13 (10 by the end of the election cycle) of the 17 Councillors shared the 22 listed appointments not including school governorships.

Organisations could be divided into several types:
- grant aided, promoting a specialist interest or activity often hoping to involve the wider community. Receiving £5,000 or more as an annual grant or under a 3 year funding agreement;
- a decision making or a collaborating Committee at District or County level and unfunded, although the Mendip CCTV Users Group is an exception to this;
- unfunded groups where there is an assumed a close working beneficial relationship e.g. Frome in Bloom and;
- groups providing a paid for service such as the Somerset Association of Local Councils – East Area.

OUTSIDE BODIES listed for 2007/08

The following cameos describe a cross section of wildly different organisations. A mixture of local groups or those closely linked to well-known national charities some with and some without Town funding or groups that offer the opportunity for the town's opinions to be voiced to the higher tiers of local government. How much benefit a Councillor can give or what opinions are voiced is difficult to judge - reports to the Town are rare and rarely descriptive. The groups involved were surveyed for their views.

General Influence and a hoped for understanding and support for their aims topped the list, hearing Council business first hand was important, as was the hoped for continued funding.

By the end of the electoral cycle (2007-11) many more were sending in reports detailing how the Town's money was spent but this is an administrative process and is unreported and unseen.

The locally run groups with three year funding:

Cheese & Grain Community Trust - the exception, was on a four year funding cycle	£35,000
Frome Association for Holiday Activities	£5,000
Frome Museum	£1,000
Frome Tourist Information Centre Ltd	£8,000
Young People Frome + Frome Youth Council	£6,500 + £3,000 in grants
Frome Festival	£5,000

The Nationally Linked Charities:

Frome and District Citizens Advice Bureau	£7,000

Groups which may or may not be funded:

Frome groups:

Frome Allotments Association	around £3,000
Frome Twinning Association	around £3.000
Frome in Bloom	not funded
Frome Public Transport Users Association	not funded
Frome Recreation and Open Ground Supporters (FROGS) funded occasionally	under annual grants

The Nationally Linked Charities:

Frome and District YMCA Centre funded (08/09)	under annual grants
Fair-Trade Frome funded	under annual grants £1,000

Local, District and County Authority groups:

CCTV Users group funded annually	£8,000
East Mendip Area Youth Advisory Committee	not funded and short lived
Mendip Play Partnership creating the Mendip Play Strategy May 2007	not funded
Frome Locality Steering Group, started 2006 finished 2007	not funded
Frome Community College Media Arts Strategic Group started 2006 finished 2007	not funded
School governors	not funded

District and County Committees:

Somerset Mendip Area Working Panel only ran in 2007-08, all Parish Councillors could speak at meetings not funded, replaced by East Mendip Community Partnership
East Mendip Community Partnership, all Parish Councillors could speak at meetings not funded

National links - the lobby group:

Somerset Association of Local Councils - East Area Town Council pays membership fees

Locally run groups with three year funding:

Long term funding gives groups a measure of financial stability, enabling them to plan and apply for grants from other organisations such as the National Lottery; Parish funding gives a confirmed level of credibility. Grants are paid annually.

Cheese & Grain Community Trust

The exception with funding on a four year cycle paid annually:

- £35,000 for general running costs
- £26,000 for external repairs and maintenance, until September 2008 when the Trust took over.
- £17,000 is paid off the Public Works Loan Board loan along with £20,000 in interest charges each year.
- One Town Council observer and one Frome District Councillor observer.
  www.cheeseandgrain.co.uk

What they do

The Cheese & Grain, in the old Cattle Market car park, is a multi-purpose 650 capacity live gig and club venue with conference facilities and day time specialist markets including: antique collectables, crafts, and farmer's markets. It programmes music from bands both national such as "Madness" and local "The Wurzels", solo artists, such as Robert Plant and tribute bands. With specialist interests from chocolate fayres to rabbit shows, from family parties to wrestling bouts. There is a licensed café and bar. The Grain is recognised as a regional centre for music.

History

Built in 1874 as the "New Market Hall" for the Frome Market Company selling locally produced cheeses and grain crops, transported on the railway running to the rear of the building. It replaced the covered market at the bottom of Cheap Street in the town centre. The weekly cattle and livestock market moved next to it until the 1990's when it moved again to outside the town at Standerwick.

Frome Operatic Society, now based at the Memorial Theatre, staged all its early productions here, beginning with "Trial by Jury" by Gilbert and Sullivan, in April 1906. The building was commandeered and turned into a munitions factory as part of the J W Singer's war effort during the First World War. Afterwards returning to markets and trade exhibitions until the late 1950's when it was bought by Frome Urban District Council who later sold it in 1963 for industrial use; BenChairs and Frontline Kitchens were the last manufacturers to use it. The building gradually deteriorated finally becoming a store for used vehicle tyres.

In the 1990's the building was bought by Mendip District Council and leased in 1997 after much wrangling over car parking spaces, to the Town Council for use as a community hall replacing a small wooden market hall popular for: antiques, collectors' fayres, jumble sales, and Women's Institute Markets, which stood in front of the town library. The Town Council borrowed from the Public Works Loan Board to repair and refurbish it. It opened with bigger markets and as an entertainments venue (September 1998). By October 2001 complaints of noise (it was rumoured by newcomers to the town) led to the building being closed for further soundproofing and acoustic works, as well as the addition of a vast new mezzanine floor for offices along with new bar facilities. The Cheese & Grain re-opened in July 2002 with live events and new markets.

Who is involved

In April 2003 the Town Council leased the building to an independent charity which now manages the building and its activities for community use.

Anyone who lives or works in Frome or surrounding villages or any of the groups using the building can become a charity member (there are around 300), the Committee of trustees is elected by the members. It employs around 20 people. As part of the 2010 lease the Town Council had 6 free hire days. The Trust has made a small profit in the last few years.

Frome Association For Holiday Activities

- Funding: £5,000 per year
- Funding pays for the co-ordinator
- One Town Council observer
  www.faha.co.uk

What they do
This play scheme provided activities for 5-11year olds during the 12 weeks of school holidays with 24 children at each of the all day sessions, providing a surprising 1,440 places over the year. Charging (£15.50 2008) per day, with free places for disabled children and in 2010 for children on free school meals. Each scheme is themed such as Easter, Halloween and Christmas providing craft projects, games and puzzles, a kitchen for cookery, and sports activities either in the indoor sports hall, or outside on the tennis courts.

History
FAHA started over 20 years ago as an umbrella organisation for the many different play providers in the town, before becoming a play scheme. It is based at the County's Youth and Community Centre.

Who is involved
FAHA has a management committee of volunteers and is applying to become a charity. The scheme and qualified staff are Ofsted inspected.

Frome Museum

- Funding: £1,000 per year
- Funding for running costs
- One Town Council observer
  www.fromemuseum.org

What they do
The museum concentrates on the industrial and social history of the town with permanent displays on:

- J W Singer & Sons Ltd whose foundry was internationally famed for its bronze statuary, such as Boudicca on the River Thames Embankment and Justice on the Old Bailey in London;
- Fussell's Ironworks of Mells one of the country's major manufacturers of agricultural edge-tools in the 19th Century, this included anything with a cutting edge from spades to in later years lawn mowers;
- Butler and Tanner, printers, who became a leading European colour book printers;
- Other collections include: Victorian costumes, many from the Horner family (of Little Jack Horner nursery rhyme fame), fossil and rock specimens from the local geology (Jurassic), and paintings of local people (17th century poet Elizabeth Rowe), or by local artists.

There are two particular curiosities: Mr Maggs Chemist Shop, Victorian splendour recreated and a 3D model of the streets and buildings of the town centre as it was in 1985. New exhibitions are mounted throughout the season.

The museum library's extensive archive of people, buildings and events from the town and the surrounding villages with maps and photographs can be booked for historical and family research.

History

Housed in an extraordinary and imposing wedge shaped, Italianate Grade II listed building on North Parade in the town centre. The museum was opened in 1869 as the Frome Literary and Scientific Institution for the further education of the professional and business classes in the town.

Who is involved

The museum, a registered charity, is staffed entirely by some 30 volunteers opening from March till the end of November. Entrance is free or by donation. The Frome Local Study Group gives history walking tours towards museum funds once a month.

Frome Tourist Information Centre Ltd (TIC)

- Funding: £8,000 per year before its absorption into the Town Council.
- One Town Council observer and one District Council observer. The Town Council funding was on a three year funding cycle, whilst the District Council funded on an annual basis.
  www.frometouristinfo.co.uk

What they do

It provides information for tourists and residents alike with leaflets of places to visit, things to do, locally and further afield, a monthly "what's on" guide and a welcome pack for new residents.

There is a booking service: for local accommodation, national and international coach and train travel plus discounted event tickets. The selection of local books by local authors and the Frome teddy (a small bear with Frome emblazoned on its jumper) are sadly gone when Town Council absorbed the Centre (2010) making it the "reception" for the Council offices; taking queries and providing limited information about the Council.

Website

In 2008, the website had 3 million hits with 45,000 unique visitors, whilst the Round Tower had 30,000 visitors.

History

Originally in a renovated circular cloth drying Round Tower of the Black Swan Art Centre. Its incorporation into the Town Council, when District funding was reduced, later saw a move (2010) to the town library.

Who is involved

Originally an independent not for profit company, and one of the 5 unrelated TIC's based in the main Mendip towns. The 23 volunteers and 3 paid employees provided a friendly, experienced and locally knowledgeable service, only the paid staff remained. (see Unknown Unknowns)

Young People Frome (YPF)

- Funding: £8,000 per year plus an additional grant of £3,000 for the Youth Council. Funding part pays for a co-ordinator and a published activity directory. The grant funded projects, including giving grants to other town organisations.
- One Town Council observer
  www.fromeactive.org.uk

What they do

YPF produces the "Frome Active" booklet, for 0 to 25 year olds, which includes lists of toddler groups, childcare nurseries, schools, clubs, offering sports, arts, things to do and things to join in with. Featuring services provided by Somerset Carers, Mendip Housing, Mendip YMCA and Wessex Counselling. Updated annually it is available at public points around the town. Since 2001, the directory is published on-line with occasional Youth Council minutes. The YPF co-ordinator provides administration for the Frome Youth Council both based at Frome Community College.

History

Created by the Mayor's Youth Initiative in 1988 it brought together voluntary and statutory agencies to provide and promote activities for young people from teenagers to those in their mid-twenties. It was cutting edge at the time. It brought, youngsters in school, with those hoping to go to university, with youngsters doing apprenticeships as well as those in work, together in a forum to help provide things to do and to give them, up to then, an unheard voice. This eventually centred around the production of an activities directory of groups and clubs in and around Frome and was delivered to every household. In 2007, the Frome Learning Community Partnership (FLCP), an umbrella organisation for all the schools in the Frome area, added extra funding to organise limited preschool and after school activities sharing resources and ideas.

Who is involved

The management Committee is made up of representatives from the Police, Rotary Club, Somerset Volunteers Network, ex-town Councillors, and Frome Community College staff.

Frome Youth Council (FYC)

What they do

It organises occasional events for teenagers such as the Rhythm for Life (May 2009) an exhibition showcasing 26 organisations providing activities for young people. The Town Council had promised to use it as a sounding board for its projects to get the youth perspective but other than a brief stint on the Christmas Spectacular Committee nothing materialised.

Since the start of Young People Frome there have been many promises of a youth café and each new YPF co-ordinator has had it as a priority, lots of venues have been chosen but it never quite happened. The local ITV television station gave the project a filmed five minute slot in its community involvement section "ITV Fixers" (2009). More talks were held with the Town Council to move it on but without success. Flourish, the local Mendip Housing Association gave the group £9,000 in 2010 to pay for a project researcher. After 23 years it opens where it was originally intended, as part of the YMCA Foyer project.

History

Based at Frome Community College it is now a small group of students from the College.

Originally it was intended to be a broad age range of youngsters (under 25s) from across the town including those in school, further education and employment meeting to discuss possible projects.

This is separate from the student year representatives elected by classmates to give an opinion on the running of the College. The name is a misnomer as the Youth Council is unelected. Over the last ten years, via the YPF co-ordinator, FYC has been involved in discussions over: the Frome Foyer Project (housing for young people), the play equipment in Mary Bailey Playing Field, the skate board parks, the Frome Festival and the Christmas Spectacular, fronting Saturday Sport at the leisure centre, promoting the Duke of Edinburgh Award, the founding of Music Mayhem and intermittent discussions on the long proposed youth café for the town.

In the past the Town Council's grant has allowed it to grant aid other organisations within the town. This was advertised for the final time in October 2008 and offered £250 to providers of activities for young people. There are no details available.

Who is involved
Made up of about seven or eight tertiary (16 to 18 years of age) students (2009) meeting about twice a term to discuss projects and involvement in town events. FYC has wanted to extend its role and be more closely involved with the Town Council, hoping to voice opinions on what is important to young people indeed there was a suggestion that there was a student on every Town Council Committee but nothing happened. FYC no longer publishes minutes of meetings.

Volunteering
There are national and local schemes which recognise the volunteering work undertaken by 16 to 25 year olds (such as the Youth Council). The number of volunteered hours are added up, any volunteering counts including meetings as well as actual projects, and certificates are given after a set number of hours e.g. 50 hours. Volunteering, is useful evidence on a Curriculum Vita, showing a level of community commitment and is useful when applying for college and university places as well as demonstrating learned skills and experience to potential employers.

One Youth Council member won both the Mendip Young Volunteer of the Year Award and the Somerset Volunteer of the Year Award.

Frome Festival
- Funding, £5,000 each year
- One Town Council observer
  www.fromefestival.co.uk

What they do
"Enthralling and spectacular, Somerset's largest community festival offers something for everyone and entertainment for all ten days of classical music, jazz, folk, indie, literature, drama, film, dance, workshops and free events starting on the first Friday in July. With household names, famous celebrities, international stars, globetrotting VIPs, comic superheroes, puckish jesters and spellbinding sorcerers." Every year brings record audiences to over 150 events in 40 different venues attracting overall audiences of up to 30,000. Bringing together venues which provide the town's entertainment throughout the year in an explosion of activity. It has become the anchor for the arts in Frome.

History
Started in the year 2001, as one man's inspiration it has become the event of the year, with far too much to see and do.

Who is involved
The Festival is a not-for-profit company limited by guarantee and a registered charity. The Friends are its members who may vote and stand for election to the Board. The Board are also trustees of the charity. The Festival is organised, promoted and in the main performed by local people with a smattering of celebrity names, many who live locally.

The Nationally Linked Charities:

Mendip Citizens Advice Bureau (Mendip CAB)
- Funding, £7,000 each year
- One Town Councillor observer
  www.medipcab.org.uk, www.citizensadvice.org.uk

What they do
The Citizens Advice service helps people resolve their legal, money and other problems by providing free information, practical help and advice.

Perhaps best known for its debt and welfare benefit advice which makes up the largest proportion of queries, it also advises on; housing, employment issues, consumer, legal, relationships, utilities such as telecoms, immigration, health, and taxation. CAB advice is independent, confidential, impartial, and non-judgemental.

The Mendip CAB website emphasised four areas of work;

- Domestic abuse, all those who feel threatened or intimidated in their own homes. Such as partners, spouses, parents intimidated by their teenage children, older people being financially used by their children and men suffering domestic abuse.
- GP Outreach Project, a three year Big Lottery Funded project concentrated on bringing the full CAB advice service to patients in five GP surgeries in the Mendip area.
- Extended Welfare Benefits Service, under contract from the Legal Services Commission providing benefit advice in rural areas from form filling through to checking benefit entitlements.
- Financial Inclusion Fund Debt Advice, offering a one to one review of finances, setting out the best options and checking welfare benefit entitlements.

History
Frome and District Citizens Advice Bureau ran as an independent office before joining the other Mendip towns in April 2005 to become Mendip CAB. This in turn is part of the national Citizens Advice network which sets advice standards and training.

Who is involved
Each bureau is an independent registered charity. A modest income of £373,000 in 2007/08 ran 5 offices, a telephone help line, a mobile unit visiting the larger villages plus requested home visits with a workforce of 17 and some 85 trained volunteers. Funding came mainly from Mendip District Council providing around £93,000 annually or roughly a third of the District Council's grant aid allowance with Somerset County Council giving around £64,000. The Parishes contributed about £23,000 with the remainder from specific targeted government grants and small amount from donations.

By 2011 the Frome bureau estimated it helped oversee £5 million of debt from mortgages, credit cards and ordinary loans.

Groups which may or may not be funded:

Frome Allotments Association

- Funding included within the town general budget around £3,000
- One or two Town Council Observers

What they do

The Allotment Association handles the day to day management and insurance of the 109 town allotments; it collects the modest rents on average £15 per allotment (adding around £300 per year to the town's income). It manages the waiting list of around 90 (rising to 120 by the end of the electoral cycle) for the Town Council.

History

The number of sites today is small compared to the large acreage at the beginning of the 20th century. (Chapter 3) petitions have been raised unsuccessfully to force the Council to create more. It had made tentative enquiries to buy land from farmers on the town's edge but thought the cost too high. Despite this some have been lost to development at Singers Knoll, and an extensive piece of Mendip owned ex-allotment land which could be licensed to allotment holders has been allowed to slip into dereliction over the last ten years (Chapter 25).

Who is involved

The Council confines itself to renewing fencing and general maintenance; the budget is rarely fully spent. The Association recently were awarded funds (2012) to provide an education outreach worker for schools to encourage the growing of food.

Frome Twinning Association

- Funding included within the general budget of around £2,500 to £3,000
- Mayor and Deputy Mayor were honorary members, now partly absorbed into the Town Council (2009)

What they do

The culmination of each year is the annual cyclical travel exchange in July. Members host guests in their homes for a long weekend and a programme of eating and entertainment. Visiting tourist spots, or enjoying sporting and musical events, often returning to stay with the same families each year forging lasting friendships. Each town takes it in turn to organise the formal Civic Reception with speeches and an exchange of gifts between each of the town Mayors, and the signing of charters the townspeople are not invited to this or any events. Frome has taken the opportunity to "open" a footpath and gardens renamed after the respective Twinned towns. Frome members share meals and go on walks in the remainder of the year.

History

In the mid 1970's Frome in common with towns up and down the country joined the Twinning movement when the continent was a still seen as a strange and mysterious place. Frome's first Mayor was chairman.

Starting after World War Two it was hoped establishing links between local communities in Britain and the Continent would contribute to a secure peace in Europe.

Twinning aimed to: encourage knowledge of another and different way of life, create the opportunity to discuss mutual problems and solutions, develop friendships, share cultures and organise sporting events centering on the annual exchange visits and above all be fun. Since its inception thousands of villages and towns in Europe indeed across the globe have established links.

The Frome Twinning Committee (later changed to Association) initially Twinned with Château Gontier in western France in 1975 adding Murrhardt in southern Germany in 1983. Château Gontier and Murrhardt, had been Twinned with each other since 1966. It was only in 2005 at the annual tripartite meeting Murrhardt and Château Gontier decided to extend Twinning to Eastern Europe which had by then become part of the European Union. Six towns were studied initially, later reduced to two Zabkowice Slaskie and Rabka-Zdroj. Both were visited by members of the Association and Councillors who had by this stage decided to take a more prominent role and in May 2008 the southern Polish town of Rabka-Zdroj was chosen. To begin with the Association wanted the Polish link to be a Partnership which would have entailed a lower level of commitment but the Town Council wanted greater involvement and to turn away from the purely social to include business and educational elements.

Who is involved
The present day Association is 50 strong and membership a modest £5. Frome's Mayor and Deputy Mayor were honorary members in order to participate in the Civic element of the annual exchange visits and sign any Charters. With its amalgamation with the Town Council the Mayor became President of the Association. Councillors are also invited to the Civic Receptions. It has been funded to varying degrees over the years by the Town, with generally an annual sum of £2-3,000 to cover the costs of the group visits. With the addition of the fourth Twin the town was assured there would be no additional cost indeed ample European funding was there for the taking (See Chapter 25, Known Unknowns).

Frome In Bloom
- Not funded
- One or two Town Council observers

What they do
It organises an annual competition celebrating the gardeners of Frome. Categories have grown to the present day 23 including shop windows, hanging baskets and a children's category for the tallest sunflower.

History – Floral displays had long been the preserve of the larger towns with Parks Departments vying with one another to produce serried ranks of white alyssum and scarlet salvias with the piece de résistance, the floral clock, often with a mechanical cuckoo striking the hour and frequently coupled with a tableau of figures, studded in plants, from either history or story books. They were part of the itinerary of every visiting coach party in the 1950s and 60s and an important tourist draw.

In the late 1970's the indomitable late Miss Jones and a small group of enthusiasts gave Frome's keen gardeners their first opportunity to enter their front gardens into a competition and started Frome in Bloom. Later, entering Frome into the nationally held Britain in Bloom competition, coupling the Front Gardens competition with the Town Council's own floral displays, hanging baskets and Park, it included commercial premises, residential homes, businesses, and allotments. Points were deducted for litter and graffiti but awarded for the neatness of the grass verges around the town.

Britain in Bloom

The Britain in Bloom competition's four tenets are to promote:

- Horticultural excellence
- Community involvement
- Environmental friendliness and
- Sustainability - using more permanent, wildlife friendly less watered planting and landscaping.
- And judging includes how graffiti and litter are dealt with locally.

South West in Bloom

The town, now entered by the Town Council takes part in South West in Bloom part of the Royal Horticultural Society's Britain in Bloom competition. Categories for the July judging are based on electoral roll numbers. For many Parishes this is the culmination of their Parish year and it is taken very seriously, many feeling their reputation depends on floral competition success.

The town gained silver in the Portman Cup (population 12,000-18,999) in 2006 with only a brief mention in 2007 but entered the St Bridget Cup (population 19,000-34,999) winning silver again in 2009.

Neighbourhood Awards

The Awards are for keen groups of neighbours wanting to sort out a neglected bit of land, with planting, or tidying up. This non-competitive scheme offers help and advice. At the end of the growing season each entry is presented with either an Award of Improvement, a Merit, or an Outstanding Achievement certificate. In 2007 three groups in Frome achieved an Award of Merit: the Orchard Street Organic Allotments, Welshmill Allotments, and the Dommetts Lane Guinness Trust housing.

Mendip in Bloom

Launched in the early 1990's, entry is automatic. It aimed to encourage community pride and increase summer visitor numbers - although never quite explaining how. An August judging uses the same criteria as Britain in Bloom offering: gold, silver gilt and silver covering a range of categories including best: town, licensed premises, shop or office, public building, private garden, village, allotment, and rural pub, plus a floral photograph category. Prize money of £1,500 is donated by local companies (cider makers, quarry companies, Glastonbury Festival and the local newspaper). The City of Wells or Glastonbury usually win but Frome was given Highly Commended in the Best Town category (2006) and a smattering of prizes since. 2011 also saw a grant of £800 given to the Town Council.

Who is involved

A small committee of volunteers oversees around 100 entries plus at least 30 allotments.

Frome Public Transport Users Association (FPTUA)

- Not funded
- One Town Council observer

What they do

FPTUA promotes the use of public transport in the Frome area and provides a quarterly forum for discussion on rail and bus public transport issues taking up problems as they arise.

As part of the Community Rail Working Party covering the Weymouth Line FPTUA works alongside the train company Network Rail and local authorities looking at ways to improve the service and the stations. Indeed they regularly clean Frome Railway Station of rubbish. The local bus companies also liaise with the FPTUA over road closures and bus routes.

History

Started in 1977 to re-instate the direct rail service to London primarily for commuters their eventual success has meant there is an early morning and late evening service. They also succeeded in persuading County Highways to adopt the very potholed and puddly Station Approach and mend it.

Who is involved

A group of around 10 enthusiasts. However, FPTUA were not included in the 3 Frome County Councillors Transport Public Forums (2011), as yet another attempt was made to gauge the extent, with a hope to tackle, Frome's perennial town centre traffic congestion and wider transport problems.

Frome Recreation and Open Ground Supporters (FROGS)

- Not Funded. Awarded £250 under the annual grants in 2008/2009
- One Town Council observer

What they do

FROGS have organised: fun days in Victoria Park including putting up bat and bird boxes in the park trees and litter picking. It organised a nature trail as a part of the Frome Festival Green Fair, a play day for a Mendip District Council public consultation into Frome play facilities and regularly tries to clear the Frome Millennium Green of brambles.

History

Founded in July 2005 FROGS are a group of volunteers (not a charity) whose aims are to provide practical help and opportunities for everyone to be involved in: improving the appearance, raising the awareness of and the care and usage of Frome's green areas so they are welcoming, well used, safe and enjoyable.

A successful fund raising group FROGS fronted an ambitious Big Lottery bid of £50,000 with the Town Council providing matching funding paying for architectural fees, project management, suppliers and some money - although not noted in the Council minutes. The town had bought the Welshmill play area from Mendip and the bid planned a children's cycle track, with new play equipment, a woodland trim trail, sculpture and seating. This was successfully completed in 2012. The first example of a true partnership between a town group and the Council.

Who is involved

6 core members organise work days to clear or tidy the town's green spaces with other volunteers joining in.

The Nationally linked Charities:

Frome and District YMCA Centre

- Funding via the annual grant application process - food vouchers for youngsters with no income
- One Town Council observer
  www.mendipymca.org.uk, www.ymca.org.uk

What they do

Mendip YMCA focuses on young people specialising in housing and homelessness issues. Accommodation and support is offered through a network of schemes to young people aged 16-25 years who are either homeless, threatened with homelessness, faced with sleeping rough, or need support to keep their accommodation. Mendip YMCA goes into secondary schools across Mendip talking to year 11 students, and organising family mediation to help prevent homelessness. A "Move On" scheme: lists available rented property, offers a deposit guarantee scheme enabling rented accommodation to be taken up, and resettlement support; it helps with finding and setting up a home and with independent living. In Mendip District, 67% of those needing help came from Frome.

"Routes" base at the YMCA gives information, advice on learning opportunities for all young people, signposting a wide range of services, e.g. housing, activities, employment, and training, again providing support, help and guidance. It helps around 550 people a year. Initially funded by Mendip District Council but later from the Big Lottery.

History

The charity was founded in 1844, by George Williams who started a spiritual and educational support group for young working men in London which later developed into the YMCA England; it maintains its Christian ethos today.

In April 2002 Mendip YMCA opened the Frome Foyer acting as the Managing Agent of YMCA England, the Registered Social Landlord to which it is affiliated. The Foyer provides 13 self-contained flats for young people aged 16–25 and provides a stepping-stone to independent living with comprehensive support to assist with basic life skills and help with accessing training, education, employment and learning opportunities. The Community Building at the Foyer on Palmer Street in Frome opened in 2003 and provided a "Routes One Stop Shop", developed in partnership with Connexions Somerset part of the national careers advice service. The long awaited Youth Café opened as per the Foyer's original plans in 2011.

Who is involved

There are 43 members of staff with around 30 volunteers; giving advice and information, including families who agree to give up to 7 nights emergency bed and breakfast. Others help with administration, decorating, gardening, and fundraising for fun activities. Board members steer the charity. Frome and District YMCA is part of Mendip YMCA which in turn is a self-funded local charity and company limited by guarantee.

An income of around £766,000 (2007/08) funded all the Mendip projects with a large grant provided by Mendip District Council. Frome has the most homelessness in Mendip District, in 2007/08 of the 482 people helped in Frome 56% were aged 17 or under.

Fairtrade Frome

- Funding via the annual grant application process
- £1,000 to publish the Frome Fairtrade Directory
- One Town Council observer
  www.fairtradefrome.org.uk

What they do

Frome Fairtrade publishes a directory of all the cafés, shops, businesses and organisations in the town that support Fairtrade principles. It organises events: promoting Fair-trade Fortnight at the end of February with a school's Cooking Competition using a mystery bag of Fairtrade ingredients.

It also gave away free bananas as part of the national campaign to increase the proportion of Fairtrade bananas sold in the UK from 25% to 50%. It has hosted farmer/producers talks to schools and run tombolas at the Christmas Spectacular indeed the Council insisted that all stalls and traders served Fairtrade products. The group hopes by promoting the purchase of Fairtrade products to boost awareness and understanding of trade issues underlining the fact that ordinary people can make a difference to the lives of producers.

History
Frome has been a Fairtrade Town since Feb 2003 and was one of 401 (2008) towns and cities in the UK to have achieved this status. The designation is proudly placed on the town entry signs. Somerset was the first Fairtrade County in England in March 2005.

Who is involved
A local group of volunteers, who have formed a steering group; it is not a registered charity.

Fairtrade
Fairtrade's stated aims are: better prices, decent working conditions, local sustainability, and fair terms of trade for farmers and workers in the developing world by persuading purchasing companies to pay sustainable prices (which must never fall lower than the market price). Fairtrade addresses the injustices of conventional trade, which traditionally discriminates against the poorest, weakest producers, enabling them to improve their position and have more control over their lives. The Fairtrade Mark which appears on all Fairtrade goods is an independent consumer label which appears on UK products as a guarantee that they have been certified against internationally agreed Fairtrade standards.

The local campaigns have a set of goals, and groups receive a certificate of congratulation from the Fairtrade Foundation - a registered charity, when they are reached. Once a local community declares its status as a Fairtrade Town (or university etc), they must be committed to continuing their campaigning and awareness raising.
There are five goals to meet:

- The local council passes a resolution supporting Fairtrade, and agrees to serve Fairtrade products (for example, in meetings, offices and canteens).
- A range of Fairtrade products are readily available in the area's retail outlets (shops, supermarkets, newsagents and petrol stations) and served in local catering outlets (cafés, restaurants, pubs).
- Local workplaces and community organisations (places of worship, schools, universities, colleges and other community organisations) support Fairtrade and use Fairtrade products whenever possible.
- Media coverage and events raise awareness and understanding of Fairtrade across the community.
- A local Fairtrade steering group is formed to ensure the Fairtrade Town campaign continues to develop and gain new support.

Neatly summed up in the five C's: Council support, Commerce (retail and catering), Community, Common Consensus (public support gained through media coverage and events), Captains (steering group).

Local, District and County Authority Groups:

Mendip Closed Circuit Television Users Group (CCTV)
- Funded £8,000 annually
- One Town Council Observer

What they do
Each of the Mendip towns has closed circuit television cameras in place in potential trouble spots to record activity on the streets and in the car parks throughout the day and night.

Image requests
- 2007/08 - 847
- 2004/05 – 351 the year the scheme started

History
Of the 847 image requests (2008) 30% were from Frome with CCTV supplying images in ¾ of incidents. By the year ending March 2008 the police had made 48 arrests as incidents were unfolding and alerted by the CCTV operators, up from the 28 from the previous year. Not surprisingly when evening monitoring started the number of incidents doubled with half or requests for Friday and Saturday evenings. The seriousness of the incidents is not detailed or how many arrests, prosecutions, convictions or fines resulted from the cameras. Crime and anti-social behaviour in the mainly rural area of Mendip is low compared to other parts of the country.

In 2009 the Users Group restated its objectives to:
- Ensure that CCTV cameras are operational and monitored;
- Provide evidence on request to enforcement agencies and officers of the court;
- Work with the police to reduce crime, anti-social behaviour and the fear of crime.

To achieve this the Users Group aimed to:
- Retain images for a minimum of 14 days;
- Provide images within 7 working days of a request;
- Provide quarterly statistics to funding partners.

Who is involved
Perhaps surprisingly, there are 7 volunteers who monitor the CCTV watching for a 2 or 3 hour shift on a weekly, fortnightly or monthly basis, supervised by a manager.

The CCTV system is funded by the 5 Mendip towns - Frome, Shepton Mallet, Wells, Street and Glastonbury, and are operated by Mendip District Council in partnership with Avon and Somerset Constabulary forming the Mendip CCTV User Group.

CCTV Coverage was an element of the Safer Cleaner Streets, Area of Action, one of Mendip's five areas listed in its management programme. Frome Town Council and the East Mendip Partnership have requested statistics, details of effectiveness, location of cameras and their spread but no information has ever been minuted.

There was a controversial cutting down of trees in the Kingsway shopping precinct, part of the Conservation area, to aid the coverage of new cameras, but, this was later denied.

East Mendip Area Youth Advisory Committee
- Not funded
- One Town Council observer

It met at the Frome Youth Community Centre, possibly for only a year, although a Councillor continued to be appointed to it for the whole of the electoral cycle. There are no minutes available.

Frome Locality Steering Group

- Not funded
- One Town Council observer, one Frome District Councillor observer

This was a multi-agency group formed to prioritise all young people and children services. Funded from the Government's Sure Start initiative and the Children's Fund and later redistributed through the Local Area Agreements. It ran for a year from 2006.

Mendip Play Partnership creating the Mendip Play Strategy, May 2007

- Two Frome Town Councillors and the Frome Town Clerk were participants
- There were no other budgetary commitments

What they did

The Partnership resulted in the publication of the Mendip Play Strategy (2007) a ten year plan running until 2017. The strategy reviewed the present provision throughout the Mendip District from the more traditional approach to play, of playgrounds and play equipment broadening to include the natural environment and public open space which provided play opportunities.

It aimed to provide an action led framework for future provision, whilst achieving the government's Every Child Matters Agenda and the aims of the Mendip Community Strategy. The Partnership and Play Strategy were an element to access allotted money from the Big Lottery Fund's Children's Play Initiative.

Who was involved

The Partnership was a discussion group, led by consultants, of 29 representatives consisting of:

- 6 Parish Councillors from 3 of the 5 main towns Street, Glastonbury, and Frome none from any of the other 62 Parishes in Mendip;
- the District Councillor cum portfolio holder (i.e. nominally in charge) for Mendip's Street and Landscape Services and a Play Champion - a somewhat silly title;

There is no explanation for the choice of representatives or even a profile, they met 3 times. It was heavily weighted with 11 County and District staff, the remaining members were from: the public sector – the police; the private sector - the church and the voluntary sector charities such as Barnardos, who also ran a consultation "away day" on the concept of Play Rangers which was later adopted and funded. Held together by paid consultants who produced a report.

History - The Big Lottery Fund's Children's Play Initiative

The Initiative allocated to each local authority across the country an amount of money based on the child population of the area and weighted by the level of deprivation. Mendip was allocated £214,000. There are several pockets of deprivation in Mendip, in Frome: Welshmill and Keyford Wards, with two Glastonbury Wards and one Shepton Mallet Ward.

The process expected a Play Strategy which identified needs through consultation, and a Partnership of interested bodies which could be consulted and also reported to – it met three times and produced a list of projects which reflected the perceived needs.

A total of 78 children, young people, parents and staff took part in the consultation process, a very small sample considering the population of Mendip is about 108,000, with 26,380 children and young people under the age of 20 years.

The issues were well rehearsed as a Play England anecdotal survey reported, only 2 in 10 children regularly play outside in the streets and open spaces where they live compared with the 7 in 10 adults surveyed who recalled that they played out as children on a daily basis. More traffic, less open space, real and perceived dangers from crime, changes in family life and new patterns of work are all considered causes. The consequences it is suggested, is children and young people suffering: increasing obesity, mental health problems and joining in anti-social behaviour; this last is contradicted by the Strategy's own results.

Play we are told is a fundamental experience promoting: health, a sense of well-being, intellectual, physical and social development.

What is there?
The Strategy lists an astonishing 113 sites. 15 are large play sites, in Frome. There are a large number of sports pitches and areas of public open space giving Frome potentially a play area greater than the Fields in Trust Six Acre Standard. This skews the overall result masking the number of very low quality, small play areas in residential developments and takes no account of the nil provision in more recent housing developments.

Six Acre Standard
Many local authorities have adopted it as their open space Planning standard. Designed so residents of all ages can take part in outdoor activities. It suggests for each 1,000 residents 2.4 hectares (6 acres) is set aside made up of:

- 1.6 hectares (4 acres) for outdoor sport and recreation space including parks.
- 0.8 hectares (2 acres) for children's play with 0.25 as equipped playgrounds.

The Strategy graded play and open space sites including sports pitches by quantity, quality, accessibility and distribution correlating this with each Electoral Ward's age range of potential users. A problematic approach as people do not necessarily confine themselves to "their" Ward (Frome can be walked across in 45 minutes) and did not account for any other myriad reasons for usage including: areas too small, poorly sited, difficult or unpleasant to use because of litter and dog fouling, or for instance all the sports pitches are on the north side of town. Neither was enjoyment "measured" nor the reasons people visited play areas discussed.

A description of some supervised play available was included in the study, but this did not extend to Scouts, Guides, Cadets, Woodcraft groups or music, art, theatre or sports clubs.

The Money
Play areas and open spaces are funded by both Mendip District Council and by individual Parish and Town Councils. Many take responsibility for some of their own play areas, funding them through their own precept - as Frome Town Council does or applying for grants which many of the villages have successfully done.

Using such sources as the now defunct Somerset Aggregate Levy Fund.

The District had a budget of £43,000 for developing and upgrading play and £88,765 for maintenance and inspection. However, these costs are charged out to the Parishes that have Council-owned play facilities through the Special Expenses Rate (SER) which is listed separately on each Mendip householder's annual Council Tax bill. SER also includes the upkeep of churchyards. The District's four skate parks are funded in differing proportions by the District, the Parishes and the skater groups.

Planning Obligations or Section106 agreements allow Planning authorities to ask for contributions (often financial) to be made to offset the impact of any development. With new residential developments this can include new, or improvements to existing and future maintenance of on-site or off-site open space and play areas. Mendip District has applied this patchily and in an ad-hoc fashion. Whilst getting some new play areas built, getting them adopted and open is another matter and certainly one inadequately small playground to serve 100 houses is now filled with rusting equipment and has been closed for over twelve years on one of Frome's newest estates (the Singers Estate). Requests for action from Ward Councillors have met with no response, although Mendip itself says it will resolve the difficulties within a few months (2012).

Most recently, new housing developments in Frome have begun to charge households around £10 per month to maintain their estate's green open spaces and play areas amounting to a substantial £12,000 a year for 100 house estate. These will be run by management companies.

Unlike other authorities, Mendip does not have a formal process or an easily applied set of rules. With a target of 10,000 houses to be built by 2028 the District has needed something which could be consistently applied otherwise it would continue to fail its residents. The Government brought in new legislation, a Community Infrastructure Levy (2008), asking authorities to clearly list and set rates for financial contributions for play areas, amongst other things, to ensure proper provision is made.

Actions

The Strategy devised a range of short, medium and long term action plans plus an overall promise to upgrade everything else.

Most recommendations suggested professionalising the provision of play areas such as employing staff, devising funding arrangements, using more consultations or generalised comments which could only be delivered through the Planning system or by policy changes at Mendip. The 2 projects in Frome and Street were the only site specific items listed that would have any permanence and had already been decided through separate fundraising or the Planning system.

The three projects chosen (December 2007) were short term actions (in a time frame of 0 to two years):

- In Frome, £50,000 towards an area next to the new Community Hospital. Now tagged as a "Beacon Play Area" carrying "Town Park" status using natural materials logs and rocks rather than manufactured play equipment. Overall cost was suggested to be £130,000; the new Hospital had already contributed £128,400 as part of a Section106 agreement although £116,000 had been spent building a lit footpath. Completed 2010.
- In Street, £14,000 was given to the new Skateboard park already part funded by Street Parish Council with an overall cost of £53,000. Completed 2009.

- Play Rangers, £150,000, was a joint purchase from Barnardos with Taunton Deane, Sedgemoor and West Somerset District Councils to oversee outdoor play. Running from October 2008 to March 2011 in Street, Coleford and the Frome Keyford Ward – the only one of the three areas of deprivation in the District chosen. In Frome, weekly on Fridays between 3.30 and 5.30, 2 or 3 Rangers waited under the trees at the well-used playing field opposite one of the town's First Schools to see who turned up. Play is not organised, but facilitated, with mainly ball games. There is no registration, however Barnardos estimated between 2 and 20 children took part, depending on the weather.

With Play Rangers coming in at a weekly cost of over £380 per site it is difficult to see any real value particularly when other play spaces in the town were in such desperate need of improvement. The District had closed and dismantled the much used town centre skateboard park because of lack of funds to pay for weekly checks and any on-going maintenance reducing overall play provision, particularly for teenagers.

The villages were essentially back to their own devices, albeit very successfully, raising money from including: the Somerset Aggregate Levy Fund until its demise, the Somerset Community Foundation, and the Mendip Hills Area of Outstanding Natural Beauty. The Strategy did usefully list funding sources.

Despite identifying non-existent and poor facilities many of which were not much more than patches of worn muddy grass, particularly the very small "play" areas on the newer estates where many carried a large "No Ball Games" sign. The Strategy disappointed by not making commitments and naming sites to be improved, making it unlikely that any improvements would ever be seen and indeed that there would be little to report on or evaluate.

Strategy Evaluation
Despite initially aiming to report quarterly to its Play Partnership following up with an Annual review and later a comprehensive five yearly review. Nothing was ever reported to the Frome Town Council or to the East Mendip Community Partnership meetings.

As is in the nature of these things, the press releases surrounding the allocation of the Government grant talked of "winning" in triumphal tones and were full of self-congratulatory quotes from District staff leaving Councillors with just a few lame comments of satisfaction to make.

Frome Community College Media Arts Strategy Group
- Not funded
- One Town Council observer

What they did
The College is a secondary school with around 1,300 pupils including the Tertiary years. All the town's schools funnel into it; the only choice of education is in neighbouring towns. It became a specialist school with Media Arts status in 2002 providing a professional standard television studio, an editing suite and radio station – it was the birthplace of the radio station Frome FM.

History
It was part of a Labour Government drive to add value to the national curriculum and raise standards. The school had to raise £50,000 from internal fundraising or private companies to gain a Government grant of £100,000 for capital projects.

There was an additional £129 per pupil per year for the 4 years of a targeted development plan for additional staffing and training, although up to 30% could be spent on equipment. If schools made a good attempt to meet their targets their grants were renewed at 3 yearly intervals without the need for further sponsorship. Most schools adopted a specialism from a range. Later the Government offered further grants for schools with long term business partners and later invited high achieving schools to apply for further specialisms with extra funding. The 2010 Coalition Government ended the funding.

Who was involved
The Strategy group probably met only briefly in 2006. The school lobbied the town through the local newspaper weekly stressing how important town–wide support was, emphasising it already had the newspaper on board. Media Status funding came with the proviso to let the townspeople, local schools, community groups, use the new studio facilities and borrow equipment (although the school did not advertise this opportunity on its website or in any of its literature). Equipment could be bought to the value of one third of total funding which included one salaried community arts worker. Under-spends went into the school's general budget. By the end of 2011 the future of the Media Arts Centre was uncertain and redundancies were made.

School Governors

- Not funded
- One Town Councillor out of a possible 9 schools

What they do
Councillors have the opportunity to become a Local Authority Governor and in Frome's case they are appointed by Somerset County Council. Frome Town Council is notified of any vacancies and volunteers are called for, they may or may not be chosen to fill the vacancy.

Councillors' Declaration of Interests, showed only one Councillor out of the 17 as a Governor (March 2009), in previous years most schools would have had one Councillor volunteering for the role.

It can be a considerable additional commitment with an estimated 10 hours a term for roughly four meetings (generally two Full governing body meetings and two specialist Committee meetings). Extra time is needed getting to know the workings of the school and the education system thoroughly, preparing for Office for Standards in Education (Ofsted) inspections where they will be questioned, visiting the school whilst it is at work during the day, and joining in on school events. Many governors take on specific roles as well as a particular school class.

Local Background
Schooling within Frome is organised into three tiers. Starting with the five First schools which provide education for 4 to 9 year olds, two have a state nursery attached catering for 0 to 5 year olds enabling children to transfer seamlessly to the main school. The one Primary school (Catholic) takes pupils from 4 to 11 years of age generally sending its pupils to the nearby town of Trowbridge for Secondary schooling. A Special Needs School has a catchment area beyond the boundaries of Frome taking children from 4 to 16 years of age. The two Middle schools take children from the First schools at the age of 9 or year 5 until aged 13 or year 9 when they will transfer to the Secondary School - Frome Community College.

They can remain there to take both GCSE and "A" level exams or vocational training leaving at the age of 18 at the end of Tertiary Two.

Who is involved

There are 350,000 school Governors in England, and it is reputed to be the largest volunteer workforce in the country, Somerset County Council's website claims 1 in 100 adults is a school Governor. All Governors are voluntary, and unpaid, although expenses can be claimed such as the cost of a carer for dependent relatives whilst meetings are being attended. Employment law gives Governors the right to have reasonable unpaid time off from their workplace. Governors are appointed for a maximum of four years, and this term is renewable. No special qualification are required only enthusiasm, commitment, an interest in education and to be aged 18 or over on the date of election or appointment. Within Somerset all new and re-appointed Governors are subject to an enhanced Criminal Records Bureau (CRB) check before their appointment or re-appointment as a Governor can be confirmed.

Responsibilities

Each governing body, which can vary in size from between 9 to 20 members, can be made up of:

- Parent Governors, ideally parents of children at the school and elected by other parents of children at the school;
- Staff Governors, either teachers or support staff elected by the school staff;
- Local authority Governors, appointed by the local authority;
- Community Governors, members of the local community appointed by the rest of the governing body (except in voluntary aided schools);
- For some schools there are Foundation or Sponsor Governors, where the foundation or relevant religious body appoints Governors;
- Plus the head teacher (if they choose to);
- Associate members may also be appointed by the governing body as members of Committees, and may include pupils, school staff, or anyone else who the governing body feel could contribute to its work. Their voting rights are decided by the governing body.

The local education authority can advise on any vacancies in an area for any category of Governor.

The head teacher of the school is responsible for day-to-day management of the school whilst governing bodies are responsible and accountable for all major decisions about the school and its future. Governors have a legal responsibility to promote high standards of educational achievement and set the school's vision and strategic aims, monitor and evaluate performance acting as a critical friend to the head teacher and ensuring the school is accountable to parents, pupils and the community.

Responsibilities are defined in law and include:

- being accountable for the performance of the school;
- planning the future direction of the school;
- promoting high standards of educational attainment;
- setting targets for pupil achievement;
- taking general responsibility for the conduct of the school;
- managing the school's budget, including key staffing decisions;

- making sure the curriculum is balanced, broadly based and complies with legal requirements;
- making sure that the school provides for all its pupils, including those with special educational needs;
- drawing up an action plan after an inspection by Ofsted;
- in Church Schools, foundation governors are expected to help preserve and develop the school's religious character.

How is it done

The last twenty years have seen the progressive delegation of funding and responsibilities from local education authorities to individual schools. Schools are now largely self-managing, responsible for their own budget and accountable for all aspects of their performance. Schools generally have a delegated budget to cover salaries, running costs, maintenance and equipment; the Governing Body is responsible for managing this budget. They can decide how many and what types of staff to employ, which equipment to upgrade or replace and what the priorities are for implementing new strategies and initiatives. Governors must appoint the head teacher, and may be involved in the appointment of other staff.

Governors ensure accountability by monitoring and evaluating the school's progress, and setting its annual targets and strategies for performance with the head teacher (who sets targets for staff).

The Governing Body is led by the Chair, elected for a year or more, by the Governing Body from within its membership, though Staff Governors, including the Head Teacher, cannot stand. This is very much a "hands on" role with frequent meetings including Committee work. The Full Governing Body will meet once every half term to discuss and report on the ongoing business of the Committees, the governing body, and the school with decisions taken by a majority vote. There will be a number of Committees which will specialise in areas such as: Finance, Staffing, Admissions and Exclusions, Health and Safety, Curriculum and Premises and may cover other areas such as marketing, discipline and management. Most meetings take place in the evening.

The Clerk to the Governing Body provides advice and interpretation on the regulatory and administrative framework in which Governors work, preparing and distributing minutes and agendas, keeping records and dealing with correspondence. This is a non-voting paid post.

Local authorities provide a range of free training for Governors and Clerks to the Governing Body throughout the year. They may provide facilities such as insurance or specialist support in terms of equipment or educational materials to help schools study specific topics such as the Victorians which schools can buy into. For Church Schools the Diocese will normally provide additional support.

...Frome Watch...

Schools

The 17 schools in Frome and the surrounding villages formed Frome Community Learning Partnership (FCLP) for: discussions, the sharing of experience and resources, to broaden the curriculum, to provide a consistent approach to behaviour, and to put on preschool and after school activities.

It part funded the Young People Frome (YPF) co-ordinator, who develops and publishes the "Frome Active" booklet and website- a listings directory of activities for young people from 0 to 25 years.

New possibilities

2011, the Coalition Government widened the definition of Academy status, giving the option to all schools and ending the mandatory element of business sponsorship control. Frome's two middle schools have become Academies however, the upper school – Frome College is unlikely to be accepted as it shares its campus with the local leisure centre and theatre and does not have sufficient input into Key Stage 2. Academies will become publicly funded independent schools free from local authority control. The 10% of the budget which went to the local authority from central Government providing services such as: insurance, bulk buying of supplies, and specialist help, will now go directly to the school. The school could continue to purchase from the local authority or decide to fund its own priorities. There is also a limited freedom to depart from the National Curriculum.

At the same time state funded, (£2 million per school) independent Free Schools were launched. For all abilities, in which charities, or groups of parents or teachers decide and provide what they want and what their area needs with more control over the curriculum and teaching staff pay. Frome had two contenders:

- Frome Free School incorporating a Forest School, small at 160, for pupils aged between 4-18 years. It was one of 41 accepted from 320 applications in the Government's first round of applications. However, the school was unsuccessful and was asked to revise its plans and reapply in 2013.
- The Steiner School for over 600 children between the ages of 5-16 years was given the go-ahead. It planned to buy the now empty Victoria Hospital (the sell-off of hospital land would trigger a hoped for unexpected windfall for the Council because it had previously sold Park land to the Health Trust (see Known Unknowns)) and open in September 2012. Whilst negotiations for the Hospital site continued, the school opened several miles away in Corsley in its small recently closed Victorian School. The nearby fee paying Steiner Waldorf School in Bruton closed with its pupil's transferring to Corsley. The State schools were not happy with the concept suspecting their funding would be further reduced and they would be left with less capable children. In any case they disagreed with the Steiner ethos.

Frome also has loosely affiliated small groups of home educators using "education otherwise" enshrined in the original 1948 Education Act (repeated in Section 7 of the 1996 Education Act). Whilst education is compulsory, schooling is not. The National Curriculum does not need to be followed.

The Nationally linked – lobby group:

The Somerset Association of Local Councils (SALC)- East Area

- Funding, the Town Council paid an annual membership fee to both SALC and NALC of around £2,500
- The Mayor and deputy Mayor with the Parish Clerk go to the annual NALC conferences
- One Councillor was appointed to attend quarterly meetings
  www.southwestcalcs.org.uk

What they do

The Association provides training and assistance as well as legal, technical and specialist support and advice, together with regular newsletters and circulars, enabling Parish Clerks to have advice at the end of the phone.

The National Association of Local Councils (NALC) is a national lobby group for the promotion of the role of Parish Clerks and their councils, it is a consultee to central Government and comments on national Government policy.

History
SALC's advice and support is backed-up by the Association's affiliation to NALC. For instance in 2009, 2 Parish Clerk training weekends were held for those wishing to gain their qualifications and a conference on the delegation, via "The Power of Well-Being," of Government control to the lower tiers of local government.

The Somerset Association does not have a web-site, as it stated, *"so that there is a simple control over the release of papers and documents to those who do not subscribe."*

Who is involved
The Somerset Association of Local Councils (SALC) is an organisation of Town and Parish Councils which claims more than 80% of Somerset's 315 Town and Parish Councils in its membership.
There is a joint website of the 7 County Associations of South West of England who have organised themselves into a Conference of Local Authority Associations (SWCALCS).

National Representation
Society of Local Council Clerks (SLCC)
Founded in 1972, and now with 4,000 members. The Society provides training, advice and branch membership for Parish Clerks. Along with NALC they devise the Parish Clerk pay scales.

Local Government Association (LGA), which is more often quoted or asked to comment in the national press and media, lobbies central Government on behalf of County, District, Borough and Unitary authorities and includes the police, fire, national park and passenger transport authorities in its remit.

District and County Committees:

Somerset Mendip Area Working Panel
- Not funded
- Parish Councillors could speak at the meetings, they were not appointed

The Working Panel began in February 2007 (6 meetings) and was replaced after the first year by the County Councillors Local Initiative Budget. (LIB) (see Chapter 9).

The 12 County Councillors in the Mendip Area Working Panel notionally contributed to a pot of £180,000. The Panel meetings discussed some general issues, most notably community engagement, but principally awarded the grants on a bid basis; applicants speaking for their bid. The Panel had an uncertain start, with long running squabbles as to who chaired the Committee; disputes over its procedures, purpose and decisions.
It lasted a year as the running costs were prohibitive, with up to 12 staff members from both County and District in attendance plus representatives from other "stakeholder" bodies such as the police, and the NHS, making at one point 35 people.
In the end the funding decisions were taken by "officer delegation" based on the November panel of 4 Councillors recommendations, allowing members with prejudicial interests as sponsors of groups asking for funding, noted at the meeting's start, to take part in discussions.

East Mendip Community Partnership

- Not funded
- All Parish Councillors can speak at the meetings, they are not appointed

All the District Councillors within the geographical area of East Mendip met at bi–monthly meetings in Frome, to discuss randomly chosen issues, to make resolutions and listen to explanations and presentations given by District Council staff. Parish and County Councillors as well as the public could attend and speak. For a time the Committee sanctioned the Frome Area Regeneration Fund, which held a small budget (around £20,000) and held occasional public forums on controversial Planning issues. The Regeneration Fund ceased with Mendip District's budget problems in 2009. The Partnership was criticised by the District Council Scrutiny Board for poor public involvement (see Chapter 9)

OUTSIDE BODIES – the Past

As times have changed some organisations such as the Blue House have abandoned the use of Councillors, some such as the Vallis Vale Standing Committee had become unnecessary as others too had run their course.

The Blue House

Alongside the town bridge, unusual for having shops along its length, is The Blue House, a Grade II listed building. Re-founded by the Lords of the Manor – the Leversedges, in 1728 as an almshouse. Originally it housed the elderly ladies of the Parish. They lived in the wings whilst the central part of the building was a charity school for boys, named, because of the colour of their uniform, The Blue Coat School. The equivalent institution for old men and girls, now demolished, stood at Keyford to the south of Frome town centre. Two sculptures of young women were rescued and now stand to the side of The Blue House whilst the two central figures on its frontage, of an old lady and a young boy are a reminder of the buildings original foundation.

The original building funded over the centuries by public subscription from Frome's wealthy has in more recent years been renovated and modernised by the trustees in 3 massive public appeals one of which caught the generous attention of Prince Charles. It now provides 18 warden controlled flats for both men and women who qualify by currently living in the Parish. The trustees were originally drawn from the surrounding Parish Councils including Frome, each nominating one Councillor. The trustees also run 3 educational charities giving annual awards for local youngsters: the Keyford Educational Foundation providing (around £1,600 annually) for school clothes, musical instruments, school trips or bursaries; the Stevens prize for English and most recently the Clark prize for Mathematics.

Vallis Vale Standing Committee

Vallis Vale is a deep wooded valley, a Site of Special Scientific Interest, popular for Sunday afternoon strolls and a picnic spot since the 1800s. The Committee comprised of Parish Councillors, Mendip District Council staff and representatives from Hanson (the then quarry firm which owned a series of disused quarries in the valley).
It met occasionally for a gentle walk up the valley and the chance to try out the rope swings across the river.

Bridget Parker (Olympic) Commemoration Fund

Named after local horsewoman and international competitor Bridget Parker.

Mrs Parker still lives in Frome training horses and riders and is a selector for the British Olympic Team. The Bridget Parker (Olympic) Commemoration Fund sometimes called the Bridget Parker Trust was set up after the British equestrian team's success at the 1972 Munich Olympics winning the team gold in the Three-Day Eventing.

Film Career

Cornishman V had a successful film career appearing in *"Dead Cert"*, the Dick Francis thriller in 1974, and later with a starring role in the showjumping film *"International Velvet"* (1978) alongside film star Elizabeth Taylor.

In the team were: Bridget Parker on Cornish Gold - whose offspring Bridget still trains, Captain Mark Philips (the then husband of Princess Anne), Richard Meade, who also won the individual gold medal - the only British winner until Leslie Law in 2004 to do so and lastly, Mary Gordon Watson on her horse Cornishman V. The same team also came in second at the World Championships in 1974 at Burghley.

The Fund was set up to promote and inspire youngsters who had showed sporting promise by representing the County or England in their chosen sport to achieve sporting prowess. Raised from an annual request for monies from the surrounding rural Parishes it was administered by trustees (generally Councillors) and was unique because each Frome Town Council Clerk acted as Secretary or administrator.

In 1977 the small rural Parishes of Downhead, Leigh on Mendip, Mells and Norton St Philip (which included the hamlets of Hemington, Hardington and Foxcote), each gave the then sizable sum of £20.00 (around £150 today) with Frome donating £50.00. Adverts placed in the local newspaper, the Somerset Standard, brought in four letter requests 3 from boys who were each awarded £15.00 and one from a girl who received £12.50p! Most youngsters wanted help with travel expenses, equipment or training fees. At the year's end year there remained a substantial balance of £1,000 from a starting sum of £864.

The fund was wound up in 2007 with the Town Council deciding the final distribution of around the £8,700 remaining. Half went to the local Riding for the Disabled, and the remainder, rather than being distributed to sporting youngsters in Frome or the surrounding villages was given to the Somerset Community Foundation.

Somerset Community Foundation

The Somerset Community Foundation, one of 80 foundations nationwide, manages a wide variety of funds on behalf of national government, charitable trusts, individuals and businesses. It distributed just under £1.9 million to small voluntary and community groups in Somerset between 2002,(when it was set up) and 2008, Mendip receiving £440,502 of the total.

What do Parish Councillors think?

Because outside organisations are such a large commitment, the 2007-11 Frome Parish Councillors were asked to comment on their experience and asked.

1.   What prior knowledge of the organisation you joined did you have?

2.   Why did you want to be appointed?

3.   Were you given any information before the first meeting?

4.   Were you given the opportunity to discuss your role?

5.   Has the organisation asked you to undertake a specific role or area of responsibility?

6.   Are you there to oversee the spending of the Town Council's grant money (if applicable)?

7.   How many meetings are there in a year and how many do you get to?

8.   Is there enough time for you to be involved?

9.   What do you feel you brought to the organisation you were appointed to?

10.   Do you feel your contribution has been useful and how do you rate your contributions? On a scale of 1 to 10, (1 being the lowest)?

With too few replies to make any generalisations Councillors did feel they were contributing to the town whilst ensuring value for money and keeping the Council informed.

Datafile

Volunteering,www.vinspired.com
Somerset Youth, www.somersetyouth.org.uk
Landshare, www.landshare.org.uk
South West In Bloom, www.southwestinbloom.orgse
Somerset Association of Local Councils, www.southwestcalcs.org
Society of Local Government Clerks, www.slcc.co.uk
National Association of Local Councils, wwwnalc.org.uk
Local Government Association, www,lga.org.uk
Somerset Community Foundation, www.somersetcf.org.uk
Frome Active, www.fromeactive.org.uk
Somerset County Council,www.somerset.org.uk
Governors website, www.governornet.org.uk
Frome Free School, www.fromefreeschool.co.uk
Department of Education,www.education.gov.uk
Education otherwise, www.education-otherwise.net
Twinning,www.twinning.org.uk- European website
Local Government International Bureau (LGIB), www.lgib.gov.uk
Connect Youth International, www.connectyouthinternational.com
European Parliament, www.europarl.org.uk
European Commission, www.cec.org.uk, www.europa.eu
Europe for Citizens Programme 2007 – 2013, eacea.ec.europa.eu

ST JOHN'S CHURCH FROME

9 – PEOPLE - Other bits of Local Government

Parishes have not relied totally on their precepts but have funded specific projects from the higher tiers of local government. There was a web of schemes and Committees that shared out carefully measured amounts of money.

At District Level - East Mendip Community Partnership

Anxious not to be remote from its population and responding to Government directives to be more accountable, Mendip District divided itself into 3 forums, or Community Partnerships, centred on the major towns.

Frome dominated the East Mendip Community Partnership with 11 Councillors from its 6 Town Wards (College, Berkley Down, Keyford, Park, Oakfield, and Market) whilst only 6 came from the rural Parish Wards assigned to it, creating a geographically awkward area because Frome's nearest village, Nunney - just 3 miles away, was allotted to a different Partnership.

The Government, determined *"to build community engagement and empowerment"* passed more legislation in 2008 and Mendip responded by inviting County Councillors to Partnership meetings to take up any issues.

Frome was in an interesting position with half (8 later 9) of its Town Councillors also Mendip District Councillors and later in the County elections of 2009 it increased from 1 to 3 Town Councillors as County Councillors (2 of which were already District Councillors). It held the Partnership chairmanship giving the possibility of tremendous influence from the town into the Partnership, and from there to a strategic level at Mendip, as well as informing policy at County. Yet despite this terrific fire-power the Town Councillors cum District appeared to influence little, in fact the Partnership found it near impossible to get any information, statistics or updates it asked for.

Meeting bi-monthly with an early evening start and lasting just a couple of hours it had a roving brief of anything local giving unprecedented opportunities for town participation not seen since the demise of the Task Force ten years earlier. This was a County Councillor led informal forum around tea and sandwiches held in the early evening at the Mendip Lodge Hotel. It brought together schools, police, public organisations such as the job centre, businesses, community groups and townspeople. A popular talking shop covering car parking in the main, with often explosive rows, it too was unable to achieve anything.

Unusually, there were three levels of participation for speakers to put a case or make a presentation: at the start of each meeting the usual 3 minute slot for townspeople and any Councillors; a 3 minute slot specifically for Parish Councils although rarely used; and an Open Forum with a generous 10 minutes per speaker.

The Meetings

Packed with presentations from: single issue groups; Government agencies; Mendip District reports (and staff, up to a dozen per meeting) explaining current work; community groups with questions; and statements from the townspeople - that mostly go unanswered.

The subjects covered are random and eclectic but do make good reading. Partnership resolutions are few and requests for information ignored such as Mendip's progress on climate change or police prosecution successes due to CCTV coverage. The Partnership's scrutiny role was minimal with little follow-up. Councillors from the rural Parishes rarely made use of it and the townspeople only turned out in good numbers over the major housing and supermarket schemes. It was not the force for change that might have been expected.

The new beginnings for the Frome centred Partnership in **2006** is also the beginning of the long haul for the Saxonvale redevelopment which runs its entire history; the beginnings of the long awaited new hospital controversially on the Cheese Showfield site, a much taken for granted open space, and the even longer awaited Collegians football pitch, with the remaining Section106 money, part of the hospital deal, left over for a playground; the beginnings of the Vision for Frome - a wide ranging three year long consultation on the town by the town; and FROGS a group determined to gain appreciation for the town's open spaces.

There are heavy weight Outside Bodies to be appointed to such as: community safety, the Leisure Centre and the Frome Education & Training Centre. It shared the responsibility of holding the town regeneration plan, an incoherent wish list, which brought a trickle of money with it, some from Frome's precious Section106 agreement money distributing it, perhaps a little unimaginatively, when £4,500 goes on litter bins.

Presentations and explanations are made by Mendip staff including: Business Support (BS) which told of its 17 business enquiries in 6 months, the 3 £500 start-up grants it allocated and how its success was measured by the number of new VAT registrations across the area. The Partnership thought this odd as it was outside BS's influence; and a report on the unexpected selling off of 31 parcels of odd corners and verges of District land: some to the Parishes, some to householders for gardens and some to developers.

In **2007** the emphasis shifts and the Bailey Bridge (to demolish or not to demolish) is a constant keenly followed in the public forum. Reports are presented including the general look of the river, with banks uncut, and litter everywhere, the Partnership suggests the Town Council take on the unkempt riverside Château Gontier walk. The Town Council's reasonable request for the reuse of the abandoned allotment land on Oakfield Road is never answered. Mendip's Budget and the vital role car parking charges play (an annual reminder of the town's retail struggle) in providing cash to run Mendip is explained (17% of Mendip's income is from car parking in 2007). Consternation when the Partnership realises its own regeneration programme grant aid budget is lower than its sister Partnerships so demands more. The Vision for Frome consultation gets underway and CCTV in Frome is explained but no one is sure how effective it is.

A busy **2008** as the Partnership hosts major consultations to huge public galleries. Kicking off with the redevelopment of employment land for homes and shops with Terramond at Saxonvale, then Bloor Homes at Garsdale. Questions are asked: where will people work, where will their children go to school (the nearest school is full and there is no land to build more classrooms), will the town's small shops be killed off? Councillor reaction is muted when townspeople raise issues of design and practicalities but there is no confidence that the architects or developers will take comments on-board. Vision for Frome also holds a large consultation exercise on community values, but no-one has any questions for Mendip's Chief Executive Officer who makes a special visit.

Bailey Bridge demolition is confirmed, there will be no new bridge, then it is reprieved and the Partnership asks for a pedestrian bridge. The cost of around £150,000 is a problem as every additional £100,000 spent by Mendip is equal to 2% on the Council Tax we are told.

Mendip reports include: Butler and Tanner, - world famous colour book printers - the last of the town's historic employers, goes into receivership. Many assume the land will go to housing. The town is so shocked, a march is organised through the town centre even the MP joins in. The last time so many people turned out was in the 1980's against the Poll Tax (public meetings, marches, town centre rallies, hilltop bonfires, T-shirts, tax boycotts, magistrate cases and liaison with other anti-poll tax groups) and in the 1990's when a man was charged with ill-treatment of a dog. 287 jobs in publishing are lost in the April. By August it is rescued and 80 re-employed. Mendip is part of an action group with Citizens Advice Bureau and Jobcentre Plus, but only 19 opt for retraining, most melt away finding jobs via friends, or start their own businesses; Mendip's poor record on affordable rural housing is highlighted, only 85 since 2001 but this will now be boosted by 29 in nearby Coleford - perhaps.

Mendip decides to scrap the town centre skateboard park. Despite its closure creating a huge gap in the number and type of play areas provided. Recent repairs of £2,650 and the daily inspections costs of £70 a week are said to be too expensive. Anyway, Mendip says, the Town Council wants it to go.

By **2009**, the Partnership is beginning to run out of steam. There are fewer presentations: a new affordable housing scheme is mulled over (Singers Knoll) – no one seems to notice the allotments (always enthusiastically supported elsewhere), will be reduced; Grants are given; a Bailey Bridge enthusiast applies to have the Bridge listed, but two Frome/District Councillors get to finally sign off on the replacement. Mendip wishes to move the weekly Charter stall market - which has also run out of steam, to a Thursday - Frome's quietest shopping day and half day closing.

Mendip announces a Budget deficit of £½ million and unveils a scheme to give Gypsies and Travellers loans of around £40,000 to set up their own sites, solving Mendip's under provision and obligations under the 2004 Housing Act. There is concern that those already in homes will leave them to take up the offer. There are workshops on planning Frome's housing until 2026 for the Local Development Framework. Mendip Strategic Partnership reluctantly gives a very brief explanation of itself – no-one is any the wiser. It doesn't know it will soon be scrapped.

Presentations mainly, but little is really discussed in **2010/11**. Most intriguing is a scheme which puts reusable fake shop fronts in empty shops, "pour encourager less autres" to revitalise the Market Place. Allegedly enthusing entrepreneurs to invest into taking empty shops by illustrating what a shop could look like and acting as a useful reminder to shoppers. Frome Councillors are keen to give this a go - £3,000 the suggested fee is thought worth paying. Car parking is discussed in depth, Frome contributes £380,000 in income to the District, the value to Mendip is emphasised, but Frome shops say parking costs puts off customers, and is expensive for staff. The car parks are rarely full, but neighbouring streets are.

Frome Area Regeneration Programme

Every Committee to be a proper Committee, needs money and the Partnership was given a small amount of core funding plus a little from Section106 agreements.

Its annual distribution was to the odd mix of projects that made up the Frome Area Regeneration Programme. This largely ignored the rural Parishes until the final couple of years. As is often the case, the cost of employing staff to organise this was as great as the grants distributed.

East Mendip Community Partnership Budget

In 2008/09 £90,000 was allocated to all three Partnerships by Mendip District. East Mendip only received £30,000 despite its greater population and much to its chagrin. Money from Section106 agreements had disappeared.

Years	Core Funding	Section106 agreements
2006/07	£18,300	£11,000
2007/08	£18,500	£11,500
2008/09	£30,000	none
2009/10	Funding down to £20,000 in this final year	none

The Partnership did not suggest projects or debate a plan but relied on applicants shoehorning their proposals, into Mendip's targets.

In the initial years, 2 of the 5 Key Objectives of the District Council written in something of a punchy tone:

- Safer, Cleaner Streets - that is, lighting, signage and footpaths and,
- Greater Prosperity - which is tourism based.

After 2008 this is re-jigged into 4 alliterative, bookish and all-encompassing priorities:

- Enhancing Mendip as a place to live;
- Enabling an environment where individuals and businesses can prosper;
- Encouraging and supporting communities and individuals to improve the quality of their lives;
- Ensuring value for money is provided in all services.

Over the four years, 2006-10, funds were given to:

- Frome Festival's ten days of music, literature, art, talks and activities (£11,700);
- The Mediaeval Fayre focused on Catherine Hill with costumed stallholders and stalls, shops, music and entertainment (£1,250). The Fayre ended after a dispute with the Town Council;
- Frome Town Council for the Christmas Lights and the Christmas Spectacular late night shopping, music and entertainment (£12,500).

Or one off grants to:

- Frome Creative Network to develop a Community Interest Company website, and directory for the 96 strong artists group (£2,000);
- Memorial Theatre refurbishment (£1,000);
- Millennium Green an open space, for public liability insurance (£1,800);
- Frome in Bloom (£1,800). Unused and later given to the Town Council;

- Frome Foreground, to put on visual art exhibitions with an education programme. (£2,000);
- Sustainable Frome's re-usable "Frome" bag (£300);
- Frome Community Radio, broadcast license fee (£2,000);
- Friends of River Frome, for the maintenance of trees, litter picking and flower planting (£2,000);
- Cheese & Grain, toilets and seating (£2,000).

The majority of funding was allocated back to projects generally under District Council control:
- Welshmill Riverside Walk, lighting and resurfacing (£8,000),
- Château Gontier Walk planting (£4,600),
- National Cycle Path route NCN24 (£10,000),
- Vision for Frome (£5,000),
- Signs, artwork and maps next to the new "Beacon" toilets (£4,000),
- Towntalk website hosting Town Council details and listing local businesses (£5,600),
- Frome Education and Training Enterprise (FETE), a post -16 training provider (£2,000).
- The annual shopping guide (£1,300).

Small amounts were set aside for:
- Alcohol restricted zone signs,
- A gate to St John's churchyard,
- Dog poo bins,
- Cycle racks by the Cheese & Grain,
- St John's church hall Planning fee,
- Mendip Food Festival - which never included Frome.

From 08/09 and for the first and only time the village Parishes received grant aid:
- Stoke St Michael, a footpath (£600),
- Wanstrow, for landscaping and village notice boards (£2,600),
- Norton St Philip, several footpaths (£7,000),
- Leigh on Mendip, a village welcome pack, spring bulbs and youth club craft materials (£1,800),
- Coleford, for landscaping (£2,500),
- Batcombe, a notice board (£589),
- Mells, underwriting the community run village shop (£3,000),
- Rode, to start on its Parish plan (£1,000),

£1,011 was kept back for general contingency!

What is Regeneration?
Regeneration is the sum of 3 connected but sometimes competing goals: physical change, economic development and community renewal.

Budgetary problems at Mendip in 2009 saw the end of the Regeneration Programmes and the staff which oversaw them and with the effectiveness of the Partnership again questioned in 2011, it was the end of the East Mendip Partnership.

Blame was widely spread: was lack of publicity responsible for little town interest, although the redevelopment of the major areas of the town centre gathered huge audiences and lively debate; the over formality and unresponsiveness of meetings; the lack of proposals to take forward or the lack of any achievements to discuss; perhaps the perspective was too District based. However, Mendip still needing to be accountable decides Frome can run its own Forum, though it does not explain how or when.

Strategic Partnerships

Powerful, unreported, unelected, effectively unaccountable independent groups. They become the unseen power setting the social and economic priorities for their area, deciding what actions and initiatives were needed on local issues and requesting from the Councils they steered that there was the funding and resources in place to achieve them.

Principal Councils (the higher tiers of local government) had been told by the Local Government Act 2000 to devise Community Strategies by setting up Strategic Partnerships. Later in 2007 Government adds sustainability to the mix and labels them Sustainable Community Strategies. The Partnerships were made up of invited organisations from voluntary and community groups, businesses, health, the police, environmental groups, faith communities and a few Councillors. But, with the Coalition Government (2011) changes are made and their power ends. Many unexpectedly dissolved themselves, others changed tack and turn on the authorities they once ruled looking for financial savings from within their own Councils.

Somerset County Councillors and Grants

By now the giving of small grants had become endemic. For the canny fundraiser on Parish Councils or in community and social groups, the endorsement of their area's County Councillor released funds.

Three funds of unnecessary complexity were available until the financial storms of 2009:
- The County Councillor's Local Initiative Budget (LIB) and
- The County Councillor's Community Budget which when combined together could distribute a surprising £1,160,000 each year;
- The Somerset Community Chest.

Unadvertised and little known about, indeed one County Councillor made unsuccessful, desperate pleas to the Town Council to come up with a project he could fund. The largest Councillor fund, the Area Working Panels (AWP) would turn into the County Councillor's Local Initiative Budget. Started in February 2007, it pooled the allotted funding of £15,000 per County Councillor. The Mendip AWP, one of five covering Somerset, had a funding potential of £180,000 from the 12 Councillors within its area. 28 projects made a bid with 23 funded. Many projects already had part funding from other funding bodies or, if a Parish Council, from the precept.

In its only year of operation funding centred on Parish Council proposals: play areas, village hall upgrades, rural footpaths and bridleways. A surprising 16 villages requested electronic speed warning signs to slow traffic entering their villages; this was funded and renamed the Mendip Road Safety Improvement Programme!

Two funded arts projects were Frome based:

- The community radio, Frome FM (a CIC) broadcasting over the internet. With volunteer broadcasters it offered music - much from local bands and musicians, aired local issues and presented wide ranging magazine programmes.
- Frome Foreground Ltd, (a company limited by guarantee) exhibited 7 newly commissioned contemporary art installations by national visual artists alongside an education programme (May/June 2008). The exhibitions caused controversy as blue and yellow "wallpaper" was plastered over the windows of empty shops and buildings and outrage as lines of poetry containing swear words was exhibited next to a churchyard.

Mendip Strategic Partnership (MSP)

A seemingly shadowy unreported group which was rarely given anything more than a passing reference in the East Mendip Partnership meetings. Unelected (if you do not count the one or two local Councillors on its Board) its Sustainable Community Strategy provided the priorities and guidelines for the District Council and the participating board's organisations.

Mendip's Board membership of around 20 was made up of Councillors, police, Jobcentre Plus, community and youth organisations, charities, schools, environmental groups, and the Primary Care Trust. Membership was added to on an ad hoc basis by invitation only. It later added Councillors from the Mendip Partnerships as observers. The Board met quarterly to update its progress. The afternoon meetings (whilst open to the public) were not listed on the calendar of Committees on Mendip's website MSP had its own website, however, the Board membership had not been updated since Feb 2005 and the last of the occasional minutes had been posted in May 2007 (March 2011).

As with any Committee, there was a pot of money to be distributed, although MSP did not see itself as a grant maker, despite this funding dominated the few minutes which are available. In 2007/08 a £100,000, money raised from the second home Council Tax - £78,000 from Somerset County Council and £21,000 from Mendip District Council, was divided between projects which had applied under the MSP's five priorities, which also operated as sub-committees:

- Affordable Decent Housing for All,
- Investing in Children and Young People,
- Regenerating the Mendip Economy,
- Strengthening the Voluntary and Community Sector,
- Tackling Climate Change Locally.

With the "Sustainable" labelling added priorities were rejigged and renamed with new upbeat titles:

- Thriving Market Towns and Vibrant Villages,
- Economic Prosperity,
- Safe Communities,
- Healthy People,
- Suitable Decent Affordable Housing,
- Environment.

But by 2010 the money to give away was reduced to around £40,000. After this the Partnership disappeared.

Datafile
Mendip Strategic Partnership, www.mendipstrategicpartnerships.org.uk

The County Councillor Local Initiatives Budget (LIB)
The Initiatives Budget gave each Councillor a direct opportunity to support projects and initiatives with up to £15,000 of funding for projects costing more than £2,000 in value. 5 projects could be supported in any one year and Councillors could combine their allocations together. In its first year 2008/09 the Budget funded 42 projects.

Projects were judged and scored against a set of criteria using Somerset's Sustainable Community Strategy grouping its priorities under six cryptically named themes of:
- Making a Positive Contribution,
- Living Sustainably,
- Ensuring Economic Well-being,
- Enjoying and Achieving,
- Staying Safe, and
- Health.

Each theme contained a detailed list of Somerset's Local Area Agreements (LAA) - measurable targets – these were the County's and Government's priorities for action in Somerset. The LAAs were designed to reflect the needs and aspirations of the community and were different for each County Council. They were simple self-evident statements e.g;
LAA Priority 1.3 - *Community and voluntary groups have the capacity to meet their aspirations and local people's expectations of them; they also have the self-reliance to continue.*
Projects claiming grants tried to cover as many statements as possible.
But with County elections in 2009 and under its new Conservative administration the LIB disappeared. Giving, in this the final year, a share of £38,000 to: Frome FM Radio, Frome Selwood Tennis Club, Foreground and the funding of Frome Town Council's Green Business Seminar. The following year the Coalition Government abolished this method of delivering change (via LAAs).

County Councillors' Community Budget
This time, Councillors have £5,000 of discretionary funding for voluntary and community group projects and local initiatives. When added to the LIB, each Councillor had a potential of £20,000. But with the LIB's disappearance in 2009 the Community Budget doubled before it too disappeared in 2010. The 3 Frome Councillors £26,000 final year legacy included: supporting a new football pitch for Frome Collegians, Frome FM Radio, the Town Council's contribution to the Cobble Wobble cycling event, new books for schools, Home in Frome – an oral history project and the Frome Festival.

The Somerset Community Chest
The Chest funded community projects throughout Somerset that cost under £12,500 with a maximum grant of £750. However, applications could only be made if funding was refused or only partly met by the LIB and/or the Community Budget. In its last year (07/08) the Chest spent around £14,000 with just £700 in Frome for Frome FM Radio.

The Somerset Aggregate Levy Sustainability Fund (SALF) whilst not needing County Councillor support, was a major County-wide Parish funding body until abolished by the Coalition Government in 2010.

Somerset Aggregate Levy Sustainability Fund (SALF)

In 2002 the Government introduced a tax of £1.60 on every tonne of freshly quarried stone sold in the UK. Whilst there are quarries throughout the County, there is a particular concentration in the Mendips. Somerset produced and sold over 9 million tonnes in 2007. Other quarrying counties includes Leicestershire, Derbyshire, North Yorkshire and Staffordshire. From the considerable sum raised across the country a proportion was diverted to the Aggregates Levy Sustainability Fund administered initially by the Department for the Environment, Food and Rural Affairs (DEFRA) under five themes.

Five Themes:

- reducing the environmental impact of quarries, on land, and
- off shore,
- the careful use of resources e.g. recycling of aggregate,
- the transportation of aggregate, and
- compensation for the local communities affected by the impact of aggregate extraction.

It was the last which the Somerset Levy Fund addressed.

After 2008 the Government included it in the Annual Area Based Grant which all Counties received to fund all their services, ensuring grants made were also subject to Local Area Agreement (LAA) priorities.

Funding was ended very promptly in 2010 by the new Coalition Government, having distributed around £2.5 million. The annual budget of around £300,000 is sorely missed particularly by small rural communities as it funded some 40 projects each year from a wide range of organisations, revolving around social and environmental tasks such as: village hall and playing field improvements, sports equipment, wildlife conservation and information projects, youth clubs, building restoration, car parking, school computers, and larger schemes such as Mendip Bridleways (routes for horse riders) and the National Cycle Path (Sustrans), and surprisingly included Somerset County Council's own conservation projects and legal costs. The fund took around £20,000 annually for its own administration. The projects were judged by a panel drawn from the aggregates industry, countryside organisations such as the Campaign for the Preservation of Rural England and Councillors.

Frome has had several successes including:

- The Memorial Theatre, built by subscription to commemorate the fallen in World War One, received £10,000 for refurbishment, part of its long term rebuilding programme. The 850 seat theatre is one of the few theatres in the country managed and run by unpaid volunteers and is the base of the Frome Amateur Operatic Society and its junior arm Spellbound. It draws in performances of national and international household names as well as local talent.
  They took on the mammoth task of completing the building which stopped in 1929 as money ran out.

The Frome Urban District Council (it was a trustee) added the Assembly Rooms after it sold the Frome Water Works to Bristol Water to avoid losing the money from the town when local government was reorganised in 1972.

Vulnerable, it was a cinema for a while and a bingo hall whilst in the late 1990's Mendip District Council made strenuous efforts to demolish it to make way for sheltered housing, hoping to siphon off money to refurbish the nearby derelict Rook Lane Chapel which it wanted to preserve instead. This of course rallied calls to, "Save the Theatre". Self-funding as opposed to the town's Merlin Theatre which received District, County and Arts Council Grants (until these were abolished 2011). The Town Council had always refused to support it with grants; the reason somewhat unclear. It was assumed the Memorial Theatre's popular and more entertainment based programme was less valued than the Merlin's "Art" focused programme with a dance specialisation given to it by the Arts Council. 120 volunteers help run it.

- The Town Council received £10,000 to replace play equipment in Mary Bailey Playing Field. The whole scheme was costed at £150,000 with the remaining sum raised via the precept.
- Frome Canoe Club was awarded £10,000 for a new Club House an ambitious project totaling over £319,000 raised over many years from their own fundraising, Sport England and the British Canoe Union.
- Over £102,000 went to the National Cycle Network - an infrastructure project for cyclists and walkers which uses former railway lines, country lanes and footpaths, co-ordinated by the charity Sustrans. The Colliers Way, running from Dundas Aqueduct outside Bath to Radstock and on to Frome is part of Route 24. Mendip District Council also supported the route via the Frome Regeneration Fund. At the Elworthy Park housing development a new foot bridge crossing the river linking the path alongside the river to the main road shortens the distance by 200 yards. The development also provides £30,000 from a Section106 agreement for the "station spur". A plan to upgrade the Railway Station entrance, but not completed.
- The "Missing Link" a planned section of the Colliers Way from Great Elm to Frome following in part the river through the town is incomplete but with landowners consulted, the route surveyed and two new bridges contemplated, Planning permission is sought by a local group of volunteers - part of Sustainable Frome (December 2011). A considerable undertaking costing up to £½ million.

10 – PEOPLE - Grants – A History of Giving

As national governments have become accustomed to inventing initiatives and organising the country via funding schemes and funding streams, national charities have sliced and diced the population into a complexity of issues, each with tailor-made funding solutions. This gathering sophistication has shaped local government which has rapidly followed suit with the Parishes too beginning to recycle money, precepting, in order to give money away. The easy, instant pleasurable justifications for doing good will make funding, as it becomes entrenched, difficult and controversial to undo in future years.

National Funding
27% of charities receive ¾ of their funding from Government (2011).

There are easily well over 150 groups, clubs, societies, organisations and sports listed in the Mendip Directory (April 2008), run in the main by volunteers. This extraordinary variety of activities covers every possible interest or cause, implying, that perhaps a third to a half of the adult population of the town formally belong to something. Not taking into account, unlisted groups, evening classes, informal gatherings, ad-hoc lectures, talks, concerts, workshops, etc which also take place. They all give extraordinary value for money achieving amazing things on a shoe-string. Hopefully giving the Town Council cause to silently reflect on the £3.35 million it spends (2007-11 electoral cycle). However, the Town Council is emphatic in its belief that its funding of societies is pivotal and unaided they would falter, with the implication that groups are inherently weak and dependent rather than canny and opportunistic. They have a tremendous impact on the town.

More History
By the end of the 2007-11 electoral cycle harsh financial winds had blown through as District, County and national funding was cut, a serious problem for the Black Swan Arts Centre and the Merlin Theatre who cut staff and were thrown back on to rallying battalions of volunteers to fundraise again as they had done so successfully in the past. But, the past also had had its ups and downs.

Mendip, faced with the embarrassment of a Grade I listed building Rook Lane Chapel becoming increasingly derelict enthusiastically supported the setting up of a Jigsaw Puzzle Museum (1998), though it was not so keen to support the suggested Western Industrial Collection of Conservation Artefacts and Documentation in the Lamb Brewery, a building many thought was abandoned but was in fact an office furniture warehouse and salerooms. Frome Museum strongly supported the proposal and needing new premises (it had looked at the old Feather Factory on Willow Vale) planned to combine forces to create The Lamb Heritage Centre. A request to Mendip for £100,000 of funding was airily dismissed, they could be not be involved in funding such a project despite the Museum saying it would have to close its doors by Christmas. Today the Lamb Brewery is housing.

Rook Lane was rescued, in the 1990's after years of indecision in which the interior of the building disappeared, and various developers failed to get permission to turn it into flats. Indeed the Civic Society had formed in 1973 to rescue it but the Frome Urban District Council instead spent the monies raised from the sale of the Water Works on refurbishing and extending the Memorial Theatre.

The 1991 intense fundraising campaign raised for the Chapel what seems now a modest £63,000 with a chunk of money (£500) from Prince Charles - still proudly remembered today. With contributions from English Heritage (£100,000) and a loan from the Architectural Heritage Fund (£100,000) under the umbrella of the Somerset Preservation Trust, who it was agreed would sell Rook Lane Chapel on to Mendip District Council once it was restored and thus pay back the loan.

A use which would include the community was now needed the local Textile Group who all used hand looms looked ideal. But unable to get the funding in place and after much dithering, an innovative Jigsaw Puzzle Museum was proposed (1997) becoming a Mendip District obsession. It would be a tourist draw and *"would be the making of Frome."* The 9,000 jigsaws were in private hands, the partial financing of the scheme by Mendip was hotly debated, as was a home for the curator - a bungalow behind the Chapel with access via the Memorial Theatre's car park. The division of the Chapel interior and the problems of car parking meant the Planning application and Lottery bids went to the wire several times. After two desperate Lottery attempts, the first one - for £450,000 - but without any contributing outside cash it failed. The second, for £790,000 was thrown out despite match funding of a substantial £250,000 from Mendip to the horror of locals. Again it failed to secure any other funding and the Puzzle Museum faded away. Today, it is the offices of a local architecture firm with the community aspect preserved by Rook Lane Arts with exhibitions and concerts.

An article in a December 2001 edition of The Somerset Standard newspaper on local fundraisers calculated that £433,000 had been collected during the year, but a staggering further £2-3 million was still needed by the reported handful of projects it listed:

- Frome Victoria Hospital Centenary Fund, had raised £120,000 from events organised by the Hospital Friends and a multitude of groups and individuals. This gave the Fund at the year's end £370,000 from a target of £485,000 which had to be raised before the Primary Care Trust would fund a new hospital.
- Trinity Church, raised £140,000 to refurbish their church hall, kitchens and toilets from their target of £250,000.
- Memorial Theatre, raised £80,000 to rebuild the frontage of the theatre similar to the original plans of 1925.
- Black Swan Arts, raised £115,256 to refurbish the galleries, shop and restaurant areas from a target of £162,000.
- Harry's Hydro, raised £30,000 for a purpose built hydrotherapy pool and sensory centre for disabled children and adults taking the total to £63,000 from a target of £170,000.
- The Frome College Media Studies bid, raised £70,000 in pledges towards gaining Media Arts Status.
- St John's Church, raised £3,000 towards restoration work to the church, church yard and the church hall towards a target of £842,000.
- Merlin Theatre, raised £6,543 in cash and gained £3,900 in kind (value of work received which in other circumstances would have been paid for e.g. a volunteer carpenter making something).
- The Julian Wort Appeal, raised £10,000. The Appeal was started as a memorial to Julian by his bereaved family buying heart monitoring equipment for local doctors' surgeries.

There were many other projects with lower profiles raising funds in the same year.

Ten years on:

- The completed Hospital was opened in 2008, £700,000 raised locally and fund raising continues;
- Trinity Church Hall was successfully completed and in 2011 it launched a further £800,000 project to provide a mezzanine floor in the church;
- The Memorial Theatre is funding further improvements and is currently replacing all its seats;
- Black Swan Arts now fundraises to replace its lost grants;
- Harry's Hydro, building started in 2011 after the Town Council guaranteed funding for the next 10 years;
- Frome Community College gained its Media Arts status but this was later abolished by the Coalition Government;
- St John's Church funded over £500,000 of repairs to the exterior of the building particularly the roof, so the church is water-tight and structurally sound. The appeal continues particularly to revamp the Church Hall.
- The Merlin Theatre now fundraises to replace lost national Arts Council, Mendip District, and County Council grants.
- The Julian Wort Appeal has raised almost £30,000 and donated through CRY (Cardiac Risk in the Young): two ECG Machines one to the Frome Medical Practice and one to the Frome Hospital plus two defibrillators to the Frome Hospital.

How do they do it?

Most groups fund themselves from their own membership or by fundraising. In the past the mainstay was jumble sales - which were a weekend must, or the sponsored event, today these have generally been replaced by music concerts. Groups have also developed more sophisticated constitutions in order to access the growing variety of funding and grant making bodies both locally and nationally, many which demand goal setting targets, definable community involvement, an educational element and specific and measurable effects or outcomes.

However, groups can resort to the Town Council to supplement their income and for many this has become an important element in their budgets. Over the electoral cycle the amount of money gifted has slid, from £65,650 to £55,637 even though the Town Council Budget doubled. Some organisations were funded for a set period of years giving them added security and access to other funding sources. The distribution of the remaining money is dependent on who applies. Groups who take funding may be asked to take a Councillor onto their management team or simply to write a report of their spending.

Groups can organise themselves in several ways: with a simple constitution, using unpaid volunteer executive officers such as chairman, secretary and treasurer; or as a Community Interest Company (CIC) (introduced in 2005) with paid directors and a management structure combining a business approach with social action, or; as a more traditional charity managed by voluntary unpaid trustees which have chosen a specific area of concern, some paid management, a high dependency on volunteers, with or without a trading arm.

The formal structure of the CIC and the Charity should make access to a range of grant aid funds easier.

The traditional charities structure is however, more transparent thence more accountable than the CIC, as a wealth of information is displayed on the Charity Commissions website and in the annual reports sent in by the charities, (although only by those with an income over £10,000). The Annual Report outlines their activities, future aims, and lists trustees, volunteers, income and expenditure and make excellent reading. A CIC will be registered on the Companies House website but the information available is limited and there is a charge for some of the detail.

Community Interest Companies (CIC)

Community Interest Companies (CICS) are limited companies which either run businesses or associated activities and want to use their profits and assets for a community benefit and are not driven to maximise profit for shareholders and owners. A Community Interest Test is applied to ensure profits and assets are "Asset Locked" and can only used for community purposes. CICS are cheap, flexible and easy to set up. They are sometimes misleadingly called "not for profit companies", but it is the surplus or profit created which is used for the public good. These social enterprise companies which include co-operatives and mutuals principally tackle a wide range of social and environmental issues and needs using business solutions.

A CIC can take a number of forms such as a private company limited by guarantee, or by shares, or a public limited company. A CIC limited by shares can pay dividends to its shareholders, although these are capped. Alternatively, some CICS may depend on grants or donations to enable it to carry out its social purpose. A charity can not be a CIC, but can register a CIC as a subsidiary company.

As a limited company a CIC must comply with company law generally and will be registered at Companies House, as well as complying with the CIC legal requirements. Registration had to be approved by a Government appointed independent Regulator who had a monitoring and enforcement role, but promised a "light touch".

By March 2009 2,544 Community Interest Companies had formed nationally. 3 of which were in Frome; Frome Creative Network CIC, Frome Community Productions CIC, and Sustainable Frome CIC. By 2012 the number had doubled to 6.

Charities

There are over 166,000 with around half having an annual income of less than £10,000. All registered Charities, must by law demonstrate that their aims have an identifiable public benefit and a charitable purpose using the broad areas of potential charitable activity set out below.

The Charities Act gives the following descriptions of charitable purposes:
- the prevention or relief of poverty;
- the advancement of education;
- the advancement of religion;
- the advancement of health or the saving of lives;
- the advancement of citizenship or community development;
- the advancement of the arts, culture, heritage or science;
- the advancement of amateur sport;
- the advancement of human rights, conflict resolution or reconciliation or the promotion of religious or racial harmony or equality and diversity;

- the advancement of environmental protection or improvement;
- the relief of those in need, by reason of youth, age, ill-health, disability, financial hardship or other disadvantage;
- the advancement of animal welfare;
- the promotion of the efficiency of the armed forces of the Crown, or of the efficiency of the police, fire and rescue services or ambulance services;
- other purposes currently recognised as charitable and any new charitable purposes which are similar to another charitable purpose.

Charities have a legal requirement; if their income is £10,000 and over to send an Annual Return and a copy of the Trustees Annual Report and Accounts to the Charities Commission. These are published on the Commissions website. Charities with incomes of £10,000 and below only need to keep registration details up to date. Charities can not make a profit but can run a trading arm which does.

Parish Grants

To justify the spending of money raised from the precept via the Council Tax, Parish Councils use a range of specific statutory spending powers and duties (see Chapter 3) given under the 1972 Local Government Act when the present local government system was first set up, this has been tweaked by more recent legislation (see Chapter 9). Most Parish spending can be made to fit those original categories, particularly Section 137 which allows spending on anything the council considers worthwhile, if it can find no other power to use with the assumption it will bring, *"direct benefit to the area, the community or any part of it."* There must be a match between the money spent and the benefit to local people - a difficult judgment.

Definition of powers and duties
A power: something that the Parish/Town Council can choose to do but is not compulsory.
A duty: something that the Parish/Town Council must provide.

Indeed NALC, in the "The Good Councillor Guide" (2006), describes Section 137 as *"a treasure"* allowing Parish and Town Councils to spend up to a statutory limit per elector (£6.15p in 2009/2010). In Frome this gave a spending potential of around £126,000.
The Town Council website of the time used the following parts of the Local Government Act 1972 to explain some of its grant expenditure in 2007/08:

- Section 137 Power of local authorities to incur expenditure for certain purposes not otherwise authorised. i.e. a Council can spend on anything a Council considers worthwhile, if and only if no other power can be used.
- Section 142 Provision of information, etc, relating to matters affecting local government
- Section 144 Power to encourage visitors and provide conference and other facilities
- Section 145 Provision of entertainments i.e. provide a dance hall, concert hall or theatre, maintain a band or orchestra, develop arts and crafts, providing programmes and refreshments for them.
- Section 176 Payment of expenses of official and courtesy visits, etc.

Datafile
Charity Commissioners, www.charity-commission.gov.uk
Community Interest Companies, www.bis.gov.uk/cicregulator
Social Enterprise Companies, www.socialenterprise.org.uk
Companies House, www.companieshouse.gov.uk
Statute Law, www.statutelaw.gov.uk

Town Council Annual Grants

Whilst applying for grants from all levels of governrnent has become the norm and often one of the first ports of call. The majority of Parishes in the past have relied upon money from either the wealthier members of their community to fund what was needed or from raising money by subscription.

The town's almshouse, The Blue House, founded by the Lord of the Manor, William Leversedge in 1728, replaced an earlier building housing the poor of the Parish. It has been updated in subsequent years via 3 major public appeals. Much too was achieved in the 1800s as subscriptions were raised to fund: a new Cottage Hospital, the Victoria Park and the town's Swimming Baths, whilst the town's many chapels were paid for by their congregations. The Literary and Scientific Institute was gifted by John Sinkins, a clothier, for the town's enlightenment and education and the Boyle Cross by Mr and Mrs Boyle in fond affection of Frome. Individuals like Thomas Bunn spent an entire lifetime trying to cajole the rich into providing for the poor, gave generously himself and despaired of the poor whom he found to be difficult and exasperating.

...Frome Watch...

The increasing reliance of those without means on the Poor Relief required drastic action and it became the practice for Parishes to encourage their poor to emigrate, Canada initially and later Australia.

Emigration to Canada

Letters published in book form (sold for 6d a copy) from enthusiastic emigrants entreating their family and friends to join them, and describing this new land *"overflowing with an abundance of the substantial blessings of life"* fuelled a surge of emigration of Frome's poor (around 400 in 1831/2 alone).

Reports described vast quantities of all types of food - meat was said to be cheap, cider and even wine could be enjoyed in a pleasant climate. The land providing good crops - even without manure, plentiful fish and game which could be taken unhindered (no harsh punishments, poaching back home was a crime). With no taxes or tithes and with churches of every persuasion. There was social equality for labourers enabling them to sit with and share meals with their master's family. Where a labourer on a wage of 6 shillings a day could easily save for a farm of 70-80 acres within 5-10 years and those with a trade were even better off, a carpenter could earn 10 shillings a day in *"a land of liberty and plenty."*

Frome offered 15 months pay to any poor family on Parish relief wishing to go to Upper Canada (today's Southern Ontario) providing the sum did not exceed £600. Some news reports estimate there were 5,000 paupers in Frome with Parish relief reaching £13,000 (around £1,2 million today) with a further sum of around £4,667 (around £437,000 today) given in casual relief. It still stood at a staggering £11,723 in 1831 (about £1 million today) as the local economy continued to slip providing for around 900 persons, quite a burden on the then few ratepayers.

However, *"the benevolent ladies and gentlemen of Frome"* provided in addition to money, a well filled pack of clothes, bedding and tools. Indeed the emigrants were escorted to Bristol and personally seen on to the ships for the 6 weeks journey to Canada.

This also meant they did not slip away with the money and turn up later to be a further burden on the Poor Rate. In 1834 the Poor Law Amendment Act ensured instead that accommodation and food were provided for up to 350 persons in Frome's newly built Workhouse, for both the poor of Frome and its surrounding Parishes.

The Warmer Frome Scheme was an unexpectedly innovative idea for a Parish Council providing a generous annual £25 (£35 in today's money) grant for nearly a decade. Previously the Town Council had offered bus tokens but their abuse by 1987 led to the money given being halved and then only given to pensioners and the disabled. The Warmer Frome grant part paid the electricity bills of around 700 pensioners aged over 70 with limited savings. It was part of a larger project administered by Age Concern which also provided smoke alarm installation and a battery replacement service. The Scheme had given rise to accusations of unfairness as neighbours accused each other of claiming twice, having too much in savings or a working relative living with them so making them ineligible. Ending in 1998 as the new Labour Government introduced winter fuel payments, at the slightly less generous rate of £20 for single and pensionable couples. This, together with the deregulation of the electricity industry into 27 separate companies and the tightening of local government auditing arrangements made the scheme too difficult to administer.

By now the funding of a tapestry of organisations had become commonplace. At one time money helped pay for unexpected one-offs or specific projects rather than the day to day running costs of a group although this became increasingly routine. Money was given to benefit the people of Frome (national charities are generally excluded and in any case, swoop-in, in t-shirted splendour (chuggers) to siphon off the town's goodwill): as "seed corn" to kick-start new projects; to support the Council's own Strategic Plan; or by providing a 3 year funding commitment allowing groups to tap into other funders - something that has become increasingly essential. But many question why the town pays for others hobbies.

It should not be forgotten that most groups just get on with it themselves, such as the "Talking Newspaper" which provides service to the blind and partially sighted. 8 groups across the town varying from the Drama Club through sport to the Local History group get to together every week to read the Somerset Standard newspaper onto tapes for distribution, broadcasting twice a week via Frome Radio Station and as an easily accessed downloadable programme.

Most small groups ask for only a few hundred pounds, with some groups applying annually often for the same things each year, such as that hardy perennial, tents for the Scouts, or – inadvertently - as the result of Government legislation. When nationally play groups were asked to keep their documentation secure and easily retrievable the dozen or so groups in the town all applied to the Council for new filing cabinets.

In later years, for the most part, funding has been skewed towards the arts or activities for children especially projects offering an educational element.

At the specially arraigned Grants sub-committee applicants had the opportunity to give a short verbal presentation justifying their requests. Successful groups were also asked to account for their spending with a written report on the project's completion.

Some do by citing the Council's corporate objectives, *"Aim 4: to develop and facilitate partnerships which assist in building a sound stable yet diverse community"* as the town underwrites a musical theatre production or pays for artist fees for a handful of children to take part in a day workshop. Others just send in copies of invoices such as for building tools whilst others, uncertain of what is needed, confirm the money was spent!

Grants awarded 2007-08 were decided in the autumn of 2006, and paid in June 2007. The total of £65,650 was broken down between annual grants of £25,150 to 17 very diverse groups plus the three year funding agreements made to 9 organisations amounting to £40,500.

The Council, adding up all it spent, reckoned it distributed the sizable sum of around £160-170,000 a year including £82,000 to the Cheese & Grain (combining the grant with the Council's own loan and interest repayments on the community building in the total) *"a great resource and something rather special"* although this view would change by the end of the electoral cycle.

2007-08 shows an eclectic mix:
- Mendip Community Transport (MCT) - £3,000

To continue providing a minibus service for the elderly, disadvantaged registered users and youth groups
- Frome and District Physically Handicapped and Able Bodied Group - £300

To part fund 20 members attending the S.W Conference with travel and accommodation costs.
- Frome Gateway Club (MENCAP) - £650

To fund outings to places of interest.
- Age Concern Frome - £2,500

To continue to provide information and other practical services to the elderly in Frome.
- Frome and District Day Centre - £3,000

To provide a two course lunch twice a week plus after lunch entertainments.
- Frome Society of Disabled Artists (SODA) - £300

For expendable art materials for a community art group open to all ages.
- 5th Frome Scout Group - £1,000

To buy a large timber shed to store camping equipment.
- Friends of Rowden House and Critchill Court - £400

To hire a disabled lift coach and wheelchairs for resident's outings.
- Jackdaws Music Education Trust - £1,000

A 5 days project for Frome young people, who will select a story then represent it musically and dramatically in the style of a classical composer.
- Frome Youth Council - £3,000

To provide a Youth Café for Frome.
- Frome Memorial Theatre Trust - £3,000

To refurbish and update the "covered link" between the Theatre and the Assembly Rooms.
- Frome Support Stroke Group - £300

To organise activities such as quizzes and board games, plus purchase exercise equipment.
- Frome Twinning Association - £2,000

To host the Annual Tri-partite meeting between the three Twinned towns.

- Merlin Theatre Trust - £2,000

Core funding to enable the theatre to continue its range of activities.

- Black Swan Trust - £1,500

To continue to develop an education programme that focuses on the young or disadvantaged people in Frome.

- Mendip Moving on Group - £200

To purchase a digital camera to take publicity pictures to attract new members.

- Fairtrade Frome - £1,000

To print and reissue the Frome Fair-trade Directory.

Three Year Fixed Funding of £40,500. Starting in April 2006 ending in March 2009:

- Frome Museum - £1,000

For general running costs.

- National Children's Homes – A Quiet Place - £3,000

To develop "A Quiet Place", a counselling service for Frome's children and young people.

- Young People Frome - £6,500

To continue and expand the Frome Youth Council, to continue the Frome Active information service and to enable young people to go to conferences at local, regional and national level.

- Positive Action on Cancer (PAC) - £3,000

To continue providing a free professional telephone and face to face counselling and bereavement service for all people affected by a cancer diagnosis. Funding the volunteer co-ordinator post for 14 hours per week to oversee a growing number of volunteers. To promote the work of the charity and increase its local profile. To provide opportunities for volunteering and to raise funds with a local volunteer workforce.

- Frome Association of Holiday Activities. - £5,000

To provide supervised play schemes during the school holidays for Frome children aged 5-11. Offering a variety of activities including: arts, crafts, music, sport, cooking and games. Staff are trained in play work and /or child care.

- Frome Festival - £5,000

A community festival. To underwrite, the World Food Feast, events in the Park and children's activities

Starting in April 2007 ending in March 2010:

- Mendip CAB - £7,000

Running Costs

- Frome Tourist Information Ltd - £8,000

Running Costs

- National Children's Homes – Frome Toy Library - £2,000

Running Costs

Fixed funded organisations not previously listed:

Positive Action on Cancer (PAC)

- Funded on a 3 year funding cycle £3,000 each year
  www.positiveactiononcancer.co.uk

What they do

PAC offers free one to one professional counselling to anyone affected or bereaved by cancer.

Either adults or children, including family, friends and carers as well as those with a cancer diagnosis to help them to come to terms with the impact of cancer upon their lives. Up to 16 counselling sessions are offered initially. Support and home visits are also offered across neighbouring counties.

History
A local charity founded in Frome in 1994. PAC offers a specialist children's service including play therapy and an adolescent service for young adults.

Who is involved
The 14 volunteers organise fundraising, information events and activities.
Income in 2007/08 was £76,000 with the adult service dealing with 106 clients. PAC had 10 employees include 4 adult counsellors and one play therapist for younger children and an adolescent psychotherapist to work with young people supported by administration staff.

National Children's Home (NCH)
- "Quiet Place" funded on a 3 year cycle £3,000 each year
  www.actionforchildren.org.uk

What they did
The "Quiet Place" was a face to face children's listening service where children could talk about things that were bothering them to trained counsellors on a one to one basis either in school or at the Wesley School Rooms where the NCH had offices before it closed in 2008.

History
The National Children's Home was founded by Methodist minister Thomas Stephenson in 1869 in London to provide a family environment for abandoned children as an alternative to the workhouse. The NCH has since moved away from children's homes towards supporting families, creating children's centres and providing services under contract to local authorities. It changed its name in September 2008 to Action For Children. 2007/08 showed a national income of £200 million with 6.500 employees and 11,000 volunteer days recorded.

Who was involved
Children used the service at the suggestion of their school, via the Youth Service or by word of mouth. It was also funded by central Government, the Children's Fund and local schools.

Frome Toy Library
- Funded on a 3 year cycle £2,000 each year.

What they do
Toys were provided on a borrowed basis from the town's 2 Children's Centres and a community advice point (ex-neighbourhood shop).

History
Originally under the umbrella of the National Children's Home (NCH) at the Wesley School Rooms. It started in the late 1990's. In 2009 it was absorbed into the County Council.

Who was involved
Around 125 families or approximately 200 children took part in the scheme.

Other grants given

Other grants funded from the general budget:
- The Cheese & Grain (see Chapter 6, Outside Bodies);
- Mendip CCTV Users Group (see Chapter 6, Outside Bodies);
- Frome Allotment Association (see Chapter 3);
- Police (see below); and
- School Crossing Patrols (see below).

Police Community Support Officer

- Later changed to an office
- Funded as part of general budget annually, £10,000 rising to £12,000

What they do

Police Community Support Officers take on a range of roles, tackling anything from the most trivial misdemeanour to the most serious crime with a blend of social work including: victim support, dealing with truants, graffiti, missing person inquiries and more cryptically by *"contributing to the regeneration of communities."*

They can impose on–the-spot fines for a wide range of minor offences including cycling on pavements, littering and breaching dog control orders. Other powers – some of them discretionary - include drug seizure, detaining suspects for up to 30 minutes, and stopping and searching people under terror laws when supervised by a police officer. Few carry handcuffs and none batons or incapacitating sprays to defend themselves or restrain suspects.

History

The Avon and Somerset Police Authority is funded by the precept, as a separately listed item on the annual Council Tax Bill. Frome households contributed close to £1.5 million in 2008 (by 2011 as police budgets are squeezed the Government points out 1 pound in 7 goes to police pensions.). However, in the recent past the Government keen to involve communities in policing, encouraged Parish Councils to give additional funding suggesting this could be used to cover specific problems. Frome hoped to specify what problems needed a more concentrated approach but this was never achieved.

Founded in 2002, the 16,000 PCSO's in England and Wales work alongside nearly 142,000 regular officers. Their main role, described on the Home Office website, is dealing with low level crime and antisocial behaviour by supporting the work of local police officers and providing a *"visible and reassuring presence on the streets."* Indeed latest police figures (2012) say the police themselves only spend 25% of their time on the streets.

A diverse range of powers puts the PCSO's somewhere between the ordinary citizen and the formal police, with an identical uniform it can be difficult to distinguish between them, – PCSO's have a red badge on their caps. Patrolling in pairs on foot and in marked police patrol cars these officers have the same right of arrest as any other citizen but it is at the discretion of individual police forces to advise them whether to use it or not.

With a starting salary of around £17,000 and a lower age limit of 18 years for joining it is an attractive career. The demise of the traffic wardens in Frome meant that many became the new Police Community Support Officers (Traffic wardens were later resurrected (2012) as a County function with the money for fines now going to the County Council).

Frome Police composition
Frome police area (2011) is made up of: 5 Response Teams (1 Sergeant and 3 to 4 Police Constables in each team), 1 Beat Team (1 Sergeant, 3 Police Constables, 9 PCSOs), a District Targeting Team with a front office clerk. There are 7 Special Constables (unpaid) and 3 police volunteers assisting. It is a 24/7 response service, with a non-designated custody unit holding prisoners for up to 6 hours.

Who is involved
Recently the police focused on presenting a higher public profile, setting up Partners and Communities Together (PACT) meetings held in each of the town's Wards for residents and Councillors to speak directly to the police about any concerns, of the original 6 none remain.

For a time a police officer joined Councillors at Full Town Council meetings to answer any queries – none were ever minuted. The police authority also produce their own chatty newsletter and indeed undertook a survey asking the public to rank what responsibilities they would like the police to undertake from a list ranging from caring for victims to solving neighbour disputes.

The locally run police "Splash" holiday scheme ran for a month each summer in the mid to late 1990's. Youngsters had the opportunity to try ice skating, caving, pistol shooting, horse riding, abseiling and the ever popular 6-a-side football tournament. Parents paid a nominal fee and the Town Council gave £1,000. It aimed to reducing anti-social behaviour and keep children off the streets. The Council also arranged summer coach trips to Weymouth on the coast for anyone of reduced means which met with equal amounts of criticism, outrage in the newspapers and delight – many taking their first opportunity to visit the seaside, these failed as take-up was embarrassingly low.

In the scheme's later year's businesses and social services added money and staff. By its end 200 youngsters were taking part. The police added monthly discos as youngsters complained there was nothing for them to do and no where they could go but these faltered and whilst other music promoters took over still not enough youngsters took up the opportunity and they remained unviable.

Frome has a low and decreasing level of crime revolving around speeding, traffic congestion, and anti-social behaviour – these made around about half of complaints, plus some theft (although little from homes). The detection rate has risen; the Avon and Somerset Constabulary now rank 27th. The newly launched national crime map website has made it possible for everyone to check the level of crime in their own area by postcode. There are between 200 and 300 reports a month across the whole town using the sites 6 crime categories. Anti-social behaviour is persistently high - between a third and half of reports, whereas burglary and robbery are consistently low, with theft from vehicles a low but a constant irritant. Confusingly the police use the old Parish Ward names (Fromefield, Berkley Down, Keyford, Park, and Welshmill) so townspeople looking for their Ward may not find it.

Epilogue
In 2009/10 the Town Council changed its funding focus renting a small office from Mendip District Council for a Police Post in the Market Yard Car Park as a bolt hole for the police and for occasional crime reduction surgeries. It was not open to the public until in 2012 when around 20 volunteers staffed it handing out advice leaflets, dealing with lost property and taking messages. It won a volunteering award from Mendip District Council.

With the closure of the Magistrates Court (2011) the Police Station was also expected to close. Built in 1952 as the Divisional Headquarters its survival over the last two decades has become increasingly uncertain especially since arrests were transported to Yeovil - 32 miles away. It is assumed the land will be sold for housing. The Court however is owned by the Crown Prosecution Service and it does not want to sell. With the Coalition Government public spending cuts Avon and Somerset Police have been tasked to save £40 million over the four years to 2015.

Datafile

Home Office, www.homeoffice.gov.uk
Avon and Somerset Police Authority, www.aspola.org.uk
Avon and Somerset Police Constabulary
www.avonandsomerset police.uk
www.police.uk

School Crossing Patrols (SCP)

- Funded as part of general budget up to approximately £5,000 each year

What they do

Each year Frome Town Council provides between £3-6,000 in funding towards school crossing patrols (often called lollipop men and women). Usually sited near a school, they help children and, since a change in the law in January 2001, other pedestrians to cross the road. All school crossing patrols are employed by the schools they operate from.

History

Familiar in their long fluorescent coats and carrying the "Lollipop" sign with Stop and a symbol of children beneath, SCP wait for a break in the traffic before stepping out into the middle of the road with arms outstretched and the sign facing the traffic bringing to a halt any that approaches. Pedestrians then cross in front of the Patrol. They generally operate twice a day between approximately 8.30am to 9.00am and from 3.20pm to 3.45 pm.

Abusive, intimidating drivers and faster traffic has resulted in recruitment problems in some areas of the country. There is a move countrywide to have a 20 mph speed limit safety zone around all schools. There is currently only one in Frome. More vulnerable schools also have warning signage and flashing lights so drivers know they are approaching a school crossing patrol. Failure to stop is an offence with a possible £1,000 fine, 3 penalty points on a driving license and possible disqualification.

Somerset School Patrols

Somerset County Council will provide grants to cover the costs of a patrol and in the past businesses have funded some. Where the school has a voluntary patrol the County Council can provide insurance and will give the money they save to the school to spend how it wishes e.g. new bicycle parking. The County has 70 Patrols. It also provides a Safe Routes to School service which devises individual school travel plans for children travelling to and from school on foot or by bike.

Who is involved

4 of the town's First schools and the 2 Middle schools.

Datafile

Somerset Road Safety Partnership, www.roadsafetysomerset.org.uk
www.roadsafetyhub.co.uk

Other Funders in Frome

Today the townspeople as individuals or groups provide fun and entertainment whilst raising thousands of pounds for local people and the town's own good causes. Organising pub quizzes and skittles evenings, or sponsored haircuts, or groups running marathons or cycle rides. But there are also organisations common to many towns which are dedicated to be of service to their local communities:

The Lions Club

The Lions Christmas float is an awe-inspiring sight and a favourite amongst small children as it tours the town and villages on December evenings. High atop a flat-bed lorry Father Christmas on his sleigh, originally drawn by a giant Showerings' "Babycham deer" and later replaced by a pair of traditional reindeer, tours in a blaze of light accompanied by the blare of Christmas carols which can be heard several streets away. Escorted by a posse of collectors, it negotiates steep streets, parked cars and very awkward junctions collecting loose change from small children and parents who come out to look and wonder. With helpers from Rotary and the Carnival it raised some £8,000 in 2011.

Formed in 1967 the 27 strong group runs amongst other things: golf tournaments, quizzes - a monthly winter favourite and fetes raising funds for local charities such as the air ambulance, the local hospice, cancer counselling, riding for the disabled and outings for the elderly.

Rotary Club

A mixture of social and fundraising with membership drawn from local businesses and the professions There are two Clubs: Frome Rotary founded in 1925 with around 54 members is men only, wives can join the Frome Inner Wheel Club; and Selwood Rotary with both men and women founded in 1990 with around 20 members.

Frome Rotary which twinned with the Rotary Club de Bayeux in 1968 fund-raises to provide health care for Indian, African and South America countries. It organises an annual Kids outing for 900 disadvantaged children from across the area to nearby Longleat and runs local public speaking competitions, designers, engineers and young chef awards. Bursaries are provided for youngsters to live and work abroad on development projects. It headed the funding of the new Community Hospital raising a staggering £700,000 for equipment.

Selwood Rotary also raises funds for local and international charities. Fund raising from wine tastings, fashion shows and concerts, provides support to local cancer charities and local families.

Freemasons

With traces of Frome Freemasonry as early as the 1790's the present Royal Somerset Lodge which includes Frome dates from 1863. The Lodge provides around £25,000 each year, for the whole of Somerset with organisations applying on a quarterly basis. Aiding: hot lunches for the elderly, youth clubs, children's play, Guides, Scouts, disabled groups, the air ambulance and cancer charities.

And Frome has groups unique to it:

Frome Community Lottery

Launched in October 2000 the Lottery has given around £72,000 funding 60 local groups.

These include: the Millennium Green, Frome Festival, Young People Frome, Home in Frome, Harry's Hydro, Black Swan, Frome Tennis Club, Frome Museum, the Memorial Theatre and the Guides. The Lottery's 16,000 cash winners have shared £67,000. Each £1 entry attempts to predict the temperature in six locations across the world. With a recently increased top prize of £25,000, the Lottery hopes to attract more members and raise funding to £10,000 a year.

The Woodlanders

For 35 years a group of talented enthusiasts have presented Music Hall to enthralled audiences in a packed village hall on the edge of Frome for one week in mid-October. The evening's entertainment, which once included a sandwich supper, retains the traditional sing-along, topical humour and glamour of the Edwardian Music Hall. Over the years more than £100,000 has been raised to provide funds for West Woodlands village hall and church and Frome voluntary groups. The £4,000 raised in 2010 was distributed between 16 diverse groups from playing fields to the Carnival and from a rural bus service to a story telling group.

Frome Carnival

Frome crowds line the streets whatever the weather to watch the illuminated carnival floats go by, warmed by the blaze of lights on a late September evening. It is a uniquely West Country tradition and marks the end of summer.

Perhaps originating back to the celebrations following the failure of the Gunpowder plot in 1605, today, 20 Somerset towns from August to mid-November show off the results of a whole year's work by their Carnival clubs with extravagant costumes and brilliant set designs all set to music on a stationary or moving tableau lit by thousands of light bulbs. Originally on hay carts pulled by tractors then flat-bed lorries, today's floats are often 30 metres in length negotiating the hills and winding streets of Somerset's market towns.

Founded in 1926, and now part of the Wessex Grand Prix circuit, Frome Carnival is the highlight of the third week in September originally coupled with the annual travelling fair coming to town, and the annual Cheese Show. It followed on from the choosing of the Carnival Queen with her Carnival Princesses, and the Carnival Granny still forming the centre piece of the parade. The separate Children's Carnival with small children dressed in extraordinary costumes from nursery rhymes, television characters and parents' imaginations have their own Carnival Queen and Princesses. The judging of costumes takes place on a Saturday afternoon in the Park followed by a parade through the town later joining the evening procession.

Sadly local firms no longer delight their customers with their own idiosyncratic contributions. Instead majorettes have become the significant new feature interspersed with marching bands, groups of friends, neighbours and children who dance and parade their way through the town centre. The most irreverent is Saturday Afternoon Theatre Company who have constantly surprised over the years including their famous synchronised swimmers, danced to "Swan Lake" and their Frome fertility dance.

Pennies collected by families throughout the year were thrown at slow moving lorries draped in white sheets to collect them, with small children racing in and out picking up those which miss their target. These today been replaced with 80 or so collectors shaking buckets along the edge of the crowd interspersed with balloon sellers and light wands. £6,000 was collected in 2011.

Carnival costs £10,000 - £12,000 to put on each year and the money the street collection raises is distributed to local people in need, providing carpets, washing machines, fridges, microwaves and wheelchairs.

…and an unexpected one:

Flourish Homes
A housing association which took over the running of local authority housing in Mendip also puts money aside funding an extraordinary range of projects and groups from village shops to drumming workshops, playgroups to sing-alongs for the elderly, originally with a pot of £50,000 it dropped to £25,000 reflecting the difficult national financial climate.

Datafile
Frome Lottery, www.fromelottery
TheWoodlanders,www.thewoodlanders.org.uk
Carnivals in Somerset Promotion Project, www.cispp.org.uk
Frome Lions, www.fromelions.org.uk
Rotary, www.rotary-ribi.org/clubs

SIDNEY HOUSE CHRISTCHURCH STREET WEST FROME

11 – POWER - Duties and Powers

Allotments
What you can expect "them" to do, what you can do, and a round–up of Planning, the Parish Poll and the Annual Parish Meeting

In truth Parish Councils do not have to do anything. There are few duties or statutory responsibilities for Parishes to carry out:

- provide allotments;
- hold an Annual Parish Meeting for the electors of the Parish, hold four council meetings a year - of which one can be the Annual Council meeting;
- appoint independent auditors for regular internal audits and comply with annual external audit rules;
- think about the likely effect on crime and disorder of decisions, keeping prevention in mind;
- think about the protection of local biodiversity when making decisions;
- think about adopting a closed churchyard if requested by the parochial church council.

Parishes can also take the opportunity to be a "statutory consultee" on local Planning applications and voice local opinions to the Planning authority.

In all other matters Councillors have a choice in what they do and this pivots on the amount of money they feel they are justified in spending. It really does depend on the personalities involved as to the depth and extent of a Parish Council's activity. This is a serious responsibility as decisions made resonate down the years long after the particular Councillor whose enthusiasm it was has left. Often funding once established, and the original reason half-forgotten or indeed no longer relevant still continues. A robust regime in place to look dispassionately at spending is essential. Without the financial capping mechanism of County or District/Unitary authorities, who can be penalised by central Government for overspending. Parish Councils can raise what funds they like only limited by an amount per elector if Section 137 (Local Government Act 1972) is used. For some Councils (those that qualify) the Power of Competence (Localism Act 2011) overrides it.

Many Parishes have an historic dimension with often major historic buildings or land bequeathed in perpetuity by generous benefactors in previous centuries. Now charities or trusts they were set up specifically for the relief of the poor, providing grants often for housing or education. Councillors may act wholly as trustees or as representatives of the Parish on a charitable board. These functions are unique to their place and often involve particular closely defined conditions imposed by the original benefactor.

More recently, Government has encouraged Parish Councils to provide extra funding for day to day services it already funds, or is funded, by the higher tiers of local government. It was suggested Parishes could ask the police to target specific concerns in return for extra money to fund an officer, or to pay for additional school crossing patrols where there are road safety concerns. Once a Parish Council has decided on what it wants to spend money on it creates a budget which may be modified by taking money from reserves - its savings, often left-overs from previous years' budgets.

It is not considered good practice to tax or precept purely to create a surplus as taxation should only be raised for specific purposes. From the resulting sums, taken with the number of households in the Parish, the level of precept is arrived at and collected by the District /Unitary Council on behalf of the Parish.

There is a long list of powers supported by Acts of Parliament which a Parish Council can use as a framework to provide voluntary responsibilities. These will often be covered by the District and County/Unitary Council legal responsibilities and run concurrently. Some of the Parish powers and duties are listed as follows:

Parish Council Powers
Not including Health and Safety, employment responsibilities, equality legislation, data protection or Freedom of Information.

Access Land
Power to enforce byelaws made by another authority.
Which Law - Countryside and Rights of Way Act 2000 s.17.

Allotments
Duty to provide allotments. Power to improve and adapt land for allotments, and to let grazing rights.
Which law - Small Holding & Allotments Act 1908, ss.23, 26, and 42.

Baths and washhouses
Power to provide public baths and washhouses and bathing huts.
Which law - Public Health Act 1936, ss.221, 222, 223 and 227.

Burial grounds, cemeteries and crematoria
Power to acquire and maintain, Power to provide, Power to agree to maintain monuments and memorials, Power to contribute towards expenses of cemeteries.
Which law - Open Spaces Act 1906, ss 9 and 10; Local Government Act 1972, s.214; Parish Councils and Burial Authorities (Miscellaneous Provisions) Act 1970, s.1 Local Government Act 1972, s.214(6).

Bus shelters
Power to provide and maintain shelters.
Which law - Local Government (Miscellaneous Provision) Act 1953, s.4.

Bye-laws
Power to make bye-laws in regard to: Pleasure grounds, Cycle parks Baths and washhouses, Open spaces and burial grounds, Mortuaries and post-mortem rooms, Public conveniences.
Which law - Public Health Act 1875, s.164. Road Traffic Regulation Act 1984, s.57(7). Public Health Act 1936, s.223. Open Spaces Act 1906, s.15. Public Health Act 1936, s.198.

Clocks
Power to provide public clocks.
Which law - Parish Councils Act 1957, s.2.

Closed churchyards
Power to maintain.
Which law - Parish Councils Act 1957, s.2.

Commons

Powers to contribute to expenses to regulate and manage.
Which law - Commons Act 1899 s.5.

Common pastures

Powers in relation to providing common pasture.
Which law - Smallholdings and Allotments Act 1908, s.34.

Conference facilities

Power to provide and encourage the use of facilities.
Which law - Local Government Act 1972, s.144.

Community centres

Power to provide and equip buildings for use of clubs having athletic, social or recreational objectives.
Which law - Local Government (Miscellaneous Provisions) Act 1976 s.19.

Crime prevention

Powers to install and maintain equipment and establish and maintain a scheme for detection or prevention of crime, Power to contribute to police services e.g. PCSO's, Duty to consider crime reduction in every policy and action.
Which law - Local Government and Rating Act 1997, s.31 Police Act 1996 s.92 Crime and Disorder Act 1998 s.17.

Dogs

Power to make Dog Control Orders and to take enforcement action.
Which law - Cleaner Neighbourhoods and Environment Act 2005.

Drainage

Power to deal with ponds and ditches.
Which law - Public Health Act 1936, s.260.

Entertainment and the arts

Provision of entertainment and support of the arts.
Which law - Local Government Act 1972, s.145.

Flyposting and graffiti

Power to take enforcement action against those who flypost or graffiti.
Which law - Cleaner Neighbourhoods and Environment Act 2005.

Financial assistance

Duty to require information.
Which law - Local Government Act 1972 s.137A.

General Powers

Power to incur expenditure for certain purposes.
Which law - Local Government Act 1972 s.137.

Gifts

Power to accept.
Which law - Local Government Act 1972,s.139.

Highways

Power to maintain footpaths and bridle-ways. Power to light roads and public places. Provision of litter bins.

Powers to provide parking places for bicycles and motor-cycles and other vehicles. Power to enter into agreement as to dedication and widening. Power to provide roadside seats and shelters. Consent of Parish Council required for ending maintenance of highway at public expense, or for stopping up or diversion of the highway. Power to complain to highway authority as to unlawful stopping up or obstruction of highway or unlawful encroachment on roadside wastes. Power to provide traffic signs and other objects or devices warning of danger. Power to plant trees and lay out grass verges etc and to maintain them.

Which law - Highways Act 1980, ss.43,50. Parish Councils Act 1957, s.3. Highways Act 1980, s.301. Litter Act 1983, ss.5,6. Road Traffic Regulation Act 1984, ss.57,63. Highways Act 1980, ss.30,72. Parish Councils Act 1957, s.1. Highways Act 1980, ss.47,116. Highways Act 1980, s.130. Road Traffic Regulation Act 1984, s.72. Highways Act 1980, s.96.

Investments
Power to participate in schemes of collective investment.
Which law - Trustee Investments Act 1961, s.11.

Land
Power to acquire by agreement, to appropriate, to dispose of land. Power to accept gifts of land.
Which law - Local Government Act 1972, ss.124, 126, 127. Local Government Act 1972, s.139.

Litter
Provision of receptacles Power to take enforcement.
Which law - Litter Act 1983, ss.5,6. Cleaner Neighbourhoods and Environment Act 2005.

Lotteries
Powers to promote
Which law - Lotteries and Amusements Act 1976, s.7.

Mortuaries and post-mortem rooms
Powers to provide mortuaries and post-mortem rooms.
Which law - Public Health Act 1936, s.198.

Open spaces
Power to acquire land and maintain.
Which law - Public Health Act 1875, s.16.4 Open Spaces Act 1906, ss.9 and 10.

Parish documents
Powers to direct as to their custody
Which law - Local Government Act 1972, s.226.

Telecommunications facilities
Power to pay public telecommunications operators any loss sustained providing telecommunication facilities.
Which law - Telecommunications Act 1984, s.97.

Public buildings and village halls
Power to provide buildings for public meetings and assemblies.
Which law - Local Government Act 1972, s.133.

Public conveniences
Power to provide.
Which law - Public Health Act 1936, s.87.

Recreation
Power to acquire land for or to provide public walks, pleasure grounds and open spaces and to manage and control them. Power to provide gymnasiums, playing fields, holiday camps. Provision of boating pools.
Which law - (see Local Government Act 1972, Schedule.14 para.27). Public Health Act 1875, s.164. Public Health Acts Amendment Act 1890 s.44. Open Spaces Act 1906, ss.9 and 10 Local Government (Miscellaneous Provisions) Act 1976, s.19. Public Health Act 1961, s.54.

Town and country planning
Right to be notified of Planning applications.
Which law - Town and Country Planning Act 1990, Schedule.1, para.8.

Tourism
Power to encourage visitors and provide conference and other facilities.
Which law - Local Government Act 1972,s.144.

Traffic calming
Powers to contribute financially to traffic calming schemes.
Which law - Highways Act 1980, s.274A.

Transport
Powers in relation to car-sharing schemes, taxi fare concessions and information about transport. Powers to make grants for bus services.
Which law - Local Government and Rating Act 1997, s.26, 28 and 29. Transport Act 1985, s.106A.

War memorials
Power to maintain, repair, protect and alter war memorials.
Which law - War Memorials (Local Authorities' Powers) Act 1923, s.1; as extended by Local Government Act 1948, s.133.

Water supply
Power to utilise well, spring or stream and to provide facilities for obtaining water from them.
Which law - Public Health Act 1936, s.125.

These make fascinating reading and chart the concerns of local government over time resulting in an odd mix of possibilities.

...Frome Watch...
Frome Town Council (2007-11 election cycle) used its duties and powers to budget for:
On-going:
- maintaining allotments
- grant aiding town organisations and clubs
- commenting on Planning applications
- maintaining a park with a bowling green, a putting green, boule court, tennis courts, and a bandstand. A playing field with children's play equipment and a riverside field.
- planting roadside verges and hanging baskets

- maintaining two public toilets
- providing Christmas lights and a Christmas event

Occasional:
- bus shelters
- litter/grit/dog poo bins
- street lighting
- occasional additional entertainment events

Towards the end of 2007/11 election cycle the council added tourist information and a tea room in the Park, extra grit bins and in its last year it transferred the previously District maintained riverside walk and two play areas into its care.

Section 137 is the power of last resort and commonly used as a reason to fund all sorts where no other power exists. The National Association of Local Councils (NALC) best sums it up in "The Good Councillor Guide" (2006), *"There are very few activities that a Parish Council cannot undertake; the trick is to ensure that there is a legal power for every action of the council. If the council cannot find a specific power, then Section 137 (Local Government Act 1972) is a treasure."* Spending must be balanced by the benefit gained and money cannot be lent to individuals. There is a set amount per elector (£6.15p 2010/11) which rises annually with the Retail Price Index. Councils should list their Section 137 spending as a separate item within their Budgets.

Datafile
"The Good Councillor Guide", 2006 published by National Association of Local Councils
Department of the Environment, Food and Rural Affairs, www.defra.gov.uk

Allotments
Allotments are the jewel in the crown of a Parish Council and its only statutory duty a Parish has to undertake (enshrined in the 1908 Act) indeed it has a duty to provide allotment gardens where there is unsatisfied demand, upon the written representations of six electors or alternatively by the resolution and voting of ten electors at the Parish Annual Meeting.

By definition an 'allotment garden' is wholly or mainly cultivated by the plotholder producing fruit or vegetables for himself and his family, chickens and rabbits can also be kept. Interestingly at one point there was a no flowers rule. An allotment should not exceed "forty poles" (1,210 square yards/ ¼ of an acre/0.10 hectare) today it is generally assumed the average plot is 300 square yards (250 sq metres or 10 rods). This should comfortably feed a family of 4. The rents, generally very low, are set at what a person can be *"reasonably expected to pay."* Allotment land (statutory) cannot be sold without consent of the Secretary of State.

Types of Allotments
The majority of allotments are owned by local authorities and fall into two categories:

Statutory, originally purchased or appropriated for allotments, and if sold land must be provided to replace the lost allotments, or
Temporary, where the land is ultimately meant for some other use.

The various Acts of Enclosure and Commons Acts between 1750 and 1860 allowed landowners to enclose roughly a third of all agricultural land in the country. The rights of the peasantry were consequently swept away. They were no longer able to pasture a cow or keep pigs and geese on the commons or use it to cut and collect gorse, bracken or wood for fuel or cultivate crops, creating a landless labouring poor. Overall there was very little sympathy for the poor although more progressive landowners did set aside land for allotments. The 1806 Enclosure Act was the first to stipulate that a portion of land should become allotments to make up for the loss of the Commons. Seen as a success as the demand on the Parish Poor Rate lessened, it was hoped the rise in crime would also reduce. As time progressed landowners realised they could rent land out giving themselves a greater return as the popularity of allotments grew apace, particularly with the introduction of the potato as a food crop. The 1819 Select Vestries Act gave discretionary powers to Parish Wardens to buy or lease land for letting at reasonable rents, with the 1831 Act increasing the area from 20 acres (8 hectares) to 50 acres (20 hectares).

...Frome Watch...

In 1820 the Marquis of Bath let 6 acres of grassland in Frome dividing them into allotments with no rent, rate or tithe to pay. The first year went well but during the second year, some allotment holders complained of being robbed, others demanded their Parish poor pay as well, whilst others stopped cultivating their plots, complaining that the gardens were too distant, considering the few leisure hours they had available. The experiment was abandoned. Later attempts in the 1830's were equally fraught with the last attempt providing allotments for 150 tenants. Each being, it was reckoned, large enough to feed a family of 5, overall growing food for 750 persons. The rents however, proved impossible to collect. The Society of the Friends of the Poor, made up of Frome's wealthy, collecting the rents on behalf of the landowners – the Earls of Cork and the Marquis of Bath, were very vexed having to make up the shortfall, some £66 (around £6,000 in today's money) at one year's end.

The Poor Law Commissioner's Report of 1834 detailed the opposition in some quarters by landowners, farmers and clergy to providing allotments. Many thought it would make the labourers too independent, and demand higher wages, or act as an inducement to an early marriage and thus more children with a bigger burden on the Poor Rate. Equally, labourers were concerned it would result in low wages and slave like conditions. The Report also detailed the successes finding happy productive workforces with a reduced burden on the Poor Rate. The General Enclosure Act of 1845 saw the further development of allotments under the control of the Parish Wardens. Although the fields were often distant, on poor ground, and with high rents, the allotments could still be a useful supplement to meagre wages; benevolent landowners were still taking a major role in allotment provision. After the Allotment Extension Act 1882 church charity lands were also included.

Throughout Victorian times their popularity spread, despite, in some cases, the high rents. Allotment gardens had become part of a working class ethos particularly in the towns and cities. As leisure time increased, flower and vegetable shows started alongside the formation of clubs and associations. In the countryside the Rural Sanitary Authorities in the 1887 Allotments Act could now acquire land and even compulsory purchase it.

Enthusiasms had grown such that the elections of 1889 became known as the "Allotment Election" with candidates standing according to their position on the subject, those who were in favour of allotments, won!

This resulted in a further Act in 1894 giving further powers for both the voluntary and compulsory creation of allotments.

It was under the 1908 Smallholdings and Allotments Act, (confirmed by later Acts of Parliament) that Councils were forced to be proactive, to discover what land was needed and to buy or obtain it. It is this Act which states categorically that allotments must be provided, there is not a choice. Parishes can buy, lease or accept gifts of land, or alternatively compulsory purchase or compulsory lease. Some have used the Lottery "Awards For All" scheme to fund the buying of land.

Smallholdings and Allotments Act 1908
Section 23 provides that if allotment authorities *"are of the opinion that there is a demand for allotments ...in the borough, district or Parish, the council shall provide a sufficient number of allotments to persons...resident in the borough district or Parish and desiring the same."* In determining demand an authority must take into consideration *"a representation in writing by any six registered parliamentary electors or rate payers."* However, there is no time limit set in which to provide them.

Allotments can be provided by:
- principal local authorities, County, District or Unitary,
- the 10,000 Parishes,
- councils leasing land to independent allotment societies,
- Trusts, and other public bodies,
- private landowners.

Allotment gardens were at their height of popularity by the time of the First World War when there were one and half million plots; this held steady, resurging during the Second World War.
By 1949 4 acres of allotment land per 1,000 head of population was recommended. In 1969 the Thorpe Report recommended a minimum of 15 plots per 1,000 population but allotments continued a steady decline, to about quarter of a million plots today.

Now, Government sees allotments as a health benefit and part of its overall public health strategy, particularly for the over 50s the age-group which traditionally dominate the age profile of allotment holders. With growing concern about food miles, and the future security of food supplies, the predicted shortage and security of energy supplies, combined with governmental promises to reduce the nation's carbon footprint, allotments should be a potent force. However, Governments have not been proactive in defining land or insisting on the inclusion of allotment land in new developments, although all Planning authorities are obliged to include allotments as part of their Local Plans.

However, responding to the estimated 100,000 people currently on allotment waiting lists nationally, some Parishes have set up garden share schemes. The National Trust (2009) provided a 1,000 new allotments available through the Landshare website which "match-makes" between potential growers, landowners and helpers.

...Frome Watch...

Frome is built on the clays and limestones of the Jurassic Forest Marble, producing the distinctive north facing escarpment up which the main streets of Bath Street and Catherine Hill wind from the valley bottom of the river Frome. This produces a light, brown, alkaline soil somewhat stony often with sizable pieces used for rubble walling, house building and splitting into stone roofing tiles. In places the soil is under laid by heavy impermeable clay. Only the present day Welshmill allotment site is on the alluvial silts of the river valley bottom.

The 1903 Ordnance Survey Map shows 18 allotment garden sites set amongst the fields to the west and south of Frome town centre; part of a network of market gardens, smallholdings and nurseries. The allotments provided around 40 acres (16 hectares) of land for a population of, in 1901, around 11,057 (the population had dropped from 12,240 in 1831 in harsh economic climes).

Frome, 1903 allotment areas:
- one off Dyers Close Lane,
- one off Robin's Lane,
- six along Oakfield Road,
- two on Park Road,
- one off Summerhill,
- four on Locks Hill
- one behind Garston Road
- two near the railway station

All have been turned into housing, much of it local authority, for Frome Urban District Council (UDC). The abandoned Garston Road site with adjacent industrial land being the last to go providing 187 homes (2010).

The current Frome (2011) "allotment rate" of around 4 per 1,000 population is half the national average of 7 and considerably smaller than the Somerset average of 15.

The 110 plots over 8 allotment sites (about 10 acres/4 hectares at Cranmore View, Queens Road, North Hill, Mendip View, Orchard Street, Welshmill, and Vallis Road.) are managed and administered by the Frome Allotments Association for the Town Council who have a nominal involvement:

The Singers Knoll site was a recent transfer from District. (2008). Both Queens Road and Singers Knoll are remnants of the larger 1903 areas - used for housing by Frome UDC.

A Strategic Review by Mendip District Council (2004) concluded that any remaining town allotments should be passed to Frome Town Council for a nominal sum. With one exception the Ring O'Bells site (named after the local pub) long abandoned next to the Police Station and Magistrates Court complex on Oakfield Road. Not marked as such on the 1903 map, and at around 3 acres it is the largest site after Welshmill and could accommodate at least 50 allotments. Landlocked, plotholders were asked to vacate it in the early 1990's as the site was needed for housing. However, this will only be possible with the demolition of the Police buildings - something which has been constantly threatened and is increasingly likely. The District in the meantime has refused numerous requests to allow the land to be cultivated or even leased on a temporary basis. Since the closure of the Magistrates Court (2010) and now the suggested relocation of the Police Station families who have "guerilla gardened" cultivating and creating gardens on the land and providing play space for their children are in danger of losing something precious.

Ironically, a District Council commissioned report -"Allotments Strategy for Mendip" (2002) emphasied the importance of allotments to the development of sustainability, as open spaces, for biodiversity, and for their health, educational and social benefits adding that any proposed housing which threatened allotments should be reviewed but if allowed, replaced with a site that is of similar quality and accessibility.

The value of agricultural land doubled between 2001 - 2011 from £2/3,000 to £4/7,000 with pony paddocks fetching £10,000, and those with water £12,000 or more an acre making it, the Town Council felt, too expensive to purchase.

There are fewer private sites today than in the past, as land behind Rodden Road and on Innox Hill have gone out of cultivation. The newest is at The Leys on the western edge of town, where there are informal plots on an 18 acres (7 hectares) smallholding, part of an ambitious project of community involvement in food growing, tree planting, biodiversity, and education including - for a time - a local vegetable box delivery scheme.

A Frome Allotments Association plot offers extraordinary value for money at around £15.00 per annum per plot bringing in around £300 per year for the town. There is however a considerable waiting list, up from 30 in 2007, 65 in 2008, 80 in 2009 to 120 in 2011. A petition to the Town Council in 2009 did not receive a reply although the Council's website boldly recognised its duty to provide allotments. In answering a question at the Town Annual Meeting (May 2009) the council stated it had written to all surrounding landowners asking to buy land but with no luck.

Enthusiasm is still high, with Food Frome, first set up in 2005 investigating and recording the past and present food culture of the town and the newly formed (2007) Sustainable Frome's Food and Land Group promoting the production of local food.

Datafile

Growing our Own, Food Frome,2008
Allotments by Twigs Way, Shire Publications, 2008
The Allotment Chronicles by Steve Poole, Silver Link Publishing Ltd, 2006
Securing Food Supplies up to 2050 – The Challenges Faced by the UK, at Planning Resource.co.uk/doc 2009
Allotments, www.allotments.org.uk
National Society of Allotment and Leisure Gardeners, www.nsalg.org.uk
Department for the Communities and Local Government, www.communities.gov.uk
Federation of City Farms and Community Gardens, www.farmgarden.org.uk
Landshare, www.landshare.channel4.com
Food Frome, www.foodfrome.org.uk
www.allotmoreallotments.org.uk

12 – POWER - Planning Matters

The Planning system impacts everyone's daily life from the development of airports to house extensions, from tree felling through to the Change of Use of the local newsagent into a take-away. Set up in 1948, it gave control of land usage to the State in a hope of creating economic prosperity in a country levelled by the Second World War.

Legislation has been added endlessly, so today there are vast tomes of finely nuanced regulation which have become a trap for the unwary. In doing so Planning has become: a political football, a way to get at the neighbours, a system to protect the environment, or a way to legally despoil it. Whilst legislation provides the framework, it is the guidance notes issued at intervals by Government which provides an explanation of the rules. These in turn are challenged using the Planning Appeal system and the Courts providing in turn "new rules" which can alter substantially the way future decisions are made.

Planning is the key activity most people associate with Councils and most only get involved when they wish to do something or wish to prevent someone else from doing it. The Department for Communities and Local Government definition takes in a wider perspective, *"Planning shapes the places where people live and work and the country we live in. It plays a key role in supporting the Government's wider social, environmental and economic objectives and for sustainable communities."*

There are two stages to consultation: the Planning authority and the Parish. The Planning authority, (District, Unitary or County) receives Planning applications and begins the process of consultation sending details to a variety of bodies:

- in local government such as Highways and Environmental Health,
- to Government departments such as the Environment Agency, or English Heritage,
- local such as Civic Societies and national lobby groups such as Campaign for the Preservation of Rural England or the National Trust,
- Parish Councils and
- neighbours for comment.

Parish Councils as statutory consultees can only hope their opinions and recommendations are listened to by the Planning authority. They do not as yet have Planning powers of their own.

Planning is regarded with a mixture of cynicism and exasperation by all who find themselves grappling with the process which is often regarded as akin to the "dark arts", as the whole mysterious process unfolds. This is not helped by the often, stilted nature of public meetings, too often resulting in a stylised, theatrical, and an often unexpectedly adversarial approach. They frequently lack a purposeful debate or any attempt to create a considered meeting of minds. It is not always the round-table discussion, thrashing out vital issues, looking for a consensual way forward it should be or an audience might expect, much in the end comes down to the personal preferences of Councillors.
For the watching audience it can look inept, slightly embarrassing, and floundering, as Councillors peer at and shuffle through plans and papers in apparent surprise, vaguely unclear and self-conscious, hoping someone will use a telling, carefully learned Planning phrase they can at least all agree on, *"over development"*, or *"detrimental to visual amenities"*, for an easy start.

However, Planning is the most popular Committee for both Councillors and the public. It is a subject everyone has an opinion on and wishes it to be heard for personal or political reasons, or even in the hope of being quoted in the local press. It does offer Councillors the opportunity for a wider influence, so there is usually lots of competition between Councillors to be appointed to the Planning Committee. Many Planning authorities offer training, with the Parish or Committee Clerk giving guidance on the Planning authorities' processes.

With discussions limited, certainly at Parish level, by Councillors own knowledge or bias, television programmes watched, shock-horror pieces in the tabloid newspapers or on experience gleaned on a piecemeal basis from previous Planning meetings. Inaccuracies of fact and inconsistencies creep in, often heatedly debated. Unchallengeable by the listening audience, who can only speak for 3 minutes in the Public Forum before an application is discussed. Causing great frustration as misinformation is batted backwards and forwards across a meeting. Lengthy agendas are tiring and it is difficult to critically analyse application after application when meetings run to 4 or more hours. Much could be solved by visiting the application site at both Parish and Planning authority level to look at the context of schemes.

The Application

Planning Considerations
Planning officers balance the applicants' wishes with:
- the public interest,
- the Local Plan previously called the Local Development Framework. It allocates areas of land use and areas of potential change. If no Local Plan exists the National Planning Policy Framework is used,
- set against national and any regional Government policies,
- case law i.e. High Court and Supreme Court legal rulings,
- visual effect such as design, appearance and layout,
- the impact and effect on neighbouring properties,
- highway safety and traffic,
- conservation of buildings, trees and wildlife,
- environmental problems such as noise, dust, smell, pollution,
- economic viability, and hopefully
- the Parish Plan and Parish Design Statement which were often combined. These expressed specific local views on housing and jobs and particularly the design, setting, and use of local building materials. Government expected local Planning authorities to make these views part of the decision making process. The Localism Act 2011 brought in Neighbourhood Plans generally similar to the Parish Plan again outlining local views. These are seen by the Parishes as pivotal.

Planning applications received by the Planning authority – not the Parish Council, whether written or filled in on-line are validated (if all the information requested is present), listed (lists may be published in the local newspapers), given a number, and allotted to a Planning officer who will be the point of contact for the application as it goes through the system.

Once registered the clock starts and the officer has 8 weeks (or 13 weeks) in which to research, visit and present a report to the Ward Councillor or the Planning authority's Planning Committee (for a Committee decision) or reject or approve it themselves if they have delegated powers.

Possible supporting information for Planning applications
(some authorities list over 2 dozen):
- bat, bird, slow worm and badger surveys,
- archaeological reports,
- economic viability reports,
- travel plans,
- environmental impact studies,
- noise studies,
- landscaping details.

Planning officers can - depending on a Planning authorities' way of doing things, give advice to applicants beforehand – this is increasingly being charged for, and discuss the concerns and issues of objectors and Councillors not just Planning Committee Councillors. Not all decisions happen quickly or within the specified time, of 8 weeks (small applications) or 13 weeks (large applications). For particularly complex developments, or potentially unpopular ones decisions may take several years. Some indeed disappear rarely to resurface.

The government time target for applications (8 or 13 weeks) is the basis of the statistics by which Planning authorities are judged allowing them to be listed on a league table. If they drop below a certain value government can send in a specialist squad to take over decision making, much in the way as they do for failing schools.

Once the target has been missed there is no rush to decide an application because there are applications coming up behind which need to hit their time targets. Applicants can agree to a time extension gambling the result may come more quickly or be more favourable. Confusingly after the 13 or 8 weeks deadline there is a further 6 months when applicants can go to Appeal (see failed applications) because no decision has been made (non-determination). This is an additional expense, applicants can claim their costs but so can the Planning authority, neither may get them. Applicants can alternatively just sit it out and hope something is decided soon.

Third Party Right of Appeal
With no third party right of Appeal there are few avenues for an outraged community:

Calling-In an application
Anyone, including MPs, can call-in an application up to the point the Planning authority makes the decision. It is free. The issues should be of more than of local importance preferably with a national scope or policy. There is a general reluctance to meddle with local decision making.

The Secretary of State (SofS) decides after a Public Inquiry held by a Planning Inspector and this can be based on the Inspector's recommendations. The SofS does not have to agree. Numbers have dropped from a high in 2007-08 of 29 to 3 in 2012-13.

There is anecdotal evidence of call-ins happening more frequently in Conservative marginal constituencies.

The SofS can also "recover" an Appeal intervening before an Appeal decision has been made. Again the decision is based on the Inspector's recommendations and again a "recovered Inquiry" would be around very high profile issues of national, infrastructure or policy importance.

Judicial Reviews (JR)

Anyone, although usually it is an action group, can ask the High Court to review a grant of Planning permission looking at whether the processes and procedures have been properly applied such as a failure to consider certain information.

JRs are by far the most popular route for challenges to the legal system. With around 12,400 (2012 including immigration, asylum and criminal cases) requested each year, Planning makes up a very small proportion averaging around 150. Of these some 35% "have merit" and are allowed to proceed and of these 25% are successful.

Despite such a small number the Government sees Reviews as a brake on development and investment with publicity seeking objectors perversely delaying the implementation of Planning permission or even over turning it, with the subsequent huge cost to developers in defending their permissions.

From July 2013 the time allowed for a challenge was halved from 3 months to 6 weeks (some developers did not start development until the "risk" period had ended). A judge still decides if a case should proceed that is it "has merit". The court fee has been raised from £60 to £215 for a second judge in a second hearing to examine the paperwork if the initial JR application was turned down. Cases without any merit are now banned from the second chance hearing. Both sides will need to employ specialist lawyers to argue the technicalities. It is a slow expensive process often taking more than a year to resolve.

2014 saw a specialist Planning Court begin, so there is, the Justice Secretary stated *"a crucial check on the powers that be but we cannot allow meritless cases to be a brake on economic growth. That would be bad for the economy, the taxpayer and the job seeker, and bad for confidence in justice...but unmerited, costly and time wasting applications (will) no longer stifle progress."*

Revoking Planning permission

Planning permission can be revoked after it has been granted but heavty compensation would be due and the process is very rarely used.

Design and Access Statements

These short comprehensive narratives accompanying the application explain the thinking behind the proposals. Answering a series of questions about: layout, scale, appearance, access and landscaping. Why things are where they are, how they look, the overall setting and what influenced the design. How people will move in and around a site, connections to the surrounding area, what consultations have been done and how the resulting opinions were incorporated including what Planning policies were used. Sometimes accompanied by photographs and diagrams. The Statements should be read first to get the real flavour and meaning of a proposal.

The resulting Planning authorities Report may recommend approval (with conditions), refusal or a deferral for more information. The Report's conclusions may be discussed with the District/Unitary Ward Councillor, who may also be a Parish Councillor, if the application is straight forward it may be approved under delegated powers, if there are some objections these can be discussed and solved between the Planning officer, the applicant and the Councillor, again with approval or refusal under delegated powers. Complex issues, particularly where there are lots of objections, or an application is in some way controversial or at the Ward Councillor's suggestion (including when an application is from a Councillor or council employee), is discussed and decided at the Planning authorities Planning Committee.

For the applicant there is a long list of possible types of information which can be requested before the applications is even validated and hopefully the applicant has already spoken to the neighbours to allay any fears.

Decisions are sent to the applicant, posted on the authorities' website and may be listed in the local newspaper. A list of decisions is sent to the Parish Council, but objectors are not routinely told of the outcome.

Making opinions heard
By understanding the system, by speaking out, by writing or by joining with other individuals or groups.

Material Planning Considerations
The Planning authority has to take into account "material Planning considerations" when making a decision and these can of course be used as a basis for objections these include:

- Previous Planning decisions, including Appeal decisions and any compensation or awards of costs against the Planning authority at Appeal.
- Loss of light or overshadowing,
- Overlooking or loss of privacy,
- Visual amenity - but not loss of private view,
- Loss of trees,
- Landscaping,
- Nature Conservation,
- Archaeology and Heritage Assets,
- Effect on Listed Buildings, Heritage Assets and the Conservation Area,
- Layout and density of building/buildings,
- Design and appearance,
- Materials used,

- Road access,
- Highway safety,
- Traffic generation,
- Disabled access,
- Adequacy of parking, loading or turning including for emergency vehicles,
- Noise and disturbance resulting from use,
- Hazardous materials used or found on site,
- Smells,
- Local, strategic, regional and national planning polices,
- Government circulars, orders and statutory instruments,
- Policies in the Local Plan.

Issues which are not Planning considerations are:
- Assumed loss of property value,
- Loss of a view,
- Private disputes between neighbours,
- Construction work i.e. noise and dust, but measures such as hours of work can be made to lessen the impact,
- Competition between businesses,
- Ownerships disputes over rights of way,
- Fence lines and boundaries,
- Restrictive covenants,

The applicant:
- Nuisance or annoyance previously caused (unless permission is retrospective),
- Any profit likely to be made,
- Reasons or motives in applying for permission (such as it is purely speculative)
- Race or ethnic origin, sexual orientation, religious beliefs, political views or affiliations or any other personal attributes,
- Identity, behaviour, personal morals or views.

Perhaps the easiest argument to voice and one that causes most concern is high density or overdevelopment especially any "garden grabbing." Since June 2010 this is back as grounds for refusal and can be coupled with what it looks like (visual impact) and the effect on the character or personality of a neighbourhood. Akin to this is the adverse effect on neighbours' enjoyment of their homes such as by noise, disturbance, overlooking, loss of privacy, or overshadowing (but not noise or disturbance from doing the building work itself). Especial care should be taken in Conservation Areas, near Listed Buildings and in Areas of Outstanding Natural Beauty. Design can be cited, including bulk and massing, detailing and materials or if the proposals are over-bearing, out-of-scale or incompatible with buildings already existing. Again a higher standard will be expected in a Conservation Area, near Listed Buildings or in Areas of Outstanding Natural Beauty. Loss of views by neighbours as an argument for objection can be a question of degree.

Highway safety or inconvenience to road users is decided by the Planning authorities' technical department but always comes up high on objectors lists. It is difficult to use unless backed with expert opinion.

The Public

Of all the committees, Planning draws an audience to watch the discussion or to speak in the Public Forum at the meeting's start. Planning authorities and Parish Councils ask speakers for advanced notification, so no one is missed out, setting aside 15 to 30 minutes in 3 minute allotted slots or as a set amount per issue. With lots of people wishing to speak either for or against an issue an appointed spokesperson emphasising the collective viewpoint is more effective than a trail of people repeating the same points. This will need a bit of organising. Individual speakers not associated with a group can feel very aggrieved and stripped of their democratic rights if not allowed to speak because time has been given to a group and angered at the assumption they will dully repeat points already made. Most comments are about personal or neighbourhood concerns rather than overall policies and sound disconcertingly flat when met with a blank silence from Councillors.

Unless a confident public speaker it is generally best to write, short, snappy points which can be read easily, rather than falter part way through to be cut off unceremoniously by the Committee Chairman. It surprises many that the applicant can also speak in support of his own application. There is no right of reply, no way to correct or query what anyone says or ask questions. But to sit, listen and hope the "right" decision is made. There is no third party right of appeal, so for objectors this is the end of the road.

Councillors can ask questions but discussion is discouraged until the main debate. The Committee Chairman may curtail statements if he feels they are too repetitive, or rambling. Inherently confrontational nothing can describe the sense of frustration, futility and helplessness felt by objectors, certainly over larger schemes, or by the applicant, when confronted by a sudden and unexpected unleashing of vitriol. The Planning meetings themselves can take on a surreal almost Kafkaesque quality.

Whilst Parish meetings can be intense and passionate, this is sadly not translated into the official minuted comments made by Parish Councils which are often, too brief, terse, and too often written in a faux Planning language, missing the central arguments, discussion or supporting detail carefully made by neighbours, objectors or applicant, failing to give a true reflection of local opinion. This perhaps explains why Parish comments can be so easily discarded to the chagrin of all.

There is a common misconception that there is a right to know about new developments. However, Councils will be criticised if they do not adopt best practice and make some attempt to inform the public of planned developments. Most District and Unitary authorities list applications on their websites and put up site notices (giving the application number and the briefest description) on the nearest lamppost to the application site – so there is a need for constant vigilance and close regular examination of local lampposts – most of the time these will turn out to be notices about lost cats.

Action Groups

An action group can collectively:
- research the subject,
- create a list of reasons for objection,
- suggest modifications to design, layout, landscaping or materials.
- suggest things the area needs to mitigate development: play and open spaces, allotments, footpaths, a shop,

- delegate others to write,
- have a spokesperson,
- go to meetings,
- speak to the Planning officer,
- speak to the developer,
- speak to the Ward Councillor,
- speak at Parish meetings,
- speak at Planning authority meetings,
- understand the policies in the Local Plan,
- read the applicant's Planning file,
- support each other,
- raise money for posters, or leaflets to reach a wider audience,
- hire professional help to hone arguments,
- form a limited company for objectors,
- distribute information,
- arrange photographic moments for the local press,
- write press releases,
- start a website,
- encourage letter writing,
- organise a protest march.

Planning applications are often hidden away on Planning authority websites under "Environment Directorate", Environmental Services" or "Development Control." Many local newspapers publish lists and some development changes appear under "Public Notices." Many authorities inform neighbours by letter asking for comments.

Councils are more comfortable dealing with organisations than with individuals – whom they appear to view as "difficult", so no matter how small a group: elect a Chairman, come up with a good gutsy name or even better a catchy acronym.

Letters either objecting or supporting (this should be clearly declared otherwise a letter can end up in the wrong category) should be written to individual Councillors, the Planning Department (who will forward them to the staff member overseeing the application), the Parish Council, the Ward Councillor and any Councillors representing the Parish at District/Unitary level who are on the Planning Committee keeping strictly to the applications Planning issues. A lobbying round-robin letter or information pack can be written and sent to all Planning Committee members and it is wise to state this clearly as Councillors can be easily upset and feel compromised. Letters may or may not be read or acknowledged but at least view-points have been explained directly and not filtered or summarised by the Planning process. Otherwise if mass letter writing letters is undertaken they should be individually written, not a signed pre-printed or standardised letter, as this might be seen as a petition, in which case only the top letter is counted.

Petitions are generally disregarded partly because they too frequently include people not local or who have been invented.
However, the Local Democracy, Economic Development and Construction Act (2009) asks local authorities to give more weight to petitions so presumably this means Planning petitions as well.

Letters posted or e-mailed are not confidential and may be published on the Planning authorities' website (if it has this facility) or read in the applicant's Planning file, which is open to all.

Many feel they should write to their Member of Parliament however this is a waste of time. They cannot arbitrate or mediate or act as a sort of appeal tribunal. Again Councillors can be prickly about the possibility of this type of "outside interference." Whether they can provide some influence on their political Party's Councillors is a moot point.

Responses vary; many people put a lot of effort into well researched, carefully crafted letters providing complex documentary evidence. Not all objectors are necessarily negative, many do suggest modifications; however, such reasonableness has the inherent danger of making them ignorable. Letters of support though rarer are not unknown. Issues raised in letters, are not, as may be expected, always dealt with on an argument by argument basis in the Planning officers' reports, but by using local Planning policies which outline the general intent of the authority.

However, local people's perception of what is important in their surroundings does not translate easily into the generalised wording of policy statements but, it does make objections easier to dismiss and townspeople may disappointingly see their views brushed aside.

Comments received may be listed on a roughly scored basis (such as, 6 objections made on density, 2 on overlooking etc), often only the first reason of a series of reasons is used or comments may be simply divided into three categories:

- **For**- straight forward letters in support,
- **Against** - letters which only contain objections, or
- **Undecided** - letters which give a reasoned and balanced argument weighing up the pro and cons and concluding as against. However, letters suggesting modifications can be categorised as undecided, or equally as a letter of support.

If Councillors have not read the views of local people the impact will in any case be lost. But importantly the Planning authority has consulted.

The list of the reasons for permission or refusal is posted to the applicant and the Parish Council informed. If neighbours do not like the decision there is little to be done, there is no third party right of appeal. If the procedure i.e. the paperwork, was incorrectly dealt with it is possible to complain to the Local Government Ombudsman (LGO) who can award compensation, but cannot change the decision. The LGO cannot look into complaints about Parish Councils, so they are effectively free from scrutiny.

If the decision was reached unreasonably a judicial review through the Courts can be requested within six weeks of the decision with an upfront fee of £215 however, the whole procedure is very expensive – running into £1,000s and rarely undertaken.

Developers and Development
Developers, as a genre, strike terror into the hearts of most communities often characterised as unreasonable, bullying and deaf to the opinions and needs of local people.

They vary in size from the local builder building one or two houses on small plots of land, the local housing association providing rental housing, through to regional builders who take on larger areas, and national house builders who develop complex sites. Large sites will probably have a Planning brief attached to them which a developer will be expected to follow.

Public consultation, although increasingly popular is usually limited to, at the minimum, a few pre-application exhibitions with the ubiquitous sticky post-it notes for comments. Complex or very large sites should at least offer surveys of opinions, visits to the site, workshops for concerned groups, updating via newsletters, websites and the media - crucial before and as the application progresses through the Planning system. How effective local opinion is in influencing how and what is built is never clear, the public is generally very cynical but, still gamely turn out.

Development can contribute:
- Affordable housing, so young families can stay in their home Parish - they are being increasingly priced out of rural areas;
- Cash for a new local playground, or a revamp of an old one, sports equipment and changing rooms; additions to the community hall, bus shelters, a new open space or allotments;
- Planning fees for cash-strapped authorities, at around £400 per house per application. When permission is granted authorities impose conditions (what should be done first or done to an agreed standard), these have to be discharged (or agreed that they have been completed) with some authorities charging £90 for each condition. More and more authorities also charge around £100 an hour to give applicants preliminary advice;
- New with the 2010 Coalition Government is the New Homes Bonus (NHB). This is calculated as the Council Tax of each new home, revived empty property or traveller's caravan times 6 and is given to the Planning authority spread over six years. It is primarily an incentive or "reward" from central Government for the granting of permission for new homes. The Planning authority (Districts share the "reward" with their Counties) and may share some money with the Parish affected;
- The Coalition devised an enhanced Community Infrastructure Levy (CIL) raising money for local infrastructure. The Government suggests around £10,000 per house but some authorities have set this considerably higher. Planning authorities should have a list of approved set charges, avoiding the problem of the Planning staff deciding. However, few authorities have set theirs up (just 9 by 2012) so consequently their area and Parishes loose out on considerable sums of money - the Parish concerned shares either 15% or 25% if there is an adopted Neighbourhood Plan. Combined, the two schemes (NHB and CIL) give Planning authorities and their Parishes substantial sums to upgrade and provide their communities with infrastructure, facilities and services.

The Planning Committee
The Chairman, if in a kindly mood can help those waiting to speak by jiggling the agenda so the relevant comments are with the relevant application allowing objectors or supporters to watch the discussion of "their" application. This also avoids facing the Committee with an indigestible confusion of comments in Public Forum. Contentious issues are usually considered first. Even so, certainly at Planning authority level, a wait of an hour or two is not uncommon.

Parishes with stand-alone Planning committees and long agendas along with many Planning authorities use early evening 6 o'clock starts whilst other authorities meet on weekday afternoons instead, both tricky for any attending audience. All Planning levels can and do arrange special meetings to discuss difficult or controversial applications.

Decisions Decisions

Hopefully Parish Councillors have read the application forms, plans, and any letters of support or objection sent in to the Parish, read the accompanying reports, looked at the illustrations and photographs and even walked round the site to gain an understanding of the issues before the meeting; essential when making life affecting decisions in the few minutes set aside. The comments made by individuals in the Public Forum should provide the detail. Councillors can, if there is uncertainty, defer a decision asking for more information although with only 3 weeks allowed (Planning authorities may be persuaded to extend the time limit especially in controversial cases) for the Parish to comment this leaves little room for manoeuvre. Crucial to decision making, for Planning authorities, is the possibility of a Planning Appeal if an application is refused, with the fear of an award of costs for unreasonable behaviour.

Applicants who feel unfairly treated by their Planning authority can complain to the Local Ombudsman (after first complaining to the authority's Chief Executive) for "maladministration" if they think that procedures have not been correctly observed, but not if they simply do not like the decision. This does not apply to Parish Councils. The Courts can be asked to undertake a judicial review (the Coalition Government to discourage reviews now only allows a 6 weeks window of opportunity and has included an upfront fee of £215) of a decision by the applicant, to see if the law has been correctly applied, but this is very expensive and unlikely to succeed. In any case the authority is simply asked to reconsider the issue and may still up hold its previous decision.

Impartiality, at both Parish and Planning authority level is still paramount. Until the recent Localism Act, lobbied Councillors could not give an opinion in case their objectivity was seen to be compromised; they faced the possibility of complaints to their Standards Committee. Now they are free to lobby fellow Councillors, take up local causes, support individuals and publicise issues whilst remaining prepared to listen to arguments and evidence before making a final decision. Indeed public and Parishes alike should take advantage of their District/Unitary Councillor who hopefully is a frequent visitor to Parish meetings either to lobby or to ask advice of. So much is often reliant on asking the correct questions.

Similar difficulties may arise for a Planning Committee, if a Committee member's employment is in a profession closely involved with local Planning issues – not uncommon. The Committee consequently may be judging a fellow Committee member's work, with staff dealing with a Committee member as both Councillor and applicant. Therefore, care must be taken by Councillors to declare disclosable pecuniary interests; and to have these noted in the Committee minutes, Councillors should not take part in the discussions or voting, and should preferably leave the room; the details are laid out in each District/Unitary and/or Parish Code of Conduct.

The watching audience waiting for a decision of approval or refusal and seeing dismissive nods and the vague gestures of Councillors rather than a distinct raising of hands will be often unclear who to blame or who to lobby next time.

The Parishes rarely monitor as a matter of policy what is built, although they may grumble and it is left to enthusiastic individuals to follow the twists and turns of construction to make sure what is built is what was approved - for which they get scant thanks.

Approval is the most straightforward with perhaps an added comment of pleasure. Refusal less so, as Planning related reasons need to be given, not neighbours' frequently used reasons: such as the assumed devaluation of local property, the loss of a personal view or "sunlight." Uncertain how to comment "catch all" generalised Planning phrases such as *"access"*, or *"overdevelopment of the site"*, or *"detrimental to visual amenities"* are used rather than the detailed reasons specific to the application. Parish Councillors may even be heard to say, *"we will come up with the reasons later"* or *"use whatever we said last time."* It is tempting to add large numbers of reasons which do not always square with the issues, in order to add weight to an argument or to please the listening audience. Reasons frequently become formulaic and every Councillor will eventually learn a list.

Increasingly Parish Councils try to act as their own Planning authority citing elements from their Local Development Framework (renamed Local Plans (2012)) and the now defunct national Planning Policy Guidance Notes/Planning Policy Statements (referred to as PPG's/ PPS's). These documents set out in broad terms national policy against which decisions were made and measured; there were around 25 for example: PPG2 - Green Belt, PPG19 - outdoor advertisement control. Now largely swept away and re-crystallised in the National Planning Policy Framework (NPPF 2012)).

At the end of the day a Parish Council has 21 days – some will not change their meeting dates and run out of time if meetings are infrequent - to make recommendations that reflect local opinion. The legal decision is taken by the Planning authority. It will let the Parishes know the results of applications including if a disappointed applicant goes to Appeal giving the Parish Council the opportunity to take an active part in the Planning Appeal process – very few do.

Quality of decisions
A Planning authority draws on Councillors from across the whole of its area and even this Committee may be managed to reflect the political balance of the Council. Many Parishes see a fundamental unfairness in decisions taken by Councillors from other towns especially without a visit to the application site. Some Planning authorities do organise site visit coach tours with Planning staff to explain the main issues. Controversial applications can be deferred for a whole Committee visit to fully understand what is at stake. Otherwise much discussion time can be taken up in Committee by Councillors explaining to each other aspects which would be obvious if there had been a site visit beforehand, and often exhausted by these endeavours a deliberation of the issues becomes perfunctory. Despite a multiplicity of rules and policies in the Local Plan to follow there is much inconsistency in decision making. Many Parishes and particularly local people feel it is a lottery in which they all loose.

...Frome Watch....
The Decisions
Mendip District's Planning Board decides: Planning applications; including tree preservation orders, advertisements, and listed building consents plus the adoption of development briefs.

Made up of 21 Councillors from across the District, Frome was well represented with 5 Councillors in 2008 rising to 7 by 2010 including two Frome Town Council Planning Committee members.

Frome delegated the discussion of Planning applications to 7 Councillors sitting on Frome's Planning Committee. Meeting about 16 times a year to keep up with the District Council's Planning Board 3 weekly cycle of meetings.

In the past Frome's applications were decided locally by the Frome Area Board. This was hugely popular and great fun, with the townspeople of all ages turning out in large numbers (many forced to sit on the floor in crowded meetings) despite meetings often being some 4-5 hours long. It was axed as too expensive and much of the general interest subjects pushed onto the East Mendip Partnership Committee, leaving Mendip with only Planning applications. Discussed now in a more sedate fashion with little input from the town as the distance to the Shepton Mallet meeting (12 miles) seems too great

Applications and plans can be examined, but not taken away, at the Town offices and the Mendip's Town Library Information Point or at the District Council offices where a duty Planning staff member may be on-hand to answer any queries. In common with most Planning authorities: the forms, plans, supporting documents, letters of objections or support from neighbours, local groups, and other statutory consultees etc could be viewed on-line until a website update did away with all comments.

Despite Frome's deep distrust of Mendip District Council and in particular its Planning Board to deliver anything good for the town Frome's own Planning Committee comments were (and are) surprisingly few and then rather terse. Too frequently deciding to leave it to the Planning officer despite often impassioned views from the townspeople. Comments were not posted on the town's website either or included in the archived minutes so there was no easy way of discovering what comments were made other than travelling to Mendip's offices to view an applicant's file after giving 48 hours notice.

Frome and District Civic Society (part of the Frome Society for Local Study (335 members)) fields a small dedicated team to comment on all Planning applications before the Town's Planning Committee. A considerable undertaking for a voluntary group. It looked at 239 applications in 2009 (270 in 2008) including two major housing, shopping and commercial redevelopments and two extensions to the Conservation Area. Its commentaries are integral in forming both Town and District opinions.

The Society also commented on Mendip District Council's 160 page Consultation Paper on the Local Development Framework – "Time to Plan", which set out the future residential, economic, and environmental issues for the area whilst set within governmental parameters for change and development over the next 20 years. Eventually a Core Strategy (renamed in 2012 the Local Plan) will be produced, to replace the current Local Plan (dated 2002), covering the years 2006 to 2028 and it is against this that Planning applications will be judged. By the end of 2011 it was heading for its 4th consultation!

The Society has successfully publicised issues through the local paper, mounting most notably a campaign to save Critchill Grange, a Victorian Villa of historical interest in its large garden from demolition and redevelopment; a cause which local Councillors took up somewhat belatedly.

The Society developed Local Listing with Mendip District Council (suggesting the idea at an East Mendip Partnership meeting back in 2007) allowing the townspeople to put forward suggestions of buildings and street details such as walls, railings, lampposts, milestones etc which are not on the English Heritage Listed Building list, but are well loved landmarks or just thought important locally.

These will be mapped and an inventory made which can be referred to in future Planning application discussions. Local Listing was initially piloted in the five Mendip towns - as yet (December 2012) nothing has happened.

The Society also has membership of the Mendip Conservation Advisory Panel, an area wide group of mainly retired architects looking at all applications within and neighbouring the Conservation Areas or Listed Buildings, including buildings which could be described as "Heritage Assets." The Panel comments and suggests improvements based on design materials and sustainability. "Heritage Assets" are now equal to English Heritage Listings since the introduction of the National Planning Policy Framework. The Framework also suggests every Planning authority has a Design Review Panel similar to the Mendip Panel but perhaps with a wider, broader base of professions from transport, engineering, landscaping, and urban design to review and assess all applications and provide pre-application advice.

Frome has 369 Listed Buildings, more than any other town in Somerset, ranging from elegant cast iron Cockey street gas lights lamp standards which were once manufactured in the town, to the terraced cottages of the wool workers and the large houses of the merchants and mill owners. Two Grade 1 buildings: Rook Lane Congregational Chapel and The Blue House – an almshouse for the poor of the Parish. Marston Park to the south of the town is listed as a Historic Park and Garden as is Orchardleigh to the north.

The Town Council had requested the Listing of all the remaining unlisted Cockey street lamps in the town. However, it included many reproduction lamp standards on its list and later abandoned the project. A small group of local enthusiasts requested the Listing of the Town's Bailey Bridge, only 1 of 3 of its type in the country; unfortunately it was demolished by the District Council before an English Heritage appeal decision was made.

Frome, along with the City of Wells, is one of a handful of Parishes which belong to the Historic Towns Forum. It provides good practice guidance aimed at principal authorities, lobbying national policy makers and providing discussion groups for areas of interest such as sustainable tourism.

But not all goes well. "The Orchard" - a small apple orchard seen as a neighbourhood green space surrounded by older housing. A cramped site with a proposal for 11, two and a half storey houses. A previous application had been refused at Appeal. Now 87 letters of objection were received for the new application plus a detailed commentary from The Civic Society. The Planning report however, recommends approval on the basis that the Planning Inspectors points of refusal (overlooking and the size of one house) have been met. The Inspector had dismissed the neighbours' views that it was a valuable wildlife haven, countering with the belief that the small gardens with each house would suffice. Of the possible 7 Frome District Councillors on Planning only 2 were present, one stating the points of refusal had not been fully answered and left before the vote, leaving the remaining Frome Councillor's proposal, to refuse the application, without a seconder. The motion failed, and the Planning Board voted to approve the application 7 votes to 4, no Section106 agreement was suggested. The local newspapers reported Councillor reservations but also the Council's Planning officer and solicitor's fears of costs to the Council if a refusal went to Appeal as, in the officer's opinion, the Inspector's criticisms had been met. Local people hoped they could still object but it was all over.

An October 2007 application to demolish Critchill Grange and build 10 homes was met with massive protests, 800 objected whilst 134 supported approval. Originally named Critchill Villa it was large, gabled and surrounded by trees. Built in 1858 by local architect William Brown (he has several examples Listed in the town) for master brewer William Knight.

"A house of good quality...clearly some merit" said English Heritage although it would not add it to the statutory List. Whilst the Planning officer approved, 13 of the 16 Councillors voted against to a public gallery of 20 protesters on the grounds of loss of trees and no bat survey.

The applicant appealed and the independent Inspector dismissed it because of harm to the character of the area, poor design and no Section106 agreement for a local play area. To give the Grange more protection the Conservation Area was later extended and it also came under the new category of "Heritage Asset." Despite further design reservations by the Mendip Conservation Advisory Panel at the end of 2012 two 4 bed homes were built hard against the garden boundary.

What can possibly go wrong?

For those hoping for something thoughtful and considered it is too often an unsettling and irrational process. Although not lacking structure and guidelines these can be haphazardly applied:

The System

- Too many people feel the "system" is loaded against them and there is a truth, which has become a superstition, which states once something goes wrong it will continue to do so. Applicants frequently become deeply paranoid.
- Inconsistency amongst Planning staff, across applications or even in the same one. If one approves, another will want odds and ends or even major proposals changing especially if the staff member overseeing the application changes.
- Second guessing what the Planning officer means from their cryptic comments.
- Second guessing what the Government means when it uses finely nuanced wording.
- Increasingly more evidence and reports are requested to support each application. The Coalition Government has asked Councils not to overdo it but many still have a tick box mentality i.e. a flood assessment for a proposal to join two second floor rooms together.
- Applications towards the end of meeting agendas have a tendency not to do well as Councillors tire. A different day, the same Councillors, and there could be a different decision.
- Section106 agreements (s106), the legal documentation often takes months to prepare, meanwhile for the developer costs on borrowed money mount. Once agreed implementation is still not guaranteed, that may take years or not at all and is frequently not enforced. Residents worry s106 will be too weak or poorly drafted with not enough demanded to cover the full impact on residents leaving the developer "wriggle room." Parish Councils are not quick enough to extract advantages for their communities particularly when they are objecting and do not necessarily have a wish list as a fall-back position if permission is granted.
- Section 106 agreement money if not spent by the Planning authority within a set number of years is handed back to the developer which will mean planned improvements are not made. Too few Parishes bother to monitor the situation.
- "Localism" has been snatched up as a watch word and brandished by all. When combined with the new "relaxation" of the Planning rules a gross over-simplification has been created which will take years to play out most probably through the Courts.

- Sustainability with its uncertain meanings has taken over as the new yardstick by which everything will be judged and is competitively repeated by Councillors, residents, and developers to support all viewpoints.
- Consultation is an industry. Never before have quite so many people and professions spent quite so much time drawing up plans, conducting and repeating surveys, writing reports and initiating impact studies. Detailing in design features, always in the vernacular, and subjecting them to systematic scrutiny to end up with yet another mish-mash of clashing unresolved styles, stagy theatre sets illustrating a favourite historical period against which shopping is paramount and using the clever ruse of not providing enough parking to somehow resolve car ownership and usage problems. Everyone fights a desperate rear-guard action.
- A vast variety of reports (e.g.bat surveys, economic viability, and environmental impact) can be produced by applicants to back their case. These are produced by a raft of experts and vary in quality, at their worst increasingly glossily produced, with lots of photographs and full of hyperbole. Reports can be too easily accepted on face value. In the past Planning authorities frequently commissioned their own. Objectors are left to challenge what is written.
- Large schemes are problematic many applications are put in in outline, so the details, which are the most concern to locals, such as: layout of homes, roads and open space, the size of shops, industrial buildings, the number of storeys, security lighting, screening, and landscaping are decisions for another day. Often the principle in large applications is the only issue for Councillors to decide. Parish Planning meetings leave local residents wading through quantities of plans and reports not knowing what it will mean or how to make protests meaningful.
- Planning blight, when proposed routes or areas are put aside and protected for major infrastructure projects figures high in the mythology of Planning history. Houses and businesses become difficult or impossible to sell and blight can rumble on for years as decisions are not made. There is no compensation for projects, such as by-passes, which are later abandoned.
- It is a curiosity of the system that although Councillors may vote approval at a Planning meeting, often to the relief of participants, it is the issuing of the decision notice which counts and until that point the decision is in jeopardy and can be recalled. Again months can pass.
- Equally success at Appeal with an award of costs for the applicant against the Council does not mean the money will be received. Councils will still argue, often for years, meaning everyone has to go back to the Courts again.
- It is an oddity that small issues will be magnified and fought over whilst large strategic decisions sail through unhindered.

The Applicants
Are, as always inventive.
- There are applicants who feel the rules should not apply to them because, *"we are the right sort of people"* with pure intentions or *"anything we do is bound to be fine."*
- Every Parish has one lovable character who makes changes without formal permission and is indulged *"It's ok it's one of George's, he never applies"* or again, *"they are our sort of people."*

- Many applicants feel their applications will be treated more favourably if they are friends with Councillors especially the Committee Chairman - despite rules to guard against this. However, this could be useful when making decisions at the Neighbourhood Planning stage.
- Owners of listed buildings may find the procedures intrusive and over-personal as every decision and detail is picked over not only by the authority's Conservation department, but local history societies, and ad hoc locals, everyone has an opinion and wants to interfere. Conservation officers can follow relentlessly their own favourite building style.
- Crying and forlorn looking or pregnant applicants can easily sway a Committee. Getting permission by gaining sympathy votes for: wishing an ailing granny to live with them, or wanting a country home at the bottom of the garden for grown-up children and prospective grandchildren, or alternatively, young parents wanting a house extension in order to have room for a long awaited and hoped for new baby. Or wanting a home on a spare piece of land to save an ailing business, or a single parent with children who is widowed or divorced and needs a home for the children and to be on the site of a fledgling business to keep an eye on livestock or plants. Generally in circumstances where permission would normally be refused, most frequently in the countryside. Once achieved many sell within a year or two.
- Some may snaffle parts of a neighbour's garden or highway verge because it has been included incidentally on the plans or it just looked handy.
- A constant winning argument is that any proposed business or retail development will bring jobs – this is never checked up on and a loosely drawn permission means there will be "development creep" where unintended buildings and uses will happen or hours of working gradually extended – with the subsequent problem of traffic, noise and lighting, a more noticeable problem in rural areas.
- Ambitious business plans may not necessarily stack up but Councillors sometimes find it difficult to be party-poopers.
- Business owners closing a business may liquidate their land assets by turning them into housing losing future employment land.
- Proposed development discussions can go on for years; often Parish Councillors may not be party to them or come too late in the day to have any influence. Newly elected Councillors can be out of their depth.
- Developers can change details often quite radically by making amendments without further consultation of the Parishes or residents. Equally they may ask for conditions on an approved permission to be set aside as no longer relevant.
- Developers may threaten to pull out if discussions take too long or Planning conditions are too onerous, this can make it unbuildable – good if you did not want it in the first place, bad if you have promised the regeneration of an area.
- It is a curiosity of the system that applicants do not need to own the land or buildings under scrutiny.
- "It's just a game you put it in, take it out, jiggle it a bit, put it back and everybody is happy." Large controversial applications or small ones which arouse intense local opposition are put in, withdrawn to everyone's relief but later a watered down version is applied for which will sail through.

Everyone congratulates themselves on their success.

- Approval may not mean anything is built, particularly galling if neighbours have fought a long arduous campaign. Three years is allowed (it used to be 5, the 1997 Labour Government hoped the reduced time would ensure more house building - it didn't) before a Planning permission dies, until then it is an asset to be lodged with a bank and borrowed against. But a rudimentary start can keep a permission alive indefinitely.
- Cambridge Rules. For a site to be successfully developed land adjoining may need to be used (perhaps to widen a road) but is owned by someone else. In this instance the owner of the adjoining land, who now has a ransom strip, can claim, traditionally (initially based on a 1961 Lands Tribunal decision) a third of the whole site value. Clever negotiators may be able to raise this to 50% or more.

The Objectors

Today, objectors know not to be entirely negative, but the window of opportunity to object is still a narrow one.

- Merely not wanting or disliking change is now not enough, demonstrable harm needs to be proved. Everything pivots on the balance of benefits to harm against the background of sustainability.
- Localism is strongly cited at every opportunity and to support every objection.
- Localism has sanctioned a more combative approach to new plans.
- There are rounds of applause as Councillors see sense in Planning Committees but it is the receipt of the decision notice and what it says and the conditions imposed which is crucial and not discussed at Committee. Breathes are held for the months it can take to issue it.
- Speculative applications are always regarded with horror against a background of *"they are doing it for the money"* when applicants apply on the off chance of getting permission.

Homes

Design, Design, Design. Large scale developments, with the subsequent sense of loss of control for local people, are daunting especially when large proposals lack sufficient details or visualisations of the finished scheme.

- Housing is planned either with a touch of picturesque irregularity creating a modest range of narrow fronted homes that could have accreted over time and grown organically or a pastiche of the leafy suburb squarely regular, predictable with plasticky features that promise solidity and are copied across the country. It could be anytown.
- Crumbling listed buildings, both in town and countryside which no-one does anything about.
- Many will notice the scattering of small, uninteresting often brick built bungalows in the countryside. In odd corners of fields or to the side of farmyards – this is "farmers vernacular."
- Closeness to neighbours with small or no gardens is an oddity particularly in more rural settings. It is the details that jar, the wrong shaped windows and doors, the wrong type of stone or wrong coloured brick – it's a surprise these things are never noticed. There are the bits which are never completed such as chimneys stacks which give a familiar finish to homes – which in many cases are generally fake and hoisted, already complete, into position by crane.
- Odd looking new buildings which have no relationship to their surroundings.

- The housing code's (energy and resource efficiency standards) importance in providing better buildings is rarely emphasised.
- Amenity planting a term which has become the cliché of awfulness. Landscaping unfinished, trees poorly planted and abandoned to die or left to grow at, often, crooked angles or trimmed mercilessly each year.
- Trees chopped down on new developments after, often long, protracted arguments to keep them.
- Trees dying after building materials, huts etc have been stored over their roots causing soil compaction.
- If the site is sold the new owner may not keep to the original permissions directives or may ask for change so well-rehearsed arguments are run through again with no guarantee of the "right" decision being made.

Road Signage

Recently, Berkley school just outside Frome (built in 1864 with today 92 pupils) set amongst fields and orchards, with a charming 18th century church and Manor House and two neighbouring farms – there is no village, was targeted by Somerset County Council. There are now 107 road verge warning posts and 18 large school and speed warning signs within several hundred yards of the school entrance where previously there had been none.
Costed at around £4,500.

- Despite exciting, innovative materials available the big 6 house builders keep to a few well-worn standards.
- Social housing, is too often given to people with no connection to an area splitting up extended families who would otherwise support one another. This can be rectified in s106 agreements so local people do get local housing. It is up to the vigilance of Councillors. Of course some villages want none preferring to keep the "riff-raff" out. The promise of social housing can be used as a bargaining tool to get a one off permission for something which would not normally be given.

Countryside

Design, Design, Design. Combined with a clash of culture as urban solutions and values are helicoptered in and foisted on rural locations.
- The balance between new and old, integrating large numbers of new people or extra industry whilst bringing much needed employment is often at odds with those retiring to their rural idyll. However the industrial expansions that takes place are not necessarily what government had in mind of pleasant country flavoured pursuits in rural surroundings when it is large sheds or haulage yards, with all night security lighting and 24/7 working.
- Diversification and the pressure to encourage jobs certainly in agriculture can bring new buildings and housing to provide security. These jobs may be short-term but the applicant has gained a valuable property if the commercial use is abandoned. Alternatively the next owner may want to build more.
- There are always incomer complaints about countryside noises and smells, sheep bleating, cows lowing, church bells ringing.

- Bits of fields fenced off to become gardens exacerbated by the colourful plastic of children's' toys or wooden seating can result in general outrage and rapid Planning enforcement action.
- Start with a small field, a ramshackle shed, a couple of sheep, then add a few chickens, another shed, a pony, another shed, some ducks, extra sheep, a very small caravan and a small holding is born and a Planning problem.
- The use of the wrong coloured profile steel sheeting to clad buildings - why white which can be seen from miles around.
- An enthusiasm for a multiplicity of road signs where every bend is a hazard and needs its own personalised set of arrows.
- The assumption that wildlife habitat lost through development can be mitigated by making a new one or by merely planting more trees than those felled – biodiversity offsetting. Misunderstanding the richness, complexity and interdependence of the natural world.
- Cycle paths also accumulate their own signage and may be only a few hundred yards long but were included in a development to make it "acceptable" and tick a box.
- Roadside hoardings and banners – proliferating with the changes in national economic conditions (the economy is always heading for a downturn or starting to pull out of one). These need Planning permission but this is generally ignored.
- Verges are part of the highway but can disappear as enthusiastic home owners surreptitiously mow them adding them to their gardens with surrounds of wooden stakes or painted stones, planting trees and daffodils. If these cause damage the Highway authority is liable for any insurance claims.

Neighbours
- The current enthusiasm for the newly coined term of "Localism" has become equal to any local opinion.
- It is sometimes forgotten that District Councillors can be formally asked to represent local opinions.

Councillors
"Sometimes difficult decisions have to be made." Often it is a case of deciding between the least worse options. It is a fragile relationship easily upset if either applicant or objector misjudge Councillors' mood by: too much bluster, appearing too knowledgeable, criticising staff, giving too high powered a presentation, too aggressive, or presuming a little too much.
- Councillors can play to the gallery of anxious objectors or impress their visiting local MP whipping themselves up into a *frenzy "Let us test this at appeal Mr Chairman."* Crowd pleasing (occasionally receiving rounds of applause from the audience) often reckless refusals can land a Council with costly bills *"why must we keep rolling over."* But this is also "Localism" in action, *"we can work up some reason to refuse."*
- Resolutions are not always properly made; *"you know what we meant"* is used when wording is contrary to what was intended. Grumbles about details from Councillors, Parish Councils and authority staff do not necessarily make it into the final recommendations.
- Decisions can look superficial as Councillors dash on to the next application.

- Uncomfortably quick decisions give rise to accusations of "backhanders" and dark mutterings form the public.
- The behind the scenes horse trading *"I'll support yours if you support mine"* or the pressure brought by political parties to support an ideological view, to embarrass the opposition or to play to an audience at election time, will mean applications get refused for reasons other than their merits.
- Worrying too much about applicants going to a Planning Appeal if an application is refused.
- Councillors can add a precept to the Council tax to fund objections at Planning Appeals but few really want to go that far, easier just to grumble.
- Failing to insist on good design or adopting policies which will ensure this.
- Debate is too often non-existent, rules and procedures not understood or worse misunderstood and common sense totally lacking, Councillors if they do not know enough often just repeat each other's comments.
- Adding objections outside their jurisdiction e.g. parking or access – which is Highways, flooding - which is the Environment Agency.
- Curiously, whilst developers are derided certainly in private and their agents thought not much better, architects are held in awe. Perhaps it is their masterly ways with large sheets of paper which they can fold with just a flick of the wrist.
- Whilst all architects are plan drawers, not all plan drawers are architects.
- Developers only need to emphasise new jobs for Councillors to fall in line, wider impacts are not necessarily looked at and there is still a tendency to see an area in isolation – an island mentality and ignore solutions which are "across the border" which collaboration with neighbouring authorities could solve.
- Planning Councillors may see themselves as gurus or at the very least "consultants" with some touting for business when Planning applications have failed offering to shepherd the renewed application through the system. Whilst they may leave the room during discussions it is still their colleagues making the decisions. Mendip's Planning Board at one time had 3 of its 21 members acting as "Planning consultants."
- Some Councillors have a tendency to agree with whom-ever they are speaking to either applicant or objector so both sides feel confident that they have Councillor support.
- It is worrying that on controversial applications Councillors who could speak for their electorate may not turn up to the meeting or provide a fellow Councillor with a written statement of views leaving their area "unprotected."
- Councillors have been heard to say if it is not in their area they are not concerned.
- Changes in national policy are often seen as an inconvenience and unhelpful when deciding local issues.
- It is not uncommon for housing Planning permission to be given to stave off business failure. Councillors can be very sympathetic.
- Councillors sometimes just make up rules. Farm worker's homes are a particular sticking point if too ambitiously large – too many bedrooms, a large lounge or plans which include a swimming pool (swimming pools as a genre are not looked at favourably). A Committee may think this is somehow unreasonable and "above their station in life" and refuse the application. Alternatively certain professions such as doctors will be looked on more favourably.

- Planning may be used to solve perceived problems which generally solve themselves.
- Surcharging of Councillors and Council employees ended in 2000. Up to then misappropriated spending, mismanagement and poor decision making could result in heavy fines even bankruptcy of those involved as the external auditor attempted to recover a Council's financial losses. The 1997 Labour Government legislated abolishen after several notorious cases involving Labour-led Councils who had refused to implement Conservative Government policy such as increasing council housing rents. Culminating in the mid-1980s in the high profile cases of Liverpool and Lambeth Councils whose refusal to implement a rates cap resulted in prosecution and heavy fines for the whole Council.
- Many wish it was still true. Developers may hint at this possibility even today. This is not to be confused with the non-personal costs incurred by Councils through the Planning Appeal process or the possibility of fines after police and court investigations into allegations of Councillors benefiting financially from their authorities decisions. The level of proof will be high and will rely heavily on a Councillor's colleagues and any suspicions from local residents. The Government claims it is a robust system.
- "Localism" has been seized on by the Parishes who have honed and repolished previous Neighbourhood Plans or have bid for grants from Government and their local authorities to proudly produce their first. Employing battalions of consultants and mobilising the local populace into filling in yet more surveys through workshops and forums. But with so few finished Local Plans by Planning authorities, which would provide the framework, the work put in by the Parishes could yet be wasted as Planning authorities dither. Mendip District Council has employed five people over 6 years to draw up its Local Plan and was surprised to discover it was unfinished.
- Canny Parish Councillors realising the new National Planning Policy Framework demanded a five year housing supply campaigned to have their villages delisted as a settlement to avoid any new housing development. The previous excuse of "premature to the Local Plan" no longer holding water.

Planning Terms

A brief summary of some of the more frequently encountered terms:

Planning Permission

Planning permission is a formal record of what you want to do and how you must do it. Most applications are registered by District Councils or Unitary Authorities (there are some exceptions – such as mineral extraction and waste disposal which are decided at County). Comments are requested from: other departments such as Conservation, or Environmental Health, Government agencies such as the Environment Agency, and other authorities such as Highways. Near neighbours and local groups, such as the local history society are routinely included as are national organisations such as the Georgian Society, or the Victorian Society in towns or the Campaign for the Preservation of Rural England in the countryside and of course Parish Councils. The general public's only notification is to spot a notice tied to a fence or on nearby lampposts or possibly in local newspaper listings. The public only have 14 days in which to comment. Planning authorities are expected to decide the majority of applications within 8 weeks and complex applications within 13. This they do with varying degrees of success.

A Planning application may seek permission in one of two forms, outline or detail:

Outline Permission

This looks at the principle of building. This considers at a minimum a notional site layout and content backed by relevant reports such as the impact of increased traffic and is used to find out at an early stage whether or not a proposal will be approved before substantial costs are incurred drawing up architectural plans so details can be sparse. Permission comes with "conditions" attached such as time scale for the build, approval of samples of materials and there will also be "reserved matters", not included in the grant of outline permission. These must be approved before work starts on site.
These can be:

- the appearance - how a building looks, the materials used, including the exterior of the development and its links to the surrounding area;
- access - covering all routes to and within the site and linkages to roads and paths outside the site;
- landscaping - the improvement or protection of the area near to and surrounding the site such as open spaces, play areas, wildlife areas, tree or hedge planting. Trees can be given tree preservation orders to protect them from change.
- layout - buildings, routes, open spaces, the spaces between buildings and their relationship to one another and the surrounding area.
- scale - the size of the development including the height, width and length of each proposed building.

Approval, of "reserved matters" is effectively the same as the granting of detailed or full Planning permission. Reserved matters are sent to the Parishes for comment, the Ward Councillor may be asked for comments and some Councils, usually with large applications will return them for discussion to their Planning Committee. If the application for outline permission contains all the necessary information the authority can grant detailed permission.

Some Councils may try to insist on more detail or written reports (flood assessments, bat surveys etc) if an application is controversial, but the Government has asked local authorities to keep these to a minimum in case it holds up new developments. Parishes worry that once permission is given developers will sell on the land – which now has an increased value, and the new owners will apply to intensify the usage or start again.

Detailed or Full Permission

This includes internal layouts, materials, design, landscaping etc. Permission may be granted with "conditions" these may be similar to "reserved matters" and are discharged or carried out within a strict time frame before development can start or in planned staged phases during development.

The "conditions" are set out in the Planning officer's report confirming elements of the submitted application with the authorities Planning policies. Surprisingly the detailed decision of what buildings will look like, probably the most important aspect to everyone living locally is, in some authorities left to after permission is granted and is a discussion between the developer and the Planning officer. Roads, open spaces and playgrounds are eventually adopted by County or District /Unitary authorities who will maintain them.

The developer may give a "commuted sum" to pay for a number of year's maintenance of open space or play areas as part of a Section106 agreement.

Applicants have 3 years from when permission is granted in which to start work, before needing to reapply. Permission is not necessarily a forgone conclusion the next time, Planning rules and circumstances do change.

There are around 450,000 Planning applications submitted annually. In extreme circumstances and for very publicly controversial decisions an application can be "called in" taking the process away from the Planning authority and giving the Government Minister in charge an opportunity to review and decide. Now rare, numbers have dropped from 50 to 25 a year (2011).

Enforcement
Perhaps surprisingly, applications are not routinely monitored by Councillors or Planning staff. If building work has started without permission or has deviated from an already granted permission an Enforcement staff can be asked to investigate, if the applicant is found out. Prosecution in the Magistrates Court can result in fines and in occasional cases the demolition of the offending building. However, retrospective permission can be applied for, this is generally seen by Councillors as unfair and deserving of a punitive response, but if it is otherwise within the rules permission will be granted. In some cases the number of years which have passed since the development started is crucial, as a complex set of rules apply and again, if within the rules, permission is granted. Mendip District Council had a back log of around 300 cases (2012) to investigate making a rapid resolution of problems impossible. If an Enforcement Notice is appealed against the procedures are the same as for Planning application Appeals.

Building Regulations
These follow on from gaining Planning permission. Whereas Planning permission covers what can be built or the use of land (as set down in the rules), and includes the appearance and scale of proposed buildings, the impact on the general environment and neighbouring properties. Building Regulations set minimum technical standards for the design and construction of buildings, their stability, materials, means of escape and fire precautions so they are safe and healthy for people to use. The Regulations cover weather proofing, energy efficiency (up to code 6 in the Code for Sustainable Homes) sound insulation, plus access and facilities for all users including those with disabilities

Change of Use
Planning organises commercial activities into Use Classes. New owners wanting to carry out a different business are changing categories from for example: shops to offices such as estate agents, newsagents to take-aways, or public houses to residential and will apply for a Change of Use. Such changes can fundamentally alter the character and viability of an area so need careful consideration. If too many shops become offices the footfall for the remaining shops will decrease and businesses become marginalised and fail. The Coalition Government in 2013 swept away the carefully constructed considerations of the past and announced a 2 year moratorium of the rules. No-one knows what will happen.

Right to Light
A popular myth, the "right" only exists if it is clearly stated in a properties deeds or leases.

The Prescription Act (1832) gave householders a general "right" to maintain a degree of air and light to their property.

This skylight rather than sunlight is acquired if there has been uninterrupted enjoyment for at least 20 years. There is no "right" to maintain the exact same amount of light only to retain a reasonable proportion which will vary in each case causing on occasions Planning applications to be amended.

Compulsory Purchase Orders (CPO).

Feared across the country as homes, businesses and lives have been blighted, often for decades as the routes of large infrastructure projects such as airport runways, motorways and by-passes have been argued over. CPO allowed Government and local authorities to buy land and buildings against their owners' wishes; it was often felt at knock-down prices.

Today, the compensation received, including legal and valuation advice, should leave owners in the same financial position after CPO as before the process began. The purchase should be in the public interest and the process take about 3 months but there is a right of appeal. Local authorities have to complete the purchase within 3 years, although by using a slightly different legal framework this can be extended to 6 years. Compensation can also be paid to those affected by projects near to their homes but this can be tightly drawn leaving many suffering from an unexpected drop in land values but without, they feel, due recompense.

Failed Applications

There are 6 months from a refusal of permission for applicants to decide to: either re-submit an application or go to Appeal.

The "fast-track" 12 week service is solely for householder Appeals over the alteration or extensions to existing homes and is a review of the paperwork with an unaccompanied site visit.

Planning Appeals

Appeals in 2008/09

- 405 Local Planning Authorities (LPA)
- 20,389 Planning Appeals broken down into:
- 79% as Written Representations,
- 16% as Hearings,
- 5% as Inquiries,
- 34% were allowed nationally.
- 1,700 or c8% of Appeals asked for costs.
- c2% of Appeals are awarded costs, roughly 300 to appellant and 100 to LPA.

In Mendip of the 75 Appeals 37% were allowed and of the 20 Enforcement Appeals 30% were allowed, so in the majority of cases the LPA decision stood and the Appeal dismissed.

Still a free service, the Planning Inspectorate an independent government body chooses from three types of Appeal: Written Representations, Hearings or Inquiries.

Councillors can send or give evidence to all three and all participants can send in additional written evidence before the case is heard. The Coalition Government keen for the Appeal system to be open and transparent encourages the recording or photographing of proceedings as they unfold. Indeed Inspectors go out of their way to be inclusive and encourage participation whilst maintaining fairness and balance.

Written Representations
As the name suggests, these are written statements from the appellant, the local Planning authority and any third parties wishing to comment, including the 'statutory' consultees (e.g. the County Highways, English Heritage, etc) neighbours and local amenity groups. The Inspector visits the site.

A Hearing
Used for less complex, small-scale proposals. This round-table discussion, with the Inspector acting as chairman, starts with a summary of the appellant's and local Planning authority's case. To keep costs low, legal representation is not normally allowed. The Inspector takes part in the discussions to ensure that all points are fully explored. Anyone can ask to speak, but not ask questions, there is no time limit. Copies of what is intended to be said should be given to the Inspector, the Council and the Appellant. There is an accompanied site visit, only if the proceedings are adjourned rather than closed can discussions continue on site.

Inquiries
These are formal; with the Inspector listening to the evidence and to witnesses including third parties such as Councillors in a court-like setting. The appellant and the local Planning authority can employ legal representation and experts to help present their case, this increases costs substantially. Anyone can ask to speak, but not ask questions, there is no time limit. Copies of what you intend to say should be given to the Inspector, the Council and the Appellant. There is an accompanied site visit but no further discussions.

A Report is written based on the written evidence and the Inspectors verbatim notes and judgement given several months later, participants can ask to know the result. If either the appellants or the local Planning authority feel the "other side" was unreasonable and "wasted valuable time and resources", they can ask to be compensated by an award of costs, but rarely do. The Government decides, in a late move, Inspectors can make their own award of costs if they feel either party has behaved unreasonably causing unnecessary Appeal expense.

Theoretically Appeal decisions can be challenged by third party objectors in the High Court within a 6 week time frame. But it is unlikely an Inspectors decision will be quashed. Costs will run into many £1,000s and when eventually the case is re-run the same conclusion may still be reached.

Parish Councils and their Councillors can represent their Parish views at a Public Inquiry or be called as witnesses, they do not have to have legal representation. Indeed, Parishes have sweeping powers to represent Parish views at any Public Inquiry.

The Government (August 2013) anxious to bring new meaning to local government democracy announced the public could blog, film or tweet openly and discreetly during Hearings or Inquiries with the proviso that some residents may not wished to be filmed and could opt-out. This does not apply to Councillors or Council staff.

A previous attempt in the June for all Council meetings to be open to digital and social media reporting had been ignored by many Councils who on occasions used the police to clear meetings or banned citizen journalists (bloggers). Various procedural excuses were made (see Accountability) prompting the Government to name and shame Councils.

The Planning Development Brief

For large sensitive areas, such as town centres, Planning authorities can provide a comprehensive set of rules and guidance (the Planning Brief), for potential developers to follow. Developers are not necessarily the landowners; but speak on their behalf assembling sites with the agreement (although surprisingly not necessarily) of a number of landowners in order to put together a comprehensive scheme.

It is not totally unheard of for Planning permission to be sought and received on land without the landowner's express permission.

Hopefully, there is public consultation on what is to be built, its purpose and overall design covering: shopping areas, open spaces, play areas, residential and work area mix, parking and roads. In particular how a new development will blend into the existing surroundings with particular attention paid to local architectural or historic details and materials. This can either result in innovative designs or a faux "localism" where local people are supposed to believe the proposals reflect their history and their community within a manufactured sense of place.

These wish lists written into a Brief are developed by the Planning authority in conjunction with the Parish, hopefully referring to the Parish Plan/Design Statement and now the Neighbourhood Plan which contains local aspirations and are a way of solving long held frustrations. Briefs are often a way of re-developing large Brownfield sites within towns.

Expect to see:
- housing, with a percentage as affordable i.e. given over to a Housing Association for rent;
- shops: perhaps offices and the increasingly popular live/work units providing "cheap" employment opportunities and a "soul" to what would otherwise be empty streets;
- public open space with perhaps a play area for children – these are always minimal and the first to go if costs rise;
- a legacy, a public building such as a town hall - very popular with Councillors or a meeting hall to create an instant sense of community and as a "pay off" for the development. Councillors love them, the quality varies and they can be hideously expensive to run;
- a piece of art – often perplexing, often of a local hero nobody has heard of. The result of a competition, frequently chosen by Councillors and the result of a consultation survey and as ever via workshops for local school children
- parking is usually kept to a minimum as everyone will be assumed to be using public transport - tricky in more rural areas, or using bicycles.

There could be substantial Community Infrastructure Levy (CIL) and Section106 agreements to pay for the additional infrastructure needs, such as school places, highway changes, play areas and leisure facilities plus the New Homes Bonus as a "reward."

Developers in response will claim to have incorporated all the requested elements in their plans whilst reflecting the areas historical links and materials, these, curiously, can look very similar across the country, in can be anytown. They will argue to minimise both CIL and Section106 agreements claiming the prohibitive cost of redevelopment due generally to land contamination (inevitable when building on Brownfield sites) so communities may get a lot less additional benefits than anticipated. It is the landowner, who the developer is negotiating on behalf of, who actually pays for any improvements out of the price received for the land.

Sheaves of drawings are produced which are often difficult to understand, with artist impressions of the finished development sketched in watercolours, and populated by groups of happy families and trees artfully dropped in. Not enough use is made of 3D computer imaging or holograms, on the occasion cardboard models are made, they do usefully throw up the most obvious problems. Public consultation can be minimal which many people see as paying lip-service. However, the Localism Act has unintentionally encouraged gathering squalls of well-informed objectors who expect to be listened to and who view the Planning process and Councillors as blinkered and obstinate.

The finished development is down to the negotiating skills of respective council staff, the persistence and imagination of Councillors and the lobbying of local groups, media coverage is often minimal and rarely analytical. If negotiations falter, and it can take years, a developer only has to mention economic regeneration and the jobs a development contributes to bring authorities into line, although the jobs produced frequently use a lower skill base and do not truly replace or use the craft skills of the industries now lost and if multiple retail shops are favoured this adds an additional nail in the coffin of any remaining independent and more traditional shop owners and the beleaguered High Street.

Landscaping and Design

...Frome Watch...

A town of mellow Jurassic limestones in buffs and cream has in more recent years been subject to each developer's re-interpretation as the incorrect stone is used: front porches built in the dark grey limestone of the Carboniferous - out by a few hundred million years, creating a jarring note; "Frome ears" lugs at mid height on dressed stone window surrounds, a cosy unique detail giving a sense of place often ignored as inconsequential. The over use of render - now universal, and brick, at one time limited to the few houses built around the time of the arrival of the railway.

Supermarket design varies wildly with Frome getting the poor end of design spectrum however, landscaping of the local ASDA is a triumph of trees whilst Sainsbury took out its maturing trees replacing them with desert planting an unfortunate note for a countryside edge site. Locally, landscaping is poorly treated, trees die and are not replaced, some areas becoming weedy and uncared for except for an annual trim which scalps plants within an inch of their lives.

New shop fronts are a universal problem as corporate signage drowns out the unique settings of small market towns.

Generations of wiring, old junction boxes and odd bits of abandoned shop fronts festoon the fronts of older Frome shops. Frome's Chamber of Commerce in the late 1950's produced a design guide which successfully tackled the problem for a couple of years. Other towns such as Lavenham in Suffolk also ambitiously removed telegraph wires when there was a general movement to reduce street clutter in the 1950s vastly improving the way the town's ancient buildings look today.

Most people hope for a blending of the old and the new into a lively ensemble, done with empathy and a profound knowledge of local historical and architectural traditions. Interpreting the past with moderate modernisation, adding unfamiliar elements as "new flavours" to give strong looking buildings with a distinct mood which will settle into their surroundings to become an orchestrated whole. Landscaped, with well-designed open spaces of trees, water, paths and play areas, giving a development shape, integrating it with its surroundings and making it enjoyable for those who live or work in it, as well as for passers-by. Single trees and ancient hedgerows thoughtfully incorporated into a development avoiding householders later applying to have them felled or lopped as inconvenient.

Costs of Materials
Costs /m2 for building facing materials:
- Render - £25
- Brick - £45-67
- Reconstituted Stone - £48
- Local Stone - £75-£120
- Rubble Stone or Flint - £90

The choice of new trees or hedgerows are usually limited to native species in well-worn set proportions creating a visually bland uninteresting setting for homes. Landscaping is too frequently abandoned after the first enthusiasm and in any case is often too small an area to be effective much of it odd corners and edges or "left over" land. Planning permission contains the proviso for dead trees and planting to be replaced by the end of the first 5 years of a new development. Bunds or mounds created as screening banks either dissolve away or with odd trees scattered along their length or collect wind driven piles of abandoned tree guards (many are recyclable) looking as intrusive as the buildings being screened. There is no effective checking mechanism other than an authority's enforcement procedures and it is something Parishes could easily monitor but don't.

House designs claim to follow the local vernacular but this is inconsistently achieved when the obviously wrong materials – type of stone, colour of bricks, roof tiles or slates are used. The Localism Act with its emphasis on consultation hopefully gives the opportunity to, yet again, improve both house design, ornamental details and layout although Councillors can be too easily persuaded that good design is too expensive.

Housing density, is invariably a contentious issue, with the previous government minimum of 35 houses/hectare giving rise to small gardens and cramped interiors, whilst cars line the roads and parking dominates neighbourhoods. Small details are important whether in building design such as window and door surrounds or road names. It is important for communities to keep local associations such as field names, local industries or local families all too often whisked away and replaced with bland names, such as "Valley Heights" - for a new riverside housing development.

Backland development

Small landlocked sites behind already established housing either garden land or open space are unpopular with neighbours and generally treated with distain by Councillors. Neighbours hate the unexpected loss of privacy, the loss of familiar trees, and the extra noise. Councillors often vie with one another to be the first to announce an application as Backland development thus confirming their innate wisdom. It is an easy plus for a new Councillor to achieve allowing them to feel part of the Planning Committee team. On the whole Committees see Backland development as almost immoral and the loss of a garden contemptible.

Infill plots

Small gaps between existing buildings are filled in the endless pursuit of occupying spaces often by something incongruous, an architectural gesture or a counterpoint. Committees are saddened but often sympathetic to the applicant, bowing to the inevitable. The loss of a garden is unfortunate.

Both Backland and Infill development have been treated gleefully by Planning authorities in the recent past and were termed "windfall sites," helping to achieve Government set targets without the hassle of allocating sites. Most authorities have assumed and planned for a percentage to be developed over the life of their Core Strategy (some 20 years). Although obviously not knowing how, where or when or even if, they would appear, it was an act of faith which actually did work. However the Coalition Government in its new National Planning Policy Framework wanted certainty and has insisted that there is always a "ready-to-go" 5 year supply of residential building land and has implied it is bringing to an end the building on garden land.

Conservation

Listing Numbers
In England there are 374,081 Listed Building entries.
There are also:
- 19,717 scheduled ancient monuments
- 1,601 registered historic parks and gardens
- 9,080 conservation areas
- 43 registered historic battlefields
- 46 designated wrecks
- 17 World Heritage Sites

Listed Buildings

Every Parish has buildings which are historic, architecturally interesting, well-loved and locally exceptional. It is a subject which raises great passions. Many of these will be Listed by English Heritage on behalf of the Government and range from bridges to stately homes, mile stones to lamp posts, buildings of national architectural importance, or regional buildings showing local traditions.

Buildings are chosen because of their age and rarity, so the fewer the surviving examples, the more likely they are to be Listed. Buildings generally have to be over 10 years old – to be eligible.

Listing includes:
- All buildings built before 1700 that are in or near original condition,
- Most buildings between 1700 and 1840,
- Buildings after 1840, but some selection is made,
- Post 1945 buildings need to be of exceptional importance and under threat.

Additional considerations:
- Architectural Interest: buildings which are nationally important because of their architectural design, decoration and craftsmanship; or illustrating specific building styles and techniques;
- Historic Interest, this includes buildings which illustrate facets of the nation's social, economic, cultural or military history;
- Historical Associations with nationally important people or events;
- Group value, especially where buildings are part of an important architectural or historic group or are a fine example of planning (such as squares, terraces or model villages).

Buildings are classified into 3 grades:
- **Grade I** buildings are of exceptional interest, sometimes considered to be internationally important. Just 2.5% of all Listed Buildings;
- **Grade II star** buildings are particularly important buildings of more than special interest. Just 5.5% of all Listed Buildings;
- **Grade II** buildings are nationally important and of special interest. 92% of all Listed Buildings are in this class and it is the most likely grade of Listing for a home owner.

Perhaps not surprisingly 55% of Listed Buildings are owned by the churches.

A Listing will describe, in a much abbreviated, and slightly tricky to understand wording, the features which are thought to be important such as the windows, roofs, ornamentation and materials used. Listing protects the whole building including the interior and in addition any building or structure which belonged to the main building when it was Listed and which was built before 1st July 1948. These "curtilage Listed Buildings" include outbuildings and boundary walls. If the use and ownership of them changes – they are still Listed because of the original historic connection. New additions such as conservatories attached to a Listed Building come under Listed Building control.

Listing does not prevent change, but acts as a pointer to which buildings need a careful assessment, it is a balance between the historic importance and past and future uses, looking at the fabric of the building and seeing what can be retained. Listing ensures Listed Building Consent is applied for so all the arguments can be aired. Listed Buildings can be altered, extended or in exceptional cases demolished, the arguments raised are very passionate. Grants for repair are variously available under Government initiatives, from grant making trusts and even television programmes.

In addition there are buildings and parts of the townscape and landscape which are considered to be "Heritage Assets." Although not English Heritage Listed or necessarily in a Conservation Area, they are loved locally and are part of an area's sense of place. Planning authorities now need to consider carefully any changes in and around them looking at the use of design and materials to be used.

Listed Building Consent

Everyone knows of horror stories of plastic windows or strangely painted front doors or "stone" cladding of brick buildings which cause consternation and letters to the "paper." Consent is needed for any work which affects the special architectural or historic interest of a Listed structure and is part of the Planning process. Small scale repairs using matching materials and methods or replacement kitchen or bathroom fittings where the building is not altered do not need consent.

Other work does including:

- externally: the often notorious replacement windows and doors, conservatories and extensions, walls and gutters;
- internally; the moving of internal walls, alteration of fireplaces, doors, floors, stairs and fittings.
- additions: alarms, satellite dishes, signs.

Not obtaining permission is a criminal offence with heavy fines or imprisonment. Most authorities have a conservation expert who will visit and give advice. Conservation teams and English Heritage can be thought pernickety advising on materials to use even paint colours for rooms and insisting that additions such as new interior staircases can be removed easily at a later date, if needs be, to protect a building's original fabric.

Request a Listing

A building does not have to be in a good state of repair to be Listed, and buildings are being added to the register all the time, English Heritage dealt with 2,000 new Listing enquiries in 2009. These may have been overlooked in the original survey or the result of new information. Anyone can request a Listing (spot-listing), the public, local authorities, amenity groups or owners. Based on a detailed description and photographs English Heritage will research, visit the site and consult before making any recommendations. If a building is at risk of demolition or unsympathetic alteration local Planning authorities can issue a Building Preservation Order. This lasts 6 months allowing the Secretary of State to decide whether to formally List the building.

Buildings at Risk Register

Protection is not guaranteed and some neglected Listed Buildings or Monuments are also included on the national Buildings at Risk Register as well as a local one and yet even this does not mean local authorities will take action.

Urgent Works and Repairs Notices

If a building is in severe state of repair the Planning authority should issue a repairs notice on the owner. The owner has to comply within a set time period to make the building safe and weather proof; this often involves just covering it in blue plastic sheeting. If the owner does not act the authority can do the work themselves and charge the owner. To encourage local authorities to be more proactive and prevent endangered buildings deteriorating beyond the point they are economic to repair English Heritage runs a grant scheme to underwrite some of the costs.

In extreme cases local authorities will compulsory purchase endangered buildings ensuring their restoration, this can be a very long process taking several years.

…Frome Watch…
Frome's Historic Buildings

Frome has only one building on the national Heritage at Risk Register, a Drying House on Willow Vale, a remnant of the cloth industry. Mendip District Council publishes its own "At Risk" list. Of the 44 entries (2008) three are in Frome: an outbuilding to the Lamb and Fountain public house and two C19th warehouses: one in Merchants Barton and the other on South Parade.

Scattered throughout the town are the remaining cast-iron Cockey street lamp standards which brought gas lighting to the town in the early 1840s. These elegant art nouveau lamps, now incongruously converted to sodium lights, were made in a local foundry one of the town's major industries in the 19th century. 25 are already Listed, but there are replicas as the Council discovered as it tried to List a further 52.

The Bailey Bridge served the town's Market car park for decades first as a road bridge then later as a footbridge, closed when the surface wooden planking rotted. In 2006 a small group lobbied to have it repaired but it was later condemned as structurally unsound and plans were made to demolish and replace it. Later the £150,000 replacement cost was thought too high and not a priority so demolition was confirmed in 2008. Although a popular landmark everyone admitted the new bridge 50 yards away served as well and the lobby group continued to argue the Bridge could be repaired. At this point BT, the telecom giant reminded the District Council that the Bridge carried its cabling. The lobby group still hoped for repair, but more money was unexpectedly found to build a new one. The lobby group started the Listing process discovering that the Bridge was only one of three of this particular design. The District Council demolished the Bridge and gave it to the Buckinghashire Canal Trust where it has been reused. The Listing failed as did the subsequent Appeal as by then it had been dismantled.

The Frome Historic Buildings Trust was perhaps the first attempt by local people to breathe new life into dilapidated cottages creating new homes. Later in the 1990s the Town Council, Mendip and County with various government grants gave building owners within the Conservation Area 50% of costs towards exterior and largely cosmetic improvements.

Local Listings

Every Parish has historic, artistic, architectural buildings and archaeological landscapes which are not on the statutory lists held by English Heritage. They add an unquantifiable interest, richness and character, and are much loved elements in local streetscapes and landscapes and would be sorely missed and any unsympathetic change regretted.

Local Listing gives the community the opportunity to nominate, research and photograph what is important locally including: individual buildings, whole terraces, boundary walls, archaeology, monuments, or street details creating character statements for each Heritage Asset. After discussions with local historians and heritage experts the finalised and adopted Lists can be used by Planning authorities and developers to help improve and conserve an area's sense of identity in future development proposals.

The new National Planning Policy Framework suggests Heritage Assets deserve the same protection as the statutory English Heritage Lists.

…Frome Watch…
Mendip Conservation Advisory Panel

A group of a dozen or so people from the District's local Civic and Amenity groups which includes the Frome Civic Society.

A resident from each of the five towns with knowledge of heritage conservation and a Councillor from the District Planning Board form the Panel. It is unelected and extra members are invited to join as needs be. It meets about every six weeks.

The Panel comments on Planning applications affecting the character, setting and appearance of a Listed Building or when an application is in or near a Conservation Area, primarily from a design, materials and historic viewpoint. It has a wide ranging brief considering pre-application proposals, changes of use, development briefs, policies, highway works and Conservation Area changes.

An application's shortcomings are listed and the Panel suggests refusal or acceptance with comments passed to the assigned Planning officer. These are not always acted upon and the Panel has frequently expressed its severe disappointment.

The Local Listing of Heritage Assets started in the autumn of 2009 but as yet there is no List-December 2012. With the Government's enthusiasm for local accountability the Panel could form the basis of a Design Review Panel as outlined in the new National Planning Policy Framework which would look at all applications from a design perspective.

Conservation Areas

Familiarly centred round the historic cores of villages, towns and cities a Conservation Area can also include historic parkland, model housing estates and even canals. These areas of special character not only include individual Listed Buildings but how buildings are grouped together, with their paths and boundaries, trees and gardens, even the spaces in between which make up a familiar scene are given a broad protection. As with Listed Buildings the idea is to manage change and every Parish will have its own idea as to how well this works.

Application numbers
There are around 32,000 Listed Building Consent applications a year. 90% are approved.

First created in 1967 there are now over 9,300 Conservation Areas in England these are mapped and designated by District /Unitary Councils or in London by English Heritage. Whilst the boundaries are reviewed regularly there is no statutory requirement to consult.

A Conservation Area gives the Local Planning Authority (LPA) several extra controls over:
- demolition, there is a presumption in favour of keeping buildings which add to the character of an area,
- minor developments, this will include changes normally allowed elsewhere such as satellite dishes - frequently ignored,
- trees, whether cutting down, or loping. The LPA can also make a Tree Preservation Order to give additional protection to a tree or a group of trees.

Article 4 Directions
Many homeowners can make alterations to the outside of their homes without Planning permission, known as "Permitted Development Rights", this includes such things as changing windows and doors and demolishing boundary walls. Unfortunately these changes slowly alter the special feel of an area as street details are lost. Planning Authorities can remove these "Rights" by making an Article 4 Direction so Planning permission is required before any alterations can be made. This is most effective in Conservation areas where ill-suited plastic windows and doors can then be avoided.

Trees

Trees or groups of trees can be protected by a Tree Preservation Order (TPO) these are mapped and numbered, listed and described by the Planning authority. Trees are protected because they add so much to the local streetscape or landscape, or because they are rare, or perhaps because they are screening an eyesore. Planning permission is needed to fell or prune a TPO tree.

When a tree is in the Conservation Area but without a TPO, six weeks' notice must be given in writing, detailing the species, the location and the work to be carried out. Carrying out works to protected trees without approval is a criminal offence with heavy fines. However, there are exceptions if a tree is dead, dying or dangerous and action needs to be taken quickly for safety reasons.

A TPO can be applied for by anyone, including local people or the Parish Council. A tree can be spot listed in an emergency but felling often takes place over Bank Holidays when Planning authority offices are closed.

Local Development Framework (LDF) renamed Local Plan (2012)

In 2004 the Planning and Compulsory Purchase Act introduced a new system of plan making. The old system of County Structure Plans and District Local Plans which set policies and priorities on, the amount and type of housing and employment areas, leisure facilities and tourism hopes, schools and highways was replaced with the new Local Development Framework process covering the same policy areas. It was also based on rounds of local consultations and re consultations: with the general public - using exhibitions, Parish Council comments, input from local amenity groups, local organisations, businesses, Planning agents and developers, landowners and individuals over a period of years.

The resulting plans were expected to span about 20 years and were set within the context of Government Regional Planning policy (now abandoned) particularly and often most controversially housing, where new-build housing targets were set. Some towns were told to expect growth whilst others were given a minimum; smaller hamlets lost their residential status and were not allowed any extra housing. The finalised Core Strategy became the yardstick against which all Planning permissions were judged and any funding directed.

Swept away by the Coalition Government with the abolition of regional targets. Local Plans (2012) were re-instated covering the same areas, with housing and employment targets decided locally.

It is a peculiarity of the system that as the LDF/Local Plan ages and comes to towards the end of its Plan period the weight or relevance given to the policies in it lessen or even cease. Hopefully there is a new Plan being formulated to replace it, an "emerging Plan" this gradually gets more important until fully ratified (it is looked at in detail and in public by a government appointed Planning Inspector who can send it back to be rewritten).

There can be a gap between the old and the new Plan where no rules appear to apply and Planning applications may be passed which would normally be refused.

...Frome Watch... Housing

Housing numbers for 2006 to 2028 (Frome's allocation is 2,300) were calculated in a novel way:
- 332 have been built,
- 460 have planning permission in place,
- 971 are provided through sites already allocated in the old Plan,
- 228 will be "windfall" sites,
- 309 are left as a shortfall so sites will need to be found.
- Mendip calculated around 600 houses were built in the electoral cycle 2007-11.

The National Planning Policy Framework has thrown this method of calculation into disarray.

... Frome Watch...

Frome and the Local Plan

Consultations started in 2008 on the 2006 to 2028 Plan and was still on-going (2012) entering a 4th consultation. This has so far produced a series of predictions or visioning (loosely based on a 1970's behavioural psychology theories that suggested imagining what the future town will be like will help the authority achieve it) of what will be accomplished by 2028, these are curiously exactly the same as the previous plan, so it is baffling why it takes so long to produce.

Change is not a gentle continuum but a series of sharp changes with nothing much in between. However, the vision is written in pleasing generalities: stating for instance that the town should build enough housing, landowners are asked to suggest their land for development; the work force should be trained and discouraged from working out of the town (it is estimated 50% do) and new businesses encouraged. There is no acknowledgment that all the major applications approved over at least the previous 10 years has allowed the majority of industrial and commercial land within the town to become housing, destroying the town's industrial base and scattering its skilled workers. Any small new businesses starting up have been a matter of luck or serendipity.

Land is promised for allotments – despite Mendip owning previously used allotment land but refusing to rent it out. There are some numbers: the need for 2 or 3 new County funded schools (this is before the rise of the Free Schools) and rather precisely 4.8 hectares (11.9 acres) of open space. Because Frome is built in a bowl ringed by escarpments and a bypass; there are few easy decisions left.

As the Local Development Framework (now with a name change and morphing into the Local Plan) will provide a template for all the changes in the coming years it should in some measure be aspirational although whether to the point of ignoring Parish realities is an area for much discussion.

Housing numbers are certainly keenly watched and this is where the crux of the matter lies leaving the allocation of land for jobs as a secondary issue with the rest, schools, open spaces etc. as window dressing. Frome, as with any Parish is asked for its opinion, indeed many authorities specifically ask their small Parishes what their housing needs are as worryingly their young people and young families are being lost from their home Parishes. Land allocated in the past rarely seems to be reviewed indeed many allocations carry on over the decades from Plan to Plan with the original reason long forgotten or irrelevant saving the Planning authority finding different useable sites and giving the landowner a bankable asset. The Coalition Government's new regime demands a five year "ready-to-go" with Planning permission housing supply, creating a lot of very difficult decisions ahead.

Councillors indulge in low level grumbling when told what to do by their principal authorities seeing their Parish issues misunderstood or ignored. Townspeople could therefore reasonably expect a chunky document carefully worded with a thorough, reasoned and detailed commentary with arguments set out to steer the Planning authority in its deliberations. But, they will be disappointed by the sparse, vaguely incoherent offerings from the Parishes. The retort, *"they will only ignore us anyway"* is barely an excuse.

Indeed Frome's Planning Committee offered no observations on where houses, employment land or open spaces, allotments or play areas should go. No comment on the problems thrown up by the last Plan or that the same issues still need to be resolved. Having written its own Strategic Plan it is surprising it did not want to see these ideas incorporated. Instead it stuck to odd details and avoided giving numbers. Instead taking tourism as its focus, it wanted acknowledgement that the Town Council's activities had successfully raised the town's profile. It did remark on problems of house building in the floodplain and ended with arbitrarily agreeing the towns traffic congestion as well as its bus and train connections needed improving and to complete Frome's educational take, a university should be approached to set up a branch.

However, a lone Councillor by the end of the election cycle Frome had begun tentative steps to come up with a town Design Guide.

Parish Plans and Design Statements

Both Plans and Statements (pre-Neighbourhood Plan) harnessed the energy of local involvement and the determination for real and thorough consultations, from the design of the initial leaflet logos by local children, to regular updates: in Parish magazines and newspapers, with flyers, and brochures; with discussion days and presentations to local clubs, societies and businesses, to websites; updates on Parish notice boards and at Parish Council meetings using Councillor representation on the Plan or Statement steering committee to give detailed feedback. Everyone could be involved.

Parish Plans were a Government sponsored initiative to encourage people to come up with community led ideas for projects that would make local improvements. Parish Councils asked local people to form action groups to research areas of interest, concerns and needs. With these responses drawn up into a questionnaire every household was asked for its opinion. Summarised, these are redistributed for further comment and this feedback forms the key ideas and the basis for a Plan. Realisable projects are listed alongside suggestions on what to do. The Plan is adopted by its Parish Council who will be part of making it work. Every household is given a formal summary of the finished Plan and an invitation to help implement it.

Village Design Statements, encouraged by Planning authorities, asked local people to decide what their area should look like and how it should develop. Village teams researched areas of interest, sent out questionnaires and held design days fundraising to publish the finished statement. The resulting Design Statement traced how the Parish had changed over time including: employment, shops, clubs and societies, churches, open spaces, footpaths and highways, important landscapes and views. In-depth research, area by area, by dedicated locals looked at buildings describing: how they were built, the materials used, and any quirky detailing which helps make a place unique. Including the surroundings such as trees, the spaces between buildings, walls, verges, and wildlife as well as housing densities and included affordable housing needs for local people.

The resulting recommendations were intended to stand alongside the Planning authorities' Local Plan and Design Guidance.

Most Statements, unsurprisingly, want the new to respect the old, any changes to enhance their immediate surroundings, and designs to be sensitive to what is unique to each Parish.

If the Localism Act (2011) wasn't enough to unsettle everyone, the National Planning Policy Framework, hot on its heels (March 2012) tore up the old rules - some 7,000 pages with their well-worn certainties for the uncharted territory of local decision making and the presumption in favour of sustainable development, providing guidance in 58 pages. Together they create a new Planning landscape with the Neighbourhood Plan as central (see also Politics), The Coalition Government boldly stating, *"We will devolve power to the lowest level so neighbourhoods take control of their destiny."* However, the more recent easing of General Permitted Development Orders elbows aside policies in Local Plans albeit for a limited time, but who will monitor these changes?

...Frome Watch...

Vision4Frome's 120 project Community Plan provided a pick and mix of ideas to be added to Frome Town Council's new Neighbourhood Plan (2012) but this was unfortunately not taken up. As one of the national frontrunners it received a Government grant of £20,000 to buy in expertise from Mendip District Council, £20,000 from Mendip itself and an additional £20,000 from reserves. A steering group was set up, and several consultant led Citizens Panels (townspeople were paid £10 each per meeting and the late afternoon start meant only the retired or those working in the professions attended). Plus Planning workshops with opinions sought from invited groups and organisations arranged. The "hard to reach" townspeople remained elusive – they were probably at work. But it all has to wait for Mendip to finish their Local Plan into which the Neighbourhood Plan should dovetail. This will be a couple of years down the line.

After a referendum and if on gaining the support of more than 50% of those who vote it will become part of Mendip's Local Plan (the old Local Development Framework).

Neighbourhood Plan

Now, with the full weight of Government behind them and led by Parish Councils, or if one does not exist a Neighbourhood Forum of resident associations and community groups. Looking at the by now familiar themes of: homes, work, transport, green spaces, play and leisure. Asking what the whole community would like, where it will be and what it will look like using a raft of consultations and focus groups. The result should be prescriptive stating clearly what and where things should go and why. It is a statement of the obvious. Too often the finished glossy reports dwell too much on the philosophy of the Council, the history of the area and the pleasantness and enterprise of its inhabitants.

But the Plan will still need to dovetail into the Planning authorities Local Plan which needs to be completed and then approved by an independent Government Inspector first (nationally, only 40% are).

Excitingly, Parishes can now decide to permit the development they want to see by-passing the need for Planning applications using Neighbourhood Development Orders (NDO).which will detail the type (such as new homes or offices) and extent of new development.

Community Right to Build Orders are a type of NDO for community groups and will be site specific small scale developments such as businesses, community halls, renewable energy schemes or affordable housing with a housing association as a partner. Any income could fund other local facilities such as playgrounds or community halls.

The Plans and Orders are independently checked and a referendum held with a 50% pass rate of those who vote for the Plan or Orders to succeed.

Localism Act 2011

Now, at last, there is to be a real shift of power from central government and its bureaucrats to local people who for too often had *"awaited the arrival of top down plans that seem never to arrive or seem to involve them."* The Act gives some new and some revamped opportunities (see Politics):

- New powers with Neighbourhood Planning and accompanying Neighbourhood Development Orders (NDO) and the Community Right to Build Orders (CRBO) by-passing the standard application process. Subject to a referendum with a 50% pass rate. A grant system of £17.5 million provides funding to push start CRBOs;

- Community Right to Challenge, an old familiar is given an extra push encouraging community groups, the Parishes, even council employees to bid to run local services and float ambitious ideas. There is a grant system of £10.5 million to help groups take up the challenge of running services effectively;

- Community Right to Bid for Assets of Community Value, a response to the outcry as village or corner shops, pubs and even local fields disappear. Local people can now nominate much loved "community assets" such as libraries, swimming pools, shops, pubs, markets or land to be on a community asset list. If they come up for sale locals will be given time to raise the money to buy them with the Parish Council or a community group set up as a charity or a Community Interest Company continuing to run them.

- Building on the concept of Community Asset Transfer which was given a big push in 2008. The higher tiers of local government can lease or transfer property or land ownership (generally community halls, allotments or playing fields) to Parish Councils, community or voluntary groups, charities or community enterprises to run. Groups generally already use these buildings, so with local pride and knowledge, hands-on management, enthusiastic volunteers, the resulting frequently lower overheads offers better value-for-money and a more involved community. Some authorities looking for savings came to local agreements about libraries, Somerset sent a round robin letter to all its Parishes asking them to take on and subsequently pay for hitherto County responsibilities. Frome replied tartly it could not afford it without a subsidy from County.

- Consultation, new developments will now demonstrate how local opinion on design has been incorporated into schemes.

- The Power of Competence replaces the Power of Well-Being. Now Parishes can do virtually anything. Judged by, if it is lawful for an ordinary person a Parish can also do it. But, the Government rather playfully, but firmly, explains, the ownership and use of nuclear weapons on a neighbouring Parish is still forbidden. However, the scope is huge and needs the support of the electorate.

Parishes can:

- provide a cost effective or innovative service, such as selling energy to the national grid, setting up a co-operative or a company to run it;
- trade, such as running a community shop or post office;
- lend or invest money, perhaps by way of a development grant to a community enterprise or by helping a struggling business by buying it's shares, alternatively giving a loan and having an income via the interest;
- overlap with another authority's statutory duty such as education, waste collection, highways, or social services perhaps: forming a community trust to run a school, or joining forces to cut highway verges;

The Power can be used anywhere, even outside the immediate Parish although the electorate may object.

National Planning Policy Framework (NPPF)

NPPF creates a presumption in favour of sustainable development:
- **sustainable**, defined as ensuring better lives today without worsening the lives of future generations and;
- **development**, defined by Government as growth i.e. earning a living and housing a growing population.

Now with Neighbourhood Planning the Coalition Government brings decision making to communities: no longer remote, elaborate, or forbidding, the preserve of specialists and based on centralist targets.

There are 12 core Planning principles to be incorporated into all Local Plans, mostly common sense written in an upbeat optimistically vague way repeating much of what has gone before in previous legislation. Whilst much is protected; the countryside, valued buildings and open spaces all decisions will still be a balance between the benefits given and the harm done. Local Plans, we are told, will be creative, flexible, whilst bearing in mind the need to reduce, recycle and reuse under scored by a building and landuse map (see Politics).

There are highlights: good building design is a requirement and a 5 year "ready to go" housing supply; the Green Belt is specifically protected; locally important heritage buildings and archaeological sites which are not listed by English Heritage or Natural England are now their equivalent; town centres at the heart of every community can be protected; alternative transport promoted; specific business allocations made backed by an "economic vision."

General Permitted Development Orders
By 2013 the Coalition Government, with the national debt at over a trillion pounds and the annual overspend only reduced by a third, decides the Planning rules are to blame for sluggish economic growth and gives a further tweak to the rules.

This time using General Permitted Development Orders. There has always been a list of things homeowners could do without asking their Planning authority such as build small extensions or garages under General Permitted Development Orders.

Now and for 3 years only (until May 2016) the rules have been relaxed (but not in Conservation Areas or the ANOB) with the Planning authority given only a limited opportunity to object and then only able to consider, transport, highway, contamination or flood risks. The nearest neighbours will be consulted (still 21 days) with their opinion crucial. Local Councillors will not be asked. Only if the neighbours object will the authority need to decide if the impact is too great.

New Rules

- Home rear extensions can now be double their previous size, unexpectedly there is no fee.
- Now offices can become affordable homes. It is hinted this may be further extended to full market price homes and also to empty shops (generations of Frome shop keepers have been doing this as their businesses have become uneconomic. Keeping the shop fronts and building walls behind. The Government hopes to use, *"the untapped potential in the many disused existing buildings"..."to provide much needed homes and businesses."*
- Offices, shops, restaurants and industrial units and warehousing can also double their previously permitted size.
- Businesses have always been ruled by Use Classes and have had to stay within their category. Once crucial and sacrosanct, generations of Councillors have agonised and debated over the hopes of new entrepreneurs when trying to fine tune their High Streets either avoiding too many of one sort of business or not allowing changes between categories. Now, but for 2 years only, businesses in the Use Classes which includes: restaurants, cafes, pubs, takeaways, offices and financial services, can become whatever they would like to be before changing back at the end of the 2 years. Now shops can become restaurants.

It is assumed a range of vibrant entrepreneurial pop-up ventures (these have recently burst onto the High Street often only lasting a few weeks) will rapidly appear taking advantage of this new business landscape testing their viability before the premises revert back to their previous Use Class at the end of the 2 years. No-one explains how the process will be reversed in practice and what the hoped for successful businesses will be able to do next.

- Agricultural buildings can now become shops or offices or cafes as each farm has the potential to develop into an enterprise hub perhaps undermining the Government's support for High Street rejuvenation
- Any building can become a Free school for an academic year.

For most prior approval is needed and it is assumed with less detail demanded decisions will be easily made within the 56 days allowed if not the development can go ahead by default.

Much of the above has been the bread and butter of every Planning Committee. These Councillors will have less to do and no influence on issues over which people in the past have looked for leadership.

Planning authorities' income will initially reduce, pressuring budgets and sharpening anxieties as a more proactive and positive economic stance is demanded.

Money

Section106 agreements (s106) and the Community Infrastructure Levy (CIL)

Planning obligations or s106 agreements were originally designed to solve the problem of local authorities being unable to afford to build the infrastructure needed for new developments such as schools, access roads, or sewers or even hospitals. The developers' contribution enabled developments to go ahead; developers considered it a tax and the necessary price of permission with local people fearing Planning consent was being bought.

Planning authorities aiming "to lessen the impact of a development" fund local infrastructure or services such as: road improvements, school places, play areas and open spaces or the mundane such as bus shelters. The law says there should be a direct relationship between what is requested and the development. Permission cannot be bought to make the unacceptable acceptable. If a children's play space is not included on site a contribution could be expected to buy additional equipment to improve a nearby park or provide extra bus shelters to encourage the use of public transport!

Most authorities had affordable housing policies setting out the number of houses to be transferred to a housing association for rent with each residential Planning permission. The trigger point was set nationally at 15 houses over which there was a set percentage (nationally 15% but authorities varied). However, developers have gained permission for housing over a number of years using separate permissions on adjoining sites avoiding triggering the threshold or claimed a Brownfield site was too contaminated and therefore too expensive to develop if affordable housing was included. The Coalition Government's new rules will enable Planning authorities to ask for contributions from all sizes of development from the single house to the new housing estate.

Community Infrastructure Levy Charges for Housing 2012:
Torbay, £100 per square metre,
Wimbledon, £385 per square metre,
Bath, £98 per square metre in the city rising to £196 in some of its rural areas.

Section106 agreements are secret negotiated agreements and rely upon the skill of the Planning officer and the persistence of Councillors in asking for money for facilities and local improvements. Many authorities use a set amount per square metre per house. Nationally only 14% of residential Planning permissions and 7% of office and light industrial developments (2009) made contributions. This was generally the larger schemes some offering specific things, too often simply funding for a play area, inevitably with this system there was a shortfall. Indeed, if the Planning authority did not spend the allotted money within a set time period, frequently 5 years, it was returned to the developer.

Affordable housing
For people who are unable to rent or buy on the open market, it used to be called social housing.
Providing:
- Housing at a cost low enough to reflect local incomes and local house prices;
- Homes that remain at an affordable price for current and future eligible households.
Affordable housing includes:
- Homes for rent via a housing association;

- Shared ownership with a housing association;
- Homes sold but kept below market value, generally 80%, in perpetuity.

By 2012 the central government grant of £50,000, previously given to build each affordable home, had gone reduced to £15,000 Housing Associations now rely on this and any contribution from landowners.

Since April 2010 Government expected Planning authorities to set, publish and implement Community Infrastructure Levy Charges (by 2014) suggesting between £5,000 and £10,000 per house. By 2012 only 9 had a scheme running.

It focused on increasing the scope of support to a wider area not just the immediate development, even adding together contributions from separate developments. The Planning authority now has a specific monitoring, reporting and enforcing role. Section106 agreements will be kept to provide affordable housing contributions on new housing sites. This will give nomination rights to Parishes so local people can live in their home village and not loose their family connections. In all cases it is the original landowners who pay the levies as developers' claw back any payments made.

Developers could always re-negotiate s106 agreements but by 2013 the Coalition Government decides if developers say the level of affordable homes is too great, making building uneconomic, the numbers required will be eased for 3 years only. Government hope this will "unblock" 75,000 stalled homes.

With the Localism Act (2011) a more robust CIL eases the rules; money can now be asked for all sorts and will be expected to fund infrastructure, local services and facilities. Parishes which agree to new developments begin to look forward to huge "windfalls", thousands of pounds are suggested, and they also discover this applies to housing already planned for their area.

Government suggests 15%, or 25% if there is a Neighbourhood Plan in place, to spend, as the Housing Minister explained, on *"what the hell you like,"* although in reality it is expected to fund infrastructure. It is Parishes on the edge of towns who will benefit most as those towns expand.

Commuted sums
Planning authorities have a responsibility and a statutory requirement, to claim maintenance payments from developers to cover future costs for a set period of years; this can include play areas, signage, public art, bridges, hanging baskets, paving, and highways. These are one–off payments, some of the money may be passed to the Parish Council.

Percent for Art
Hailed as bringing culture to communities "Percent for Art" is still included in large development project briefs and will be a part of s106 agreements. Discretionary on local authorities it was aimed at being 1% of the total development budget and was seen as part of a general move towards public art as an expression of local feeling and traditions. Celebrating a sentimental view of the past or an historical event, perhaps a local hero, or an attempt to become a focus of civic pride and identity, or, the proud centre-piece of a new public space.

They tend to be a piece of statuary on a plinth as short-listed artists shoehorn their usual offerings into the art brief. Often commissioned as a result of a competition and frequently controversial "Art" was later expanded to include community involvement in the concept, design and the execution with practical "skills" workshops for adults combining with an educational element - school children being particularly useful for this. Councillors enjoy unveiling the finished works of art.

New Homes Bonus

A generalised local authorities income before the New Homes Bonus and CIL:

- Council Tax – 25%
- Business Rates – 24%
- Fees and Charges – 18%
- Central Government – 33%

A new Coalition Government funding scheme (April 2011). Based on newly built homes, including affordable homes which get an additional annual premium (£350) and empty homes brought back into use, including traveller pitches, caravans and student accommodation (supported by an extra £160 million of investment aid). Government matches the Council Tax raised for the following 6 years. Effectively replacing some of the, now reducing, central Government funding. It will become a crucial local funder and an important part of the process when deciding housing Planning applications.

Government aims to increase house building, which had slumped with the continuing financial downturn (120,000 built in 2009), and "reward" areas which agree to extra homes. Local authorities are expected to consult Parishes on how this "windfall" is spent, the Parishes are hopeful of great things; thousands of pounds are again suggested. The Government recommends a 20/80 split, 20% to the first tier authority – the County, with 80% to the second tier or Districts, reflecting who provides services and infrastructure. Spending ideas range from: reducing the precept, extra rubbish collections, extra swimming pools, refurbishing libraries, or providing new affordable homes. Many fear too much will disappear into general spending. It is not ring-fenced.

...Frome Watch...
New money, new possibilities
Mendip received just under £1.5 million in the first two years of the New Homes Bonus and eventually announces how the Bonus will be spent:

- 40% will be invested in something which will provide the District with an income in years to come;

- 30% can be bid for from a Local Legacy Fund (£250,000). New projects from £10,000-£100,000 qualify, these can be run by Parish Councils, voluntary and community groups including social enterprise companies. Aimed at supporting businesses, housing, solving rural isolation providing strategic and community leadership, aiding health, education work opportunities and the quality of life.

The Parishes will have to prove they welcomed the new housing in order to qualify and match funding will also be looked favourably upon;

- 1% will go to groups and societies for local small scale community environment projects. Decided and distributed by Ward Councillors as *"an example of Localism and Councillor leadership."*

Councillors can pool their allocations reminiscent of the defunct Somerset County scheme. £100,000 is anticipated over the first 2 years, or £2,000 per Councillor.

The Town Council is furious and demands all the money from the Bonus for all the proposed housing, an estimated 2,300 homes (2006-28). It estimates around £10 million and a petition is launched. It has misunderstood.
Whilst the Community Infrastructure Levy (CIL) was discussed in 2009 nothing was ever approved. Mendip missing out on an equivalent amount of money to its New Homes Bonus "reward."

Neighbours
A vital element in any Planning application. Those closest to any change will generally be informed by letter but it may be best to speak to those most immediately affected personally, otherwise any suspected slight will magnify into a fully-fledged objection. There are a few "neighbours golden rules"; do not fall out, try to be realistic about what you are doing perhaps underplaying any improvements, consider helpful suggestions and promise to invite them round immediately it is finished.

Country neighbours can be especially difficult when those who have bought their rural idyll find themselves woken at unlikely hours by sheep bleating, cocks crowing and the full force of the dawn chorus exacerbated by the sound of tractors and farmers doing agricultural things including leaving colourful piles of plastic and machinery in odd corners of fields. Indeed the 1997 Labour Government legislated to encourage farmers to tidy up farm yards and reduce rusting piles of machinery and the colourful plastic. The Planning authorities Enforcement officer generally deals with these complaints if there is time.

Ward Councillors
Planning applicants need their support so they should be asked for their opinion; they may have previous experiences of similar applications and can help in discussions with Planning officers or if a refusal seems imminent applicants should push for the issue to be debated at Planning Committee. They will welcome being a willing ear but be aware there may be a hotch-potch of reactions: some will decide on merit, others will stick to their prejudices, those belonging to a political party or faction may feel forced to toe the party line and be dragooned into support or refusal. They are able to suggest Planning conditions, or items for s106 agreements.

The Village Envelope
Is a line tightly drawn around houses and gardens, outlining the edges of a settlement. Any changes and development normally only takes place inside the envelope (affordable housing for rent can be the exception). Fields or open spaces which have fortuitously been included may be developed but usually not without controversy.

Housing and Homes
Much Government credibility rests on housing numbers, as the need for housing constantly grows – the fastest forming households are single people who now make up 30% of homes. The 1997 Government boldly promised to build 300,000 new homes a year although in reality it had little influence. Actual numbers struggled to reach half that as the financial crisis hit and house builders locked into contracts to pay (on reflection) too high a price for the land could not afford to build.

Perhaps surprisingly self-build is a growing force providing around 10% of homes; nationally most of Britain's housing is built by the 6 national house builders. They have provided cheaply built, poorly designed, small, energy hungry homes built on average in 12-15 weeks. There is not the long term commitment a self-builder has to build to a higher standard. Again with the average stay in a home of 7 years homeowners do not have the incentive to improve their homes especially when investment in energy efficiency has a long payback time.

In an effort to boost these more easily affordable homes the Coalition Government has begun to provide short term loans out of a £30 million fund. Councils will be expected to provide self-build land allocations (although Mendip has chosen not to). On average in Europe 50% of homes are self–build with Germany topping 80%.

The General Development Process

Sometimes the roles of landowner, developer and builder are combined.
In general:

- The landowner owns the land.

- The developer will assemble a site or sites, raise the finance, produce a masterplan and the designs of the houses and may sell the Planning permission on.

- The builder and/or developer will build the whole site or a number of builders will build a proportion of plots. These are built in stages so as not to undermine the value of the development.

Finally there is the purchaser and/or the renter. The development may be sold as individual houses or as a whole or in part to an investor. Perhaps leased or rented or passed to a Housing Association as homes for local people.

It was the penny levy on the rates in 1919 to build "Homes for Heroes" for returning soldiers after World War 1 that brought housing into the political arena. With the beginnings of local authority owned public housing gaining pace after the Second World War until 1980 when 5 million council house tenants were given a "Right to Buy" as the Government switched housing funding to Housing Associations and out of local authorities' political control.

Facts and Figures 2007/08

Types of homes in existence:		When were homes built:
Detached	22%	4% Before 1851
Semi-detached	32%	15% Between 1851-1918
Terraced	28%	19% Between 1919-44
Flats	17%	22% Between 1945-64
		24% Between 1965-84
		6% Between 1986-2008

Who owns what

In 1918	In 2008
89% private rented	7% private rented
10% owner occupied	84% owner occupied
1% social /public rented	9% social/public rented

The 1960's saw Government set standards (Parker Morris Standards) for homes including a minimum room size only abandoning them in the 1980's hoping market forces would continue to raise standards – they didn't. The 1997 Labour Government set the number of houses at a minimum of 35 per hectare and homes become even smaller. Today's average home is the smallest in Europe at 87 square metres only London sets a minimum size of 35 square metres. Surveys quote three top wants in a home: outside space, room size and nearness to local services.

Housing targets have come and gone as the Regions haggled with Government and Districts argued over numbers with Regional Planning Authorities for years. Until in a masterly breath-taking stroke the National Planning Policy Framework (2012) did away with regional targets in a move to dispense with rules and have decisions made locally. With a proviso that if not enough housing was allocated Government would penalise them by moving their self-imposed allocation forward increasing the number of houses that should be built.

With the lowest level of house building in England and Wales in peace-time since 1923-24 and the cost of a home having doubled between 1997 and 2007, a 5 year "ready to go" housing supply hopes to correct this. The Local Plan should indicate where. Housing numbers based on a needs survey of the Parishes are now a minimum. The excuse a Planning application for housing is premature to the Local Plan to stop unpopular applications is gone.

...Frome Watch...

How many Frome homes

Mendip has spent 4-5 years, far too long, cogitating over its Local Plan only to discover it has lost control over where housing should be built. It does not have the 5 year housing supply in place demanded by the National Planning Policy Framework, so now the long held excuse of "premature to the Local Plan", a handy way to get rid of uncomfortable applications, cannot be used. Parishes fear the flood gates opening and being swamped by large numbers of houses too difficult for their small communities to absorb.

Frome, District assumed, would need 2,300 new homes up to 2028 – but this is no longer a target, as under previous legislation, but a minimum. 792 already have permission or have been built. Now no longer able to include in the count previously allocated land – those with lapsed Planning permissions or rely on the serendipity of "windfall" sites 1,508 would now be needed instead of the 309 previously guessed at.

In a double blow Mendip without an adopted Community Infrastructure Levy charging structure has "lost" the same amount as it has gained from the New Homes Bonus.

Housing Codes

Levels of energy efficiency/ CO2 emissions
level 1 - 10% - inefficient
level 2 - 18%
level 3 - 25%
level 4 - 44%
level 5 - 100%
level 6 - zero carbon - ultimate efficiency
Code for Sustainable Homes

With worries of climate change, flooding, dwindling resources, the environmental impact of new homes and governmental targets to reduce carbon emissions a national Code describing the overall sustainability of new homes was produced in 2008. Using a 1 (low efficiency) to 6 star rating system it sets minimum standards for energy, water and resource use with points collected to achieve each level. Code 4 should be achieved by all new homes by 2012 and Code 6 by 2016.

A home's sustainability is measured against 9 design categories:

Energy:
- aiming to limit the amount of CO2 given into the atmosphere therefore making a home more energy efficient as per table above;
- limiting heat loss through insulation and airtightness or by building flats or terraces until no energy is used in heating - creating a "PassivHaus" (only 100 have been built nationally by 2012);
- using energy efficient internal and external security or decorative lighting accounting on average to 10-15% of an electricity bill;
- providing a space for the natural drying of clothes;
- choosing "A" or "B" rated energy efficient white goods;
- using local energy generation from renewable resources which themselves use low or zero carbon technologies - 10% is suggested so government can hit its own target;
- providing secure cycle storage to reduce car use - most car journeys are less than 5 miles;
- providing a home office, with two telephone points suggested – to reduce travel to work. Surveys suggest over 25% of workers have worked from home at some point.

Water:
- reducing the consumption of potable water by re-using grey water or harvesting rain water – 10% of UK water is used to flush the loos and for washing;
- rainwater collection for garden watering.

Materials:
- building roofs and walls from low environmental impact materials. Considering the mining/harvesting of materials through their processing, to usage, reuse, recycling and final disposal over the assumed 60 year life cycle of a home;
- Ensuring that 80% of materials which provide the basic building elements - walls, floors, roofs and the finishing elements - windows, panelling and doors are responsibly sourced. All timber should be legally sourced.

Surface Water Run-Off:
- Avoiding, reducing, and delaying rainfall going into sewers and watercourses, certainly no more than when the site was undeveloped, perhaps achieved by recycling rainwater;
- using pervious paving for parking and green roofs for buildings;
- encouraging house building in low flood risk areas whilst reducing building in medium to high risk flood areas. Flooding is already twice as likely as a 100 years ago with 5 million living in flood risk areas in England and Wales.

Waste:

- providing indoor and outdoor storage of recyclable and non-recyclable household waste;
- reducing building construction waste on site by reuse, recycling, recovery and composting. 13 million tonnes are unused and thrown away annually;
- providing facilities to compost household waste thereby reducing landfill - which in turn reduces toxic liquid leachates and methane – 27 times more powerful then CO_2. 30% of household waste can be composted.

Pollution:
- reducing global warming by using thermal and acoustic insulating materials with a low global warming potential. The Kyoto protocol set limits on 6 specific gases;
- reduce nitrogen oxides (caused by burning fossil fuels) by choosing suitable space and water heating systems.

Health and Well-Being:
- Enhance quality of life by using daylight and warming the house naturally so reducing the need for artificial light;
- providing sound insulation by careful internal design - neighbour complaints on noise is the most common cause for disputes;
- improving the quality of life by providing a secure outdoor space, some of which is partially private and suits a range of occupants – older, disabled and children. Curiously the minimum is 1.5 metres by 1.5 metres of garden space for each bedroom and 1 metre by 1 metre of shared space;
- Homes should be easily adapted and accessible to all types of householders through the life of the building.

Management:
- A simple householder user-handbook helping to use the home efficiently;
- protect the quality of life by designing homes and estates so they feel safe and secure, so crime and disorder or fear of crime does not undermine community cohesion;
- construction sites should be run in an environmentally, socially accountable and a considerate manner with monitoring for dust, water usage, CO_2 emissions, energy use, and pollution with care taken with the use of timber.

Ecology:
- developing land with limited wildlife value whilst discouraging the use of ecologically valuable sites;
- making changes that improve the wildlife value of a site whilst protecting it from damage during site clearance and construction;
- making the best use of both the land and the building footprint by maximising the useable space.

...Frome Watch....

Housing
The new proposed Core Strategy for Frome (2006-2028) expects 2,300 new homes to be built mainly on the few remaining employment sites.

It is an oddity of accounting that many of these are already built or are in the pipeline. Indeed if any of these are holiday homes they will also be counted as full time homes. The twenty years between 1991 and 2011 gave a new homes target of 2,590 of which 2,229 were completed (a 14% shortfall) with few s 106 agreements the associated loss runs into £thousands.

A list of Mendip agreements (1997 to May 2008) gives 7 sites in Frome with s106 agreements and 3 with commuted sums for very modest amounts totaling £318,144.96. There is not an easily accessible list. A request for an updated version resulted in a demand of around £1,600 to supply the information plus copy charges. Most Councils follow government recommended best practice of 10p a copy sheet or have free downloadable on-line access. Mendip is not alone not knowing about its 106 agreements, its adjacent sister District of South Somerset discovered no-one was responsible for agreements, or knew what agreements had been made or if they were completed or if or where any money had been spent. Mendip's requests for monetary support seems limited to play areas in only one known instance translating into new equipment on the Edford Playing Field (£53,000) an already established area to serve an extra 100 new homes.

As early as 2009 Mendip District Council Cabinet agreed the charges for monitoring the proposed new Community Infrastructure Levy (CIL) charges (10% on top of cash requested and £500 for each non-monetary contribution) but nothing was finally approved. Each Planning authority will develop their own and widely differing schemes. Nearby Bath has settled on a charge of around £7,500 per average home, Torquay on £8,700 and Wimbledon in London £33,500. Mendip's Planning Department estimated it would have netted a very modest additional £25,000, if charging had been in place over the previous few years. Seemingly missing out on a huge opportunity and potential which would be equal to the New Homes Bonus it receives today. It still does not have a set of charges in place (2012). The Audit Commission in 2009 gave Mendip a rating of 1 out of 4, for resource management i.e. Performs Poorly, stating the authority did not meet minimum requirements.

Art
Frome has had mixed experiences with the very little public art it has on show, perhaps unexpected, as the town sees itself as a creative centre. The most successful was the Boyle Cross donated to the town by Frome devotees Mr and Mrs Boyle (she designed it herself) in 1871 becoming the centre piece of the Market Place. Made of pink Devon marble, the Market Cross above its 8 sided fountain bowl is now sadly without its water, but was used in the past by fishmongers to wash fish. Vandalised and broken into several pieces in the 1990's an outraged town demanded its restoration and a local quarry company offered to fund it, although the opportunity to restore the water was not taken, it is again filled with summer flowers.

The Millennium celebrations brought together the odds and ends round the town including newly commissioned pieces into an Arts and Crafts Trail. Most notably a tall natural stone wall, (hiding some toilets) although not in local stone despite being bought as a job lot from a local reclamation yard. At waist height, a glass frieze, a line of dense, blue glass bricks have buried industrial components (from Singers – brass sprinkler heads, from Bussman Cooper – glass fuses, and from Notts Industries – swarf) inset in them. Celebrating the town's industrial past and originally designed to be lit, it proved unaffordable. Today many of the glass bricks are broken (2012).
A set of 5 elaborate specially commissioned – from local ornamental blacksmiths - tree guards protecting a line of new red oaks in the Market Yard car park have since disappeared to the Park although the two welded rusting crucibles balanced on one another, remnants again from the Singers Works, in the "library square" remain.

The Millennium Green high on the side of the river valley is a wild area with a sculptural centre piece, with other carvings including poppy seadhead seats in wood scattered around. Perhaps notable are the carved quotations taken from Christina Rossetti's poems (she lived and taught in the town for a time) and Siegfried Sassoon (the war poet buried in nearby Mells) with a group of cherry trees donated in memoriam by relatives and listed in the Lions Club Book of Memory.

Centre piece to the Trail was the Singers Links the sad reminder of an industry which was the heart of the town. Beginning in 1848, Singers – the local foundry - at its height produced the best bronze sculptures in the country, exporting across the world, from, most famously, Boadicea on the Embankment in London to the Rhodes Memorial in Cape Town, South Africa, with church bells and church lecterns for the local market. Its town centre factory edged the river for hundreds of yards. The last castings were mostly soldiers for First World War memorials. The only example in Frome is of Charlie Robbins, an employee, standing outside the new edge-of-town Singers factory which now makes water sprinklers.

The site redeveloped for housing in around 2000 left two office buildings for conversion and rescued 4 pieces of "typical" machinery, (now graffitied) – a fine Pilkington Power Hammer, a Factory Gantry and Railings, a Scarp Kiln and a Sand Blast Box - boxy metal shapes in unlikely pastel shades plus a 1980's miniature bronze copy of a camel (General Gordon's of Khartoum fame) perched on top of a bright blue fluted column overseeing where the original statue was cast and the still as yet unopened children's play area. The planned interpretation boards were never provided and the idea petered out. Unexpectedly Mendip District Council ran a survey in the town (2011) asking if they should be scrapped, relocated or retained. There are no results available and the "Links" have yet to be adopted into Council care.

The Trail included the repaved Apple Alley with its mediaeval pigeon lofts and jettied Tudor buildings but is really a mess of litter bins and back entrances to shops. The prettily decorated Valentine Lamp in Catherine Street, the town's only remaining gas street lamp was the result of a one man's enthusiasm. It is lit with great ceremony and celebration every Valentine's day. The fine mural of the history of Frome in the Westway precinct is sadly missing – it was unexpectedly painted over when the precinct was refurbished.

An earlier sympathetic Town Council in the 1990's provided a set of outdoor boards for graffiti artists in the town and for a time even various shops sported newly commissioned works on their metal window shutters.

The Saxonvale Planning Brief gives a further opportunity for art in the proposed un-square-shaped new "town square."

Mendip District Council's list of Section 106 agreements and commuted sums 1997-2008 for Frome

Area of Frome	Type of development providing money	Amount available in £s	To be spent on
Section 106 agreements			
Wessex Fields	supermarket	10,000	Unknown
Singers site	136 dwellings and four shops	20,000	Offsite skateboard park and sound insulation for the Cheese and Grain community building
Vallis Road	housing	55,170	Off-site play area
Coloroll /Elworthy Park site	housing	30,000	Station spur upgrade road to Railway Station
Showfield site	hospital	128,400	On-site footpath, lights, bins, seats and play area
Naishes Street	12 apartments	10,560	Off-site play space
Portway	23 houses	24,230.50	unknown
Commuted Sums			
Rosedale Walk	houses	5,313.96	unknown
Horton Street	unknown	4,000	unknown
Brunel Way	houses	30,470.50	unknown

In the Countryside

There is a confusing raft of terms, designations, organisations with attendant acronyms all intending to protect the rural character of the countryside, from wetlands to rolling downland, mountains to deeply hedged country lanes, celebrated, iconic and quintessentially British and recognisably home. It is suggested around 45% of the countryside is covered by some sort of national designation. The following are some of the more commonly encountered terms:

Green Belt

Green Belt – generally sparsely populated farmland on the edge of some large towns, and probably the most familiar term in Planning. Green Belt is not as widespread or as powerful as most people think however, the land is protected by normal Planning controls and against "inappropriate development." This does not mean nothing can change, but new uses of existing premises or additional development is rigorously scrutinised to see if the benefits outweigh the harm. Seen as repeatedly under threat, indeed there have been calls to replace it with green wedges and corridors in order to provide more land for housing; the Green Belt has enthusiastic public backing headed up by the Campaign to Protect Rural England (CPRE).

Green Belt Aims:
- to protect the countryside from urban sprawl and ribbon development and prevent towns from merging together;
- to provide open space and recreational opportunities and enhance the landscape;

- to encourage new developments to locate and regenerate sites within towns and cities and protect a town's country setting and historic character.

There are 14 green belt areas in England encircling the major cities: covering 13% of the land area of England (2009), (there is one in Wales, 6 in Scotland and 30 in Northern Ireland). The first green belts established were around London, Birmingham and Sheffield in the 1930's. By 1955 Government was asking local authorities to define areas as Green Belt. The preservation of "openness" is the main criteria, challenged by the recent push for renewable energy projects these are thought inappropriate but not impossible. The National Planning Policy Framework suggests new Green Belts for new towns and suggests new Local Green Spaces are written into Neighbourhood Plans. Offering protection to small special areas of beauty, wildlife, history, tranquillity or even just a playing field as long as it is "special and significant to the community."

Greenfield Site
Land which has not been developed and has probably been used for agriculture.

Brownfield site
Garden Land
Homeowners with more than 0.5 hectares (1.25 acres), may pay capital gains tax, of up to 40% of the sale price, even if only a portion of garden is sold. Generally garden land sold before a house is not taxed but could be payable if fenced off for development at the time of sale.

Land which has had a previous use most probably industrial, either in the town or the countryside - not including agricultural, forestry land or buildings. The 1997 Government wanted Brownfield sites to be redeveloped before Greenfield setting a target of 60% of all new development to be on Brownfield sites from 2007. The cost of demolishing redundant buildings, coupled with often very severe land contamination problems from, for example heavy metals, is complex and has to be dealt with before any development can take place. Decontamination is expensive and the responsibility of the landowner who may wait until land values have risen sufficiently before putting land forward for re-development. In 2000 the Government controversially included gardens as Brownfield sites this increased the number of houses built on gardens from 1 in 10 to 1 in 4 by 2008. The 2010 Coalition Government reversed this but not before many large single houses in large gardens had either been demolished or had had small houses squeezed onto them.

National Parks

Costs
Cost to the taxpayer per person per year (Mendip AONB 2010)
AONBs   18p
National Parks 80p
The Queen   60p

There are 15 areas designated National Parks in the United Kingdom. They cover areas of beautiful countryside, rich in wildlife and include towns and villages within their boundaries. Owned by the people who live there - the Park Authorities own very little.
The Parks are managed by Members made up of local Parish Councils, who produce five year management plans.

Specialists are employed such as rangers, planners, and educational staff backed by volunteers who are involved in practical activities such as: leading walks, dry stone walling or surveying wildlife.

Each Park Authority makes the decisions on all Planning applications within their area. The first National Parks, the Peak District, the Lake District, Snowdonia and Dartmoor were designated in 1951, the newest, the South Downs in 2010. Funding is from central Government.

Areas of Outstanding Natural Beauty (AONB)

Similar to National Parks, again owned by the people who live in them, these are also landscapes with a distinctive character and beauty, rich in wildlife and history and again include villages and towns. AONBs main purpose is to conserve their beauty. Managed by advisory committees of Partnership Panels; made up of their local authorities and countryside organisations overseeing a management plan based around discussion forums. They do not make decisions on Planning applications although they are consulted.

A small paid staff is funded from Natural England - who designates them, DEFRA and their local authorities. Again there are volunteering opportunities such as: dry stone walling, species surveys and path patrols.

There are 51 AONBs in England, Wales and Northern Ireland the first was the Gower Peninsular in South Wales in 1956. Scotland has its own areas called National Scenic Areas, there are 40.

...Frome Watch...

Mendip ANOB

Frome is at the eastern end of the Mendip Hills, an area which is still actively quarried. Despite having its own share of interesting landscapes and charming villages the Mendip AONB only covers the western half of the range, There have been attempts to extend the AONB with the eastern Mendips making tentative noises to be included.

The Mendip AONB Partnership, as does any quasi government organisation, offers grants. Its Sustainable Development Fund donated £65,000 in 2010 to 17 projects from: tourist leaflets, owl surveys, education packs, village hall solar panels, and fencing to the Parishes and organisations within its area.

Sites of Special Scientific Interest (SSSI)

These are some of the country's very best wildlife habitats chosen for their animals, plants or geological rarity. These Sites, which are often small, give protection to very fragile environments or even to a single species. There are over 4,000 SSSIs (127 in Somerset) covering around 7% of the country's land area.

... Frome Watch...

Frome SSSI

Frome's nearest SSSI is the town edge Vallis Vale, a deep valley of ancient woodland following the Mells stream. A habitat for crayfish, kingfishers, dippers, kestrels and bats. It was "the" place to be seen to stroll or picnic in the 1800's and the subject of "picturesque" watercolour paintings. Still popular today with rock climbers, small children and dogs. It has the few remaining intact lime kilns in the area.

Enthusiastic landowners can nominate their own land putting together a management plan with the Government's conservation body, which in England is, Natural England. It reports on, monitors and advises on how best to protect these fragile areas.

Although ostensibly protected from development this has not stopped the destruction of many by new roads, or housing as they are considered to have a nil monetary value. However, public outcry in some instances has led the threatened species to be moved to a new site!

Special Area of Conservation (SAC)

The international importance of the majority of SSSI's has given them European recognition and included for special protection under the European Union's Habitats Directive listing of Special Areas of Conservation. Each EU Member State compiled a list of its most important wildlife areas, part of global efforts to conserve the world's biodiversity, giving protection to a variety of wild animals, plants and habitats.

Local Nature Reserves

From ancient woodlands, flower rich meadows, coastal headlands these are areas which give locals the opportunity to learn, study, research or enjoy whilst conserving what is special. Principal local authorities can lease, buy or just form an agreement with a landowner and can delegate this to their Parishes (there are 1,500 in England, 41 in Somerset).

Horses

Horses are not considered agricultural unless they are to be eaten or are living wild but are instead a leisure pursuit. Surprisingly controversial even in the countryside as fields are sub-divided into small paddocks by copious amounts of wooden fencing. Stabling and the use of stripped jumping poles criticised as unnatural intrusions in the countryside. Thwarted horse owners unable to get permission for stabling may take revenge on neighbours by selling land on for unfriendly occupations.

Footpaths - yellow waymarkers

The whole of the UK has an extraordinary network of paths (Scotland has a tradition of unhindered access to open countryside).These are centuries old routes taking workers to their fields, factories, churches, mines, markets, as well as to the next village. Fiercely protected by walkers and local groups of the Ramblers Association, paths have been kept open against the encroachment of brambles and scrub, unfriendly landowners, ploughing and unpredictable livestock. Familiarly way-marked by finger posts in towns and countryside, they are supplemented by coloured plastic arrows or more cryptically by spots of coloured paint on field fence posts and styles. Footpaths are for travellers on foot only.

County and Unitary Highways Authorities duties

Are to:

- Maintain for inspection "the definitive map" which shows all public Rights of Way in their area;
- Signpost and way mark paths - often with the help of individuals and voluntary groups;
- Maintain the paths, but not the styles, gates and bridges, this is still, perhaps unexpectedly, the responsibility of the landowner, who can recover 25% of the cost from the Highway authority.

Alternatively if local groups and landowners, provide a workforce the Highway authority will provide the styles and gates in kit form for installation. The Highway authority can as a last resort, after giving a landowner 14 days notice, undertake the work and charge the landowner accordingly.

Many Parishes appoint volunteers to report on the conditions of paths in their area. Rights of Way have to be kept open all year round;

- Establish a Local Access Forum (a statutory body) of volunteers which discusses supports and influences what the Highway authority does.

"Beating the Bounds" is an annual church walk which follows the Parish boundary of each Parish church, many footpaths follow these old boundaries. Traditionally, before maps, children were beaten all the way round to help them remember where the boundaries lay with prayers held at certain points.

Ordnance Survey maps are most commonly used reference source but can be out of date if paths have been stopped, created or diverted by the Planning authority often because of new housing, industrial development or a film celebrity has bought a house near a route. The Highways authority can also divert or extinguish a path for specific reasons such as protecting an SSSI. The public and the Parish Council can object to any planned changes.

Somerset Local Access Forum

The Forum (there is one for each county or Unitary authority) looks for volunteers among users, landowners and those with tourist, health and educational interests. The 16 strong Forum includes 2 Councillors and meets twice a year. The public have a 2 minute slot for questions. Appointments are for 3 years. There are no minutes of meetings or the statutory Annual Report filed (2012). It helps define the County's Rights of Way policies.

Government estimates 10% of Public paths are unrecorded. These historic Rights of Way were mistakenly left off when the first definitive maps were created in the 1950's. But, there is an opportunity until January 1st 2026 to map those missing from the list, although this deadline looks likely to be extended. Groups of enthusiasts including Parish Councils can collect and submit evidence; it is a lengthy and expensive process (£4,000-£10,000). If designated the new path is the responsibility of the submitting group or Parish. County and Unitary authorities do have compulsory powers to create footpaths and bridleways compensating the landowner, or by coming to a written agreement. The Coalition Government however is funding a new grant scheme" Paths for Communities", to encourage new paths and an improved network to boost tourism and rural businesses.

Recording missing paths
Using:

- Documentary, evidence from a range of sources including old maps and tithe awards, aerial photographs, books and Council records.
- Usage, 20 years of uninterrupted use along a linear route - at least six witnesses will be needed.
- Common Law, where less than 20 years of use or where crossing Crown Land. This is dependent on evidence of the amount and frequency of use and toleration by the landowner.

Footpath problems
Minimum widths:
- Cross field paths are set at 1 metre with bridleways at 2 metres
- Field edge paths are set at 1.5 metres with bridleways at 3 metres
- Carriageways are 3 metres wide

Densely overgrown footpaths, or footpaths blocked with bits of rusting junk, with rickety styles or strands of barbed wire strung across them, or anything that deters such as a lone bull in a field, should be reported to the principal authorities' (County or Unitary) Rights of Way Officer who has a duty to remove the blockage and can fine the person responsible. The public can force a reluctant authority to act by applying for an order via the Magistrates Court. Newly ploughed paths and bridleways should be reinstated within 14 days (with 24 hours allowed for each subsequent disturbance) with the line marked and the surface flattened to the minimum width. Growing crops, such as maize at its full height, must not encroach to cause inconvenience to users. The Highway authority can do the work and charge the landowner. Anyone, including Parish Councils can bring a prosecution through the Magistrates Court for failure to make good the surface and mark the line, the maximum fine is £1,000.

...Frome Watch...

Wild Boar

Sightings (June 2011) of up to a dozen or so wild boar - of unknown origin, closed a bridleway on the town's outskirts as Somerset County investigated complaints by walkers and horse riders of sudden confrontations in the local woods. The boar who cunningly hid themselves amongst grazing cattle to avoid detection, even eating their cow-cake, have been shot by worried landowners and the meat sold at the local market.

Other Rights of Ways:
- Bridleways - blue waymarkers

For travellers on foot or with a horse and are marked on the Definitive Map.
- Byways Open to All Traffic (BOAT) – red waymarkers

For walkers, horse riders and cyclists. Motorised vehicles can use them, though they are generally inaccessible to the ordinary car, these are not unclassified roads and are marked on the Definitive Map.
- Restricted Byways – plum waymarkers

Used by walkers, horse riders, including horse drawn carriages, and cyclists, but not motorised vehicles such as cars or bikes. Up until 2006 and previously known as Roads Used as Public Paths (RUPP), motorised vehicles could be used. These are marked on the Definitive Map.
- Permissive Paths

Landowners can allow walkers, horse riders or cyclists use of a path over which there is no public right of access. These paths may be closed for a token one day a year against a claim of continuous public access which could turn the path into a statutory Right of Way via a Planning application.
- The Right to Roam or Open Access Land – brown Access symbol

This gave walkers additional rights over uncultivated land such as mountain, moor, heath, downland and registered common land, under the Countryside and Rights of Way Act 2000 (CROW), these areas may be closed by landowners for 28 days each year.

CROW was extended in the Marine and Coastal Access Act 2009 which hopes to create a new round-England coastal path 4 metres wide with an additional "spreading area", increasing public access over the next ten years from around a disputed 50%, - Natural England's website (countryside organisations say it is nearer 80%), it is at present. In 2012 the 870 mile footpath round the Welsh coast was opened.

...Frome Watch...

Village Greens

Of Mendip's 62 Parishes 7 have registered Village Greens. In 2011 worried members of Frome Recreation and Open Grounds Supporters (FROGS) applied for registration of the Frome Cheese Showfield which was leased to Mendip District Council as an open space.

Popular with walkers, kite flyers and children it is the home of the Frome Cricket Club and the newly built Frome Collegians football pitch.

FROGS pointed out that ten acres had recently been sold to provide a hospital and new health centre, with more land disappearing than was initially anticipated as the health centre re-jigged its position and increased its land take. It had been allocated a site behind the hospital but was able to grab the moral high ground and got its way to move to the front of the newly completed hospital. Destroying the Showfield's sense of openness and grassy views carefully preserved through long years of public consultation, cutting through the newly planted landscaping of trees, and plonking itself on the edge of the cricket pitch opening up the possibilities of long running battles in years to come. The town was exasperated.

There had been plans in the past for a supermarket and rumours of housing, indeed Mendip's own research inadvertently showed it to be the most favoured spot in the town for development. The Showfield owners - The Frome and District Agricultural Society, felt the application for village green registration showed a lack of trust in their goodwill and guardianship of over a century, the Collegians were concerned they would not be able to add facilities - such as changing rooms in years to come as Registration overrides any Planning permission. The Town Council itself decided not to support the application even though FROGS had amended its application to exclude the health centre site – which would have jeopardised construction which had already started to take place.

Village and Town Greens

An essential of country living conjuring up thoughts of long hazy summer afternoons of cricket matches and village fêtes under the shade of ancient trees, a place which through the passage of time local people have played games and sports, held picnics and fêtes, and walked dogs. There are around 3,650 in England, in about a third of all Parishes - many owned by Parish Councils. There are just 220 in Wales.

Anyone can register any area of land as a Green including perhaps surprisingly tidal beaches. Registration was free to the applicant including landowners who can register voluntarily through their County or Unitary authority in England but it was little used until the late 1990s. Applications now run at around 200 a year.

A Green is land which by custom has been used for sports and pastimes from dog walking to children playing, "as of right without permission, force or secrecy," uninterrupted for 20 years. There was 2 years grace (reduced to one year in 2013) if usage has been ended by the landowner. Evidence is based on witness statements, photographs and descriptions of activities.

Once registered, the application is advertised and if there are objections, a Hearing is arranged to sift through the evidence. Time-scales can be uncertain, often running into years, with particularly controversial cases ending up in the High Court. Once registered, a Green is protected.

Many communities have felt betrayed especially if Council owned, open space has been sold for development into housing or supermarkets.

But, the Government sees Green applications being used as a stick to stop the development of important local services listing schools or health centres; whereas more often the controversy is about profiteering from housing or supermarkets. Buildings started after a Green application date have been in danger of demolition if the Green designation was successful. A Government consultation (2011) modified the rules in 2013, applications will be charged for and Green applications will not be allowed if Planning permission has already been sought.

Common Land
Open, unfenced and now frequently remote they are a remnant of the mediaeval farming open field system.
Essential to the livelihood of every Parish they gave the people rights to:

- graze sheep or cattle (herbage)
- take peat or turf (turbury)
- take fallen wood, gorse or furze by hook or by crook (estovers)
- take fish (piscary)
- allow pigs to forage for acorns or beechmast (pannage)

It was from Common land enclosure that the need for allotments grew. These unimproved pastures contain a wealth of wildlife and archaeology (covering around 4% of England and Wales). Today some 7,000 remain, with the largest in the Lake District, the "Right to Roam" confirmed general public access. There also remains 24,000 Commoners whose deeds state their retention of rights over the Commons. The 6 Commons in Mendip, listed on the national register are quite small, only two are grazed. Scotland has its own system with 33,000 crofters sharing and working land in common.

Gypsies and Travellers
It was novelist Barbara Cartland who, whilst a Conservative County Councillor on Hertfordshire County Council (1955-64), campaigned for gypsy children to have the right to attend local schools and for gypsies to have a permanent place to live which helped drive changes in the law requiring local authorities to provide camp sites. Hertfordshire led the way by setting up 14 camps and other authorities followed; Barbara Cartland gave part of her country estate to provide a camp - Barbaraville which opened in 1964 and still runs today.

Every Planning authority researched and was expected to provide permanent camp sites. If there were insufficient, gypsies frequently bought their own land providing for themselves bypassing the usual Planning procedures. Otherwise living in isolated spots, on scraps of fields, wasteland and verges with room for ponies.

The 1997 Labour Government guidance had suggested Councils should not take enforcement action against unauthorised traveller sites applying Planning rules depending on an individual's background.

Changes by the 2010 Coalition Government attempted to stop the use of retrospective permissions on unauthorised sites by providing £60 million of funding for new sites. However, Government statistics stated there were 2,200 gypsy and traveller caravans on unauthorised developments in 2011.

...Frome Watch...

Travellers in Frome

Ad hoc Traveller camp sites are a summer problem especially on the Showfield.

Wide verges, green spaces and field gates in and around the town have massive boulders strategically placed to prevent camping. However, verges and tree planted highway land still provide grazing to collections of piebald and skewbald ponies.

And Finally......

The Annual Parish Meeting

The Annual Parish Meeting is *the* opportunity for all the registered electors of the Parish to meet, discuss, make comments and suggestions on the Council's previous year's activities. Current issues, future proposals or anything can be discussed, resolutions proposed and voted on giving a useful measure of accountability. Non electors can watch but not take part.

There are a few rules: the meeting takes place between the 1st March and the 1st June, not earlier than 6'oclock in the evening or on premises where alcohol is sold and if a schoolroom is chosen there is no charge. Meetings generally last a couple of hours.

This is not a Council meeting. It is the only opportunity electors have to run an agenda, to take part in round table discussions and to put any resulting resolutions to the Parish Council.

Councillors do not have to attend, but as electors themselves, they may raise questions and make comments. But, as the purpose of the meeting is to enable the ordinary elector to have a say, Councillors should not be allowed to dominate the meeting.

The Parish Chairman or Vice Chairman chairs the meeting but if not present the meeting can elect from amongst the electors present. The Chairman gives a brief end of year report summarising completed, on-going and future Council projects.

Questions can be asked on the night, even though it is all too easy for Councils to scupper a discussion and not answer a question properly by claiming lack of warning. An offer at the very least should be made to answer in writing and to follow up information reporting back to both the individual and the Council. Many Councils prefer questions, which are generally answered by the Chairman, a designated Councillor, or the Parish Clerk, in advance so an answer can be prepared.

Sparsely attended meetings make awkward stilted affairs and the frequently chosen lecture theatre style seating layout will feel confrontational, signing a register adds an unexpected layer of formality to an atmosphere which is already "them and us" with the voting public at a distinct disadvantage.

NALC suggests persuading local groups perhaps those who receive Parish grants or popular organisations such as the Women's Institute or the local Drama club to put on exhibitions or even give presentations at the meeting's start.

Using this as an opportunity to celebrate local activities with a glass of wine and canapés. This will get more people along as at the very least someone has to staff the stalls and will therefore provide an audience. However, it does move the meeting a considerable ways from its central purpose which is holding the Council to account with the discussion of local issues by local people.

Resolutions and Decisions

Electors can discuss, frame a resolution and ask for a vote on any issue.

Ten electors are needed to support a resolution which is decided by the vote of the majority. Resolutions do not bind the Parish Council to any action unless more allotments are voted for, then the Council has a duty to provide them. Resolutions are taken to the next Full Council meeting for discussion and decision. The meeting can call for a Parish Poll.

What is a Parish Poll?

The Parish Poll (from the Parish and Community Meetings (Polls) Rules, 1987) gives all local electors an opportunity to give an opinion on a specific subject either by giving an answer to a specific question or the appointment to any office

The Parish Clerk only takes the minutes if his/hers predecessors have. Otherwise the minutes can be taken by the Chairman or an elector. The minutes are signed annually although it will be impossible to agree on accuracy with the passage of time particularly as the same people may not be present. The press can attend as it can at all public meetings.

Other Meetings of the Parish

In England Parish meetings can be demanded in other ways: by the Chairman of the Parish Council or the Parish Meeting (those Parishes which are too small for a Council), or any two Parish Councillors, or a District Councillor, or any 6 local government electors at any time, but these are rarely used.

...Frome Watch...

The Frome Annual Town Meeting

The Annual Town meeting is heralded as the electorates' opportunity to hold Councillors to account. It was held with great trepidation in the past by Councils not knowing what would be asked and knowing the one or two usual suspects would turn up and ask the same question each year. It was something many Councillors avoided. The Mayor read out a brief round-up of the previous year and a general steer for the coming year. The register for the electorate to sign was solemnly circulated; questions from the floor taken and after a general discussion promises made to chase up queries and report to the next Full Council. Few townspeople turned out, but then most would not have known it was on.

By 2007 changes had begun, in the previous year's meeting the old Council had met with heavy criticism as it attempted to explain a large precept rise going into some detail to an increasingly hostile audience - this would be the last time. Future meetings would now be tightly controlled. Written questions were preferred – these are usually very few and questions on the night fielded with an exasperated air often with the excuse that time would be needed to prepare a proper answer, discussions never quite get going. Questioners were now time limited as the Council put on a show.

The town's groups and societies - some had been given town money so felt obliged to go, were invited to put on exhibitions of their enthusiasms and activities; this at least provided an audience and gave new visitors an extra interest, wine and nibbles added a casual, celebratory air. PowerPoint became the vehicle of choice as the audience settled and the "top table" took turns to run through well-honed speeches, an hour or so later few townspeople could think of a question, light relief only provided by occasional equipment failure. This was not the examination or challenging of Councillor policies or the airing of town issues of old.

The criticisms of 2006 followed on into 2007 as further attempts were made to get explanations and a discussion on spending going, the precept had risen by 29% but, as the townspeople knew, this was only the price of a loaf of bread as the Council attempted an explanation suggesting it was just 56 pence per resident per week. Indeed the Mayor criticised the turnout - 15 residents, as typical of "voter apathy." Assurances that the extra was being saved in Reserves, to fund new offices at a future point plus employ two extra staff met with puzzled protests, particularly as there did not seem to be an itemised spending plan just rough guess work budgetary figures. The Council's higher precept was, the townspeople were told, *"so we don't get caught with our pants down."* Opposition continued but discussion was curtailed, without creditable answers. But, enough was enough and the Mayor told protesters to write in so the meeting could press on with presentations from two of the town's voluntary groups.

The next Council was more careful, repeating what had already been said in its newsletters and the written Annual Reports. Covering the mundane day to day concerns of the 3 Committees: Planning - mainly Planning applications and various bin deployments; Policy & Finance with its grants, Christmas festivities and Twinning; Recreation & Properties with its oversight of the parks, grassy areas and play equipment upkeep and repair, with the park refurbishment a constant reminder each year.

No attempt made to equate this year's budget with past years, no explanation of what the river project was, or the ins and outs of outside hanging basket watering, or who contributed to the town design statement bearing in mind the extensive electorate involvement the surrounding Parishes had undertaken in producing theirs, or even why whole budget columns remained unspent or considerably underspent. But always ending the meeting as it always did with a slightly ominous final warning, that only the Council could provide for the town.

The end of an electoral cycle - May 2011
In this, the last year of the electoral cycle the outgoing Mayor's final report sums up the Council's achievements. Four years and £3.35 million later, which includes an extra £833,000 to spend as the controversial 2006 rise carries through, it can be said little has changed. The precept (budgeted at around £915,000 in its final year) is, the town is told, a response to demands for a high level of service by a densely populated (25,000) and rapidly growing town (around 600 extra houses), providing what is popular and important.

Highlighting:
- The £100,000 (actually nearer £116,000) given to 28 community groups, the police, CCTV, school crossing patrols and the Cheese and Grain - "a great resource and something rather special."
- The Christmas Lights and Christmas Spectacular success;
- The (unexpected) purchase of 3 pieces of land - vital for a densely populated town as a green riverside lung with consultations in the offing to ask the townspeople what they want from the sites;

- Maintenance as the Rodden Meadow brambles are cut back and 12 new trees are bought and planted along with wild flowers. The replanting of Château Gontier Walk and at Welshmill, the woodland is thinned;
- Money, as £59,475 is still awaited part of a Section106 agreement from the building of 70 houses on the Slipps Nursery site and allocated to Mary Bailey Playing Field;
- The Tourist Information Centre now run by the Council as Mendip funding ended (it in fact only decreased). Now in its new home at the town library, the footfall had increased to a spectacular 200,000 from 20,000;
- The 260 planning applications discussed in which in 81% of cases Mendip was in accord with Frome's opinions, with 12% against! The beginnings of a town design statement - encouraging high quality design, preserving local character in new developments to eventually link into the Local Development Framework to which the Council had also sent a brief opinion;
- The 5 dog poo bins, 7 litter and 23 grit bins deployed with a further 20 waiting in the wings;
- The request to English Heritage to list an extra 55 Cockey lamps (Nov 2010, later withdrawn);
- The 150 town events the Mayor and Deputy Mayor attended and the startling success of the Mayor's facebook page with its 2,600 followers and the Mayor's fund-raising for the Air Ambulance.

But ending with the by now familiar final stern warning, with no Town Council none of the above would have been possible and "a gap" would exist. And it is the Council and only the Council that, "can fill the gap" other groups could step in, but they would not be answerable to all the people of Frome. The Mayor raises the question what value does a precepting Council bring? The activities it lists are to a degree or were certainly in the recent past wholly covered by local groups and societies.

The Parish Poll
Parish Polls are referendums and are an additional opportunity for local electors to express an opinion on a specific subject. A Poll can be demanded at any Parish meeting, if the meeting Chairman agrees or by 10 electors or one-third of those present, whichever is smaller, in effect one elector can demand a Poll. The meeting Chairman notifies the Returning Officer (at District /Unitary) who organises it.

A Poll can be on any issue including the appointment to an Office. The request for a Poll is not voted on but the wording of the question is. The resolution proposed at the Parish meeting is reproduced as a question on the ballot paper and is phrased so a YES or a NO is the only answer that can be given; for example;

"Do you agree to F...... Parish Council obtaining a Public Works Loan of up to One Hundred and Fifty Thousand Pounds to assist in funding new Council premises for F...."

Key Features
More than one question can be asked if needed:
- A Parish Poll cannot be combined with any other type of election;
- There are no polling cards, or postal votes or votes by proxy for Parish Polls. This means that electors who want to vote need to do so in person at the Polling Station. The votes are counted immediately afterwards;
- The polling time is short between 4pm and 9pm;
- The expenses are paid by the Parish Council or Parish Meeting and the Council should have the powers to deal with the subject of the question and consequently the decision;

- The Parish meeting proposal is copied as the question on the ballot paper and it should be possible to give a YES or NO answer;
- The result is not binding on the Parish or the District /Unitary authority but Councillors do have a gauge of local opinion before taking a decision;
- The day for the ballot is fixed by the Returning Officer between 14 and 25 days (inclusive) after the day on which the Poll was demanded;
- A Notice informing the electorate about the Poll is posted at least 5 days before the Poll, which gives little time to organise support;
- Turnouts are much lower than for local elections, perhaps because they are little understood or as a voter commented *"they will do what suits them anyway so what is the point."*

Local Polls

In Shepton Mallet, Frome's sister town, a Planning application by the supermarket chain Tesco on a site next to the town's Cenotaph cast an uncertain future over it with suggestions that it should be moved from its commanding position at the top of the High Street.

The monument unveiled on Armistice Day 1920, mirrored the design of The Cenotaph in Whitehall London, and bears the names of the 200 local people who died fighting for their country during the First and Second World Wars.

A Parish Poll was called in October 2005 with the question;
"Do you want the War Memorial (Cenotaph) moved?"
From a population of less than 10,000 the vote was: Yes 204, No 388.
A protest camp which hoped to protect dozens of trees close to the Memorial failed and they were felled to make way for the Tesco shopping development. However, the subsequent Section106 agreement provided around £57,000 for a landscaped area with paving, seating and planting around the Cenotaph and was completed in 2010. Now a charity, it is maintained by the Town Council and "Friends of the Cenotaph" who regularly lay fresh flowers. Recent Grade II listing has given the monument added protection.
The cost of the Parish Poll was around £2,200.

Perhaps the success of the first poll tempted Shepton Mallet to try again.
This time with:
"Do you want Shepton Mallet Town Council to build a new civic centre/community rooms in Shepton Mallet by using the Town Council's reserves and raising loans over the next 20-25 years?"
Councillors had laid ambitious plans for a new public building encompassing a "town hall" for offices and meetings, weddings and a café to spark a town centre revival – although it was not to be built in the old town centre marketplace but nearer to the new Tesco town centre. Shepton had ironically been the focus of a television series plotting the changing fortunes and decline of the shopping High Street and the rise of the supermarkets.

The Town Council's own working party had spent 9 months without arriving at a conclusion although it was rumoured, many Councillors supported the scheme because of party loyalty whilst assuming nothing would happen. An anti-campaign of worried citizens was keen to knock the idea on the head even offering to pay half the costs of the Parish Poll. Concerns over the possibility of spending £1.5 million with a possible repayment time of up to 50 years were not without foundation.

Shepton had been given a choice back in the 1970's when another attempt to revitalise the town centre was on the drawing board. A choice between a row of colonnaded shops in a Georgian style or more modern boxy style of glass and concrete common at the time.

Shepton chose the modern look and the town's kindly benefactor (from the Showering family - of Babycham fame) added a community building to be the centrepiece of civic and cultural life aiming to do – what the new scheme was promising, to revitalise the High Street. Built in a Brutalist style it continues to loom in the corner of the town's marketplace overshadowing the charming mediaeval church. It was a financial disaster as Mendip District which took on the running of the building constantly juggled with poorly drawn up leases, high running costs, growing debts, long closures, and constant refurbishments until eventually selling it off.

So in November 2011 Shepton Mallet went to the polls to consider what was already an emotionally fraught question. Many Councillors thought the referendum too soon explaining it should wait for the Working Party report. With a lower turnout than for the Cenotaph Poll (just 488 voted or 6.48%), of the votes cast 50 were for the motion with 438 against firmly rejecting the plan.

Whilst some Councillors argued the low turnout invalidated the result, forgetting many of them were voted in by a similar number of voters. Still without the Working Party Report the Council voted £15,000 for a feasibility study, an extraordinary sum for a normally modest low spending Council. The cost of the Poll at £2,275.50p was irksome and remembering a townsperson speaking out and pledging part payment at the Public Meeting which first called for a Poll, the Council decided to pursue the possibility of passing on some of the cost.

The windswept upland village of Priddy, its scattered homes set in a landscape of Neolithic monuments surrounds a village green on the top of the Mendip Hills. Famed for its annual sheep fayre and pub food it was posed a simpler question:
"Are you in favour of establishing a 30mph limit with legally required signage in the village of Priddy?"
With 35 for and 160 against, the proposal was lost but with an extraordinary 38% turnout. The cost was £607.

Datafile

Urban Forum, www.urbanforum.org.uk
Planning Aid, www.planningaid.rtpi.org.uk
Department of Communities and Local Government, www.gov.uk
Planning Inspectorate, www.planning-inspectorate.gov.uk
Frome Society for Local Study,www.fsls.org.uk
Images of England, www.imagesofengland.org.uk
Somerset Historic Environment Record, www.somerset.gov.uk/her
Conservation Area Appraisals, Mendip District Council (Shepton Mallet, Frome, Street), www.mendip.gov.uk
Historic Towns Forum, www.historictownsforum.org.uk
Somerset Urban Archaeological Survey, www.somerset.gov.uk
English Heritage, www.english-heritage.org.uk
Planning Portal www.planningportal.gov.uk

Local Authority Building Control, www.labc.uk.com
Locality, www.locality.org.uk
Heritage Lottery Fund, www.hlf.org.uk
National Parks, www.Nationalparks.gov.uk
Areas of Outstanding Natural Beauty, www.aonb.org.uk
Communities Infrastructure Levy www.communities.gov.uk
Sites of Special Scientific Interest, www.sssi.naturalengland.org.uk
Campaign to Protect Rural England, www.cpre.org.uk
MAGIC, www.magic.gov.uk
Civic Voice, www.civicvoice.org.uk
Ramblers' Association, www.ramblers.org.uk
Open Spaces Society, www.oss.org.uk
Mendip Hills AONB, www.Mendiphillsaonb.org.uk
One Place, www.oneplace.direct.gov.uk
Fix My Street, www.fixmystreet.com
The Tree Register, www.treeregister.org.uk
Natural England, www.naturalengland.org.uk
Commission for Architecture and the Built Environment, www.cabe.org.uk
Directory of Grant Making Trusts published by the Charities Aid Foundation
Our Countryside the Future, November 2000, www.defra.gov.uk
Public Art, People, Projects, Process by Eileen Adams funded by Arts Council of England 1997
The Buildings of England Somerset: North and Bristol by Andrew Foyle and Nikolaus Pevsner 2011
Thinking the C20th century by Tony Judt and Timothy Snyder

ROOF LINES

13 - MONEY - Money

Who has got it and where it goes

Councillors define themselves and their Councils by their spending. Indeed Councillors judge their own value from the scope of their good intentions and ambitions, judging that, *"it is for the people of…"* to be a sufficient justification for any spending and if criticised quickly point out they are volunteers. The electorate can only judge from the results seen.

…Frome Watch…
What does it go on?
Frome electors astonished to realise that the annual precept of over £800,000 hid a higher budgetary figure (£914,879 in 2010-11) and discovering spending in the four year electoral cycle (2007-11) topped £3.35 million; electors could reasonably ask the question, "what did they do with it":

- wages around £1.4 million,
- around £500,000 was given away,
- around £500,000 was added to the Reserves,
- around £250,000 on Park equipment and refurbishment,
- around £200,000 repaid loans,
- around £150,000 used for events such as Christmas,
- leaving roughly £350,000 for general housekeeping.

Without a portfolio of buildings earned income is small, with only occasional small sums from grants.

In small Parishes spending revolves around community halls, playing fields, footpaths, war memorials and perhaps cemeteries. Principal councils may provide some grant funding as do Government initiatives, any lottery opportunities are there primarily to extend and refurbish village halls and playing fields. Small Parishes have become adept at finding grant funding and are naturally disinclined in any case to ask for money via the Council Tax and consequently construct modest budgets. Large Parishes, many with substantial number of buildings providing a steady income from rents, inevitably try to be bolder, employing more staff and competing to offer a wider range of spending choices.

…Frome Watch…
Responsibilities
Frome's main Budget responsibilities are:

- The town office and flat,
- 2 recreation grounds and a meadow. An extra playground, a kick about area and two path were added in 2010,
- Allotments,
- Managing the public conveniences at Merchants Barton (later closed) and the Park,
- Repayment of borrowings,
- From 2010 managing the Tourist Information Centre.

Spending, alongside Planning, is today where any Councillor's influence lies and Government has encouraged them to be bolder in their ambitions, to take on new responsibilities using the opportunities in the newly introduced "Power of Well-Being." Decisions should still be underscored using the "Value for Money" criteria and the three "E"s of: Economy, Efficiency and Effectiveness.

"Well-Being" was replaced by the Coalition Government in 2011 by the "Power of Competence" which extends spending possibilities. Indeed Government assumed asking for more information to be published; two types of audit and a torrent of consultation would act as a brake on any rashness and create a culture of accountability.

The Budget

The Budget is made yearly in advance of the following financial year using comparisons with previous years. Councillors list items they feel obligated to spend on alongside a wish list of projects, using guessed at spending totals to make a Budget, whilst a commentary or explanation would be useful it is not necessarily supplied. Decisions should be a balance between value gained against the liabilities incurred by the action taken. Decided by the ruling group or maybe concocted between the Clerk and the Chairman a Budget can come to Committee or Full Council in its final form, hopefully all Councillors will have had some input but there is often an air of resignation as the "opposition" goes through the motions of a robust interrogation. Whilst some niggles are expressed, debate is discouraged, as the Clerk and Chairman with barely concealed exasperation hurry things on, it will go through on the nod. Proposals, initially trailed in the press as: *"bright new future for," "bold plans announced,"* or *"Parish gets boost,"* are not followed up and what actually happens lays unreported although may hopefully appear in the Parish's Annual End of Year Report.

...Frome Watch...

Earned income

National Association of Local Councils (NALC) estimates that on average, non-precept funding makes up one third of Parish council income. For Frome this would be about £266,000 (2009/10), whereas in effect it was the surprisingly small amount of around £23,000.

With past obligations taking much of the Budget there is a scramble between competing Councillors and Committees for the often small amounts not spoken for. When extra Precept is called for, and to field any criticism, the rise is always compared dismissively to the price of a loaf of bread. However, the percentage rises can be eye watering, but, there is nothing anyone can do.

The new fashion for Action or Strategic Plans - a "to do/wish list," focusing on a range of exciting things for the coming year or years can throw some light on future Budgets and are Councillor reflections of what is important to their community. New Councillors, barely able to define let alone cost their thoughts in election leaflets once elected assume barely rehearsed ideas are now acceptable, affordable and implementable.

Useful Definitions

- Capital Expenditure
  Money spent on buildings or equipment (not a repair). These become assets and have a value which depreciates with time.
- Revenue Expenditure
  Day to day running expenses including the cost of borrowing.
- Earmarked Reserves
  Set amounts of money put aside for a named purpose for spending within a known timescale.
- General Reserves

Where money for day to day running is kept - the precept, plus end of year surpluses, income and a notional set amount for the unexpected.
- Reserves are invested whilst waiting to be spent. (Frome regularly includes proposed items of expenditure which end up in Reserves at the years end).

Parish Council elections create new spending opportunities with perhaps the possibility of changing inherited spending plans or, if enough newly elected Councillors form a majority, a totally fresh approach. However, there is a tendency to feel obligated to follow what previous generations of Councillors have always done, merely adding an annual percentage based on the national inflation rate. Some Councils try to break the mould raising a sum of money before deciding how far it will stretch, however, it is not considered good practice to budget for a surplus, a Council should budget for agreed costed projects. Other Councils somewhat resigned, claim there is nothing to be done or smugly decide they will never raise enough to do anything worthwhile and drift along. Neither is a good approach to budgeting.

Expenditure will balance income with responsible Councils checking, monitoring and discussing progress regularly during meetings against the agreed Budget as the year progresses, monthly is suggested best practice. Larger Parishes may have specific group of Councillors who sample and review decisions however, Councils will vary.

Income
The Budget determines the Parish Precept and this becomes the Council's main source of income; it is listed as a separate item on the Council Tax bill sent to all domestic households. Parishes can look for other sources of funding such as: grants from their District, County or Unitary Council; lottery funding or money from Government initiatives including quasi funding bodies; sponsorship from businesses; or taking on paid responsibilities such as: toilets, highway sign or bus shelter cleaning, grass verge cutting, or pothole and street lighting fault notification. Additional income is most commonly from hiring out the community hall or collecting burial fees and is held in General Reserves.

Reserves
Any savings are kept in Reserves. It is an oddity of accounting that proposed Budgets can contain amounts that are transferred to Earmarked Reserves, to be in effect savings. Whilst money is taken out of General Reserves to reduce the overall impact of the Budget and keep the precept within bounds. This is frequently heralded as a saving in local newspapers. Whilst simultaneously budgeting, by using often wildly guessed at figures, to have a surplus over actual expenditure to be sent to General Reserves.

Earmarked Reserves, sometimes called Rolling or Capital funds are not ring fenced but Parishes will try to avoid spending them on anything else. Money left over at a project's end is added to General Reserves.

General Budget areas may not be wholly or even spent at all, so surpluses again are kept in General Reserves alongside earned income. Overspending can be solved by taking money out of General Reserves or by "vire" between Budget categories, taking money from one area of surplus and putting it into the Budget area with the shortfall, always controversial and results in loud accusations of bad management. A Council by law has to have at least a 3 months spending buffer in Reserves. Curiously Budgets do not have to be published.

The Precept

Council Tax	
Valuation Band	Property value ranges as of 1st April 1991
Band A	Up to £40,000
Band B	£40,000 to £52,000
Band C	£52,000 to £68,000
Band D	£68,000 to £88,000
Band E	£88,000 to £120,000
Band F	£120,000 to £160,000
Band G	£160,000 to £320,000
Band H	£320,000 and over

Historically it was the rates – based on the notional rental value of a property, which funded local Councils. This was replaced in 1989 by the Community Charge popularly known as the Poll Tax. This was a fixed tax per adult resident, so some households with a large number of adults (parents with grown up children at home) were suddenly confronted with a massive bill. This was thought particularly unfair as people in large houses and presumably wealthier would now be paying less. Chaos ensued: people did not register to vote to avoid the tax; those who rented would be gone before the Council caught up with them, large numbers refused to pay, the Magistrates Courts were clogged with prosecutions and there were mass protests across the country culminating in what turned into confrontation with the police in Trafalgar Square and a riot. The Charge was abolished and replaced in 1993 by the Council Tax levied on the capital value of a home.

...Frome Watch...

The Poll Tax

Frome joined the national anti-Poll Tax campaign; organisers were warned their phones would be bugged by the police so each area operated as a separate cell. Public meetings were held and suggestions made to slow down the payment process. The audience which packed into the Memorial Theatre were mainly the elderly and felt this was not what they had fought two world wars for. The police were ever present waiting outside packed into their white vans. Thousands turned out for the marches through the town with rallies and speeches in the Market Place, beacons were lit on hilltops as a mark of solidarity and buses provided for well-wishers giving moral support to non-payers when they appeared in the Magistrates Court in nearby Shepton Mallet – many dragged out payment for years.

Each Parish sends in its Precept request to its District Council/Unitary authority (by the end of January). These may be published under a the handful of spending categories chosen but, as each Parish uses different spending categories detailing their individual Parish Budgets, comparison between Parishes becomes impossible. Equally a Parish may change the names and make-up of its Budget categories each year making comparisons between different years impossible.

But, expect to see the Budget total, Parish income and any money taken from Reserves to balance the Budget – giving the impression of reducing spending, to give the new Precept amount alongside a comparison with the previous year.

...Frome Watch...
Precept comparisons

Frome has historically had the highest precept of all the Mendip Parishes and one of the highest in Somerset.

April 2006 to 2007
Frome Band D - £9.86
Mendip Band D - £130.97

April 2010 to 2011
Frome Band D - £8.61
Mendip Band D - £141.28

12% of houses are Band D with only 9% in the higher Bands above. Any high percentage increase therefore, Councillors say, barely effects anyone.

The Council Tax is locally set based on the price a property would have fetched in 1991 in England, (2003 in Wales). Various authorities such as: Parish, District, County and Unitary Councils, passenger transport, fire, police and national parks authorities can each raise a Precept, and this will be listed as a separate item on the Council Tax bill, collected by the District Council/Unitary authority and funnelled to the precepting body.

The Precept collected by the District/Unitary Council as part of the Council Tax is described in press releases as the cost per band D household. The Valuation Office Agency not the Council carries out the valuations and properties are placed in one of eight Bands, from A to H. The Council Tax on a Band A property will always be one-third of the Council Tax on a Band H property, rising in set proportions through the Bands in between. A bill will therefore depend both on which Band a property is in and the Councils' spending decisions.

Recently homes in Wales have been reviewed and revalued giving an overall rise of around 30%. A similar review was scheduled for England but was shelved (2009) after protests in the press suggested the extent and the intrusive nature of the review including valuing items such as, the addition of double glazing, home improvements, views from windows and the pleasantness of a neighbourhood. The 1991 valuation had been substantially carried out as a drive-by.

Special Expenses Rate and Double Taxation

Some Parishes look after their own playing fields, cemeteries and churchyards. These are funded through their own Parish Precept. Other Parishes rely on their District Council/Unitary authority, to provide them with these services with these in turn spreading the cost over all their Parishes. The result is double taxation, with some taxpayers paying twice and is obviously unfair. This is easily solved by the authorities only charging the Parishes that use their services, a Special Expenses Rate; again listed on the Council Tax bill as a separate item. An alternative is to give the self-funding Parish a concurrent grant.

...Frome Watch...
Special Expenses Rate

Out of the 62 Parishes in Mendip, the District maintains 19 churchyards plus the 3 cemeteries in the main towns as well as some closed churchyards. In only 9 Parishes does Mendip maintain the play areas (2010/11).

In Frome the Special Expenses Rate raised £67,737 in 2010/11 having more than doubled in the course of four years from around £31,923 in 2006/07 when the town's 15 play areas were added to the cost of the town's cemetery. There are no closed churchyards.

Councillors, electioneering (May 2011), were vociferous in their condemnation of the Rate, viewing it as a stealth tax and roundly criticised Mendip although they were part of the administration that set it.

Nearby Stoke St Michael Parish was charged £4,500 annually by Mendip for cutting the grass in the churchyard. The Parish Council successfully found a cheaper alternative halving the cost.

Frome:
The Budgets 2007-2011
Tricky to understand as spending estimates are swamped in details of recharged salaries and overheads, transfers in and out of earmarked and general reserves, along with charges for depreciation as items appear and disappear under unfamiliar headings. When the accounts were first challenged with an additional audit there was a suggestion to provide an explanatory workshop for the electorate, but, this never materialised. Certainly a commentary would be useful or just a more straightforward list.

Budgets rose year on year (45% across the 4 year electoral cycle – see The Profile) followed by their accompanying Precepts, once the mould had been broken in the more optimistic times of 2006/07. With the Budget set, it is a political decision what the Precept will be and much is made of the fact of keeping it "low". Whilst the Precept hovered a shade lower (5%) than the Budget, in the electoral cycle's final year there was an 18% increase. No one seemed to notice this huge rise. Councillor comments concentrated on the Precept remaining roughly the same as the previous year and the town's stoic success when faced with national financial storms.

The Budget is reduced notionally by financing from reserves and income. But in truth by spending less or in some projected areas not at all, all without explanation. Most years have successfully produced a surplus for the Reserves, a startling £434,000 in the first two years, suggesting the Budget has been grossly overestimated and set well above costs.

Income
Little has ever been earned apart from two small contracts: one from Somerset County Council (£4,000) for road sign cleaning and for the reporting and monitoring of potholes etc in the roads and for a time from Mendip District Council (£120) for footpath weed spraying.

Most income is from rentals: in the Park, (at its height around £2,200) from the tennis courts, with a little from the putting and bowling greens; and a steady sum from the flat (around £4,000) over the town offices. In the early years there was bank interest on the town's Reserves or savings but this reduced (to around £5,232) as the banks recapitalised their balance sheets in the financial crisis. Mendip gave grants over many years for the Christmas Lights, (£12,500) from Section106 agreement money or as part of town regeneration. Frome's Chamber of Commerce also made modest contributions (around £700 annually). The Tourist Information has latterly provided an annual income (around £24,000) including grant aid (£10,000) from Mendip, the new Park café may provide a small contribution in future years. With income from Allotment rentals (£300 annually), Hanging basket sponsorship (£229) and Christmas Spectacular income (£1,015) even a grant from Mendip in Bloom (£800) the town pieced together an income of around £46,000 in the electoral cycle's final year (2010/11).

There is also the strange paradox of the Council relying on grant aid brought to it by voluntary groups to fund its ambitions as in the refurbishment of the Welshmill play area where £50,000 of Lottery money was secured by a group of enthusiasts (FROGS) or with Rotary contributing to the Christmas tree.

Reserves

General Reserves.

High General Reserves resulted from over estimating costs and a constantly high Budget which in turn necessitated and justified a high 3 month buffer.

Earmarked Reserves.

These have been for specific projects, such as new town offices, park play equipment, the new park café, and toilets, they may disappear or appear as they are tidied up or renamed and as this is unminuted there is no way of following. Usually a list appears in the end of year accounts.

In Practice

Ordinarily the Parish Budget is only given a passing glance but the banking crisis in Britain has brought more scrutiny and questions about "value for money" to all areas of local government spending. National problems started in September 2007 with the failure of the Northern Rock Bank (previously a Building Society) with investors queuing for days to retrieve their savings, the Government at first denied there was even a problem. The collapse in America of Lehmann Brothers in October 2008 emphasied the depth of the crisis as Governments around the world shored up their banking systems. In Britain this led to the partial nationalisation of Lloyds and RBS Banks and in Iceland to the collapse of all 3 Icelandic banks, losing many local authorities their investments; Somerset County Council lost £25 million. Frome Town Council in common with most Parishes held its money in current or low interest savings accounts and had no investments.

Parish Council Audits

All Parish Councils regardless of size have to keep account books of payments made and income received with: copies of invoices, receipts of purchases, rents, utility bills, employees pay (but not personal information about staff), grants received and given, outside contracts, cheque books and bank statements, culminating in balance sheets, internal auditor's reports and an annual return all of which can be examined by the councils' tax payers. Much may be on-line as part of the Parish Publication Scheme (see Accountability).

There are two audits an external audit- annually and regular internal audits.

External Audit

All Parish Council accounts end on the 31st March and are approved by Full Council by the end of June when the completed Annual Return is sent to the external auditor. Between these dates local taxpayers have a specific legal right to look at and have copies of all the paperwork, sending written queries or complaints to the external auditor for investigation after first giving their Council the opportunity to explain. Objections should include as much detail and evidence as possible, however the auditor does not encourage trawling though the accounts and minutes looking for issues, this is seen as malicious!

The external auditor, an independent accountant, is appointed by the Audit Commission but paid for by the Parish Council. At one time the accounts were inspected and electors seen in person but visits have been replaced by a 3 page form, with electors expected to write or e-mail.

A Parish advertises 14 days in advance the details of the place, dates and times when the accounts can be inspected, along with the auditor's contact details and how objections can be made.

There are then 20 working days for the electors to go through the paperwork - although few do. Obstruction to viewing the accounts is a finable offence – though in reality unenforceable.

Objections can be made at any time but the auditor will wait to the financial years' end before looking at them in detail. The auditor deals with the process of decision making such as; all expenditure uses the correct piece of legislation, and noting the Council's own procedures are followed such as, three quotes received before any contracts are signed.

Disappointingly for electors the auditor does not comment on policies or projects a Council undertakes because Councils have the ultimate power to decide what to do and the way to do it. Although it will be expected to use its resources: economically, efficiently and effectively. On Budgets below £1 million, "value for money" is not taken into account.

Leaving the auditor to look at spending or income which:
- the Council had no right to spend or receive;
- was spent or received without authority;
- meant the Council's action would result in a loss or deficiency:
- was taken from, or added to, the wrong fund or account; or
- was spent on something that the Council has power to spend money on, but was so unreasonably high that it was unlawful. Although an obvious one for objectors to use auditors are tremendously sympathetic to Councillors even with a qualified full time Clerk.

An elector can request the auditor to take a number of actions:
- to apply to the High Court to confirm that an item in the accounts breaks the law and order a correction;
- to write a Public Interest Report if a Council decision or action has been unsatisfactory but not unlawful this could also result in an Immediate Report or a Recommendation;
- to order a Prohibition Order, stopping expenditure, if decisions will result in a loss or unlawful expenditure;
- or ask the Audit Commission for an Extraordinary Audit- rarely granted.

However, the auditor may decide on a simple exchange of letters, sharing with the objector the Council's responses and any decisions and courses of action that are taken. The auditor makes this decision based on:
- How significant the issue is;
- Whether a wider public interest has been raised;
- The cost of dealing with an objection because it comes out of Parish funds;
- The balance, between the rights of objectors and the rights of the Council.

Public Interest Reports are a good read. There are one or two at Parish level each year and are generally the result of past Councillors complaints over deals on land or buildings. The auditor's investigations can be wide ranging and very thorough: speaking to the objector, past and present Councillors, past and present Clerks, reading the Council minutes, briefing papers, handwritten notes, e-mails, contracts etc.

The resulting Report makes recommendations to remedy the situation and by law it is discussed at a well publicised and public Council meeting. This produces an Action Plan and a summary, and after approval by the auditor it is published in local newspapers.

Councillors and the Council officers are no longer personally liable for any financial losses made and complainants looking for retribution will be disappointed. Recommendations are limited to tightening or redrafting of Council processes or staff retraining, something of a pyrrhic victory.

The Audit Commission stated, *"the external audit is an essential element in the process of accountability for public money and makes an important contribution to the stewardship of public resources and the corporate governance of public approved services."* With the heavy emphasis on the auditing of process at Parish level, but, unable to use "value for money" as a yardstick and with the current self-certification system, accountability is, in effect, minimal. Councillors could be forgiven, and many do, for assuming that their policies are somehow approved by the annual external audit. For a concerned electorate, the Audit Commission can only offer the cold comfort of the ballot box for regime change.

...Frome Watch...

Questions are asked

The unexpectedly huge rise in the 07/08 budget of c£230,000 raised questions in the town. The first the majority of people knew about it was when the District Council's Council Tax demand dropped through letterboxes in the March (07). Although the decision would have been made the previous autumn and the District informed by the January (07).

Questions asking for an explanation, by the Frome Ratepayers Alliance, (FRA) - a small group of electors, at the Annual Town Meeting in the April (07) went unanswered in favour of presentations by the town's voluntary groups. This resulted in extensive correspondence with the external auditor and the Town Council, including an appeal to the local MP, who returned a muted response suggesting double taxation as a possible area of investigation. Councillors dismissed this avenue as preposterous and a sign of someone being "difficult".

What started as a simple request for information was discussed in Council Committees as an unwarranted attack and dismissed by Councillors as vexatious. This led FRA to request an Extraordinary Audit from the Audit Commission in order to clarify how such a high Budget, compared to Frome's sister towns in Mendip was being used. The Council's external auditor gave hints at areas which could be looked into but would not give advice. Indeed it was hinted that putting together too thorough a case would be considered malicious and therefore would not be taken seriously.

Specific issues emerged challenging the legality of some spending areas:
- Was spending undertaken using the correct Parliamentary Acts;
- Could the high running costs of the Council as a whole be labelled as "unreasonable";
- Areas picked out for querying were: outside services, Frome's sister town Shepton Mallet only paid a fifth in running costs in comparison for its park of the same size and provision, and the high cost of central administration.
- Was there the possibility of double taxation, were the townspeople paying for open space maintenance twice, once to Mendip District and again to the Town Council;
- Was the cost of grant aiding the Cheese & Grain too much;
- Were financial decisions made correctly - by barely a handful of Councillors?

- The request was denied – it is rarely granted, and appeals to higher authorities in London met with an indifferent response. But, the external auditor felt there were questions to be answered and by September 2008 he had 5 of his own which disappointingly mainly revolved around process.

Five questions:
- How were the processes behind the spending decisions made;
- What was the *Cheese & Grain* used for and under what legal power;
- Why was there a 78% increase in Reserves and what were the plans to spend Earmarked Reserves;
- What were the Council's plans to move office and
- Why was there a need for increased staffing levels?

The Council's brusque November reply explained, *"only because it had to."* The Budget was agreed by Committee and minuted as such, adding there had been no intention to increase Reserves and staff numbers were unchanged. Plans to move were on hold and the *Cheese and Grain* was a community building.

By April 2009 the auditor concluded the Council had "properly considered" its decisions whilst noting it could not comment on the Council's policies. However, the Council was asked to monitor carefully its Reserves, setting a timescale for spending Earmarked Reserves. Despite horror stories from the Council of the investigation costing tens of thousands of pounds, as Councillors in meeting after meeting indignantly protested at the affront of the complainant and the unnecessary taking up of officer time to answer questions, the auditor's simple exchange of letters cost a more modest but, perhaps a still surprising £2,203.

After two years, the Audit Commission told the Frome Ratepayers Alliance, that in reality, it only considered "value for money" in Parishes with Budgets in excess of £1 million (Frome came in just under the bar at £800,000 to £914,000) and the ballot box was the only resort. The Council felt vindicated but grumbled about the unnecessary fuss.

Internal Audit
Local residents can be asked to check their Parish's internal workings otherwise a commercial firm is appointed. An Internal audit looks at whether the processes and procedures in place are good enough to avoid errors, mistakes or fraud. A culture of care should run through every Parish's dealings, particularly today with the increased emphasis on risk management. The risk being not delivering an expected activity or service; it is common sense to identify what may go wrong, taking steps to avoid the situation or manage the consequences.

...Frome Watch...
What really happens
Frome's day to day service delivery revolves around grass cutting and summer hanging basket management, indeed concerned staff suggested colour co-ordinating the town's public and private hanging baskets and floral displays, Councillors demurred.

Since 2010 the Council has added an additional service, tourist information with leaflets and general town information including a room finding and travel booking service.

Councils can decide on the level and frequency of auditing. The auditor does not check all records or transactions but will sample, following the decision making process through minutes, competitive quotes (at least 3), invoicing and receipts, to VAT, banking and payments and may include budgeting, book keeping, payroll and insurance.

The auditor can suggest how processes are improved, but will not comment on Council decisions. As an addition, Councillors should review the effectiveness of its internal auditing processes, risk management and have oversight of the Parish Clerk and Responsible Finance Officer at least annually. Either with a working party or a committee which does random checks or looks at specific areas of decision making – very much as a Select Committee does in Parliament; as at the end of the day it is Councillors who are accountable.

End of Year Accounts.

New Regulations

In 1996 Audit regulations applied to Parish and Town Councils for the first time. By 2003 Parishes with Budgets over £1/2 million prepared their accounts the same way as District Councils. This threshold was raised to £1 million in 2006 but by this time Frome, in enthusiastic anticipation, was already using the District accounting format, by 2011 the threshold had risen to £6 million and at last Frome dropped out returning to simpler more easily understood statements.

At each financial years end (31st March) Parishes produce several documents which give an insight into what has gone on. These can be explored by the electors of the Parish, in person, for 20 working days before the end of June. And includes: all the invoices and receipts, the accounting books, deeds and contracts, bank statements etc and is an opportunity for electors to ask questions, dispute details but principally to make any objections to the external auditor. If none are made the accounts are then closed, safe from legal challenge though not scrutiny.

Statements of the Accounts

Smaller Parish Councils – those with a Budget of less than £200,000 – can produce receipts and payments accounts or alternatively choose income and expenditure accounts which Councils with Budgets over £200,000 must use. These simply list the amount of money spent and received, mirroring the Budget which was drawn up in the autumn of the previous year. Spending is grouped under the headings or the Budget areas of what the Council does such as parks, toilets, allotments, salaries, Christmas lights etc. Income will come from the Precept, interest on savings, rents and grants received. There is a comparison column with the previous year, ending with a list of the Reserves still held and an end of year balance.

As part of the overall reporting Statement, permanent assets such as buildings, war memorials etc are listed and their value given, other replaceable assets such as office and park equipment are listed with a rate of depreciation in value given which illustrates the life expectancy of the items. Service contracts, leases etc with outside firms are listed and their value given. Deeds and charitable Trust responsibilities which are administered by the Parish are listed and accounted for separately. Transparency is the key.

...Frome Watch...

Annual Financial Statement

A Council confident in its ambitions, assured of its contribution to the town it holds in guardianship, and with lofty aspirations readily adopted the complex District Council format of presenting the comings and goings of the town's money. Anticipating even greater spending and breaching, initially, the £½ million threshold and coming within a hairs breadth of the £1million budget accounting threshold.

The many paged financial statements were presented to January's Full Council, with help from the internal auditor, for approval. The Statement slotted Parish activities into incongruous categories such as: Highways, Roads and Transport, or Environmental Health, at odds with Councils main area of expenditure in play grounds and floral displays and yet this oddly peculiar practice was never questioned or discussed, begging the question did Councillors understand it?

Written in a complexity beloved by accountants the breakdowns were on the whole unhelpful and bogged down in detail whereas a simple statement detailing income and expenditure would have been more open and transparent. It did include a reassuring statement that no member of staff earned more than £50,000 a year which is the only information about wages other than a grand total which was available.

Loans

Since 1990 the Town borrowed for two buildings in the town, new Council offices in Palmer Street, £55,000 over 15 years and the community venue, the Cheese & Grain, £620,000 in four loans over 25 years all from the Public Works Loans Board. With the Council offices paid off, there was roughly a balance of £460,000 (2011) to be paid in full by 2027.

Assets

These included the mundane: office equipment, park machinery and van. Buildings: such as the Council offices and the community hall lease, land: such as the Parks, the Meadow and allotments, the War memorials and bus shelters, the Mayoral chains of office and the Bunn Pillars - entrance pillars of a proposed sweeping crescent of town houses. The Golden Knoll, erected in 1846 by Frome philanthropist Thomas Bunn, planned to rival the City of Bath crescents. All amounted to around £1 million.

Annual Audit Return.

This is a useful short summary. Councils complete the Return by the end of June each year, sending the three page statement to the external auditor who will sign off the accounts effectively closing any future legal challenge to the accounts, although details and information can still be requested. The certified form is published on-line or pinned to a public notice board.

- **Section 1**, is a statement of the accounts and lists: the precept, staffing costs, income, repayments of loans, total of all reserves, value of assets, total borrowings and amounts spent, with a comparison with the previous year.
- **Section 2**, the annual governance statement, asks 9 questions to which the answer will be "yes" covering the ability to inspect the accounts by electors, the safeguarding of public money, the monitoring of its finances, and only doing things it can legally do.
- **Section 3**, is the external auditor's signature, perhaps making suggestions for improvement.
- **Section 4**, asks 11 questions to which the independent internal auditor will answer "yes", covering the way public money is handled and recorded.

The external auditor also sees the end of year bank balances and the Council's explanations of any variations (if they are around plus or minus 10-15%) caused by: raising the precept and placing it in reserves, maintaining high reserves, borrowing without spending, the differences between the current and previous financial year perhaps resulting from changes in spending.

...Frome Watch....

The Christmas Lights

The Budget line was a controversial £20,000, (07/08), but was broken down into c£5,500 for the lease, c£6,000 to put up and take the lights down (previously something the local volunteer Fire Brigade had done) with c£4,500 set aside for repairs and electricity. This left an unspent amount of c£4,000 as a surplus to go into General Reserves.

Balance Sheets

Monthly balance sheets will show the progress of spending, against the proposed Budget for individual budget areas and should be regularly examined by the responsible Committee or Full Council. However, this is unhelpful if only explained as a percentage without any detail.

Each budget area can be seen in greater detail again, transaction by transaction and again should be regularly scrutinised as whilst spending may be within Budget it is not necessarily wisely spent. Publication sadly is not the norm.

...Frome Watch...

Past Councils

By 1977, after the Government reorganisation of 1972, the new Town Council had settled into its new offices of just two rooms, its previous home – North Hill House, a clothier's mansion, had been transferred to the newly created Mendip District Council. A new part-time Town Clerk was in charge of the bi-monthly meetings and a Committee structure was being devised, the Precept was around £10,000.

Fourteen years on and some twenty years ago, in 1991, the Council was doing very much what it does today; commenting on Planning applications, maintaining the Mary Bailey Playing Field and Victoria Park, and providing money for a variety local voluntary and social groups. This was the last year Frome Town Council rented rooms in St John's Cottage next to the church before buying an empty shop in nearby Palmer Street.

The Budget and Precept request in 1990/91 was £148,256 (Roughly doubling the amounts gives today's value) and covered a number of still familiar areas:

- Staffing, already the largest element at c£63,000.
  By now there was a full time Town Clerk with two admin staff in the office and three park staff plus summer park patrols.
- Twinning, £1,720 supporting the exchange of visitors, although at this time only with France.
- School Crossing Patrols, £1,224.
- Grants to Local Groups, £26,700.
- Street Decoration, - the Christmas Lights, £2,300

Whilst other spending areas have long ago changed or disappeared:
- The Warmer Frome Scheme £17,000.

The second largest spending area, an ambitious scheme administered by Help the Aged. Frome pensioners over the age of 73 and on benefits were given an energy cum heating allowance of £22 annually each winter. Not without its complaints as the age cut off was annually disputed and there were accusations of people claiming who shouldn't, often because they shared a home with younger relatives. The Scheme ended when the new 1997 Government came to power and implemented its own, very similar scheme.

- Conservation Area Grants £10,000.

With monies from District, County and primarily Government. This pot of money was administered by District and matched by homeowners to repair and improve homes in the conservation area of the town. A number of similar imaginatively named Government schemes continued for a further 10 years.

- Town Crier £545.

Helped with the Town Crier's expenses as he competed against other Criers across the country and attended local events. Today's Town Crier fund raises for himself and his wife representing the town nationwide, opening local events and hosting an annual national Town Criers competition in Frome.

- Street Cleaning £4,500.

Although provided by the District Council, Town Councillors were always unhappy with the quality and employed an additional cleaner, causing friction with the District and creating Double Taxation issues which everyone ignored. It was discontinued in the late 1990's.

- Street lighting, £5,678.

Councillors listed where street lighting was reported as poor and paid for the installation of new lighting which the County Council later adopted, this still happens intermittently today.

Income was modest from the Park rentals and with bank interest it totalled around £10,480. The Council held Reserves in the Building Fund for New Offices then standing at £50,410 what was to be a long cherished ideal.

1992 was the year the money-free alternative "Lets" trading scheme started. The 400 participants swapped goods, skills, and services at a set rate per hour regardless of what was entailed. Originally called "Fromes" the name later changed to "Shuttles" commemorating the town's lost industries. By the late 1990's the Council too was involved, "selling" photocopying, or hiring out the Park and tennis courts, banking a considerable number of "Shuttles" which it found difficult to spend. A sharp rap across the knuckles by the external auditor put an end to this adventure.

1995 brought bold intentions to provide a large venue for concerts and conferences - as other nearby towns had done, house the Town Council and other organisations such as Tourist Information and Citizens Advice, whilst providing an income which would supplement and perhaps replace the precept. By 1998 a community hall, the Cheese & Grain, was opened. Replacing the nearby much loved, small, old wooden hut which was home: to market day Wednesday auctions of eggs and local produce, Thursday's Women's Institute cakes, crafts and flowers, endless Saturday jumble sales and winter Christmas fayres, interspersed with antique and bric-a-brac fayres, with regulars such as the dog training club, many groups made the transfer.

The original loan was doubled a few years later to solve complaints of noise to neighbouring houses – incomers were blamed. As the Council stumbled over its running, using a budget it could never control and with mounting costs it was eventually handed to an independent charity to run and now makes a modest profit. The 3 storied rear of the building was unconverted and unused.

By 2007 a new Council with new ambitions and a steely determination, shifted into a more dynamic way of thinking. In an excited Annual Town Meeting in April 2007 the Policy and Finance chairman explained the previous year's actions and set out its spending plans for the future:

1. New Town offices.

The Palmer Street offices had, as predicted back in 1991, proved difficult, with problematic disabled access, awkward rooms, dramatically sloping floors, narrow windy stairs and atrocious parking.

The move to the *Cheese & Grain* considered in 2006 and indeed part of the purpose of the original lease back in 1997 was shelved as not large enough!

2. Two new members of staff.
Sparked by the wonderful possibility of new powers as Somerset County Council made a bid for Unitary status which if granted would sweep away the five District Councils. Frome assumed it would again take up some of the responsibilities it lost in the 1972 local government shake-up and therefore need additional staff. However the County's five Districts, including Mendip District Council, did not want to disappear and spent £300,000 on a referendum in June 2007 to support the "no" vote (150,000 voted against change). The Somerset bid eventually failed but an ambition had been lit.

3. A second assistant Town Clerk
An assistant would project manage the revival of the Badcox Toilets and spearhead a Lottery bid of up to £1 million to revitalise Victoria Park. The District Council, in line with many authorities across the country, had closed peripheral public toilets leaving just one in the town centre. The Town was already managing one (Merchants Barton) and wanted to re-open the one at Badcox, a neighbourhood shopping area. Later the projected cost of £180,000 caused the Council to shelve the idea. Eventually even the Merchant Barton Toilets much heralded as an important public service would also close.

"Parks for People" part of the Heritage Lottery Fund, encouraged Councils with large urban parks to restore their Victorian grandeur of fountains, pavilions and statuary. The Town Council had already Earmarked Reserves of £50,000 to trigger the bid of £1million and confidently assumed it was a formality. Councillors reassuring electors that a Council Tax rise was unnecessary. The bid was never made when it was realised the criteria did not apply to Frome.

Plans were funded by a planned budget increase of £232,191 or a staggering 37%. The Precept has been raised by nearly a third (29.5%) over the previous year or £173,482. This set the pattern for the next four years with Precepts rising closer and closer to a £1million were annually demanded, masking Budgets which were much higher.

A number of disgruntled electors voiced their disapproval and tried to raise a debate at the Annual Town Meeting - the electors meeting, but the Chairman of Policy and Finance countered with "*we are saving money so we do not get caught with our pants down,*" stating the bulk of the increase was to be held in Reserves. This was the last year detailed explanations were given at the Annual Town Meeting. Further debate was curtailed by the Chairman in favour of presentations on flowers by Frome in Bloom and the infant local community radio station - Frome FM.

In the following month, May 2007, the four yearly Parish elections with their new Ward boundaries swept away nine Councillors leaving 11 survivors, 8 as unelected political party appointees.

Value for Money
Difficult to judge which is perhaps why it is little mentioned but it does demand using, at the very least, the 4 questions from the "Best Value" regime which stand behind the watchwords of the 3 "E's" of Economy, Efficiency and Effectiveness.

Known as the 4C's they ask Councils to:
1. Challenge;
Why and how is a service or activity provided? Who provides it? Who benefits? Can it be done a better way or by others? If the Council stopped doing it would anyone notice, or should it be done at all?

2. Compare;

Compare with other Councils or other organisations including those in the private or voluntary sector give a better service?

3. Consult;

What are the opinions of local people and local businesses? What are their aspirations for the future? Do Council employees think they could improve what they do? What changes do potential users, partners and suppliers suggest?

4. Compete;

Could other contractors offer better value? Is the process fair and open? Have opportunities for partnerships with other public bodies, businesses and voluntary organisations been explored?

Many Councillor decisions have a lasting legacy and planned actions or requests for support need to be relevant and their wider implications taken into account. Some are easier like the demand for allotments; others can be seen as furthering the narrow interests of certain local organisations. Some attempt should be made to give a reasoned account of why public money is spent hopefully at the very least in the Annual Report to the Parish.

Knowing more information is available via the Parish Publication Scheme should allow some comparison across Parishes and make questions in general easier to ask.

...Frome Watch...

The Years 2007-2011

In the four years (2007-11).Frome's precept was two thirds of what the District Council charged for its range of statutory services placing Frome Town Council, the Town Clerk proudly announced, in the top spending 100 Parish Councils in the country.

No other town organisation has the security the Council has, with a ready source of money and ample staff. Frome, in its four years of Budgets (2007-11), budgeted to deliver £3.35 million worth of opportunity. Despite its Strategic Plan written in the broadest and uncosted terms the town's responsibilities remained much the same throughout the electoral cycle, much as they had always been. The years, dominated by rounds of summer grass cutting, the watering of pale petunia'd hanging baskets with floral beds of summer spiky grassed desert planting turning to the bright polyanthus of winter, Planning application consultations at three weekly intervals, the annual round of grant giving ending with Christmas celebrations.

To be a Parish Council is to be the master of small things, through the mundane of annual housekeeping: town office heating and lighting, the purchase of paper and envelopes, insurance and audit fees, repairs and IT updates, and the giddy prospect of new machinery. With contractors employed for: toilet cleaning (around £13,000) and Christmas lights, grass cutting, tree surgery, hanging basket and flower watering (around £12,000) and the building of floral displays, accounting and personnel advice.

The four years of high precepts had not materialised into many specific gains for the town:

- The Victoria Park and the adjacent Mary Bailey Playing Field had been the town's spending centerpiece.

Now with: a rethatched weather-vaned bandstand, resurfaced tennis courts, new play equipment, the replacement skateboard ramps-into something less exciting, the refurbishment of an old seating shelter into a resurrected summer café - a long held dream, and the new Rabka Rock garden.

Spending around £250,000, the park, with the re-instatement of all year round park patrols and town-wide hanging baskets absorbed much staff time especially the daily journey around the town on watering duties - outsourced for a time. Despite questions no-one quite explained why a similar Park in Frome's sister town of Shepton Mallet and run by a Trust, was financed annually for around £50,000. The Park now completed, the new land transfers adding new green spaces to mow which may need extra equipment – a tractor or a new van.

- The shock take-over of the Tourist Information Centre. Initially it was assumed funds would be provided to tide it over when its £19,000 grant funding was cut after Mendip re-jigged its Budget. However, its absorption into the Council at an anticipated annual future cost of £80,000 and adding another 4 staff to the payroll took the town by surprise.

- The purchase of 3 areas of open space was a policy success ("*buying anything and everything that Mendip wanted to sell*" - a key strategy), Councillors intended to follow up with the purchase of car parking spaces but time ran out

- The approach to money had radically changed, egged on by a bureaucracy that taught, to spend was to be seen as a professional and efficient Council and a high precept showed dynamic intent. Spending has always been easily justified as being "*for the town's benefit*" or "*as an investment in the future,*" and therefore beyond dispute, or "*if we are to do anything significant we need extra money,*" and when explaining increased staff numbers, "*it is important to be ready to strike at any and every opportunity.*" Anyway, it had been discovered, as an added bonus, there was nothing anyone could do to prevent it. The Double Taxation issue over the transfer of ownership of Mendip land to the town was dodged.

Teased in Parish Forums and meetings over its high Budget by the other Parish Councils. Questioned in the press by a baffled electorate realising that some acquisitions such as land had only recently been made in the final year of administration so this didn't quite explain why budgets had been so high for most of the electoral cycle. The Town Clerk still assured voters that it had all been essential to maintain services and it was the town's lack of income from building rentals that was to blame unlike its more fortunate sister Mendip towns.

The numbers over the 4 year electoral cycle had by the end become impressive:

- Over £1 million of extra spending available.
  Using the 2006 Budget as a base- £588,592 (although even this included over £100,000 put aside into Reserves for that year) rising to a spectacular £914,879 by 2011;
- £81,000 Extra in Wages a year.
  Bringing the bill up to around £318,000 (by 2011). Employment levels rising from 6 full time staff to 10 with 16 staff overall;
- £740,000 in Reserves.
  Topping out at around £740,000, Reserves continued to chase the Budget upwards. From a 2006 year end figure of £287,496 adding around an extra £453,000. A combination of Earmarked Reserves money mainly put aside and used in the Park but including the new Town offices fund which survived and was still standing at £166,000;
- £46,000 in Income at its height (2011).

From old stalwarts such as Park and flat rentals, bank interest and the County contract. With Tourist Information Centre sales added later with a mixture of small grants.

- £189,000 paid in Loans and Interest to the Public Works Loan Board as the loans, primarily for the Cheese & Grain, are steadily reduced over the 4 years.
- £35,000 controversially put into the Christmas lights display and the associated evening's entertainment each year.
- £115,000 in Grants paid, although this had decreased over time (£53.000) going to the town's small organisations.
- £134,000 placed under the optional Section 137 spend. Twinning, Youth Council, youth organisations, school crossings and some community grants are under this heading.

The Future

Voting had always been a leap of faith with precious few ideas held up for electoral scrutiny. Now with the Power of Competence replacing the Power of Well-Being, which the Government acknowledged, had largely been ignored – perhaps the silly name had not helped. A new world order had dawned; its initial showing had allowed Bideford Council to retain prayers at the start of meetings. Business minded Councils can now start their own enterprises or act as bankers.

Stop Press New Council Tax Rules

The Government wanting local authorities to be proactive decided to move to a local system of taxation and concentrate Council Tax billing authorities' general decision making on boosting their local economies and getting people into work - so reducing the number of claimants. It replaced the Council Tax Benefit Scheme – a national scheme which helped those on low income pay their Council Tax, by a Local Tax Reduction Scheme (from April 2013). Each authority would devise its own scheme.

With a 10% reduction in money from central government to pay for the new discounts – pensioners would be protected; this would leave working aged people most affected. Some of the shortfall would be made up by owners of second homes and empty homes paying more or in some cases for the first time so theoretically some Parishes might gain.

The Parishes however were taken by surprise at the unexpected and unheralded ending, they felt, to their independence, certainly those who had proudly precepted for a 0% rise, discovered their residents were in fact facing an increase of as much as 10% at Band D for the same level of spending. Rumours said the Government would introduce a cap on the Parishes if too many costs were pushed towards them. (A local referendum is triggered if there is an excessive (over 2%) Council Tax rise at billing authority level).

...Frome Watch...

National changes

The April 2013 government changes to the way it calculated the way money was allocated to Councils lost Frome about 13% of its tax base or some 1,200 households. Nearby Trowbridge lost around 15% which translated into about £300,000.

Mendip raised Frome's precept by around 18.5% instead of the expected notional inflation rate of 2.8% to provide the town with the amount of precept it had requested to make up for the expected shortfall.

However Mendip later passed on a grant from central government (it had relented and effectively replaced the "shortfall" with a grant) to Frome of £117,000 or around 90% of the imagined shortfall. This caused a quandary as Frome Town Council now had "too much money" and was uncertain what to do with it. It incidentally pushed it over the £1 million mark for the first time. No one knows if central government generosity will be repeated.

Previously homes where people were in receipt of Council Tax benefit – pensioners, single people, low income families, second homes, empty properties were counted, at least in part, in the local tax base, after the restructuring some were not.
The more claimants, this would vary from year to year, a Parish had, the less money it would receive with some "loosing" hundreds of households as the sum needed or precepted was divided between the remaining households.

The Government realising there might be problems provided a lump sum to the billing authority to make up for any Parish shortfalls, theoretically at least. The Parishes were suspicious, there were no guarantees they would receive the money. It was hoped grants would be given in an assumed proportion to the number of households "lost" over a 3 year period. The New Homes Bonus would provide additional money in any case but some authorities thought General Reserves might rise to create a buffer against the possibility of more claimants eroding their tax base still further.

Perhaps this new regime would become an election issue against previously unchallenged spending but with no mention in the media and hazy explanations by most authorities it would probably go unquestioned.

BEECH TREE IN ST JOHN'S CHURCH YARD

MARKET DAY FROME

14 – MONEY - Pensions

It surprises many new Councillors to find they can belong to the Local Government Pension Scheme (LGPS), one of the largest public sector schemes with 3.5 million members and the majority of UK local authority Council employees (the other public sector schemes are Health, Teaching, and the Civil Service). In 2007, before the world's sovereign and bank debt crisis had fully unfolded the Office of National Statistics expected overall membership to rise to 5.2 million.

In common with most of the public sector the final salary scheme was still in place (2010), with benefits based on the final year's pay and the number of years an employee had been a Scheme member. Heavily subsidised by Councils from money collected via the Council Tax, the Scheme touted the pension as one of the most valuable financial rewards of local government employment providing a secure future income, independent of share prices and stock market which would fund private sector pensions.

Most private sector employees have seen their possible pension returns dramatically reduced as businesses and companies found the cost of Final Salary Occupational Pension Schemes (Defined Benefit Scheme), too great. Large numbers of schemes closed shifting to money purchase plans. Provided by the employer, it promises a retirement pension which is a fixed proportion of an employee's salary. Employees contributed with employers paying the most.

A Money Purchase Occupational Pension Scheme (Defined Contribution Scheme), the most common company pension scheme is funded by fixed contributions from employees and employers. The amount of pension provided at retirement depends on the size of the employee's 'pot' and annuity rates at the time.

...Frome Watch.....

Contributions

Frome contributed c18% of pay rising from £21,123 in March 2007 to £37,189 in March 2011 with the money held in the Somerset County Council Pension Scheme.

The 1997 Labour Government worried at the rising costs of pensions, strove to reduce the growing liability, but by March 2008 government had only succeeding in making minor alterations: changing the standard employee contribution rate of 6% to a range of 7 gradations from 5.5% to 7.5% dependent on pay band. The old pension scheme, which had paid on a 1/80th of the final year's pay (multiplied by the number of years employed) plus an automatic tax-free lump sum of 3 times the pension, changed after April 2008 to a higher rate of 1/60th of the final year's pay (multiplied by the number of years employed) but no automatic lump sum. However, the Scheme's normal pension age of 65 remained.

It has been left to the 2010 Coalition Government to face down the unions who in November 2011's show of strength brought out 1000's of public sector workers on strike, heralded as either a damp squib or a triumph of solidarity with the whole affair unresolved by the years end.

Councillors' pensions however, are based on Career Average pay.

This averages the pensionable allowances earned over the number of years served using the pre April 2008 calculation - the 1/80th rule, increasing annually by the rate of inflation using the Retail Price Index (3.4% in 2007, 5% in 2008).

All public sector pensions had guaranteed cost of living increases, based on the September Retail Price Index figure for the entire life of the pension. The appalling public debt (£167 billion borrowed annually on top of £900 billion of steadily rising permanent debt), had, by April 2010, caused the new 2010 Coalition Government to change this to the lower Consumer Price Index though foiled by a peak in September 2011 of 5.2%. Even with this alteration the Coalition Government continued to negotiate with the unions to further reduce pension liabilities.

Members of Parliament (MP)

After the expenses scandal, attention turned to MP's pensions. In this final salary scheme MPs can contribute 11.9%, 7.9% or 5.9% of their £65,738-a-year salary (2012) into their pension pot with any shortfall made good by the taxpayer, currently standing at £13.6 million a year. The typical MP sits in Parliament for 13 years, and can receive one third of final salary or £30,000 after 20 years, there is a cap at two thirds of final salary.

Scrutiny in 2012 by the Independent Parliamentary Standards Authority put forward various suggestions for consultation on pay and pensions including: higher pension contributions, MP's with jobs outside Parliament could be paid less, higher payments for MPs with higher qualifications, and £1,000 to those who lose their seats to help them retrain for a new job!

Datafile

Valuation Office Agency, www.voa.gov.uk
Communities and Local Government,www.communities.gov
Councils' Accounts Your rights: England from the Audit Commission
Audit Commission, www.audit-commission.gov.uk
Office of Public Sector Information, www.opsi.gov.uk
Governance and Accountability for Local Councils, A Practitioners Guide 2008 Edition, from NALC and SLCC
Armchair auditor, www. armchairauditor.co.uk
Local Government Pension Scheme, www.lgps.org.uk

SELWOOD PRINT WORKS

15 - SUPPORT and PROCESSES - The Support

How it works, what to look out for, the Parish Clerk

If Parish Councillors are "unseen", the Parish Clerk is a very "shadowy" figure indeed, generally working alone and from home fitting in and around other employment or, for many, as a pleasant semi-retired position beloved at one time by retired army officers. Only the larger towns have a full time Clerk.

The Parish Clerk
All Parish Councils must appoint a Clerk, (called the Proper Officer in law) an employee of the Council (not self-employed). In the vast majority of Parish Councils the Parish Clerk is a part-time post generally only full time where there is a sizable budget to administer and assets, for example: buildings, including venues which can be hired out for social events or buildings which are a part of a charitable Trust, these are generally either educational or almshouses for the elderly and are often subject to particular rules unique to that Trust; land, often termed open space includes parks and gardens, tennis courts, bowling greens, swimming pools, cemeteries or allotments. It is often at this point further staff are employed, and often once started more are always needed.

The Clerk provides office and administrative support to all Councillors: most importantly taking minutes of meetings, issuing meeting agendas at the request of Committee chairs, either providing or accessing advice and information; implementing the Full Council and Committee delegated decisions, make small payments and oversee any contracts and leases. The Clerk sits next to the Committee Chair in meetings, available, if asked, to provide any additional information. Chairman's Notes may have been prepared in advance containing updates on issues, letters to and from the Council or notifications received to be read out during the meeting.

The Clerk makes sure: the Council's procedures and protocols are kept and decisions are carried out lawfully, maintaining enough information for a clear audit trail, so present and future Councillors and electors can understand the Council's actions; keeping the Council's books, deeds, leases and documents providing copies to Councillors or electors on request.

It may be also part of the Clerk's duty to take the minutes of the Annual Parish Meeting - which is the meeting of the electors and not a Council meeting.

The Clerk ensures the Council is seen as: transparent, accountable, proportionate, consistent, and targeted, taking action only when it is absolutely necessary. The Clerk does not take part in debates but is there to clarify legal points when asked by the Chairman.

In most Parishes there is no separate treasurer or Responsible Finance Officer (RFO) to administer the Council's finances, it is part of the Clerk's role to keep: the accounts dealing with both the external and internal audits, send the annual summary of financial information to the external auditor and organise the review of internal processes by an external auditors.

The Clerk is employed by the whole Council to carry out the Council's decisions.

It is vital that all Councillors take personal responsibility and are aware of the nature, the extent, the implications and the costs of all Council decisions not just of those Committees they attend. Councillors are often in awe of their Parish Clerk who often serve for many years providing continuity. As the Clerk answers to the whole Council, staff answer to the Clerk who manages, organises their workload and is responsible for their performance.

The Clerk may deal with enquiries and issues raised by the public and the press acting as an intermediary with independent internal auditor. Parishes should also have an audit team of Councillors who check the work of the RFO and Clerk at regular intervals through the year. The Clerk implements any recommendations made by the Councillor team, and the internal and other tiers of government and will be responsible for the Councils implementation of the Parish Publication Scheme, the Freedom of Information Act as well as data protection. If decisions need to be made between meetings generally an extraordinary meeting of Councillors is called however, Standing Orders will have outlined what decisions a Clerk can take in dealing with emergencies and the spending of small sums of money generally in consultation with two Councillors including the Chairman, in these instances the decision rests with the Clerk, Councils can not delegate to a single Councillor not even the Chairman. If they do make decisions outside a meeting they can be personally liable for the financial consequences.

Parishes may belong to the County association of the National Association of Local Councils (NALC), an association for Parish and Town Councils and or the Society of Local Council Clerks (SLCC) for expert advice on legal matters; they also provide conferences and training opportunities.

Salaries

Parish Size	Parish Budget	Parish Clerk Salary
small Parishes	budget up to £25,000	around £16-21,000
medium Parish	budget from £25,000 to £250,000	around £22-31,000
large Parish	budget from £ 250,000 to £750,000	around £32-43,000
large town	budget in excess of £750,000	around £44-69,000
Part-time Clerks have an hourly rate of between £8 and £12.		

There are no set career pathways or qualifications for a Parish Clerk, although larger Parish Councils are beginning to ask for degree level graduates. Many rely on the Certificate in Local Council Administration (CILCA) particularly if they wish to maintain Quality Council status and will support training for this to be achieved in post, there is usually a pay rise as an incentive to completion. The Certificate (CILCA) run by NALC offers mentoring and guidance. Started in 2000 it offers a minimum training standard at a low cost (£150 April 2008) and indeed both NALC and SLCC are keen that Councillors and anyone interested in local government study for the Certificate. It is competence based and involves the gathering of evidence or portfolio building to show knowledge and understanding and is similar in format to the National Vocational Qualifications (NVQ) although not part of the national framework. It is a two year part-time course.

Whilst this is the most commonly held qualification, the University Of Gloucestershire offers a Certificate of Higher Education in Local Policy. A ten module part-time course over two years, again Councillors can take this qualification. The course of study uses written assignments covering: management, law and procedure for local Councils, finance and resources, the Planning system and community action, and environmental issues.

New Parishes

New Parishes can quickly gain staff, Exmouth, with a population of around 37,000 was a newly founded Parish Council in 2007. The town now employs 7 staff and oversees a budget of about £453,000 (2011).

Both these qualifications give a Clerk "qualified status" part of the criteria in the Quality Parish Scheme. The Local Policy Certificate can also be extended to a Diploma and a Degree with further study. The University and SLCC suggest that a salary increment is paid once a qualification has been gained.

Each Parish decides what it will pay its Clerk and until 2005 salaries were based on the population size of the Parish. This was obviously silly as the workload of a Clerk is not dependent on the number of people in the Parish but on the decisions of Councillors. A new framework was devised by the two organisations that represent Parish Clerks, the National Association of Local Councils (NALC) and the Society of Local Council Clerks (SLCC).The new salary scales use benchmarked points depending on the complexity of the job. Salaries are now based on the Parish Budget, the number of staff employed, and the number of Committees. In common with public sector salaries there is an annual incremental rise plus an annual pay rise decided by Councillors. A Deputy Clerk is traditionally paid three quarters of the Clerk's wage.

Staff

Other than Clerks, Parishes commonly employ staff to take on practical jobs: looking after cemeteries, playing fields, caretaking buildings or taking the bookings for community halls. Parishes may shadow the salary rates of their local principal Council but they can set their own.

The four year electoral cycle makes Councillors unique as employers as a newly elected Council could change a Parishes priorities but the tradition of permanent contracts severely limits flexibility. With the inevitable arms-length nature of administration by Committee and a tendency for Councillors not to see their role as employers, performance related management and regular reviews become crucial, allowing Councils the only opportunity to make effective use of and changes to staff. Usually there is a tipping point when an administration changes into a bureaucracy and once brought to life; it is intent on its own survival.

With the government directive to consult more widely placed on all institutions both public and private this inevitably entails extra meetings and invariably more staff especially given the hierarchical nature of Councils (some will feel it is below their pay grade to be directly involved but will still want to be reported to). Council meetings grow as staff then report in person which somehow triggers more meetings as Councillors usefully suggest things that need discussing. There is always one Councillor who will suggest a budget which results in more consultations and further meetings to decide what to spend it on.

This in itself can turn into a full time job with the additional employee now officially fully embroiled in organising extra meetings and perhaps adding to and liaising with a raft of consultees as the consultation net widens. This is enthusiastically taken up by participating organisations who also need to be seen to be listening, consulting and negotiating and who then make suggestions of their own. By now the Council employee has become the acknowledged expert and so there is a resulting change of job title from administrative assistant to something grand such as community, or business or tourism economic development officer with an additional pay grade attached. With no time for the original job more staff are needed to take up any "slack."

"Officer" in job titles is a charming leftover from a bygone age still clung to by Councils nationally. With militaristic overtones it is immediately officious but gives a sense of gravitas or an integrity coupled with experience and soundness not necessarily borne out by the staff member. Councillors like to refer to "our officers." It is considered a better word than staff.

Staff can include:
The Parish Lengthsman
He was a local man responsible for and taking pride in the maintenance of his patch of highway, a few miles of Parish roads (or a length of canal). Beginning in 1862 when Parishes combined to form Highways Boards, to mend the roads, keep weeds down and clear ditches. It was only in 1888 that the newly created County Councils became responsible for the highways, but with increasing mechanisation by the 1960's the Lengthsman had disappeared.

Today, Parishes again club together to share a Parish Lengthsman, to paint play equipment, clear ditches, trim verges, paint signs, clean off graffiti, and do the small general repairs and highway maintenance, or tidying up as is necessary. Cost effective and easier than badgering principal authorities (who may grant aid) to take action especially in rural areas.

Consultants
Ambitious Councils support decisions with consultations. These are usually simple, small scale surveys done at random and frequently repeat previous surveys. Still seen as pioneering, they can be used to justify any future decision. We are also told consultations empower socially isolated groups and create a sense of community in deprived areas.

Occasionally consultants are appointed for specific projects to flesh out proposals and provide a "to do" list. The concluding reports can be strangely similar agreeing there is a problem and supporting the original assumption. A report's first proposal is generally to employ a new staff member. Then, as there will already be local groups working in the proposed area, the next step is to cajole them into joining a common forum under the guise of sharing best practice and providing mutual "support." This usually leads to attempts to professionalise volunteers who will find themselves on a range of courses. A budget is always needed to implement the "to do" list. The best reports will go a little further than Councillors dared enabling them to feel validated.

Apprentices
Governments over the years have financed endless youth training or employment schemes the latest is the Modern Apprenticeship. A combination of work and training *"to create a more loyal, skilled and motivated workforce."*

This is backed by a grant of £1,500 including training costs. The apprenticeship national minimum wage is £2.65p an hour with a minimum duration of one year.

Town Centre Managers

Particularly Popular in the 1990's and seen as a solution to revitalise the nation's High Streets. Providing enthusiasm, dynamism, co-ordination, communication and promotion to, *"develop a vibrant and prosperous town centre,"* generally supporting shops, markets and tourism taking over the traditional role of the Chambers of Commerce. Reactions varied some Chambers ignored them, others contributed to or fully funded the job. Larger towns are still quite keen.

Salaries

Average National Town Clerk Salaries
2003 £14,330
2009 £26,214

Somerset Starting Salaries in 2009
Midwife | £20,710
Teacher | £21,102
Police Constable £22,104

Chief Executive Officers Pay in 2012
Somerset County Council   £160,000
Mendip District Council   £92,000

Staff bring to a Council the responsibilities of any employer with: pension, sickness and holiday entitlements, grievance and disciplinary procedures and safe working practices to consider. More recent Government legislation has added increased maternity and paternity rights and for large employers training rights.

Principal authorities in particular, have increased part-time staff alongside home working in common with other government bodies – Councillors are always keen to show their enlightened side. Making decision making, for those dependent on their staff's strategic decisions, a long drawn out process. It can be tricky to co-ordinate meetings between developers, local government and governmental bodies when all work a different selection of days and different hours within those days and if travel is involved the added pressure of picking children up after school to fit in with their working hours. The window of opportunity for meaningful discussion is slim which could be solved by better management but, not when faced with managers for whom management is a pay grade rather than a responsibility and may also work part-time.

Reasons given for paying high wages to Chief Executive Officers:
- Big money is needed to get the choice of the best candidates.
- Big pay packet is linked to a Council's business success.
- Highly paid people at the top boost a Council's success.
- Respected more by staff and Councillors.
- Attempts to regulate pay would send "wrong message."
- Other Councils take us more seriously.

As employee numbers have risen inward facing bureaucracies have become adept at growing and maintaining themselves with any value becoming difficult to judge or achieve.

Traditionally the public sector has been looked upon enviously by private sector employees for its high wages - always hotly denied, perks, enviable pension schemes, jobs for life - most contracts are permanent, and an unsackability - no matter what. The Office for National Statistics recent comprehensive analysis (September 2010) blew the myth of public sector low pay apart, finding that full-time public sector staff earned on average £74 a week more than colleagues in the private sector. The difference was starker once employer pension contributions were included with the gap widening to £136 a week since fewer than half of private sector workers are enrolled in any retirement scheme compared most workers in the public sector – of which the majority are taxpayer-subsidised final salary schemes, annually index linked for life.

Training and Advice

District and Unitary authorities will provide some training for their Parish Councillors mainly in Planning. Parishes can as with any organisation buy in training for staff such as management skills, chairing or health and safety. There are also various national bodies, forums and discussion groups which a Parish can join for all sorts of advice as well as local government and employer organisations.

...Frome Watch....

Knowing what to do?

Quarterly Parish Forums, unminuted and informal get-togethers, for all the Parish Clerks and Parish Councillors give opportunities to discuss, raise issues, share and exchange ideas, Organised by Mendip District Council with presentations and points of information by Mendip staff on their areas of responsibility. As a rural area, discussions tended to concentrate on: gypsy and traveller sites and responsibilities, keeping village shops and post offices open and rural policing, as well as the more mundane explanations of how the District Council is run.

Frome's recent own whole Council "away days", were heralded as a breath of fresh air away from party politics and helped to formulate policies such as its 2½ year Strategic Plan. The town also budgets annually for both Councillor (committee chairing) and staff (software programmes) training. Only one End of Year Report gave an extensive list.

In 2007 Frome abandoned the time honoured and centuries old title of Parish Clerk, although still the legal term, for the title of Chief Executive Officer (CEO) and at the same time splitting the job making the Responsible Finance Officer into a separate post. CEO is usually used in the higher tiers of local government and in commerce. Despite horrified letters to the local newspapers Councillors decided a name change was, *"more in keeping with modern times."* However, for a Council whose main role was the mowing of grassy areas and providing summer hanging baskets it could seem a little overblown.

But with the hoped for cascade of extra responsibilities devolving from the assumed transformation of Somerset (from County to Unitary), the Council wanted to push the business model, looking for drive, acumen and strategic decision making associated with a business CEO. Parishes, however, are unique organisations; Clerks do not carry the reputation of the Council and it is not their effectiveness which is scrutinised and tested via the ballot box but Councillors, taking both the credit and the flak.

Some Councillors can be surprisingly uncertain of their role. Who leads the Council – Clerk or Councillors and will frequently back down instead of challenging?
The roles are perhaps best summed up as:

- Councillors - Leadership - doing the right thing,
- Town Clerk - Management – doing the thing right.

Discovering staff have their own ambitions and agendas can be disconcerting, putting many Councillors at a bit of a loss, but the Council offices are a pleasant warm place to spend an hour or so for a chat although others have felt trounced at every turn with the extent and deliberate slowness of bureaucracy getting in the way of getting things done or become strangely dependent on the goodwill of their Clerk.

Frome's Town Clerk turned into an unexpectedly controversial figure as a very solemn self-conscious Council slowly and meticulous called out its Full Council members (January 2011) by name, for a named vote (a rare event) to confirm the new Town Clerk's appointment. The decision on the cusp of the election cycle, it was rumoured, was so the new Council could not reverse the decision, but no-one really knew. Letters to the papers by prospective Council election candidates and rumblings in the town were questioning whether indeed a Town Clerk was needed, and the value or the need to pay a generous £50,000 - there had been well over a 100 applicants. The CEO title was remaining in place. Certainly principal authorities (the higher tiers of local government) were questioning CEO pay levels in response to Government cuts and against the background of continued rumblings of disapproval on bankers' bonuses. After years of an "arms race" of spiraling pay, many have now done away with the post, others share CEOs and still more have cut up to a quarter off their CEO's pay.

The last ten years has seen an increase in Frome Town Council staff numbers; from a part-time Clerk in 1974 to 5 members of staff by 1992 to the 16 at the electoral cycle's end. The Town Clerk (2010) was reported as declaring on leaving post, the growth of staff numbers had been the main achievement and the one to be most proud of. Indeed, in many senses the various aspects in the administration of the Council have been teased out and assigned as separate jobs. Councillors to had gained in confidence and with a desire for sophistication mirroring principal authorities renamed administration staff as portfolio holders, (generally a term associated with Councillors) covering Planning, Finance, Outdoor Services - to oversee the Council's Estate with the Town Clerk holding the Policy Portfolio.

The Council's concerns were rapidly revolving around staffing protocols and initially the Personnel Committee met as frequently as the Full Council. Overall there was no attempt to correlate tasks, with cost and value. Staffing levels had reached and passed a tipping point. With the renaming of jobs the town's bureaucracy crystallised. There would be no returning to the low key "laissez faire" relationships of the past. The bureaucracy would want to grow and extra staff provides the relief and ready justification that any additional spending brings. Easily explained as time saving and creating efficiencies, and as always, *"it will be for the good of the town."* There is little likelihood of staff numbers decreasing in the future.

Indeed a town centre manager had been hinted at and certainly the Chamber of Commerce were particularly keen commenting, they did not have the time and someone was needed to talk to and organise the town's shops. Mendip had, for a time, from the late 1990s employed town centre managers one in each of its 5 towns (5 in Frome alone over time). These later morphed into regeneration managers, administering a small pot of grant money to improve their town centres such as the restoration of shop fronts - although not in Frome, commenting on Planning applications and providing regular updates on the number of empty shops. By the end of the 2007-11 election cycle an apprentice was added to the outdoor staff.

The Town, despite growing staff numbers, has increasingly employed contractors: maintaining outside areas such as Rodden Meadow and the Park using: gardeners, tree surgeons, builders, painters, and toilet cleaners, whilst on the office side, personnel consultants.

With nearly a £1 million annual Budget, and the end of the election cycle looming there was embarrassingly little to show, the Council took steps using its grant support to nab two community assets which in the corporate world would be described as "hostile takeovers."

The Frome Tourist Information Centre (TIC) was swallowed unexpectedly in January 2010. The problems with funding had been running for some time with Mendip District removing then reinstating grants in 2009 but Mendip's own financial problems meant it would not last. An appeal by the TIC to the Town Council probably to increase funding was met with an unexpected takeover (January 2010) unknown to the town as a whole, who would have fundraised willing to keep an independent TIC. The loss of 23 volunteers with their wealth of experience and enthusiasm which underlined the very nature of the town was bitterly received, four paid jobs were kept. The TIC's in Frome's sister towns in similarly difficult financial positions cut paid jobs, increased volunteering, fundraised, increased sales or moved premises.

The Council again, in an unexpected move, nearly forced the Cheese & Grain (C&G) a community venue and charity to disband (October 2010). Initially asked to forego the annual £35,000 grant used to subsidise community events in what was labelled a cost cutting exercise - the trustees felt unable to do this. A furore arose. The grant, it was suggested, would be paid monthly and it looked likely the Charity would close giving the Council the opportunity to take over the running, but it offered to retain the 20 paid staff. This would bring the Council's own staffing total up to 36.

Certainly with absorption of the TIC and the attempted takeover of the C&G, the Council showed its determination to be an economic force, it also toyed with bringing this together with a post of a Town Centre Manager: to promote tourism, "regenerate" the town centre and develop the town's economy.

The Council, keen to be the pivotal point of the town and not doubting its own ability or judgement, coupled with the 2010 Coalition Government's desire for Localism and having around £1 million annual Budget, this was merely going to be the beginning.

Datafile

National Association of Local Councils,www.nalc.org.uk
Society of Local Council Clerks, www.slcc.org.uk
Business Link,www.Gov.uk
Department for Innovation and Skills,www.bis.gov.uk
Office of National Statistics, www.statistics.gov.uk
Association of Town Centre Managers,www.atcm.org.uk

16 - SUPPORT and PROCESSES - The Processes

All Parishes need enough processes and protocols to function efficiently, allowing Councillors to make and the electorate to follow a clear audit trail of decisions.

The Paperwork

The Agenda and the Minutes read together provide the most important as well as a permanent audit trail of the discussions, decisions and actions taken by a Parish helping both the electorate and Councillors past and present understand how decisions were arrived at. Traditionally written up by the Parish Clerk, who both implements and reports back on the decisions logged and maintains an archive. Very old records may be placed at the County Records Office.

The style of record keeping has changed, older records were often written in a verbatim style, arguments were outlined in some depth with Councillors competing to be mentioned by name and have their pithy comments recorded. They offer a fascinating insight into the decision making process and can give a real flavour of the times and the personalities involved and are well worth reading in their own right. Modern minutes are often short, increasingly only recording the resolution and the decision with little of the proceeding discussions. It can be difficult to see the flow of ideas or the options which were available before a decision was taken. As often as not it may be down to the minute secretary how items are recorded and this may be applied unevenly across a series of Committees.

The Agenda

Councillors should ask:
What is the meeting about,
What should I be doing,
What papers should I read,
What people do I need to contact,
What did I promise to do for this meeting.

Agendas both advertise and list in order the items to be discussed during the course of a meeting. All agendas state: the name of the Committee, the place, date and time of the meeting. Many, usefully list the Councillors who sit on them so comments and queries on issues can be directed at the correct Councillor on past, current and future meetings. Posted or e-mailed to Councillors at least three clear week days before each Council or Committee meeting, with paper public notices put up at the same time on the Parish Notice Boards.

A typical agenda

Evacuation procedures
Public forum
Apologies for absence
Declaration of member's interests
Minutes
Announcements

Sub-committees or outside bodies reports, if any
Main items
Accounts
Future agenda items

As topics cannot be added after the three day deadline, unexpected issues wait until the next Committee meeting that may be many months away.

Equally an agenda cannot be published too early in case there is a last minute item to add. This leaves little time for those with concerns to organise themselves or contact Councillors. Larger Parishes usefully publish a yearly list of Committee meeting dates; smaller Parishes may meet on an ad hoc basis.

The notice sent with the agenda is a summons in law and there is a duty on Councillors to attend. If there is a problem such as illness or unexpected work commitments, an apology and an explanation is sent to the Clerk to be given at the meeting and noted in the minutes, the meeting does not have to accept the reason and can ask for a further explanation. Importantly, if Councillors fail to go to meetings for six months the Council has to again formally accept the reasons for non-attendance or disqualify the Councillor from office.

Agenda items should be precise and clear stating what is being discussed and outline what is expected, such as a vote on an action or on spending, some Councils give an approximate time for each item. Decisions will be based on the discussion in Committee backed by any reports read beforehand rather than reports given at the meeting. Councillors need sufficient time to raise questions or ask for further information. No decision can lawfully be taken on any matter not specified in the agenda. Perhaps occurring in the past as items were slipped in or decided under "Any Other Business" or due to Councillor enthusiasm pledging whole Council support to an organisation following a rousing presentation. Councillors and the electorate should have the opportunity to marshal their opposition or support for a decision

The Committee secretary often the Parish Clerk sets out the agenda to a set format with "standing items" which are always included, such as apologies, confirmation of previous minutes and declarations of interests plus items unique to a particular committee. The Committee Chair will discuss with the Committee secretary any additional items. Any Councillor can add an item for discussion. The secretary or Clerk will sign and circulate the notice. If any two Councillors call for a meeting they will outline what is to be discussed and sign the notice.

Monitoring the Council's spending should be done in detail. Using general Budget headings and vague percentages is not an adequate check.

It is unwise to table important business at the end of the agenda, where there is a danger of running out of discussion time. If an item becomes especially important or is an emergency item, the Chairman can "suspend" standing orders and deal with the item first. This can be decided by the Chair or voted on by the Committee.

Minutes
The Minutes are a record of the meeting providing an audit trail of decision making. Whilst unlikely to be a verbatim record the Minutes should summarise briefly the discussion and reasoning, the recommendations made, the resolution voted on, recording clearly the decisions taken, including any time scale and financial impact. Importantly, Minutes will link meetings together providing continuity. The Minutes are written up in the same order as the Agenda by the Parish Clerk or Committee secretary.

The Meeting
Most Parishes are small, often with the minimum of 5 Councillors. For a meeting to go ahead there is a quorum of 3 needed or a third of the Council whichever is the highest.

Meetings can take place any day of the week.

...Frome Watch...

Declarations

Frome Committee Chairmen commonly made a general block declaration of their membership of the District and County Councils, at each meeting stating, *"All dual and triple hatted members made a block declaration that their views on any item on this agenda as Frome Town Council members were not necessarily those as their role as Mendip District Council and Somerset County Councillors."* The audience would not know which Councillors this related to and the statement implied that their comments, views or support were not to be relied upon, rather worrying, particularly on Planning issues.

The Public Forum

At the start of a meeting is, generally between 15 to 30 minutes in length. It is the one occasion the electorate has to voice an opinion to the Council or its Committee as a whole. However, perhaps surprisingly, the Forum is not officially part of the meeting, and therefore any comments, questions, replies, or even the number or the names of meeting observers present will not necessarily be minuted or recorded. Making it impossible to have any lasting impact on an issue unless there is Councillor support and the issue is raised as an agenda item. Equally, anyone reading the Minutes will not know what issues or discussions or viewpoints were put forward and therefore will be unable to follow up the arguments. So support or opposition will be unheard and unknown to the public at large unless there is a press report in the local newspaper or the speaker is adept at publicity and can form a group, organise a petition, or a press photo opportunity.

Presentations, often the fun part following on from the Forum, are given by: organisations, groups, or individuals, wanting written or financial support, making a point, describing a service that the Parish may like or updating the Council on progress made.

Roll call

The Committee's Councillor membership is read out and apologies made for those not present stated and recorded at the beginning of each Council meeting. Late arrivals and early departures are also recorded with the time. Many Councils have a register which must be signed.

Declarations of Interests

Often seen as unnecessary but it is a reminder to all Councillors and any watching audience where comments and opinions may be biased. With recent governmental changes failing to declare a pecuniary interest is a police matter.

Announcements

Part of Chairman's Notes, compiled by the Parish Clerk or Committee secretary for the Chairman to read out containing general things which will affect the Parish such as road closures and speed traps, or letters received from electors or local groups. It is the opportunity for Councillors to update colleagues briefly on outside events and meetings attended.

The Minutes

The Minutes of a meeting are signed at the following meeting as a true and correct account of what happened or the next Full Council meeting by the presiding Chairman.

Each page should be reviewed for accuracy and agreed by the Committee and any discrepancies noted.
Each page is initialled by the Chairman, signed and dated on the last page.

Matters arising
"Matters arising" from the minutes is an opportunity to give brief points of information or the chance to ask questions about the previous meeting. These should be genuine questions not an attempt to re-start the discussion. If "Matters arising" are covered by an agenda item the discussion will take place there.

The Committee Chairman manages the meeting by introducing each agenda item, changing the running order if necessary, inviting Councillors to speak, focussing discussion and clarifying the resolutions, proposals or motions which are voted on. The Clerk will summarise the discussion, note the formal resolutions then the decisions, perhaps noting how many were for, how many against and how many abstained, who is to action, or carry out the decision - either a named Councillor or the Parish Clerk or specific staff and setting the time frame. This should make the minutes easy to follow when re-read and items easy to progress chase.

Voting must be by a show of hands decided by a majority of Council members present and voting on each resolution. There is no secret ballot. Usually voters' names and whether they voted for or against are not minuted but this can be requested. Generally taken when a subject is controversial or where there is some political point scoring to be done. Councillors, if they have no view or are undecided may abstain (that is to not vote at all). This is poorly thought of by other Councillors. Even so the show of hands is often tentative many Councillors voting with a slight nod or shake of the head. Not easy for a watching audience to see and consequently there will no immediate way of knowing which way particular Councillors voted, not even other Councillors may know and it can be disconcerting to hear Councillors asking *"has the vote has even been taken yet."*

Reports
Complex items may need reports or briefing notes which set out the issues, list the possibilities, give costings and estimates for the work from potential suppliers (3 estimates are required). When received beforehand Councillors can plan what questions to ask and have a meaningful discussion. However, the meeting audience may not have this information so will not be able to follow the arguments. Hopefully the Reports will be referenced in the Minutes, too often not the case, and be available afterwards if not before although too late for any electorate input into the decision. Often Reports and any enclosures are only circulated to specific Committee members so other Councillors will be equally in the dark. So much decision making may be a bit of a mystery.

Standing and Financial Orders
All Parishes must have Standing Orders, rules governing meeting procedures and Financial Orders, the rules governing the way finances are run. Both are a legal requirement and Councillors should know them by heart. Perhaps the central one is the quorum, at least a third of Councillors or three whichever is the greatest must be present for a meeting to go ahead, the bar can be set higher if a Council wishes.

Other standing orders will cover:
- the order of business,
- length of meetings and the duration of speaking time,

- the schedule of meetings for the year,
- delegation (handing over of tasks) to Committees or staff,
- the number of Councillors on Committees and the meeting quorum,
- voting requirements,
- procedures for public participation,

All Councillors are responsible for the Council's financial management and should be familiar with its administration via the Responsible Finance Officer (RFO) who is generally the Town Clerk. Financial Orders ensure the RFO acts properly and avoids the risk of fraud, bad debt, or carelessness. A minimum of two Councillors must sign every cheque, never a blank one, cross referencing it with the invoice. Commonly a separate internal control committee of Councillors will over-see the RFO, scrutinising financial arrangements, checking documents selected at random and reporting back to Full Council. This is separate to the independent Internal and the External audit.

All Councils decide how to manage risk generally with a document describing the activities undertaken by the Council such as staging festivals, owning playgrounds and sports facilities, putting up hanging baskets, owning buildings, and explaining how the risks will be managed such as by insurance, checking equipment and other common sense solutions. Some Councils also include a risk to reputation so there may be protocols about what and how information is given to the press and public.

...Frome Watch...
Bureaucratic?

By the end of the electoral cycle Frome had created a complex bureaucracy with an array of protocols ranging from making media statements, health and safety, through to personnel, forming an all-encompassing "corporate" structure. However, it can be too easy to lose sight of the purpose of being a Parish Council, which still remains to represent the best interests of the Parish, and become a self-generating, self-perpetuating end in itself.

FROME CHEESE SHOW

VICTORIA PARK BOWLS CLUB

17 - SUPPORT and PROCESSES - Meetings – What to Expect

Key Points

Before
- Councillors will know the rules and procedures and be able to explain them.

All Councillors will have:
- Read the meeting papers; surprisingly many will happily admit to having not read them, taking particular pride in "doing it on the hoof." Or if the meeting Chairman, been briefed beforehand by the Parish Clerk reading through any Chairman's Notes.
- Noted which agenda items are for information, discussion or decision.
- Arrived early and if the meeting Chairman, ensured that the practical arrangements are in place such as visual aids etc.
- Arranged their papers so they can be found.
- Be prepared to start on time.

The Opening
The Meeting Chairman will:
- Ensure there was a quorum present and start the meeting on time.
- Greet Councillors and thank them for attending.
- Welcome the audience and introduce new members or guest speakers.
- Ask all members to introduce themselves to new members and note who is seated where. Most sit in the same places each time.
- Ask everyone to give their name when they speak, this is useful for the meeting's audience and the Minute taker who may be asked to read back comments.
- Take apologies for absence and have the Minutes of the previous meeting agreed or amendments recorded.

The Meeting
The Meeting Chairman will:
- Follow the agenda and introduce each agenda item. Explain its purpose or introduce the person who will present it. If a staff or audience member only needs to be at the meeting for one particular item the Chairman can propose the item is moved to the start of the meeting with the meetings agreement.
- Make sure everyone understands what is being discussed including any jargon or abbreviations   which are being used (not all will admit to not understanding). It is disconcerting to discover Councillors who have not noticed the next agenda item has been started or who have discovered they voted the wrong way on a previous item. If it is a crucial vote, such as on a Planning application, it can mean the success or an expensive failure of a venture to an audience member.

  With Planning decisions at District/Unitary level there is recourse to the Planning Inspectorate and the possibility of an Award of Costs against the District/Unitary Council.

- Have in mind a rough time limit for each agenda item, allowing more time for the most important or contentious items, within the overall time limit of the meeting. However, if an item is taking up too much time the decision can be deferred or a task group of 2 or 3 Councillors set up to look at the options. A formal resolution to revisit the issue at a later meeting should be made, giving a set time period to stop the issue disappearing. Otherwise the Chairman may call for a decision if the issue has been given a fair hearing and move on.
- Read out any motions and amendments when they are proposed and read them out again before a vote is taken.

All Councillors will:
- Focus on making decisions, concentrate and listen carefully and be aware of what is going on.
- Take notes and refer to them.
- Be prepared to ask awkward questions and highlight issues that no one else will.

The Discussion
Councillors will expect the meeting Chairman to:
- Encourage Councillors to speak and ask speakers to repeat comments when it is unclear what was said. If Councillors drift from the topic, and many can be prone to reminisce; to remind the meeting of what is under discussion and the goals of the meeting.
- Only allow Councillors to speak when called on by the Chairman and not across the meeting. This is called talking 'through the chair." The meeting should be called to order if problems occur.
- Only allow Councillors to speak who raise a hand in request, regularly looking around the room so no-one is missed out. To allocate a strict running order or list on a first come basis of those who wish to speak to ensure a healthy debate.
- Not allow a speaker to ramble on, or a meeting to be taken over by a particular individual or a group. Whilst Councillors are entitled to their views the Chairman must listen carefully and interrupt if something inappropriate is said.
- Prevent Councillors being abusive or violent to each other or to the audience or people not present. It is unpleasant to listen to Councillors being rude to those who question their judgement and cannot reply because it is against the rules or they are not present; any transgressions should be reported to the local Standards Committee. Councillors do not have "parliamentary privilege" unlike MP's in the House of Commons.
- Be tactful when asking speakers to finish speaking, thanking them for their contribution and adding a positive comment.
- Summarise a Councillor's main points, and give equal weight to all opinions, not forgetting members who are less forceful. Be constructive linking associated points together and clarifying the various viewpoints. Encouraging the debate to move on by accepting parts of ideas and asking for them to be developed.
- Summarise feelings as well as content to anticipate problems.
- State a problem in a constructive manner, not blaming anyone.
- Use concise and impartial summaries particularly before a vote and whenever a lot of people are contributing to a debate. This helps the minute taker.

Bring a topic or discussion to an end with a summary, limiting the need for further discussion. End with a statement about what will happen next; and if a decision is needed there should be a vote. After the vote, the decision should be clearly announced.

Making the Decisions

Councillors will:

- After discussing an issue make a proposal in the form of a carefully worded motion. Further debate may give rise to amendments or alterations being suggested and these in turn are discussed. Amendments to the motion under discussion may be proposed by any Councillor. Amendments are alteration to the original motion, but should not completely distort of change the meaning of the original motion. The proposed amendment must be seconded.
- At the end of the debate, voting is on the amendments first, in the order in which they were suggested or moved. If they all fail to gain majority support, the original recommendation can be further discussed, then voted on and if it gains the majority support, it becomes the decision of the meeting. If an amendment is carried, that is say agreed, it becomes the substantive motion. The amended motion can be further discussed or voted on and if carried, it becomes the decision or resolution of the meeting.
- If motions are publicised in the Agenda, research the subject for discussion, it also helps the Chairman structure the meeting.

The Meeting Chairman will:

- For each motion ask for a "proposer" and a "seconder ". Their names are minuted. If two people do not show support the motion will fail and not be discussed or voted on.
- Ask the supporting "proposer" and "seconder" to speak in support of the motion. They will say why they support it and why they want other Councillors to support it. The "seconder" may reserve the right to speak until later.
- Ask other Councillors to join the discussion.
- At the Chairman's discretion, the Chairman may only allow members to speak once on an item and may put a time limit on each contribution. If there is general agreement about a motion and to save time, the Chairman will call for any speakers against, rather than have a lot of speeches saying more or less the same thing, something Councillors find oddly enjoyable.
- At the end of a debate give the "proposer" the right of reply. This is to allow them to respond to points raised during the discussion; however, they can not introduce new points.

Voting

- The Chairman will read out the amended motion before the vote, so all Councillors are clear on what is being voted on.
- If the majority votes are in favour, state that the motion has become a resolution of the meeting and will be clearly minuted as such. Some meetings may record the number for and against a motion and Councillors can ask for a named vote which they may use later to publicise their political differences, the meeting's audience will be able to track those responsible for decisions and know who to lobby in the future otherwise the system is anonymous.

- The Chairman's casting vote is usually used to maintain the status quo (considered best practice) in other words no change.
- Ask if there are any abstentions, i.e. Councillors who will not give their opinion, although abstentions do not count in a vote they may prevent a majority in favour and so align with votes against.

Points of Order

All Councillors can:

- Use Points of Order to deal with the conduct, or procedure, of the debate but not to waste time or disrupt business.
- Call a "point of order" if they think that:
  - there is a departure from the subject under discussion
  - an objectionable form of speech is being used
  - there is a breach of the rules of debate or the meeting's own rules.

The Chairman will decide whether the complaint is justified or not and the Chairman's decision is final. However, it can be challenged by a procedural motion, which must be voted on and if carried overrides the decision.

- Without being invited to speak move procedural motions; they require no notice, but should be proposed and seconded formally and voted upon immediately and without debate.
- Propose next business at any time. If the proposal is carried by the meeting the discussion of current business ends at once and without a decision.
- Propose that a motion or amendment is voted on. If the Chairman decides that there has been insufficient or unbalanced debate there will not be a vote. If the proposal succeeds, further considerations on the current business will stop, except for any right to reply by the "proposer" of the main motion, and a vote taken.

Closing the Meeting

Councillors will:

- Finish on time.
- Agree the date of the next meeting or remind members if it has been set in advance.
- Agree on special items or unfinished business to be put on the agenda for the next meeting. or if a sub-committee, one of the Council's main Committees if it is an issue of importance.

The Chairman will:

- Thank everyone for attending.

18 - POLITICS - The Rules

"Events, dear boy events"
Harold Macmillan PM 1957-63

Government ideas and legislation, Quality Councils, creating and disbanding Parishes, Parties, who's who

There have been swathes of local government legislation over the last dozen or so years which have been constantly rewritten and have constantly repeated the same items; reorganising and cajoling principal Councils towards co-operation and tweaking what their Parishes can do. In the elusive search for community leadership. In doing so Governments have consistently underestimated Councils, who, using their particularly well-honed area of expertise; can give all the appearance of co-operating whilst completely failing to do so.

A bit about recent government legislation

The two Acts of Parliament in 2007 aiming to increase public involvement in Local Government, were further attempts at persuading the Districts and Counties to work together. The Acts gave local government more things to do and new ways to measure their activities and impressed upon them that they should work more closely with each other and with their Parishes. Not, as many Parishes had experienced, had this always been the case in the past, where there had been frequently scant regard for local feelings. Many Parishes were hopeful the Acts would allow them come into their own, at long last they would be able to propose and run their own services again, as in pre-1972 days, and planned accordingly. They were rewarded by one of the main tenets of the Local Government and Public Involvement in Health Act 2007 which extended spending powers, in the Power of Well-Being to Parish Councils. The local electorate were unaware of the changes made on their behalf.

The Local Government and Public Involvement in Health Act 2007

The Act introduced a range of devolutionary and deregulatory measures taken from the Local Government White Paper - Strong and Prosperous Communities 2006:

- Changing the two tier local authority system i.e. County and District to a single tier or Unitary authority which carried out all the functions of the two tiers it replaced (never completed). And busily redefined, updated, restated and tidied up previous legislation:
- Re-emphasising Local Standards Committees for conduct, discipline and complaints against local Councillors with the support of the National Standards Board (later abolished);
- Modernising the objections and complaints of the annual audit, in writing rather than face to face as this was now seen as old fashioned;
- Abolishing the detailed target and monitoring arrangements for Best Value Parish Councils (the list of 41 Parishes);
- Offering unfettered spending to qualifying Parish Councils with the Power of Well-Being (later repealed and replaced with the Power of Competence)

The Sustainable Communities Act 2007

Perhaps the most radical, based on a belief that local people know best and know what needs to be done to promote the sustainability of their area but with central Government having a controlling hand as an enabler.

Sustainable Communities

The 2003 Sustainable Communities Plan defined sustainable communities as: places where people want to live and work; now and in the future; By meeting the diverse needs of existing and future residents, with sensitivity to their environment, and by contributing to a high quality of life; They are safe and inclusive, well planned, built and run, offering equality of opportunity and good services for all.

The Act broadly, covered, economic, social and environmental issues designed to strengthen the role of communities. This time good ideas generated by local communities would be fed through to their local authority and a selector; (the Government suggested the Local Government Association), with both bodies short listing the proposals. The Government would respond to all the short-listed suggestions deciding with the selector which ones to implement publishing an action plan on the adopted ideas. Somewhat unwieldy it came to nothing.

In addition the Act introduced new "Local Spending Reports" designed to give quick, easy access to information about where public money is spent. Now, at last, it was argued, local people, newly informed on where the money goes, will have a say on how, what and where it is spent, coming forward with new ideas and getting value for money. After a limited number of Reports produced in 2009 it came to nothing.

The Last Ten Years or so

Since the advent of the 1997 Labour Government every other year has brought rafts of local government legislation or White Papers. Reforms which rehash and constantly repeat previous reforms tweaking this and that following the zeitgeist, but some new ideas do step forward although only too often to disappear, including:

"Best Value"

Introduced in the Local Government Act 1999. The Act demanded continuous improvement in the running of Councils using the yardsticks of Economy, Efficiency and Effectiveness. Managing what they do by: planning, monitoring, measuring, and reporting what actually happens with regular reviews plus actively challenging current service delivery. The Act brought in independent inspection to assess the effectiveness of the measures used and required the authorities to consult the public and interested groups on how services should be delivered. Based on their Parish income this only applied to 41 English Parish Councils. However, there is a general duty for all Parishes to "embrace Best Value."

New decision making structures

The Local Government Act 2000 introduced new decision making structures and with it the method of accountability for principal authorities.

It introduced an executive based system moving away from the traditional committee system of decision making. The central reform was a "Cabinet" style of governance of between 3 to 10 executive Councillors drawn from the ruling party group members, with the option of working under a directly elected Mayor, making the key decisions.

These would be separated from the majority of Council members who acting as "backbenchers" take an overview and scrutiny role.

There was a choice of structures either with the Council leader and a cabinet acting as an executive authority, or with a directly elected Mayor - either with a Mayor and cabinet drawn from the Councillors – or a Mayor and Council Manager previously the Chief Executive. Most Councils chose the Council leader and cabinet system. Around 30 local referendums were held nationally for directly elected Mayors in the cities but the majority were rejected, 12 succeeded.

The Act revised the ethical framework with the adoption of Codes of Conduct for Councillors with a local Standards Committee to implement them and gave local authorities, i.e. District and Counties, a general power to do anything likely to promote or improve the economic, environmental or social well-being of their area (The Power of Well-Being).

From 2002 principal local authorities (the higher tiers of local government) had their own assessment regime the Comprehensive Performance Assessment and later a new framework was developed which introduced Local Strategic Partnerships and Local Area Agreements.

...Frome Watch...

Mendip Mayor?
Unexpectedly (2010) Mendip carry out a survey asking its population if it wants a Mayor - outcome unknown. Mendip Councillors debating the suggestion think it is ridiculous and unsuited to a large rural area. Expensive, once the necessary accoutrements and inevitable entourage are taken into account, as well as confusing the post with the town Mayors. Councillors in general thought there would be little point to a Mayor and predict a low election turnout giving a narrow, very political win for one of the main political parties. The idea was dropped.

Comprehensive Performance Assessment

Since 2002 principal Councils had been assessed annually by the Audit Commission and their performances compared through the Comprehensive Performance Assessment (CPA). This star rated scheme (2 stars for minimum standards or "adequate" and 4 for exceptional) looked for continuing improvement and was a snapshot of a Council's performance. Now at last, local people, newly informed where the money goes, will have more say on how, what and where it is spent, coming forward with new ideas and getting value for money.

2009 heralds a new scheme and a name change; Comprehensive Area Assessment, annually assessed by the Audit Commission. This flag rated scheme (green for exceptional performers and red where there are deep concerns) looks for continuing improvement and is a snapshot of a Council's performance. Now local people, newly informed where the money goes, will have more say on how, what and where it is spent, coming forward with new ideas and getting value for money.

The Government envisaged greater freedom and flexibility for good performers and closer scrutiny and intervention for the poorest performers.

Abolished by the Coalition Government in 2010 as part of the *"slashing of Town Hall red tape and lifting the heavy burden of Whitehall oversight."* Local authorities had begun to complain about the amount of data they were asked to provide notably Leicestershire which employed 90 people collecting 3,000 data items costed out at £3.7 million annually. This would be replaced with transparency and openness as every citizen becomes an armchair auditor. Whether they could know which questions to ask or can untangle the bureaucracy would be another matter.

...Frome Watch...

Strategic Partnerships

In Somerset there were both District and County Strategic Partnerships. At Mendip District Council the Mendip Strategic Partnership translated into a broad membership of around 20, made up of Councillors, police, jobcentre plus, youth organisations, charities, schools, environmental groups, Chambers of Commerce and the Primary Care Trust. Considering the Partnerships importance they went unreported and unnoticed.

Local Strategic Partnerships (LSP)

The Partnerships were unelected, bringing together Councillors, Police, Fire and Rescue, Health Service providers, Housing Associations, voluntary, community and business sectors to address local problems allocate funding, discuss strategies and initiatives dovetailing the activity of each collaborating organisation.

The Community Strategies developed contained long term hopes based on assumed local needs covering the next 10 to 20 years looking at economic, social and environmental issues, combined with community aspirations. These fed into principal authorities' Core Strategies this in turn created medium term priorities which in turn created targets or Local Area Agreements (LAA) setting local spending decisions and translating into Council taxes which could attract Government funding.

Local Area Agreements

Simple statements: of what is to be achieved, how it will be achieved and how achievement will be measured. As such, an action plan. With the Coalition Government's abolition (March 2011) some LSP's have disappeared, others now search for cost savings within their authorities.

The Power of Well-Being

Gave, local people, via their local Councils, a sense of ownership over how their communities were run, with more say in their management and some Parish Councils unfettered spending powers.

"Well-Being" gave the power to do anything that achieved, *"the promotion or improvement of the economic, social, or environmental Well-Being of an area,"* without the spending cap per elector of Section 137. Its use could only be voted for if the Parish had a qualified Clerk and by Councillors – if 66% had stood for election and if 80% had gone on a 2 hour training course. It was set within a complex opinion gathering and community involvement framework. The Power of Well-Being was later repealed and replaced by The Power of Competence (2011) which allows Councils to do anything as long as it is legal.

Overall Councils still need to look at what they do in the light of the principle of "Wednesbury unreasonableness."

"Wednesbury unreasonableness"

This applies to decisions made by a local authority or any public body which is, *"So outrageous in its defiance of logic or accepted moral standards that no sensible person who had applied his mind to the question to be decided could have arrived at it."* Lord Diplock 1985

The Diplock pronouncement has a ring of truth and clarity about it which is often seized on by opponents of any controversial Councillor decision and is only confused by the facts. In 1947 the Associated Provincial Picture Houses (APPH), a cinema company, in Wednesbury, Staffordshire was licensed by its local authority to run a cinema on condition that no children under the age of 15 were admitted on Sundays. APPH thought this was outside the local authority's powers and took it through the courts. APPH lost but it did lay down a principle in law. "Wednesbury" is generally used in assessing judicial reviews when individuals challenge local government decisions.

The full definition was given by Lord Greene in the Wednesbury case in 1948.
".....Discretion must be exercised reasonably. He must call his own attention to the matters which he is bound to consider, and exclude from his consideration matters which are irrelevant to what he has to consider. If he does not obey those rules, he must truly be said, and is often is said, to be acting unreasonably."

Best Value Councils

After the major local government reorganisation in 1972, local authority budgets grew considerably. So the 1997 Labour Government decided to provide a structure to improve the responsiveness and accountability to local people of the workings of local government. Introducing the Best Value framework in the Local Government Act of 1999 for principal local authorities and including the Police, Fire and Rescue Services within its scope.

"Best Value" was also applied to Town and Parish Councils with an annual budgeted income of more than £500,000 in England or more than £1 million in Wales in each of the financial years 1997/98, 1998/99, and 1999/2000. These were Parishes which had retained considerable assets after reorganisation in 1972, generally buildings and land which were leased or rented out. Consequently, 41 Parish and Town Councils became subject to the Act with the extra accounting and audit regulations. Their number was never added to.

These were:

Abingdon Town Council	Fawley Parish Council
Bodmin Town Council	Goole Town Council
Bracknell Town Council	Great Aycliffe Town Council
Bridgnorth Town Council	Harpenden Town Council
Chesham Town Council	Hatfield Town Council
Chippenham Town Council	Hemsworth Town Council
Devizes Town Council	Henley on Thames Town Council
Dorchester Town Council	Huntingdon Town Council
Dronfield Town Council	Leighton Linslade Town Council
Dunstable Town Council	Littlehampton Town Council
East Grinstead Town Council	Maghull Town Council

Malvern Town Council	Swanage Town Council
Newark Town Council	Swanley Town Council
Oswestry Town Council	Tavistock Town Council
Peterlee Town Council	Totton and Eling Town Council
Seaham Town Council	Truro City Council
Sevenoaks Town Council	Uckfield Town Council
Shildon Town Council	Waltham Abbey Town Council
Spennymoor Town Council	Witney Town Council
St. Neots Town Council	Woodley Town Council
Stratton St Margaret Parish Council	

"Best Value" was a management tool to ensure value for money for the whole electorate using the watchwords Economy, Efficiency and Effectiveness. With a duty; to consult, plan, review, measure, and report against a background of continuous improvement on local needs. A framework for reviewing the activities of the Council, its contractors and any partnerships looking at cost and quality using a comprehensive set of questions (the 4Cs).

The 4Cs:

- Challenge, why and how a service or activity is provided, who provides it, should it even be provided and ask can it be done a better way?
- Compare, do other Councils or other organisations including those in the private or voluntary sector give a better service?
- Consult, what do local people and local businesses think now? What are their aspirations for the future? How do Council employees think they could do things better. What changes do potential users, partners and suppliers suggest?
- Compete, can other contractors offer better value? Is the process fair and open? Have opportunities for partnerships with other public bodies, businesses and voluntary organisations been explored?

Effectiveness was judged annually by the Audit Commission with Government hoping it could see the effectiveness of its own policies by comparing Councils. Best practice would be promoted and failing services remedied. Now at last, local people, newly informed where the money goes, will have more say on how, what and where it is spent, coming forward with new ideas and getting value for money.

Annual Best Performance Plans listed:
- what it would like to do - objectives,
- what it intended to do - targets,
- what it would cost - budgets,
- how it would judge what it had done – assessing performance using "Best Value" performance indicators (there were around 90).

The Plan detailed the year's achievements and successes against what was expected such as, how many visitors went to an event compared to what was predicted. This reset targets to achieve constant improvements against set timescales and explained each Council's priorities. The Government expected the attitudes of public services to change, no longer centred on the convenience of the Council and their service providers.

It would put local people first.

The Government emphasised, as always, the importance of efficiency and quality, with decisions taking a wider, forward looking strategic view, not merely knee jerk reactions to short term problems. It hoped Councils would be more accessible particularly via information technology producing services the public would think were important and it tacked on, as always, a promise to promote minority groups.

Although a thorough regime, it was ill fitting for most Parish Councils who do not have the scope of operation of principal Councils. Parish activities are often limited to providing hanging baskets or caretaking the local cemetery and playing field. In April 2008 with only 41 Parishes in England operating Best Value and none in Wales it was abandoned, as too prescriptive and too expensive for all Parishes to implement.

Surveys

Local people were consulted using surveys but responses were poor. In Chippenham for instance, the April 2007 newsletter reporting on Council activities included a customer satisfaction questionnaire. Sent to around 18,000 homes and businesses in Chippenham it asked recipients to rate the Town Council's performance on what it provided, only 340 responses were returned.

There was however, an alternative, the Quality Parish and Town Council Scheme first introduced in 2000, encouraging Parish Councils to achieve minimum standards. It was this Parishes would subsequently be encouraged to join.

The Local Government and Public Involvement in Health Act 2007 abolished the "Best Value" performance reviews and indicators but placed a new duty (again) on English Best Value authorities to listen to local people before deciding what to do, stating, rather cryptically, " namely informing them, consulting them and involving them in other ways."

There is still a duty on all Parish Councils to embrace the "Best Value" principles of Economy, Efficiency and Effectiveness, and follow "Best Value" practices using the 4Cs review process (Challenge, Compare, Consult and Compete). The requirement for a clear forward-looking, target orientated Plan which could be evaluated at the financial years end rather than the usual guess work budgeting and was the schemes main strength had been lost.

The Quality Parish and Town Council Scheme (QS)

The scheme was a simple list of things to do and collect underlining already existing statutory requirements and best practice - which hopefully most Parish Councils were doing anyway. It was not reliant on or based on skills, experience or performance. By providing minimum standards the scheme covered the tremendous range of Parish sizes from Pertenhall and Swineshead with 280 electors to Weston-Super Mare, with 72,000 electors both of which achieved Quality Status.

The voluntary scheme supported by government and run by NALC was launched in 2003 following on from the Government's Rural White Paper in 2000. Out of a possible 8,700 Parish Councils 542 (2008) had qualified rising to 690 by 2011.The scheme was suspended in 2012.

It provided a useful check list of what every Parish should do.

The Ten Tests for the Quality Parish and Town Council Scheme:

Test 1 the Electoral Mandate
Two-thirds of Councillors are elected. Co-opted and appointed members did not count.

Test 2 a Qualified Clerk
Who held the Certificate in Local Council Administration (CiLCA) or The Certificate of Higher Education in Local Policy or Local Council Administration (both are awarded by the University of Gloucestershire).

Tests 3 holding Council Meetings
The Council met at least six times a year with 3 clear days notification. With time allowed for public participation and draft minutes published and available for inspection within two months of the meeting.

Test 4 Communications and Community Engagement
This asked Councils to provide information on activities and included a feedback mechanism. In the Mandatory Section Councils were expected to provide a website; listing the contact details of Councillors and staff; plus the annual report. The Council's e-mail address was to be made publicly available. A newsletter published four times a year was to include the names and contact details of Councillors and the Parish Clerk and to be readily available across the Parish in shops, on notice boards, in libraries and village halls.

17 ways of "speaking" to the Parish a Council had to choose 9 from the following list:
1. The Annual report sent to every household in the Parish;
2. The Annual report which included a summary of Council activities during the year;
3. The Council involved in community led planning;
4. An information or access point providing details on local government services and Parish Council activities;
5. An information point linked electronically to District, County or Unitary Councils (This was aimed at Councils with a public office);
6. Information about local government services and Council activities distributed to every household;
7. Links established with voluntary and other community organisations;
8. A community engagement strategy published;
9. A regular weblog, or an online forum or surveys on the Council website;
10. Regular Councillor surgeries i.e. more than six times a year;
11. Residents consulted on Planning matters;
12. The Parish's principle authorities (District, County or Unitary) informed of Parish Council activities;
13. Council activities publicised in local libraries, shops and in other public places;
14. Council activities publicised in the local press;
15. Council activities reported in District Council publications;
16. Consultations or questionnaires undertaken with the electorate on local issues affecting the Parish;
17. Information leaflets or brochures provided on the work of the Parish Council;

Test 5 The Annual Report.
This included a list of Councillors and staff plus their contact details; a summary of the Council's accounts and an overview of the Council's achievements by the Chairman or Mayor. Completed by the 30th June following the financial year to which it referred and be available at the District, County or Unitary authority offices for inspection by the electorate;

Test 6 Accountability
This asked for the last audited Statement of Accounts and Annual Governance Statement plus the Internal Auditors reports, the minutes of the Committee giving approval and confirmation that the External Auditor had not (in the last three years) or would not make a Report in the Public Interest;

Test 7 Code of Conduct
This asked that the Parish's own Code including the Register of Interests was posted on the Parish website.

Test 8 Promoting Local Democracy and Citizenship
This intended Parishes to be proactive and be involved in practical innovative ways to get local people involved in the decisions making process. It emphasised the "hard to reach" groups in particular youngsters. It intended to raise an interest in voting and in standing as a Councillor, by explaining how local Councils worked and persuading people to go to meetings. The literature suggested supporting a Youth Council, school projects, as well as writing and distributing information leaflets, etc;

Test 9 Terms and Conditions
Parishes with a paid Clerk adopted the NALC/SALCC Terms and Conditions as a minimum and all staff had a written contract of employment;

Test 10 Training
Parishes decided on the training needs of Councillors and staff producing a Statement of Intent listing what was needed.

The resulting certificate and logo lasted for four years before re-assessment, with the cost based on the gross income or expenditure of the Parish (for Councils over £100,000 a reasonable £235).

The Third Sector
The Third Sector can be defined as non-governmental organisations that are value driven and which principally reinvest their surpluses to further social, environmental or cultural objectives. It includes voluntary and community organisations, charities, social enterprises, cooperatives and mutuals.

Government had realised that Parish Councils were not central to people's lives, were little understood and in general of little interest, perhaps illustrated in the low turnouts at local elections. Parts of QS were intended to tackle this, with an innovative approach: surveying and asking questions of the whole community with an emphasis on speaking to groups considered marginalised by Government such as the young and those "who are difficult to reach." Listening to the answers, Government decided, would provide effective representation creating an interactive environment rather than the perceived traditional Council role of deciding what a community should have and then justifying it.

By increasing the focus on whole community consultation, involvement, and with it education, Government hoped a wider range of people, with new skills, experience, background, age and gender would become Councillors. At present the average Councillor is a white, male professional retiree, aged around 58.

These newly energised Parishes would seek partnerships with their principal authorities, (District, County and Unitary) other Parishes and the Third Sector. With principal authorities providing detailed briefs about their current services for challenge by possible new providers and overcoming their reluctance to work with Parish Councils taking QS as confirmation of competence to work with individual or groups of Parishes to improve what was offered to communities on a solid value for money basis.

Choosing from an eclectic mix of activities:
- Control of markets
- Street cleaning
- Maintenance of highway verges, pavements and footpaths
- Litter collection and litter control
- Street lighting (other than principal routes)
- Recycling measures
- Street naming
- Parking restrictions
- Issue bus and rail passes and other transport voucher schemes
- Road safety measures
- Noise and nuisance abatement
- Tree preservation orders
- Some aspects of planning development control
- Some aspects of management of libraries and museums
- Some aspects of leisure and tourism provision

- Public conveniences
- Taxi and public entertainment licensing,

Most of the above Parishes could already offer to do. Surveys showed most interest in: grass cutting followed by play area maintenance, street naming and numbering and minor Planning applications - the last principal authorities were scornful of.

Again, there were promises to take seriously local opinions outlined in Parish Plans. More radically, to share information, facilities and staff, offer grants and at least to think about giving the Parishes things to do. Such as helping out with IT and staffing if the Parish wished to become an "Information Point". Whilst at all times mindful of "Best Value" and taking care to avoid double taxation.

With skittish pleasure, some Parishes felt they had achieved extra responsibilities because of QS. Whether these have turned into long term successes is a difficult judgement to make when long term projects or contracts could be ended by a freshly elected Council with different Councillors and with differing views and priorities to its predecessor.

Whilst there may have been some grant aid to initially help with the new service there was still a possible impact on overall costs especially staffing and therefore on the Parish precept. That may have made one off projects or those with a low level of resource and staffing implications the better bet. Whether there was a shift of power from the current hierarchical system to one with a more collaborative basis remains unknown.

The 5 guiding principles for sustainable development
- living within environmental limits,
- ensuring a strong, healthy and just society,
- achieving a sustainable economy,
- promoting good governance,
- using sound science responsibly.

The Sustainable Communities Act 2007
With new greener concerns (especially climate change) mounting Government wanted to give a sustainable edge to its Community Strategies and Local Area Agreements with their "distinctive vision and ambition of an area" and added the 5 principles of sustainable development.

This time the unseen and unknown Local Strategic Partnerships produced Sustainable Community Strategies. Providing again a blueprint for their area and feeding into Planning's Local Development Frameworks (land use plan). Setting what would happen to housing, the local economies and the countryside for the decades to come. Until abolished by the Coalition Government (2010).

The Local Democracy, Economic Development and Construction Act 2009
The Act asks Councils, again, to involve, inform and encourage local people in local decision making. This time to take seriously and respond to petitions sent to them. Government had discovered less than a third bothered to.

Now petitions, certainly at principal Council level (the number of signatures needed varies across authorities) signed by at least 1,500 electors can trigger a debate at Full Council following a presentation by the petitioners. Enabling decisions to be reviewed or courses of action proposed. Fewer signatures (750-1,500) are needed for senior staff to give evidence at a public meeting of the Council's Scrutiny Board and small petitions (50-750 signatures) are read by the relevant staff member. By the end of 2011, the financial crisis had bit across the land with arts funding and youth services cut and libraries, as always, threatened with closure. Many took advantage of this opportunity to get decisions reversed.

The Act also gives Parish Councils the opportunity to honour a valued citizen with the Freedom of the Parish. Unlike traditional Boroughs where there is a specific right, generally to herd sheep or occasionally geese through the town centre. Parishes can spend up to £1,000 on a scroll in a casket.

In a sudden bold move for transparency and openness, the Coalition Government now requires principal authorities, including Parish Councils with income or expenditure over £200,000 to list all spending over £500 detailing costs, transaction details and supplier. In reality, without any context and real details the lists can be meaningless. These are interesting and digestible at Parish level where the lists are shorter.

...Frome Watch...
Prizes and Petitions

With a Budget close to topping a £1 million, the Council has sought the additional kudos of Quality Status (QS) spending the last few years planning for it, now with a qualified Parish Clerk, QS is granted in Dec 2010.

With the Formula One World Champion Jenson Button born and brought up in Frome, the town celebrated with the Freedom of Frome (June 2010). Jenson spent the day touring the town's schools and meeting with his old teachers. After a lunch with Councillors, the hugely enthusiastic crowd waiting in the main car park, took lots of photos and watched as the Mayor gave a speech (unheard as the PA system failed) presenting Jenson with a framed scroll to celebrate his success. Frome hoped it was the first to make use of the 2009 Act.

Two petitions ran in Frome (2011) against the funding cuts proposed by Somerset County Council to end all arts subsidies and review the usage, with the possible closure of some libraries. A reduced Government grant and with debt inherited from the previous administration in 2009 resulted in £43 million of planned spending cuts reducing a budget deficit of £76 million, but still leaving around £400 million of overall debt. Whilst arts funding ended the library was saved.

New Homes Bonus 2011

Parishes are delighted when it looks like they will get "free" money for every new home in their area (newly built homes including extra again on top for affordable homes, homes brought back into use from dereliction, caravan and traveller pitches) and worry about what to spend it on. The Government will match the Council tax (using a national average based formula) raised on each home for six years.

House building in 2009 had fallen to 1924 levels, with only 120,000 homes built. There were also 4.5 million people on Council waiting lists. The Government is optimistic, the Bonus will reverse this, and suggests communities spend their "reward" on new swimming pools, revamped libraries or affordable homes for their local young families.

The scheme is not intended to make the unacceptable Planning applications acceptable – others are not so sure.

Combined with a newer more aggressive Community Infrastructure Levy (CIL), which will collect contributions from new homes, business, industrial and commercial developments on a square metre basis Councils will be able to finance themselves. CIL is shared between Districts and County Councils on an 80%/20%, split. The Districts are surprised to learn via a television news programme (an odd way to run a country) their 80% will be shared with their Parishes either 15% or 25% if the Parish has a Neighbourhood Plan in place. Many District realise they will need to revise their charges.

Government funding to the higher tiers of local government has been steadily decreased and the realisation dawns that the Bonus and CIL will be the only way of increasing local authority funding. It is the new way of financing local government. Each home has the potential of raising a minimum of £20,000. Now, every Planning application especially housing will be a dilemma for Councillors.

Localism Act 2011
There was yet one more mammoth attempt to shift power, as Government Ministers explain, from centrally controlling bureaucrats to communities and individuals, *"we will devolve power to the lowest level so neighbourhoods take control of their destiny."*

The Coalition Government swept together items from populist news stories collected over the previous few years, shook out some of the inconsistencies of local government and legislated. Mixing, as always, some new innovative ideas, resurrecting, rehashing and reiterating many old ones and discarding a lot of the familiar certainties, throwing everything up in the air giving an unexpected twist as to who now held power and underlining the essence of the "Big Society."

Now no-one is quite sure, the Act provided the scaffolding but it was nearly a year before the guidance on what it actually meant came out, followed by bulletins and ministerial comments on radio and television which nuanced the detail. Taken together with changes in the National Planning Framework, it will be expensive challenges through the Planning Appeal system, the High Court or as a last resort, the Supreme Court which will settle the scope and define legal meanings.

Decision making (and blame?) now moves to County, District and Unity level with the Parishes snapping at their heels. The Act boldly asserts everyone will, "work together effectively for the good of the community." It covers 4 areas.

1. New Freedoms and Flexibilities for Local Government:
- General Power of Competence - they can now do anything that is not illegal. Be creative, innovate and find new ways to drive down costs;
- The Standards Board of England goes. Authorities continue to write their own Codes of Conduct. It becomes a criminal offence for Councillors to deliberately withhold or misrepresent a financial interest;
- Councillors can now be active in local debates without fear of accusations of bias or legal challenges as "predetermination" is axed;
- Discounts on business rates can be offered although councils will have to find the money elsewhere;

- Authorities are encouraged to act together, again, to boost local services and economies;
- More directly elected Mayors especially for the cities to give strong leadership and also;

And perhaps contradictorily,

- Principal authorities are asked to move back to area committee systems to reduce central rule.

2. New Rights and Powers for Communities:

Aimed at the voluntary and community groups who the Government see as innovative, effective and, above all, local.

- Community Right to Challenge - Local services can now be bid for and run by voluntary groups, Parish Councils and local authority employees. The thinking is ambitious ideas and plans will be easier to achieve by these enthusiasts. The range is wide library or youth services, bus routes or car parks;
- Community Right to Bid for "assets of community value" – Local people can now register much loved local assets such as: libraries, swimming pools, shops, pubs, markets, parks, sports centres, former schools or football grounds. When assets come up for sale or a change of ownership, and to keep them as part of local life, there will be 6 months in which to raise money and make a bid to buy it.

This is a fresh take on Community Asset Transfer. Local authorities have long been able to transfer land or buildings to community groups at less than market value for them to run on behalf of the community. Again Government is especially keen on voluntary groups, social enterprises and "not for profit" groups;

Sustainable Development
The Bruntland Report published by the United Nations in 1987 was the first attempt to draw up rules for future global development,
"Sustainable development is development that meets the needs of the present without compromising the ability of future generations to meet their own needs" and are where the three constituents of sustainable development: economic, social and environmental meet and overlap. There are 5 principles:

- living within the planets environmental limits;
- ensuring a strong, healthy and just society;
- achieving a sustainable economy;
- promoting good governance and;
- using sound science responsibly.

Sustainable development should result in: job creation, increasing bio-diversity, replacing poor design with better design, a greater choice of high quality homes and generally improving living, working, travelling and leisure opportunities.

- Council Tax rises - still capped by the Secretary of State but a referendum can be held to go over the 2% limit. This does not apply to Parish increases;
- Pay - transparency particularly over local government's highest paid who will have theirs listed;
- Rubbish - collection fines and charges abolished.

3. The Planning System Reforms:

Recognition at last that the public feel they have little influence over decisions which change their lives and their area, building resentment as plans are foisted on them by people not directly affected making the system confrontational and adversarial rather than democratic and effective.

- Neighbourhood Planning - Newish and the centrepiece - as local Parishes produce simple or detailed Neighbourhood Plans outlining where new homes, businesses and shops will go, so new developments will go ahead easily. Voted on by the Parish in a referendum and needing to gain 50% for approval it still has to fit in with the local authority's Local Plan and the new National Planning Policy Framework;
- Community Right to Build - New - now community organisations can propose and build homes, to sell on the open market or as affordable homes for local families to rent, or for sheltered housing for elderly local residents, or starter homes for young families. Communities can also suggest businesses, shops, playgrounds and community halls. If agreed in a referendum no Planning application will be necessary. An interesting way of providing affordable housing with the profits from letting staying in the Parish, all to be run by community organisations;
- Consultation - Newish - now neighbours opinions will be incorporated into schemes as they are developed via consultation;
- Regional Strategies with their quangos are abolished. Started in 2004 they decided where development took place setting housing targets – these are now thought to be bureaucratic and undemocratic;
- Duty to Co-operate - neighbouring local authorities and other public bodies will now work together, for instance on flood prevention schemes, tram systems and retail parks;
- Planning enforcement should be strengthened - so abuses, such as hiding new houses behind straw bales for a set number of years before revealing them, is now illegal;
- A flexible Community Infrastructure Levy - a charge on development, in the past mainly for infrastructure such as roads and schools and has been run unambitiously in some parts of the country. New - now some of the money can go directly to benefit the neighbourhood and Parish which said yes to the development, the Government says 25% if there is a Neighbourhood Plan. Parishes are looking forward to huge "windfalls" now they have a vested interest in the outcome of Planning applications;
- Local Plans (Used to be the Local Development Framework) - now to be based on local wishes rather than regional or central Government decisions and targets;
- National Infrastructure Projects - such as train lines and power stations will be decided by Ministers and not as previously by an unelected Commission, and based on policies voted for by Parliament, presumably to speed up the average of 10 to 20 years spent in consultation.

4. Social Housing:

Provides low rent homes for 8 million people in England.

- Local authorities now decide who should be on the waiting list;
- New tenancies will be for a fixed term moving away from the assumption of a home for life;

- Homeless will have to accept private rented properties rather than expensive temporary accommodation;
- Local authorities will now keep social housing rent to maintain properties. Previously sent to central government and then granted back;
- National home swap scheme for those wishing to move, many areas are already part of one;
- Tenants Forums to become standard holding social landlords to account and backed by a complaints watchdog;
- Home Information Packs (started 2007) definitely abolished and no longer needed in order to sell a home only the Energy Performance Certificate remains describing the home's energy efficiency.

Further powers are expected to be devolved and rolled out in the coming years suggestions include street improvements, libraries, museums, parking, licensing and the arts taking Parishes back to a time before the 1972 local government changes.

Neighbourhood Planning - Into the future

Parish Plans now morph into Neighbourhood Plans. These in turn are professionalised with bands of consultants who with local government planners herd people through the process. Citizens' Panels, with their cross gender, employment, and age ranges, with particular care taken to winkle out the "hard to reach groups", are asked key questions, as always around the familiar themes of homes, work, green spaces and the fun things: shopping, leisure and transport. The first few Plans are generously grant aided by Government to ensure they that can be understood by the professionals.

Parish Councils will take the lead, those areas without one can create Forums with at least 21 members. There is a choice of drawing up a Neighbourhood Plan or a Neighbourhood Development Order (NDO) or even doing both. Development Orders are new; the community decides its priorities and grants Planning permission for new homes or offices by-passing the need for the long drawn-out standard Planning permission process.

The Plans with their Orders are checked by an independent examiner and then put to a local referendum with a pass rate of 50% of those who vote. There is a proviso; the Plans still have to agree with the local Planning authority's Local Plan and the NPPF, so nothing too outrageous is likely to stay the course and Neighbourhood Plans can not be used to block new homes or businesses but will become a crucial perhaps pivotal part of the decision making process.

National Planning Policy Framework (NPPF) (2012)

But more was to change when, hot on the heels of the Localism Act 2011, came the new National Planning Policy Framework a slim volume of guidance of some 58 pages, 82 pages if you count the appendices, which everyone is expected to follow, discarding the 7,000 pages covering 26 specific areas of Planning Policy Guidance notes and Statements built up over decades. Although Ministers later decide they may leaf through these and pick out the best bits to keep.

Long on exhortations (as these things often are) and good intentions - but short on detail it is hailed as, *"the biggest reduction in business red tape of all time"* with the promise of quicker development decisions providing economic growth.

Scarily, this will mean anything a Local Plan states will be the minimum – no negotiation such as over the number of homes to be built. The presumption is for development as long as the benefits outweigh the harm organised around 12 core Planning Principles.

Core Planning Principles
- building a strong competitive economy,
- supporting the vitality of town centres,
- the rural economy,
- sustainable transport,
- high quality communications infrastructure,
- a wide choice of high quality homes, and good design,
- healthy communities,
- protecting the Green Belt,
- meeting the challenge of climate change, flooding and coastal change,
- conserving and enhancing the natural environment,
- conserving and enhancing the historic environment,
- sustainable use of materials.

Localism and the NPPF will be the twin pillars for the UK's Planning future (see also Power).

The countryside organisations such as the National Trust and the Campaign for the Preservation of Rural England lobbied furiously accusing the Government of producing a charter to concrete over the English countryside (in its first draft). The Government demurred shifting ground to give added emphasis to sustainability (based on the Bruntland definition) in new developments (outlined in the new Local Plans) whilst keeping its pro–growth stance.
Rural conservationist inexplicably hailed the "countryside" as saved. This means local government will need a Local Plan (the old LDF) to use as a blueprint for their area; something 60% of authorities have managed to avoid doing. And they will need to do it quickly (within a year).

With the Government firmly focussed on letting local communities decide the NPPF gives a general pale wash of guidance and a re-ordering of responses to issues:

- A preference for development on land of a low environmental value whilst yet again emphasising and encouraging the use of Brownfield sites;
- A nod towards maintaining town centres by underlining the use of the sequential test, - that is town centre first for all new retail, leisure and office uses (there is a 2,500 sq metre threshold), perhaps "shutting the stable door" on the boom in out of town retailers. There had been a surprising continuation of growth of out of town stores numbers since the start of the recession in 2008;
- A vague hint towards encouraging the turning of empty housing and buildings and even offices into homes;
- An annual review of housing sites ensuring a 5 year supply is constantly maintained. Failure is threatened with punishment, by housing numbers brought forward or if applicants go to appeal, the levying of costs, no longer will authorities be able to ignore the reality of their housing situation;

- Again Councils are being told to think about planning creatively, abandoning their reluctance to co-operate across boundaries;
- Local car parking standards (parking per house) to be dusted off, now no longer centrally decided. Balanced with encouraging the use of public transport, cycling or walking;
- Local opinion to be centre stage and design to be paramount backed by robust Neighbourhood Plans with neighbours and neighbourhoods closely involved in deciding development. This is expected to be balanced with an inevitable upsurge in nimbyism;
- New powers and teeth with Neighbourhood Development Orders and the Community Right to Build Orders by-passing the standard application process;
- Invigorated pre-application consultations to be backed by proof of how consultations have fed into the resulting application;
- Buildings and landscape heritage protection kept and extended.

Perhaps place-shaping rather than application processing. With no rules, everything is up for interpretation and there are suggestions of more loosening of the rules to come.

The Power of Competence

Better than Section 137 and more powerful than the Power of Well-Being. Competence, *"the power of first resort,"* allows Parish Councils; *"the power to do anything that individuals generally may do"* as long as other laws are not broken, Government says. It encourages ambitious Parishes: to set up businesses as companies or co-operatives providing cost effective services, trading as a village shop or post office, lending or investing money to businesses and individuals – something beyond the scope of previous legislation, either in the home Parish or perhaps, unexpectedly, beyond. Whether local people will want to invest in adjoining Parishes is untested.

Funding should be raised via the Community Infrastructure Levy (CIL), sponsorship, grant funding, other authorities, by trading, or from interest on investments but not from the precept. Care will need to be taken, as always, in case the Council's judgement is challenged, or trading damages other local businesses, there will also be the risk to reputation and the risk to public money if something goes wrong, "Wednesday unreasonableness" will still apply.

The Power is limited to those Parishes where two thirds of Councillors have stood for election and there is a qualified and trained Clerk, it is renewed every 4 years but cannot be used by Parish Meetings or Wales. The assumption will be all decisions will have the backing of the electorate.

Datafile

Communities and Local Government, www.communities.gov.uk
My Community Rights, www.mycommunityrights.org.uk
Government,www.gov.uk
Info, www.info4local.gov.uk
Mendip Strategic Partnership, www.mendipstrategicpartnership.org.uk
IDEA, www.idea.gov.uk
English Legislation, www.england-legislation.hmso.gov.uk/acts

CHURCH STREET FROME

19 – POLITICS - Creating New and Disbanding Old Parishes

Forming new Parish Councils became easier with the Local Government and Public Involvement in Health Act 2007. Previously new Parishes could only be created by permission of the Secretary of State. Even so, around 20 had come into existence since 1997. Now the decision rests with the principal councils (District, Unitary and the London Boroughs). The emphasis now is devolving power; letting and getting local people involved in making local and therefore democratic decisions, with an aim to providing effective and convenient local services.

A Community Governance Review is either suggested by the principal council or more likely the result of local people raising a petition, a fixed percentage of the proposed population need to support the new Parish and this in turn will trigger the Review.

The same legislation increased the numbers of people who can be represented by Parish Meetings from 20 to 99 and enabled Parishes to be set up in London - they had been abolished in the London Government Act of 1963.

The new Parish can: resurrect a previous Parish, one which had disappeared in the 1972 local government reorganisation, when some of the larger towns lost their Parish status; or define a new area based on Electoral Divisions or Wards; alternatively using landscape and other important features such as hills, woods or hedges; new housing estates are even suggested. It has to be an area people feel is distinct and to which they feel they belong.

A public meeting will gauge support, map the proposed area, making any necessary boundary adjustments when everyone's views are known. Some principal authorities may not necessarily wish to support a change fearing loss of control whilst for others it will be a means of service delivery.

The Petition
The petitioners choose at least one recommendation which they would like reviewed such as:
- the creation of a Parish,
- the name of a Parish,
- the establishment of a separate Parish Council for an existing Parish,
- the alteration of boundaries of an existing Parish perhaps adding new housing estates thereby altering the electoral balance,
- the abolition of a Parish,
- the dissolution of a Parish Council,
- changes to the electoral arrangements of a Parish Council,
- or whether a Parish should be grouped under a common Parish Council or de-grouped.

The petition must be signed by electors on the current electoral register and from the proposed new Parish; the accompanying map must show clearly the boundaries of the area under Review:
- If fewer than 500 local government electors, the petition must be signed by 50% of the electors;

- If between 500 and 2,500 local government electors it must be signed by at least 250 electors and;
- If more than 2,500 local government electors at least 10% must sign.

The petitioners can choose a new name and style, previously the choice was between Parish or Town, now the choice is: Parish, Town, Community, Neighbourhood or Village. The powers and duties remain the same and a new Town Council chair can be titled Mayor.

The Review

The principal authority has 12 months to consult widely; from local people, businesses, public organisations such as the police, schools, health providers, the County Council if there is one and voluntary organisations such as community and resident's groups.

The new Parish should:
- reflect the community's identity and interests,
- be effective, convenient and practical,
- take into account size, population, boundaries and
- look at the effect on community cohesion.

A Review can also look at the future of redundant or moribund Parishes which are the result of not enough local electors willing to serve on a Parish Council. Reviews in any case should be considered every 10-15 years especially if there has been a shift in population.

Case Studies

St Cuthbert Out (Wells) - Mendip District Council

The Parish Council had not held a contested election for 35 years. Covering 18 villages and hamlets: the North, South, East, and West Wards of the Parish ring the City of Wells in Somerset creating one of the largest Parishes in the country (some ten miles in diameter) with a modest 3,500 population. From isolated farmsteads on windswept uplands to chocolate-box cottages in deeply wooded valleys.

The villages and hamlets in the West and North wards raised a petition with 400 signatures triggering a Community Governance Review. To end what many thought was an unwieldy situation which linked communities with little in common, stifled initiatives, was expensive (precept stood at around £43,000), remote and bullying. Comments against change countered peevishly that it would become more expensive, no one wants to be a Councillor and in any case the present Council was experienced and objective. And what would become of the assets - the cemetery and the allotments?

A vote of the whole Parish was against change even the North Ward was happy with the way things were but by contrast 53% of the West's electorate voted for change. Indeed it was anxious to present a sound case and asked for a breakdown of Parish costs commenting that too much was spent on staffing which had the Council bristling reaching for its solicitors at this impugning of its reputation.

It was the whole Parish vote that decided Mendip District Council. Whilst the current system had problems it admitted there had been an "insufficient groundswell of opinion."

Mendip had been warned by its solicitors that not following the Review's recommendations (although it has a choice) could result in a costly Judicial Review (any individual can ask the Courts for an investigation and review on the way the law was used and administered). In the May 2011 elections 7 people stepped forward for the 5 places in the West Ward, of those elected 2 were new. The Review cost Mendip around £17,000.

Durham

Durham Unitary Authority had some areas parished and others unparished. Its Review concluded the unparished areas should have their own Parish Councils, giving an equal voice to the whole area.

New Parishes start on April 1st and the local authority will have organised the transfer of property, liabilities and staff, set the new precept and appointed caretaker Councillors, a minimum of 5, until elections take place.

Norton Radstock – Bath and North East Somerset

After 75 years of trying to live together, an awkward alliance of two towns created in 1933, separating the ex-coal mining communities of Norton Radstock Town Council near Bath into three new Parishes, with the division of buildings, parks, allotments, debts and staff was convoluted. With a budget of £625,000, a population of 22,000 and 12 staff this was a sizable undertaking.

A petition of 900 signatures from Midsomer Norton in March 2009 followed a 726 signature petition from Westfield in the June triggering a Community Governance Review by Bath and North East Somerset (BANES) in August 2009; it decided to include Radstock, the remaining portion of the area, in the mix. The Town Council it was felt, was stale. Indeed of the 14 Councillors 8 had been elected unopposed and 6 were co-opted. The 3 public meetings in March 2010, resulted in 230 submissions for and against from local organisations, businesses and residents plus a petition of 120 asking for no change leading BANES to agree in the July to 3 separate Councils, Midsomer Norton, and Westfield each with 11 Councillors and Radstock with 7.

But the reallocation of Council buildings, parks, allotments, office equipment, debts and staff was belatedly begun in February 2011 and resulted in the smallest new Parish employing all the maintenance staff, as that was where the depot was - it hoped it could bill the other new Councils for maintenance work. BANES froze the precept and left the new Councils to work out the details for themselves when they gained office after Parish elections in May 2011. Despite two years of consideration the boundaries were bizarrely drawn with Westfield taking a chunk of Radstock town centre to the east and the top of Midsomer Norton in the west. The costs of splitting the old Council were initially thought to be under £50,000 but topped out at just over £82,000.

Pontefract

In May 2008 Pontefract started the process to recreate its former Town Council, lost in the 1972 reorganisation.
The Pontefract Forward steering group put forward several reasons:
- to support community groups and town attractions,
- to revive the town hall by using it as a centre for civic functions,
- to be consulted on issues such as transport and town regeneration,
- to develop the town economy and protect its assets.

Those against criticised the extra layer of bureaucracy and the expense of an additional precept. 2,300 electors signed the supporting petition which was more than the 10% needed to trigger a Review. The initial consultation resulted in 3,000 comments; this was followed by a more detailed consultation. Whilst the first supported a new Parish the second consultation failed to gain a majority. The cost was £11,000 (April 2010). Disappointed campaigners asked for a Judicial Review but received an independent report (2012) which found Pontefract's ruling Wakefield Council had behaved correctly.

Consultation is the pivotal reason given for creating a new Council with the consultation over Planning issues foremost in most minds and the electorate expecting a more radical role. Even so individuals and lobbying groups of neighbours can be equally as successful as a Parish Council.

It does offer a useful and convenient focus point for national and local authorities, local groups and organisations when they themselves need to make public consultations. Especially true if it is part of a project brief, or a group's constitution and gives access to grants and may usefully persuade a Parish Council to be dubbed a partner.

Political parties can claim a broader base of supporters if the new Council can be persuaded to politicise itself.

The Government whilst recognising that there are other ways communities organise themselves (see Chapter 20) prefers Parish Councils simply because they are elected. Whether a new Parish offers the most value for money or value for effort is in some instances finely balanced. There are simpler less formally structured often more effective ways, including community groups, residents groups or single issue groups raising interest or money for specific projects. Alternatively there are the formal structures of Community Interest Companies, charities, Trusts and Companies Limited by Guarantee. All of which can access funds not available to Parish Councils. A new Parish will inevitably raise a precept and become an ongoing cost.

Disbanding a Parish Council
The Government expects to see Parishes created rather than abolished, amalgamated to form a shared Council or degrouped if communities have expanded, even unparished areas are expected to have some sort of forum to give electors a voice.

Between 1997 and 2008 the Government received four requests for abolition, only approving one. The criteria are difficult to achieve, as local support for abolition has to be informed and demonstrated over two terms of office of the Parish Councillors, which is 8 years. Giving the Parish Council the opportunity to be judged on how it contributes to local life. Despite this however, some Parish Councils still hope to achieve their own dissolution.

Case Studies

Byfleet
Byfleet Parish Council part of Woking Borough was set up in 1989 at the request of local residents. A Parish of three wards, returning 9 Councillors, it was the Borough's only parished area. The first contested election in 2003 returned the 9 Councillors who had campaigned for its abolition and who promptly passed a resolution to abolish.

The Borough Council conducted a Review and recommended abolition to the Government who refused saying the case was not proved and it was also against Government policy.

A further survey of the community in 2006 confirmed the call for abolition. In May 2007 the 9 Councillors who again campaigned for abolition were elected uncontested and the Parish Council scaled down its operations to the legal minimum. A survey in October 2009 confirmed the call for abolition and the Borough Council formally agreed to abolish Byfleet Parish Council in December 2009.

Lickey End
In the Worcestershire village of Lickey End the Parish Council began in 2001 following a supporting petition. At the 2001 and 2003 election 10 pro-abolition Councillors were elected to power, arguing the cost of running the Council was unnecessary as the village's needs were already met by Bromsgrove District Council. The Parish Council formally resolved to abolish itself and the District Council Review confirmed this to the Government.

The Government responded that the Parish Council had not had time to demonstrate its abilities, arguing the District Council Review had produced two contradictory petitions of equal numbers and the pro-abolition election leaflets were vague.

In 2007, all 10 pro-abolition candidates were re-elected unopposed and still aim to return Lickey End to its unparished state.

Controversy in Frome

...Frome Watch...

With six Wards (Keyford, Market, Berkley Down, Oakfield, Park, and College) in the town with roughly 3,600 electors in each there is an argument for each Ward to have its own Parish Council in line with the spirit of government policy. For example Keyford Ward previously a small hamlet with possible Celtic roots is still today complete with a Manor house, shops, school and employment areas, Berkley Down Ward on the high ground to the north is a large new housing area, with shops, school and community buildings. The old, now defunct ward names of Badcox and Welshmill are related closely to historically identifiable areas of the town and could be resurrected.

There could be benefits: each new Parish would be a manageable size, nearer the size of Parish Councils nationally, each new Parish would give greater representation on a par with the surrounding rural Parishes as the minimum number of Councillors for a Parish is five, (increasing representation in the town at a minimum to 30 from the 17 at present); using the 2010/2011 Budget demand each new Parish would have an annual income of over £150,000. When extrapolated over a future four year electoral cycle each new Parish would have had over £600,000 to spend! Contrasting starkly with the little if anything spent currently in each Ward.

Datafile
Guidance on Community Governance Reviews, www.communities.gov.uk
The Local Government and Involvement in Health Act 2007
Local Government Act 1972 www.opsi.gov.uk/acts
Electoral Commission, www.electoralcommission.org.uk

A SUMMER STALL FROME

20 – POLITICS - The Politics

Councillors do not have to belong to a political party; it can be a neighbourhood group or a single issue group. Originally Councillors were staunchly Independent but over time partisan political groupings have developed leading to an eternal, titanic, life and death struggle of classical proportions played out in every Committee. This development seems incongruous as there is an obvious mismatch between policies developed for a national stage and the very locally focused world of the Parish. This does not stop the politicking which decrees any idea suggested by "them" will be ridiculed and voted down, whist maintaining to the public at large, *"we will all work together for the good of the Parish."*

Independents

Many Councillors still stand as individuals not subscribing to any particular philosophy or cause and will be described on the ballot papers at elections as Independent. As such these Councillors will feel freer to agree or disagree with lines of argument that may be made by the political groupings on a Council and may be more able to express the views of the electorate without being mindful of party solidarity or the censorship of colleagues. However, if there are too few Independents on a politically aligned Council they can feel isolated and may be sidelined in the decision making processes or in any "horse trading" that may take place or just the general gossip. The lack of a support group may make being a Councillor hard work; however there is a greater sense of personal responsibility and pleasure in pursuing aims unencumbered.

For Independents, the organisation and cost of running for election is borne by themselves. There is a set amount per elector allowed, currently £600 plus 5 pence per elector (2008). This is traditionally spent on the production of posters, leaflets and newsletters, though it is a personal decision how much, if anything is spent. Their design and statements of intent are not restrained by the formulaic approach of the political parties but does mean the delivery of election literature, or any canvassing is also personally organised.

...Frome Watch...

The IfF Factor

Modest, in simple black and white, stylish - with oddly geometric shaped posters - Independents for Frome (IfF) were an unexpected change to Frome's political landscape where the three main parties had slogged it out for years each knowing their place, picking over well practiced enmities. Their natural and only reaction was to ignore them completely.

Part of a local swing towards independence, as Parishes over the border in Bath & North East Somerset also fielded a range of very diverse candidates in protest at their current incumbents.

Unexpected, a result of the Council's confrontational attitude to the funding of the community hall, the Cheese & Grain, a small group found themselves outside the Council meeting sharing their disbelief. Six principles were rapidly put together and inaugural meeting held. From the packed meeting volunteers were asked to put themselves forward as candidate Councillors. As individual independents, with a determination to focus just on the Parish in the forth-coming elections (May 2011) and not the concurrent Mendip District elections. The use of a common logo however, did mean it had to register as a minor party.

There were promises to be different, more genuine and meaningful conversations with the townspeople asking what was wanted, and a warning, electoral success did not mean the precept would be decreased – there had been much unease and disbelief with the realisation that the Town Budget was very close to £1 million. One of the highest in the whole of Somerset. Worries were smoothed and the inaugural meeting reassured any rise would be the price of a loaf of bread – although whether supermarket basic white sliced at 25p or artisanal at £3.00 a loaf was not explained.

Indeed the Localism Act was just around the corner which promised great freedoms. Already there was the New Homes Bonus which would supply the town with the equivalent of 6 years' worth of Council Tax with every house built to spend on community projects it was optimistically suggested (the reality was a bit disappointing). Letters to the papers and town rumours struck a different tone some sneering, many dismissive, others doubtful. The basic question was asked, how could the Independents work together? Was it an alliance, a party, leftovers from the old Labour Party? The traditional parties were incredulous and a little unnerved; with no structure and no discipline, no decisions, it was said, could be made, it was not possible to have a coalition of Independents.

Rumours abounded: the expensive decisions such as the £25,000 spent on the Xmas lights was again criticised and would be a likely target for abolition; the Mayor would be abolished upsetting, it was said, the town's charities; the town would end up with 17 Mayors, the Chief Executive (Parish Clerk) would go, and this in turn questioned the effectiveness of a £50,000 salary. It would be chaos, how could they work in partnership with anyone.

The traditionalists argued belonging to a party brought consistency in voting, there are no surprises, free thinkers are forced into line, whilst a closed shop there are important allegiances to a wider party beyond the bounds of the locality. The Independents looked to a new world order of rational debate with community views to the forefront, free of dogma, promoting the town not only to itself but to a wider audience for the tourist pound and the hope of attracting new businesses.

Political Parties

Councillors who belong to a political party; and most choose from the main national parties Conservative, Labour or Liberal Democrats, can find this a mixed blessing. Councillors who fly under a political banner will be expected to belong to the national party. There may be a time delay of up to a year before standing for election is allowed however; this may be ignored if a group is desperate for people to stand and in any case a Councillor switching political allegiance is always enthusiastically welcomed.

Councillors who belong to a political grouping are not necessarily "Political" and when asked will often state, with real regret, the necessity of belonging.

Indeed political party membership has fallen by a factor of 20 since the 1970's this has produced something of a funding crisis. In the past the grass-roots supporters could be relied upon to organise and turn out for jumble sales, cheese and wine parties, garden parties, and skittles evenings. These are often a distant memory replaced in favour of Councillors pledging a percentage of their local government allowances, around 10%, to party funds providing an important steady income stream.

Political groupings may meet between Council meetings to thrash out approaches to issues, develop policies, decide on any "horse-trading", or how to unsettle or wrong foot the opposition.

This may or may not include discussions: with the local party within the area to canvass their views, or with the political grouping at District/Unitary or County Council level, or the local constituency party or perhaps surprisingly even the local MP who may not be aware of the convolutions of local issues at Parish level.

There is the sense of comradeship in belonging to a group, though this can result in a sense of a reduced personal responsibility or autonomy for decisions or policies pursued. Colleagues will expect the group line to be followed, if there are a few strong personalities then their view will hold sway and there may be no decisions to make.

There are sometimes attempts to graft national policies on to a local platform; this is generally confined to election literature although this can occasionally emerge as resolutions in Council meetings, including sending strongly worded letters condemning proposed national wars, or support for unilateral nuclear disarmament – very popular in the 1980s. Such a stand can seem either bold and progressive or ill-fitting and inappropriate and will probably reflect the crisis of the moment and the need, Councillors feel, to be seen to be taking a lead.

One advantage of belonging to a political group is that elections costs are met from Party Funds, the hassle of designing and writing election literature and posters can be done from within the party structure often using a template, set format and colours, The candidate only needing to add a personal statement. For political parties the advantage of a politically aligned Parish is being able to claim grass-roots support and knowing that there is a willing team of people to deliver leaflets and canvass an area at national elections as well as meet and greet visiting prospective parliamentary candidates or feed easy questions that reflect well on the candidate at public meetings or to the press, whilst providing enthusiastic support for photocalls and television coverage.

Once elected under a political banner these things are not mentioned again indeed much is made of being a united Council with the politics going unrecorded on Councillor web profiles, or forgotten about on the Declaration of Interests.

In Committee meetings political groups tend to sit together and this can give a confrontational feel to meetings and does perpetuate the still hierarchical approach of managing a group. Independent Councillors can of course sit anywhere and can easily unsettle and disrupt the cohesion of a political group by sitting in their midst!

...Frome Watch...

Somerton and Frome

Frome, part of the oddly shaped constituency of Somerton and Frome,- looking not unlike a high heeled boot, is the largest town with a population of about 26,000 at its eastern end with Somerton to the south west with about 5,000, there are over a 100 Parishes, scattered in and around what is a very rural community. There is no historic, economic, geographic or transport relationship between Frome and the rest of the constituency which cuts a swathe through two District Councils (the eastern half of Mendip District and the northern part of South Somerset) but is contained within the boundaries of Somerset County Council.

The constituency has returned a Liberal Democrat MP over the last four election cycles 1997, 2001, 2005 and 2010 albeit very narrowly by small three-figure majorities (812 in 2005 until 2010 when it increased to 1,800).

Although the Liberal Democrat Constituency headquarters is based in Frome and the Town Council is run by the Liberal Democrats as the majority grouping (2007-11) - with 13 Liberal Democrat Councillors -there is no input into the Town Council by the local MP in terms of opinion or guidance on what or how town issues are addressed or on expenditure or future plans. Yet many in the town feel that plans and policies must be looked over and assume tacit approval as a given. Indeed asked to comment on the Town Council's high spending the MP demurred. Equally no views appear to be given by the Town Council to the MP. The townspeople can question their MP at monthly surgeries in the town library or by telephone. There are also regular local radio broadcasts.

The 2011 Coalition Government in deciding to reduce the number of constituencies in England from 535 to 502 to create an electorate for each of roughly 76,000 planned to abolish Somerton and Frome. Confusingly Frome's focus was expected to turn north again towards a new sphere of influence and the more economically active City of Bath. Returning it to its position of 1835 and which was repeated again in 1918 joining the newly formed (2010) Bath and North East Somerset. It was expected to be a probable hold for the Conservatives. A falling out between the partners in the Coalition (2012) threw these changes into doubt.

Government Philosophy and Parish Councils.

The 1997 Labour Government decides Parish Councils are *the* dynamic force for change setting out in dramatic and loaded terminology what is expected. The creation of "sustainable communities," achieved by people having a say in the way their neighbourhoods are managed. It sets out in strong ideological terms, not a simple to do list; Parishes are now the vanguard of a new but local political world order.

There is a central tenet, the views and wishes of the local communities. Parish communities are now defined as areas with a sense of themselves, with a distinctive local identity and a sense of place capable of fulfilling their own potential and overcoming their own difficulties including; community conflict, extremism, deprivation and disadvantage. Painting a picture of small embattled communities (perhaps a governmental response to the unknown and growing terrorism threats) who will now feel empowered to respond to challenging economic, social and cultural trends, as well as demographic changes, whilst offering a safe, healthy and sustainable environment. Quite a tall order.

A "Sustainable Community"

The Government characterises a "sustainable community" in this instance as the desire for a community to be well run with effective and inclusive participation, representation and leadership. The Government explains this as:
a) representative, accountable governance systems which both facilitate strategic, visionary leadership and enable inclusive, active and effective participation by individuals and organisations; and
b) effective engagement with the community at neighbourhood level including capacity building to develop the community's skills of:
- knowledge and confidence:
- a strong, inclusive community and voluntary sector;
- a sense of civic values, responsibility and pride; and
- a sense of place, a place with a positive feeling for people and local distinctiveness.

There are now specific, some familiar and some ambitious roles for Parish Councils:

- Influencing the quality of Planning and design of public spaces and the built environment, improving their management and maintenance;
- Judging what is needed to build cohesion such as recognising social exclusion and deprivation. Empowering citizens to influence public decisions;
- Taking on community leadership, being proactive in "place shaping" responding to local challenges and opportunities;
- Providing good quality, accessible, and easily used local services (within the limits of economy and efficiency). This, it reasoned, gave service users democratic voice;
- Using the "Power of Well-Being" to promote the social, economic and environmental well-being of their area.

The Government looked around the country and decided the unity within communities was collapsing and shifted its focus towards the creation of urban Parishes; the metropolitan areas would spearhead this. Now the Parish role will include cohesion with its bedfellows integration and diversity and Government sets out how this will happen using: strong local leadership, greater resident participation in decisions and a strong role for community groups.

Community Cohesion

Cohesion; is the shared values that hold a community together, a subtle, usually unspoken sense of mutual interest and respect, partly based on a long shared history, not generally thought about, but still there, and it can be called upon when needed, something incomers would be expected to absorb as they became part of the fabric of the community and provide its future framework. This time heavy method has been replaced by a newer, aggressive brand, resulting from the impact of a more diverse society ethnically, religiously and culturally, certainly in the more urban Parishes.

The Government sets out 3 ways of living together:
- A shared future vision and sense of belonging;
- A focus on what new and existing communities have in common, alongside recognition of the value of diversity;
- Strong and positive relationships between people from different backgrounds.

Creating integrated and cohesive communities based on three foundations:
- People from different backgrounds having similar life opportunities;
- People knowing their rights and responsibilities;
- People trusting one another and trusting local authorities to act fairly.

Whether Parish Councils see themselves in this light is another matter, for most Parishes it is still the round of fêtes, church and village events and the cosy details of village societies and clubs, stick in the mud, conservative, unexciting, low key, even dull.

Government, whilst recognising in a community, flourishing societies and clubs, offering opportunities for fun, involvement, or voicing opinions and even influencing decisions, it is the Parish Councillors with their single unique fact of democratic election that is paramount. The advantage of independence from the other council tiers with their own budgets, and their own set of specific and special powers makes the Parishes the foundation stones for all the other levels of local government in England.

Other bodies, Government says, however worthy do not have whole electorate elections.

However, what actually happens is somewhat different, the turnout for voting in local elections has been steadily decreasing. National elections have seen the level of voting drop from over 80% in the 1950s to around 55% today. Many Parish elections scrape along with an ever lowering turnout many Councillors elected on a handful of votes or Parishes not holding elections at all as seats are uncontested and Councillors co-opted as necessary. This avoids the cost of elections which may be charged to the individual Parishes by their principal authority, a cost a Parish will need to precept for.

To increase electoral participation some, such as Wiltshire's Unitary authority, pay the election costs of its Parishes others are like Mendip District Council which charges roughly £1,300 per Polling Station.

Even so, there are organisations which Government feels have a value and these are generally organisations the local authority either controls or has a heavy input into:

- Area committees; these can cover a large geographical area and may decide on low level issues, street cleaning, toilets and perhaps Planning.
- Neighbourhood management; smaller than Area Committees which rather vaguely aim to improve the quality of life on issues such as the environment, young people, housing stock, community safety and employment.
- Tenant Management Organisations; responsible for rents, repairs and maintenance on urban housing estates.
- Area/ Community /Civic Forums; set up to influence decisions.
- Residents and Tenants Associations again influencing decisions.
- Community Associations; managing community centres under a registered constitution. These meet with the warmest Government approval and are considered a good democratic model.

Sustainable Frome
Started in 2005 by a group of enthusiasts, (it has since developed a Community Interest Company) who were determined to find practical and ethical ways to meet the future environmental, economic and social changes which will effect Frome. It developed a series of interest groups in: Food and Land; Transport; Green Fair; Bring Your Own Bag Campaign; Green Buildings; Eco Schools; Spirituality; Green Club; and Creative Recycling. The whole group meets monthly to share ideas.

Frome has since become a Transition Town committed to reducing its reliance on oil and has been involved with: car sharing schemes; community energy; local shops and local food production and promotion. With around 600 members it is one of the biggest grouping in town; certainly larger than the political parties.

Vision for Frome(V4F)

This holds the document of collective wisdom, in effect Frome's Parish Plan.

Started in 2007 using Regional Development Agency Funding through the Market and Coastal Towns Initiative (since defunct) with matched and additional funding from Mendip District Council giving a pot of £45,000. A steering group of interested individuals carried out surveys and extensive public consultations (collecting some 3,500 comments) creating a Community Plan to cover 20 years. Projects with the most public backing, some 130, were launched in May 2009. Under a range of 6 headings; Economy; Getting Around; Housing and Heritage; Land Use; Food, Energy and Waste; Society and Well-Being; and Young People.

Projects of varying sizes, complexities and timescales emerged: from local energy from waste schemes, free short term parking, to supporting a town centre youth café, from hopper buses linking residential areas and town centre, extra allotments, to looking at a possibility of a bowling alley, a long held town dream. Much which was familiar and repeated previous consultations and previous plans or was already partly undertaken or funded by Mendip and Somerset local authorities. The Plan is primarily used as supporting evidence or as a basis for other projects in the town to gain grant funding including Lottery Funding. V4F does not undertake projects. The as yet hoped for close ties with the Town Council (2007-2011) have not yet materialised. V4F with its 30 odd core contributors still organise periodic forums to discuss and consult on town developments and town issues.

Datafile

Strong and Prosperous Communities. Local Government White Paper. Oct 2006
Communities and Local Government, Guidance on Community Governance Reviews, April 2008
Sustainable Frome, www,sustainablefrome.org.uk and www.transitionfrome.org.uk
Vision for Frome, www.vision4frome.org.uk
The Hansard Society, www.hansardsociety.org.uk
Labour Uncut, www.labour-uncut.co.uk
Conservative Home, www. conservativehome.blogs.com
They Work For You,www.theyworkforyou.com

JENSON BUTTON BRIDGE FROME

21 - ACCOUNTABILITY - How can you know?

"the cost of freedom is eternal vigilance," Thomas Jefferson

How we know what goes on, Freedom of Information Act, Frome's minuted highlights

Accountability

All of us have an interest in the way things are run and yet there has been and still is a reluctance by Councils to listen to views or to give explanations, an unwillingness to share information, and something of an entrenched culture of secrecy where questioning is not welcomed and often barely tolerated – *"what we tell you should be good enough"* is the impression given with questioners treated like wayward children. Often there has been an unspoken determination to give away as little information as possible and certainly it is only recently that many Parishes have published their latest minutes or reports on-line. Accountability has become the new watchword for all public institutions and when going hand in hand with a much professed desire for transparency and openness, opportunities open up for everyone to be fully involved in how things are run.

Communications or how "they" tell us what is happening.

What Councillors do and what goes on in Councils particularly at a Parish level is generally a mystery, probably rarely considered by most of the electorate and on the whole not thought particularly meaningful. Information is patchy and this has often led to a "them and us" situation with suspicion on both sides. Councillors feel misunderstood, isolated, frequently isolating themselves with their reluctance to explain. They are frequently seen as an elite group, whose comments, if reported, at best sound high-handed, or pompous spoken with a certain twist of arrogance and often with an unsaid *"we know best"*; or *"if it wasn't for people like us."*

The electorate feeling doubtful or misled by exaggerated claims of success are convinced *"they are only in for what they can get out of it."* Resentful at being asked to vote for vague generalities or uncertain ideas backed by the assertion *"I will represent the people of…."* without any explanation of what that might mean. All too often, "they" disappear from view never to be seen again until the next election. This must contribute to low turnouts. The actions of the Parish Council can seem at odds with the little that is suggested on the candidate's election leaflet which is perhaps surprising as many candidates often stand for further terms and should at the very least be able to point to evidence of past success or specific future interests or intentions.

However, much has changed over the last decade with Government determined that Parish Councillors should somehow provide, albeit undefined, "community leadership;" an unintended snub to the vast body of organisations and people who are the fabric of community life in every Parish. Government has reinforced legislation to encourage a more adventurous approach. This has fuelled ambitious professional organisations to offer services or "ready-made" opinions to Councils, influencing policy and becoming part of the decision making process. Council bureaucracies have taken the opportunity to aggrandise and elaborate their own role, added to this mix is a new breed of Parish Clerk more ambitious in their own right.

But, in the first instance the Parish electorate needs to be convinced that what is done in their name is of value and there are a number of ways this may happen.

Newspapers

Most of us rely on the local newspaper for much of what we know and this in turn is reliant on the story reaching the press and again on the newspapers printing it. Nationally many local newspapers are struggling to survive (Norway subsidises local newspapers to ensure political coverage). Few these days send a reporter to cover Council Committees and are reliant on comments made over the telephone or a written statement or press release. Critical analysis and regular scrutiny is minimal and issues are rarely followed up. There is little holding of Councils to account. Indeed, many of the higher tier Councils, have their own public relations departments writing their own press releases highlighting achievements. Award winning toilets - District, potholes filled - County, and award winning flowers - Parish, with short, bouncy, cheerful statements backed up with a quotation from the Councillor responsible – at District, Unitary or County level often referred to as the portfolio holder or the Chairman of the Committee. Although generally lacking any detailed or factual information the statement should describe succinctly the: who, what, where, when, why and how of a story. Too often the short description is followed by bland quotes expressing pleasure and emphasising the importance of the Council's role in the achievement. Statements are rarely challenged or followed up at a future date.

The newspapers' letters pages are eagerly awaited by those who have courageously asked a question or raised an issue publicly hoping to raise a debate and it is disappointing if there is no reaction from the Council or Councillors. Criticisms are often ignored and the opportunity missed to provide a straightforward explanation.

Newspaper Letters
In March 2009 local Frome newspapers printed letters from Councillors resurrecting the arguments over the desirability of Somerset becoming a Unitary Authority. Accusations of a lack of local patriotism were hurled, with the assertion that fellow Councillors just wanted to benefit from the attendance allowances. The whole matter had been considered and rejected by Government in 2007.

Occasionally it is Councillors themselves who are critical, with perhaps a view to political point scoring, sometimes bringing up subjects long since dead, with a sudden explosion and flurry of writing obscuring other topics which could be usefully debated in public. These criticisms briefly become slanging matches dividing along party lines and flare up briefly, burning obsessively for a short time before dying down. This is most likely to occur around election time. Election time is also the opportunity for party supporters to create mischief with a steady drip of letter writing throwing doubt and consternation at the opposition. These exchanges can be surprisingly vitriolic as long held grudges are dusted off.

...Frome Watch...
The Media
Frome was covered by three very individual local newspapers:

- The Somerset Standard, a weekly paid for, colour newspaper, 55p (April 2010), which can trace its history back to 1886. The paper covers "feel good" stories, local schools events, charitable fund raising and diligently follows Mayoral engagements. There is a suspected covert Liberal Democrat bias. It has a large "what's on" entertainment section, with estate agents, cars and jobs adverts plus a sports section. It publishes some public notices and listed new Planning applications (Cost cutting at Mendip District Council did away with this (2012)).

The paper recently closed its Frome office moving reporters and photographers to its sister paper in Midsomer Norton losing some of its Frome focus.

- The Frome Times, a free black and white paper delivered to every home fortnightly. It started in the 1990's covering similar stories to the Standard but with generally a more detailed serious tone. With overall less advertising it also carried the Town Council quarterly newsletter.
- The Fosse Way magazine was a free undelivered paper picked up from points in the town, with a small A4 format and a colour front cover. The content was article based with fewer photographs than its rivals and covered a huge area much of South Somerset and Mendip Districts including all the Mendip towns and the rural villages in between. Frome stories, although only occasionally included, were covered in depth. It was the only paper to advertise Mendip District Council and Somerset County Council jobs and advertised Highway and some Planning public notices. It was also the only newspaper to publish Mendip District Councillors' annual statement of claimed allowances. Sadly it closed May 2011.

Free monthly glossy colour magazines could also be picked up at points around the town. "The Mendip Times" covering the geographic area of the Mendip Hills, with articles focusing on rural life and rural communities and for a brief moment "Furball", an irreverent satirical look at Frome and the townspeople, concentrating on the music and arts scene. The newest is "The List" a monthly, delivered, slim format booklet of music and arts things to do in Frome with cameos of Frome businesses and newer still "Frome Life", A5 sized with colour articles on Frome businesses.

The real change has been the rise of websites and blogs covering the town's issues such as the on-going supermarket debate. The website "Frome People" provides a reporting service and blogging opportunity on events and town meetings including some of the Town Council's. Frome TV along with the radio station Frome FM provides some coverage of larger meetings.

Most weeks, the newspapers had photographs of the Mayor, wearing the chain of office, as the town's ceremonial figure, congratulating groups on successful fundraising, making an award, handing over a cheque or opening an event. The Deputy Mayor may step in as a substitute but it is rare for other Councillors to take on this ceremonial role. There are few opportunities for an ordinary Councillor to become known and gain any press coverage unless they take on a campaigning role, which may put them at odds with their party colleagues.

Over the last few years each Frome Mayor has tried to "meet the people." Initially with a monthly stall in the draughtiest corner of the shopping precinct, supplemented with a newspaper column. Gleaning townspeople's views was originally tried in the late 1990's, with a rota of Councillors available either to chat to or to take up complaints, based at the reception desk of the Library on Saturday mornings. The experiment was of limited success, as most complaints concerned dog fouling, litter and pavements blocked by overgrown hedges and was later abandoned.

Although the promised Mayoral internet blog did not materialise the following year's Mayor's Facebook page gained 2,600 followers and was combined with a Saturday morning "meet the Mayor" at the Market Yard police post. The Facebook page was seen as a tremendous success and an example of "best practice of public engagement" – although not always an easy read, it aired everyday queries. Councillors agreed *"social sites are key to contact with townspeople."* The format looks set to continue in the following electoral cycle.

More recently the Town Council's occasional press statements: always up-beat, always exciting, always a partnership, are increasingly fronted by staff diverting the focus and ultimate responsibility away from the Councillors who authorised the Council's actions, making it unclear who is in charge (many Councillors are a bit hazy about this as well).

As the bureaucracy hits its stride there is the appearance of a Council functioning without its Councillors and an air of inevitability as Councillors distance themselves from decisions.

The Mendip District Council's help desk in the town Library offers daily advice, dealing with queries and problems interceding with District or County departments and is the place to view Planning applications. The Town Council started its own help desk just fifty yards away at the Black Swan Arts Centre when it took over Tourist Information enabling it to shut the Council office to visitors, combining two roles. Planning applications, the town's main concern were still viewed by appointment. The new Council reception had few visitors on Council business but it did act as a signpost to telephone callers. Unable to secure a further lease it moved to the town Library next to the Mendip's help desk. Unexpectedly County caused some consternation with its determination to cut its running costs by shortening library opening hours (it closed others in the rest of the County). Eventually with threats of court action many of the County's libraries were saved and opening hours reinstated.

Websites
The internet has given Parish Councils an amazing opportunity to put their views across, and for the electorate to follow Parish discussions and decisions. Websites have vastly improved over the last few years with more information available but in some instances, along with newsletters, they become part of the public relations machine with facts difficult to find and buried in trivia. Parish websites are often part of community websites covering clubs, societies, visitor information, church and Parish events. Each give a very individual flavour of their Council and a sense of place. At their best they inform and at their worst there is again the almost a perverse desire not to give too much away.

Recent legislation has set out to change this with the Parish Publication Scheme, it also applies to Parish Meetings. Expect to see: each Parishes' individually scripted and agreed Code of Conduct; each Councillors' Register of Interests which will include their partner's details; a Publication Scheme describing the information available (covering what most people would want to know such as minutes of meetings), how it can be obtained and the cost – most should be free or a small photocopy charge. Many will automatically post the information outlined in the Scheme on-line. This raises the standard overall as too many Council websites failed to post any minutes, maintain an archive or even update general Parish information, surprising when many Parishes are large and well resourced. The Scheme has been in operation since 2005!

...Frome Watch...
Frome websites
Originally the Town Council had a small entry on a general website which listed local businesses and organisations paid for out of the regeneration budget allotted by Mendip to Frome, unfortunately it was rarely added to or updated. For many years it listed Councillors who had stepped down years before. A newer website in a startling canary yellow and a bright royal blue (the corporate colour), although carrying basic information, the main emphasis was on procedures and protocols rather than budgets or Council activities and highlighted the growth of the Council's management focus.

Newsletters
The last decade has seen the rise of the newsletter first used by large companies and utilities, taken up by local Councils and political parties who have made them part of their charm offensive. Glossy and informal with short, self-congratulatory articles with a negligible factual content, loaded with photographs of smiling handshaking Councillors with small bright-eyed children or happy award winning employees – generally dinner ladies or caretakers.

Or low grade stories such as *"Your District Councillors pressures District Council (sic) into gritting road."* Promises are made, *"we listen to what you say and take action"* or *"transparency in decision making is our priority."* Every Council action is a: *"huge success," "model scheme," "award winning," "nationally recognised,"* or *"top rated"* and is a tribute to hyperbole. Claims which at the higher Council tiers reflect the growth of public relations departments within Councils, to such an extent that in some areas the viability of local newspapers has been threatened as Councils' own newspapers high-jack local advertising revenue. It had become such a problem that the 2010 Coalition Government told Councils to stop.

Political parties have used newsletters increasingly to supplement election literature between and coming up to local and national elections. Produced as a news-sheet highlighting local issues and claiming success where possible or at the very least condemning the opposition whilst using the broad brush of association with the good things that have happened. Rarely is there any reference to election "promises" made.
There are the usual photos of grim faced Councillors and potential Councillors well - wrapped up in coats massed around or pointing to: dog poo bins - a Frome speciality, car parking charges signs - a hardy perennial, or down at raised manhole covers and potholes, or up at overhanging trees or street lights – it's the other Council's fault and of course a bit on how to get in touch.

A sitting MP may also report to his constituency via a newsletter highlighting achievements but this time photographed grinning surrounded by, again, happy, smiling school children and dinner ladies or more trickily, shaking hands whilst handing over a trophy. Both newsletters increase nearer election time.

Parish Council newsletters are generally less dramatic, more low key and should offer a useful summary of what has been done and what there is to do reflecting the views of the Council, oddly Exmouth Parish Council's newsletter carried a disclaimer *"these are not necessarily the views of the Council"* strangely distancing itself from its own reported activities. Newsletters are one of the basic blocks of the Quality Parish Scheme, 4 should be published each year with at the very least the name and contact details of Councillors and Clerk.

...Frome Watch...
Newsletters

Of the political parties locally, only the Liberal Democrats published intermittent newsletters, the Conservatives only at General Election time and Labour never.

Frome's first foray into newsletter writing was early on (January 2004) and was oddly titled *"News specifically for the residents of Frome"* and outlined the triumphs of the past and the promises for the forth coming year. A relatively new Council, it was in intense discussion with Mendip District Council requesting vigorous efforts in clearing and cleaning the town of litter. A new CCTV monitoring suite in nearby Wells caused excitement with promises of new cameras indeed the Town Council decided all Planning applications of a commercial nature should be asked to install a CCTV camera as part of the permission – this never materialised.

Town grants would continue to fund community initiatives, but the Market Yard toilets would not come under Town management because a new "Beacon" toilet was being built nearby (it later proudly won 5 annual national awards).

Drinking would be banned in the town centre and a new venture tried with the Chamber of Commerce - sponsored hanging baskets but nothing came of this.

New park play equipment is suggested and new bus shelters could be installed in a new partnership with Mendip and a budget is set aside for new street lights.

Councillors were mindful to keep the precept rise low at 5.6%.

With its aim to become a Quality Council, Frome began publishing its own newsletter (3 to 4 a year) as a local newspaper centrefold. Containing the ebb and flow of the minutiae of Parish life: the good news stories already previously reported in the local papers: the fun of Twinning, the park refurbishment, snippets about town grants, Frome in Bloom victories, Christmas Spectacular announcements, and grit and dog poo bin deployment. The centrepiece was the mayoral column reflecting each Mayor's passion: green issues, touristy events, and the power of Facebook alongside possible car park land purchases from Mendip District. Each had the calendar of Council meetings and the contact details of Councillors and in one year a useful summary of the Annual Report. All to be repeated again in each year's Annual Report and as a PowerPoint presentation at each Annual Parish Meeting.

Language.
Most legislation is couched in difficult terminology, as it attempts to turn common sense into legal sounding language Phrases used in the Local Government and Health Act 2007 are typical and the following explains the role of Parish Councils:

- by giving local people more influence over the services and decisions that affect their communities";
- providing effective and accountable strategic leadership";
- working within a performance framework which supports citizen empowerment and secures better outcomes for all" and;
- leads local partnerships to provide better services for citizens."

Increasingly local government has also developed its own particular way of speaking, making in the process the obvious obscure. There are regular attempts to persuade everyone to use more straightforward wording. Here are a few favourites:

- Partnership - people we like dealing with and who agree with us, this replaces stakeholder as top word;
- Stakeholders – everyone;
- Key Stakeholders – people we would rather deal with;
- Pathfinders – sounds exciting, experimental and ground-breaking and replaces pilot (as in pilot project), but with more money. Extra public consultations may be included once the major decisions have been made. Heavy use of paid consultants;
- Ground-breaking – a rehash of all previous attempts but this time with extra staff;
- Strategic – planned;
- Performance framework – how we know what to do, when to do it and how it went;
- Leadership - management;
- Outcomes - results;
- Service level agreements – stuff others promise to do in return for something, generally money;
- Consultation – we ask you what you think, luckily we already know what the answer should be;

- Empowerment – allows you to do the things you thought you could do already, generally best said with a slightly patronising tone;
- Community – possibly everyone?
  and two particular gems:
- Wayfinding Strategy – road signs;
- Celebratory gateways – the entrance sign which carries the town or village name.

...Frome Watch...

Symbols

Symbols which represent the town to itself and the wider world are more recent:

- The town's Coat of Arms was granted in the 1950's. Various elements give a mediaeval picture of Frome: Sheep and bobbins represent the woollen industry past on which the wealth of the merchants and the poverty of its inhabitants were founded. Over the centuries diarists and commentators have wound there way though Frome's muddy streets noting its poverty, unemployment and squalor; Willow trees represent the woodland setting of the town on the edge of Selwood Forest, long since disappeared and in reality a hunting area for the King; The motto "Time Trieth Troth" or "truth will out" taken from a sundial plaque which the Hungerfords, from the nearby hamlet of Farleigh Hungerford where their castle home was, fortuitously placed on their town house. This was their only association with Frome and the family died out in 1711.

- To mark the 1300th anniversary, year-long celebrations of the founding of a monastery in Frome in 685, long since vanished, and by association Frome itself, the face of a longhaired wey-faced young Saxon was depicted. St Aldhelm: scholar, poet, linguist, international traveller and churchman become Abbot of Malmesbury and Bishop of Sherborne founding a string of churches in the West Country. He was middle-aged and portly by the time he reached Frome. He was notably the nephew of King Ine - Frome was the Wessex capital for a short while and King Edred died here. His very youthful image is still used by some organisations as the face of Frome today and can be found on railings in the Market Place.

- The 2007-11 administration went for a branding exercise (very popular at the time amongst most local authorities) choosing the colour royal blue for office paint, letterheads and website and composing a mission statement which could be reduced to a strap line. Councillors put forward various suggestions, many echoing Lincoln's Gettysburg Address, *"government of the people, by the people, for the people,"* before plumping on something more understated and bland *"Frome Town Council will work for and with local people to make Frome a better place."* Reduced to the slightly unsettling strap line, *"Making Frome a Better Place."*

- Somerset County Council entered into the spirit of things and in 2008 launched a County-wide bill board advertising campaign telling its inhabitants of the delights of living in Somerset. Under the slogan "Providing For Life" a smiling elderly couple, happy workers or cheerful small children were pictured with useful and interesting facts, such as there are 83 registry offices in the County. The cost was £150,000 and brought much criticism as the County's inhabitants thought the idea nonsensical. Again in 2010 £278,000 was spent on a new logo, only to be ditched within the 12 month.

Consultation and partnerships exercises.

Consultation is simply asking local people what they think or more usually key stakeholders, these are increasingly professional organisations who have a vested interest in the outcome.

Their decisions may provide some additional funding or even secure their own employment in a project. Views consequently may not tally with the perceptions of local people and certainly very few consultations aim to reduce spending.

Consultation serves several purposes: it acts as publicity for whatever Councillors wish to do; it gives integrity to any decisions, and can be used to demonstrate both accountability and transparency. Usefully scotching any opposition as the consultation process can always be referred to; it gives an impression of arms-length and therefore independent and informed decision making.

Opinions are collected as either random comments under broad headings e.g. "what responsibilities should the Town Information Point have?" or a survey which asks simple yes/no questions e.g. "do you think the economic climate will improve within the next year?" The last can be reported as a percentage of those who reply so even a low response rate (1%, can be regarded a good response for paper surveys) can still be read as strong support for any proposed decision. Consultations often result in partnerships.

Partnerships are often made with those key stakeholders who were consulted in the first place. After all they have a full appreciation of the issues and are not going to rock the boat or challenge any assumptions. These can develop into long term relationships. Partnerships can also briefly occur when a Council grant aids a group to provide a specific activity e.g. the repainting of Frome's old milestones by a group of enthusiasts was reported as a partnership. Both can also be referred to as exercises.

...Frome Watch...

Consultations

Consultations held over the last four years included:

- The redesign the skateboard area - resulted in a toned down less exciting park.
- The possible opening of a café in the park- very much welcomed.
- A yes /no survey web-link via the Town Council website for the Frome based "Missing Link" group to garner support to help it raise funds for the 2-3 miles into town of the Sustrans national cycleway Route 24. The cost is somewhere between $£\frac{1}{4}$ and $£\frac{1}{2}$ million depending on the complexity of the engineering and the balance between contractors or volunteers used to build it. 1,234 had signed (2011).
- A forum on the proposed designs of the replacement to the Bailey Bridge – only a few members of the public went.
- The "Vision4Frome" group were asked what responsibilities the newly acquired Information Centre (TIC) should have.
- A town survey asking - should the Christmas tree be moved back to the town centre - the 52 replies agreed.

There are always larger consultations asking for suggestions for change or improvement: the Vision4Frome action plan developed over several years and at District level: the Local Development Framework/Local Plan which has held 3 consultations since 2008 on housing, employment and leisure needs. In the recent past "Big Cake" and "Frome Fit For Future" consulted on similar issues.

Meetings and Minutes

Whilst Minutes offer a record of decision making much can still occur away from public view.

At the bottom of most agendas there is the phrase, "That in view of the business about to be transacted, it is considered advisable in the public interest that the press and public be temporarily excluded and they be instructed to withdraw." Originally intended to be rarely used and only on matters where a high level of confidentiality is paramount e.g. sensitive personnel issues, it can be used to hide embarrassment or issues which might be controversial.

The discussion will not be circulated with the published minutes or even a later synopsis provided, what occurred will be forever unknown.

Meetings throw up other problems, the public are always behind the curve not knowing until a few days before a meeting what will be discussed and a brief agenda announcement gives little time to develop an argument or present a viewpoint. The early start of meetings makes attendance awkward for an electorate with complex working arrangements or responsibilities. The days of the local factory worker finishing at 6pm or of a leisured middle management finishing at 5pm are long gone.

...Frome Watch...

Accountability

- Regular secret Leaders meetings developed where the leaders of Frome's political parties, including the one Independent Councillor, ironed out any difficulties so Council meetings could be kept controlled and short with potential troublemakers isolated and discussion minimised. Decisions became seamless and agreement given with an air of sycophantic self-congratulation, presenting a smiley face to the world. Whilst expedient, there is little for an audience to find interesting in meetings unless someone broke rank. The use of the political block vote was reinforced and for Councillors stretched across several authorities it helped ensure the success of the ruling party.

- In the past, it was the monthly Full Council meetings where the final discussions took place where arguments were ranged and there was an uncertainty of outcome as actions agreed in minutes were sanctioned. Notes on the monthly whole Council Budget were distributed to all Councillors including any watching audience of electors and press. Detailing all spending including individual staff wages making Council expenditure easy to follow; cheques for payment were listed and signed in full view. Most recently each Committee sanctioned its own often unminuted decisions making fellow Councillors and the town heavily reliant on reports in the press. The opportunity for full scrutiny had gone.

Questions... Questions

Perhaps the easiest way to understand what a Parish Council does is to write and ask them. Letters should be addressed to the Chairman of the Council, asking for the issues outlined to be discussed by the Council and requesting a reply. The Parish Clerk will reply on the Council's behalf with their comments or decision. Simple requests for information will be answered by the Parish Clerk.

Problems do arise: queries are blocked, ignored or unanswered with a variety of excuses made: *"I haven't worked here long," "it was before my time," "we probably don't have it," "I expect the meeting was cancelled," "it might be in the archive," "I don't expect it was us," "I can't find it on my computer"* or wild guesses made and the wrong information delivered. There is not always the sense of obligation to answer questions or to go in pursuit of the answer one would hope for.

Being a Councillor
Most people are intrigued why others decide to join a Council. The following is a sample questionnaire of basic "frequently asked" questions.

About You
1. How many Committees are you on at present?
2. How many hours a month, on average do you spend at Town Council meetings?
3. How many members of the public, a month, on average, contact you?
4. How many hours a month overall, on average, on all Town Council business?
5. When you were elected what did you hope to achieve through the Council?
6. Did you specifically promise an action in your election leaflet?
7. If so what was it? And did you achieve it?
8. What are this Town Council's greatest achievements? - In the election cycle 2007-2011.
9. In what way did you contribute to this?
10. What was your greatest achievement as a Councillor in this current election cycle?
11. What do you wish you (as a personal target) could have done?
12. Was the reality of being on the Town Council very different to what you expected, and in what way?
13. What is the one thing you wished you had known about beforehand?
14. What surprised you most when you became a Councillor?
15. Would you stand again and/or encourage others to.

Planning
1. What delegated powers would you like?
2. How would you improve the consultation process?
3. Do you feel you have enough influence at the District Council's Planning committee when an officer's report disagrees with the Town view? What changes would you make?
4. What areas of training would you feel are or would be most useful?
5. Any other comments on Planning

The Politics
1. Do you have, as a Councillor, any contact with either the local MP or the Prospective Parliamentary Candidates?
2. Does or has the Town Council involved the current MP in a particular issue or campaign in this election cycle?
3. Do you feel you are a politician? Please explain
4. How do you feel your party's position / manifesto translate in Frome?
5. Do your local party members ask you to carry forward their suggestions? If so which ones have been successfully applied? Do you ask their advice on issues or on solutions?
6. What advantage has there been to the Town Council's services of your political party alignment?
7. Is or should the Town Council be a political body? Please explain
8. What are the principal issues in Frome, which can be met by Frome Town Council – please be specific not general broad categories like climate change?
9. What are the main issues for your Ward, again –please be specific not general broad categories like climate change?

The Press
There have been critical letters in the local newspapers.
1. How should the Council, respond to questions asked in the letters pages of the local newspapers (e.g. as a whole. or as Committee chairs answer)?
2. Are the issues raised by local newspaper reports discussed at Council meetings?
3. Do you write letters (personally) to the paper? please explain.
4. Do you think the focus on the Mayor – in newspapers, as opposed to the whole Council is a good thing? Please explain.

Twinning
1. What has been its main achievement, in this present election cycle 2007-2011?

Other
1. Is the Council a business?

...Frome Watch...

The 17 Councillors of the 2007-11 electoral cycle were sent the questionnaire to see what it meant to them. The 3 replies were not enough to draw any broad conclusions but do offer one or two thoughts. All agreed they spent around 20 hours a month on Frome Town Council business with about 6 hours in meetings and on average answered 3 or 4 queries from townspeople.

All felt the processes had become too bureaucratic and long winded, but could point to concrete achievements: Tour of Britain race start, land acquisition, grant aid and park improvements.

In Planning all wanted Frome decisions to be made by Frome. The main issues for Frome were wide ranging but low key: open spaces, dog fouling and traffic related whilst each Ward had its own individual set of problems. Politics was thought to provide strong leadership and consistency enabling the party with the most Councillors to make the decisions. It was thought the Council or Committee concerned should respond to critics in the press but individual letters were not thought effective. The Office of Mayor was on the whole was seen as a symbol of pride in the town not the individual. Twinning's only achievement it seemed was adding Poland to the set.

Intriguingly the last question, "is the Council a business?" has taken on an increased importance as 2010 brought in severe national Government budgetary cuts. Over the last decade or so local government authorities have claimed to be businesses. Accordingly Councils have paid their Chief Executives (CEO) (who oversee the implementation of Councillor decisions) large salaries, vastly grown their workforces and in the process turned the electorate into customers. Resulting in a mind-set of enthusiastic spending impervious to criticism.

...Frome Watch...

Are Councils businesses?

Both Somerset County and Mendip District Chief Executives fiercely defended the view that they were running businesses at Frome Chamber of Commerce meetings. County could cite its advertising campaign. In answering the same question Frome's Town Clerk said the Council strongly believed it was a business and wanted to take on a strong economic role within the town. Councillors answering the questionnaire were divided.

Financial support from government has been steadily withdrawn resulting in local authorities cutting budgets and paring back services. The Parishes have been increasingly asked if they would take up the slack. Their precept rises are not subject to a percentage cap unlike local authorities (capped annually at 2%).

With the Power of Competence unleashed under the Localism Act there is an expectation that all levels of Government will develop entrepreneurial skills to improve their finances.

Strategic Plans

Larger parishes were beginning to follow the higher tiers of local government and produce strategic plans which would give a forward view with the detailed analysis that a simple budget line lacked. Plans should define and describe a Council's direction and show how the allocating of resources; that is money and people will be made and be able to outline the expected effect.

There are some basic questions:

- What does the Council currently do, how did it come about and who currently benefits?
- Define and describe new targets and objectives, outlining who will benefit,
- Describe a course of action which meets the new targets,
- Monitor, evaluate and review the results.

S.M.A.R.T

S.M.A.R.T objectives are a useful way to scrutinise plans with their focus on goals, planning and performance.

The acronym describes the key characteristics and questions used to set meaningful objectives:

1. **S**pecific – plans should be well defined and detailed;

2. **M**easurable – track what happens and be able to put a value to the result;

3. **A**chievable - what are the constraints and is it possible?

4. **R**elevant - can the plan be resourced and is it realistic?

5. **T**ime Bound – set deadlines for completion.

...Frome Watch...

Frome's Strategic Plan 2008 to 2011

Planned as a bold definitive document, the first of its kind for Frome and based on a chilly winters evening of discussion in 2007, Councillors commented it was nice to put their political differences aside round a glass of wine and a few nibbles.

The long rambling list of ideas picked its way through a rag-bag of problems and dreams which had accumulated over the years including: buying community assets such as buildings or land; allowing camping on Rodden Meadow; prohibiting heavy goods vehicles through town; and drawing up formal partnerships with voluntary groups.

These were developed over the following year into broadly drawn, wordy statements many ambitious in their thinking and sweeping in their coverage to provide a 2 ½ year plan.

What were listed as policies became in reality a list of governance and housekeeping arrangements for example, 3 quotes to be obtained before a contract is assigned, the annual return to be made to the external auditor. Also included in an act of supreme confidence were a selection of ambitions over which the Frome had little or no control including: providing an integrated, affordable, accessible and sustainable public local transport system; or ensuring that sufficient affordable homes were provided to meet the needs of Frome residents. Many project ideas were taken from the Vision4Frome Community Action Plan to beef-up the Council's offering to the town.

The Plan does define the Council's 4 corporate aims, for the first time:

1. Better Use of Resources: this is spending and staffing;

2. A Sustainable and Enjoyable Environment: this is play spaces and allotments;

3. A Safe Place to Live - a bit of a pick and mix including: improving the town centre, being "green" in this instance the Council's own office using less paper and electricity, crime and Planning;

4. Partnership with the Community - the bits the townspeople see including: grants, Twinning, Mayoral doings, and newsletters.

The Plan whilst written robustly and full of action words like produce, review and identify, and alluding to the Best Value principles (Efficiency, Effectiveness and Economy) in reality had translated into something vague and undirected.

Without the clarity a S.M.A.R.T analysis would bring, the Plan wording was always going to be at odds with what was actually noted as achievements, its outcomes could never be objectively assessed for example,

"Objective 1.1.2. Have due regard to the effect that any spending will have on the Council Tax payers of Frome." Whilst it is unclear what this means, a Plan update noted it was both completed and ongoing;

"Objective 3.1.1. Support and promote Frome Town centre regeneration." Again a Plan update noted this objective completed without explain how or what was achieved. Indeed the majority of objectives were noted as completed by the end of year 2 without any noticeable effects in the town.

The Annual Report
The Annual Report is retrospective round-up of the year. An opportunity to give a rounded view, a "state of the nation", summary of Parish Councillor activity and achievements.

...Frome Watch...
Annual Reports

The four years of Annual Reports, extended to some 60 pages each. These covered some areas in unexpected detail for example the number of grit bins deployed whilst in other areas they were oddly silent such as Twinning achievements.

The Council had no large areas of responsibility or projects and only bought 3 pieces of land off Mendip District Council in the final year of the electoral cycle. A first brave move since the leasing of the Cheese & Grain (C&G) community hall from Mendip in the late 1990's.

The Reports were composed of the lists and general information which should also appear in the Council's Publication Scheme including:
- What the Council does;
- All Councillors listed - with a photo and contact details;
- All staff listed - numbers rose from 12 to 16;
- The main Committee meetings - these varied from 27 to 39 in total each year with around 16 additional Planning meetings;
- Councillor attendance at meetings including apologies given – This showed a huge range with one Councillor making only two meetings a year, the minimum, and others attending around 30;
- Mayoral engagements - mainly local including opening fetes and new businesses, or accepting invitations from other Councils to civic services or celebrations as well as the annual Twinning visits;
- The Budget written in its awkward to understand format for the year just completed and a guess at the year to come;
- Grants paid out to some 28 local organisations out of a budget of around £162,000 each year.

  The Cheese & Grain topping the list although unfairly included is the Council's own loan and interest payments in the total (about £43,000);

- Outlines of the 3 Committees remits: Planning - mainly applications, which dropped from 355 to 260; Policy & Finance - grants and Twinning; and Recreation & Properties - parks, and play equipment. These also formed the basis of the PowerPoint presentations at the Annual Town Meetings (the discussion forum of the electorate).

The early years delight in detail had run out of steam by the electoral cycle's end, repeating the same items every year, the same park refurbishment and the continuing attempt to list the Cockey street lamp standards. All of which sound increasingly hollow considering the £3.35 million involved. Supposedly written in Best Value terms (Efficiency, Effectiveness and Economy) there was no attempt at the 4Cs (challenge, compare, consult, compete). Without any targets set or achieved this was not a review or an analysis but a general optimistic view in bright children's crayon colours.

MARKET STALL FROME

22 - ACCOUNTABILITY - Information equals Freedom?

Whatever enmity Councillors feel towards each other and the politics they support they are at least united in their distrust of the *electorate "the people of Frome elected us to make decisions not to involve them in unnecessary consultations."* There is a dichotomy, the Government is keen on civic participation but in practice those with power would prefer to keep it to themselves and restricting access to information is one way of hanging on to it.

Freedom of Information Act (FOI) 2000

Countries as diverse as Albania to Uzbekistan, and even Zimbabwe, have a Freedom of Information Act with possibly Sweden's being the first in the late 1700's. The United Kingdom was one of the last of the western democracies to adopt an FOI Act and although the legislation was passed in 2000 it did not come into force until 2005. It laid down a complex series of rules to obtain information held by around 100,000 public bodies. It has become on occasion the only opportunity to get answers to queries which in the past officials would decide were too important, or too sensitive or just too impertinent to be answered. Opponents of the Act said it would be too expensive to operate, people would ask silly questions, and officials' time would be wasted or even that secrecy is essential for a free and candid debate. It has not been a cure all but it did tip the balance of power slightly in the direction of the public. There is still not a presumption of openness; the tremendous allure of secrecy is far too great.

What to do

The Freedom of Information Act 2000 has given everyone the opportunity to ask questions of a broad swathe of publicly funded organisations such as: government departments, local Councils, including Parishes, schools, hospitals or doctors. With access to all recorded information including: e-mails, documents, videos, audio tapes or letters except other people's personal details. This includes old records as well as recent ones.

Requests made in writing letter or by e-mail should be clearly and carefully worded. Questions should be specific; "how much...," or "what is...." If the request is for documents then "the minutes when the .....decision was made," "the policies to do with...," or " a list of records held on......" avoiding mixing complaints, comments or opinions with requests. Larger Councils will ask for clarification if unsure, smaller ones are likely to ignore queries. Reasons do not have to be given or any justifications made why the information is needed however, it is sometimes better to give reasons as this helps officials understand what is wanted.

The larger Councils will certainly have the most frequently requested information on their websites including a list of the questions with their answers which the public have already asked using the Freedom of Information Act; these are always an interesting read.

Officials have up to 20 working days in which to reply (the Parishes vary considerably when it comes to observing this limit: many ignoring all requests, others offering terse replies, and a few prompt and professional) but can ask for a 20 day extension, alternatively they may say they do not have the information or transfer the request to a different department or authority that is more likely to know. Requests can be refused if it is in "the public interest" such as national security or if disclosure damages commercial interests.

There is also a range of 23 exemptions which can be given in refusal.

Most requests will be free with perhaps a charge for photocopying (10p a sheet is recommended) and postage. But requests can be refused on cost, if the authority thinks it will be too expensive or time consuming. The threshold is £450 roughly 2.5 days work at £25 an hour (£600 or 3.5 days for central government) to answer a request, below this it will be free. If the costs are above the threshold the public body can refuse outright or alternatively charge. But it is still under a duty to help by amending the request; it may have been worded too loosely, so rewording could reduce costs. However it is still a cat and mouse game.

Parish Publication Scheme

Began a significant shift towards providing information as routine. Simple, straightforward and comprehensive without the intricacies set out for the "Best Value Councils" or the fiddlyness of the Quality Parish and Town Council Scheme.

All Parishes including Parish Meetings (who use a slimmed down version) will adopt and maintain an information Publication Scheme (the Information Commission gives a template to follow). The Scheme helpfully lists, under 7 Class or category headings, information which must be made available and how it can be obtained: on-line on the Parish website - with links, as a hard copy from the Parish Clerk, on the Parish notice board or by appointment, alongside the proposed cost – generally free or with the minimum (hopefully) photocopy charge.

Parish Meetings have the addition of Parish Trustees who oversee the assets such as bus shelters or village greens which a Parish may own.

The Parish and Community Council Publication Scheme

Class 1 Who we are and what we do:
- Who's who on the Council and its Committees,
- Parish Clerk and Councillor contact details - telephone numbers and e-mail,
- Location of main Council office and accessibility details,
- Staffing structure.

Class 2 What we spend and how we spend it:
Current and previous financial year as a minimum
- Annual report form and report by auditor,
- Finalised budget,
- Precept,
- Borrowing approval letter,
- Financial Standing Orders and Regulations,
- Grants given and received,
- List of current contracts awarded and the value of the contract,
- Members' allowances and expenses.

Class 3 What our priorities are and how we are doing:
Strategies and plans, performance indicators, audit inspections and reviews. Current and previous year as a minimum.
- Parish Plan,
- Annual Report to Parish or Community meeting,
- Quality status,

- Local charters.

Class 4 How we make decisions:
Current and previous year as a minimum.
- Timetable of meetings (including Council, committee/subcommittees and Parish meetings),
- Agendas of meetings,
- Minutes of meetings,
- Reports presented to Council meetings,
- Responses to consultation papers,
- Responses to Planning applications,
- Bye-laws.

Class 5 Our policies and procedures:
Current information on protocols, policies and procedures for delivering services and responsibilities.
Policies and procedures for the conduct of Council business:
- Procedural standing orders,
- Committee and sub-committee terms of reference,
- Delegated authority to staff,
- Code of Conduct,
- Policy statements.

Policies and procedures for the provision of services and about the employment of staff:
- Internal policies relating to the delivery of services,
- Equality and diversity policy,
- Health and safety policy,
- Recruitment policies (including current vacancies),
- Policies and procedures for handling information request,
- Complaints procedures including information requests and the operation of the publication scheme,
- Information security policy,
- Records management policies (retention, destruction and archive),
- Data protection policies,
- Schedule of charges for public information.

Class 6 Lists and Registers:
Currently held.
- Any publicly available list or register,
- Assets register,
- Disclosure log (good practice is a list of information provided under the FOI Act),
- Register of Members Interests,
- Register of gifts and hospitality

Class 7 The services we offer:
(including leaflets, guidance and newsletters produced for businesses and the public)
Currently offered.
- Allotments,
- Burial grounds and closed churchyards,
- Community centres and village halls,
- Parks, playing fields and recreational facilities,
- Seating, litter bins, clocks, memorials and lighting,
- Bus shelters,

- Markets,
- Public conveniences,
- Agency agreements (with other authorities such as highway verge maintenance), A summary of services the council charges a fee for (e.g. burial fees).

Finally, additional Information, this is an opportunity for Councils to list the other things it does or belongs to including: Maps of the area, the site of Parish notice board, organisations the Council or Councillors are represented on. Local groups or societies available, local services – buses, churches, refuse collections.

If a Council will not supply the information, an appeal to it explaining why the information should be released will trigger an internal review. If this is unsuccessful a complaint can be made to the Information Commissioners Office and again if this fails, to the Information Tribunal with the Minister as last resort. The Minister can overrule the previous two bodies and have the information released.

Environmental Information Regulations
Lesser known but requests for information can be made to government departments and Councils etc under this banner which covers a wide range of information including:

- the state of the air, water, land, natural sites and living organisms including genetically modified organisms;
- emissions or discharges to the air, water or land including energy, noise and radiation;
- Information about legislation, policies, plans, activities, administrative and other measures likely to affect or is intended to protect any of the above. Including assessments of the costs or benefits of such measures and reports on the implementation of environmental legislation. Especially where human health or safety, food contamination, living conditions, built structures or cultural sites are affected.

Stop Press
"Without the sunlight of transparency, the flowering of localism will wither" the Local Government Minister said defending an independent local press coupled with robust public scrutiny against the heavy-handedness of Councils who have used the police in some cases to stop the reporting of Council meetings.

A determined Government issued guidance (June 2013) to local authorities allowing citizens to report, blog, tweet and film all Council meetings in England (but not Wales, Welsh ministers claiming openness to be *"an unhealthy obsession"*). The uncertain situation had been highlighted in various television series when programme makers had been banned from filming Councillor deliberations. The Government explained that the filming of both Councillors and Council staff did not contravene the Data Protection Act or Health and Safety and these excuses should not be used to suppress reporting and meetings should be open to a healthy dose of criticism. Filming should be open and announced at the start of meetings giving the public who wish to the opportunity to opt out.

By August the Government named and shamed Councils who continued to *"oppose an independent press."* Some Councils still continued to call the police to remove bloggers, citizen film makers or banned journalists.

Using a range of excuses, reporting would amount to a *"breach of Standing Orders"* or be against its *"agreed protocol"* and most tellingly and perhaps more truthfully the risk of *"reputational damage to the authority."* Perhaps Councillors shied away from letting a wider audience see the calibre of discussion. The Government setting an example opened up the Planning Appeals system *"a previously mysterious and rarely seen side of the Planning process."* Both Hearings and Inquiries can now be reported, recorded or filmed this includes the use of digital and social media.

Datafile

The Silent State, Secrets, Surveillance and the myth of British Democracy, Heather Brooke, Heinemann, 2010
Your Right to Know, A Citizens Guide to Freedom of Information, Heather Brooke, Pluto Press, 2005
Your right to know, www.yrtk.org
Local Government Association,www.lga.org.uk
Cycle Path,www.fromemissinglink.org.uk
Information Commissioners Office, www.ico.gov.uk
Campaign for the Freedom of Information www.cfoi.org

THE ROOFS OF FROME

CATHERINE HILL FROME

23 - ACCOUNTABILITY - Minuted Achievements

Frome - The Highlights (2007-11)

Reading Parish minutes can be like deciphering an ancient language from an obscure and distant land full of strange exotic customs. There are hints and shadowy truths we can never really fully know or understand. But may only catch a flavour of and hope a prolonged and systematic study will reveal the ghosts of the personalities involved left behind in the text. Indeed, subjects frequently arise to burn obsessively for a season or two, before giving way to others. High–minded and occasionally intuitive insights jostle alongside views of relentless pettiness.

Those who look to the minutes for closely argued points or detailed discussions will be very disappointed. Certainly looking at the details minuted and the issues raised on any agenda no-one would suspect that the Council Budget under scrutiny in 2007, was set at around £800,000 and rose within the four years of the electoral cycle to close on to a £1 million.

The archived minutes provide patchy answers but with their accompanying agendas missing, the issues and often the subject itself unnoted, discussions vague and decisions made without their accompanying resolutions, uncertain. Frome is not alone in this. Written reports are unreferenced and were only circulated to specific Committees so effectively unavailable. Verbal reports were not written up; summaries not given; conferences and outside meetings attended went unreported; updates on spending not made. Resolutions were few and even the voting was unclear it was uncertain who undertook any resulting actions, whether Councillor or staff. With no set time frames and follow up reports rare decisions are difficult to follow. Neither unfortunately was anything recorded from either Frome's District or County Councillors with no updates on the goings-on in the higher tiers of local government.

From these barest of bare bones it was doubtful if Councillors not attached to a specific committee and there on the night, least of all the townspeople, could know or understand the decisions made. They must have hoped there was a press release in the local paper to put flesh on these roughest of details. Yet there are flashes of colour, as odd details slip out, a resolution at Policy & Finance and Economic Development to have no peanuts at the Twinning lunch followed by a further resolution *"to have no nuts whatsoever,"* and in later minutes elegiac praise for the Town Clerk's *"visionary recommendations."*

Frome's three main Committees; Policy, Finance and Economic Development (P&F), Recreation and Properties (R&P) each had 7 Councillors and with Full Council dealt with the day to day irritations of town life. Six Councillors sat on Planning, passing their comments on Planning applications to Mendip District Council. These sadly were not included in the minutes of the proceedings.
All Committees were in charge of their own budgets and inevitably acted in isolation making it impossible for Councillors to be jointly and severally responsible for all or indeed any decisions.

P&F also provided half the Councillors for its three sub-committees: Personnel, Grants and the Christmas Spectacular and some six Working Parties: Civic, Investment Strategy, Committee Structure, Relocation, Editorial, and Town Strategy.

R&P also created three working parties: Rodden Meadow, Mary Bailey Refurbishment, Victoria Park Lottery Bid plus it fielded two Councillors on the Allotments Association, an outside body, all in the electoral cycle's first year. How often or even if the Working Parties met was not recorded neither were their deliberations.

Yet despite the difficulties the four years produced some memorable moments:

April 2007- 08

Policy & Finance (P&F)
Although overseeing the newly expanded Budget of £800,000 P&F met only 4 times totaling 9 hours. Whilst it set the Budget for the whole Council there were no preliminary discussions, R&P and Planning put forward their requests and the Budgets were amalgamated and presented to P&F by the Chairman with the help of the Town Clerk. Although talked through line by line there was no critical analysis or scrutiny of need or Best Value. Meetings monitored invoice payments and discussed general housekeeping but contracts were not listed or reviewed.

A number of priorities emerge which have implications for the following four years:

- Support for Somerset County Council in its bid for Unitary status (the Districts were vehemently against it). However, Frome starts to plan Parish Councillor allowances including extra allowances for the Committee chairmen. Although there are some worries about the potential legal liabilities of Parish Planning decisions. The Committee finally decides the Council would want power over Planning, regeneration, community grants, litter and transport;
- The Bridget Parker Trust is closed. Rather than distributing the remaining £4,000 of funds to enthusiastic sporting youngsters in the town or the surrounding villages – who had contributed to the Trust in past years. The unspent funds are given to the Somerset Community Foundation;
- Twinning: trips to France and Germany are planned; the arrangements for the Frome tripartite meeting decided - the lunch menu is discussed, the cost will be borne by the town; the Polish Twinning trip is organised with transport costs shared between town and Councillors; a £50 limit on gifts is made, and a no nuts rule introduced;
- The long haul starts on the granting of a 30 year lease to the Cheese & Grain community hall (completed May 2010).

The December meeting of 4 Councillors decide:
- Office relocation is critical, having considered the United Reformed Church, the meeting decides to negotiate for offices in King Street;
- Crucially a resolution is passed to buy any riverbank off Mendip District Council (Mendip) between Wallbridge and Welshmill, including Château Gontier Walk and any land and services provided in Frome by Mendip setting in tow a period of acquisition - 3 years later;
- The Precept is set with an increase of 0%.

Recreation and Properties (R&P)
R&P's mixed brief covered: alcohol restriction zones; allotments; toilets; street lighting; litterbins; floral displays; parks; Rodden Meadow; town office maintenance and the Cheese & Grain (C&G).

All contained within 3 meetings totaling just over 5 hours. This was the Council's main spending Committee.

Over and above general housekeeping the Committee set up 3 working parties:

- One administering the "Parks for People" Lottery Bid. Local newspapers report the Council's certain hopes that a primer of £50,000 will release £500,000 in grants to spend on Victoria Park and take on extra staff to undertake the bid. A search for additional funders will also be made;
- Quotes are requested to reopen Badcox toilets;
- Singers Knoll allotments are transferred from Mendip District Council;
- Somerset Wildlife Trust present a plant and animal species survey report on Rodden Meadow;
- A Budget is agreed but no details are given.

Full Council
All Councillors were expected to attend; the 4 meetings lasted about 9 hours. It principally ratified the adoption of the Council's policies and procedures and the annual Budget, there was no overall ratification or serious scrutiny of the other Committees.

However, it was perhaps the most interesting of all the Committees with around half a dozen local organisations and groups at each meeting speaking in Public Forum and giving presentations on their projects and activities. Whilst there was an opportunity for Councillors to quiz one another over Committee reports or their outside bodies it was rarely taken. Most notable in this year was:

- The beginnings of the creation of a proposed 4 year policy and business plan based on an "away day". Because the Town Council saw itself as a political Council the Liberal Democrats (as the majority group) are asked to put forward a plan for discussion;
- Letters in the press about the high Town Council Budget and the possibility of double taxation is a constant irritant. Council discussion revolve around the amount of time (and therefore cost) it takes in dealing with the correspondence from only "one" resident and states further replies will take a low priority. The Council remarks that it does not think the value of its capital projects and services are small and reiterates its budget is reasonable (for a town of its size). Explaining the 0% precept rise is effectively a decrease of 1.6% at Band D as more houses have been built!
- The January 08 meeting confirms the following year's annual Budget.

Planning
Planning passed its written comments to the Planning Authority after listening to representations from neighbours or local groups. It met 16 times for about 32 hours this year.
It dealt with the small irritating details of town life. Making it a good Committee to raise the concerns of: parked cars, traffic, drains, raised manhole covers, street lighting, bus stops, hedges, road closures, loose kerbing, waste bins, rail and bus timetables, grubby signs, water leaks, missing yellow lines, broken bollards, and fly posting. It was a kindly Committee sending get well cards to the stalwarts from the town who attended every meeting, when they became unwell.

This year's highlights are:

- The Bailey Bridge demolition discussion, Councillors comment, "replacement (is) paramount to the infrastructure of traffic movement in the town," when a local Bridge enthusiast voices concerns;
- In August Mendip District agrees to give around £60,000 of Section106 agreement money from new housing in Frome to the Council to spend on play areas, the money is eventually released in 2011;
- The licensing of street traders and street naming of new developments - so local associations are not lost, is devolved from Mendip;
- The Saxonvale Planning process starts, based on 2006 Mendip District Planning brief for shops and housing on what is a still active commercial site. Frome Council sends in a wish list including new Town Council offices;
- After two years Ley Vale's Section106 housing landscaping agreement still rumbles on, known locally as "Colditz" the hilltop crescent of white stone houses on the towns edge can be seen from miles around. The landscaping to screen them was supposed to be completed before the houses were built, although the initial plans had the houses built and hidden below the quarry edge in which they stood. The Town asks throughout 2006 and 2007 for compliance, now the new residents do not want their views blocked by trees, Mendip shuffles its feet offering to revise the plan – it is never resolved.

April 2008 - 2009

Again this year was not easy to follow and again it was impossible to see how decisions were arrived at, whether things hinted at ever occurred, including the proposed list of land and buildings the Council would like to buy. Councillors went to conferences and Twinning events without explanation or analysis. Occasionally the minutes state "Cllr P... comments were noted", but no written record exists or "Cllr P.. was thanked for his report" again no back-up paperwork. Without even the subject of reports noted a reader could only guess at their significance. Questions remained unanswered, bald statements languished in isolation, how Councillor actions were costed was a mystery. However, ambitions had been fuelled and a distinct District Council flavour was developing with the Council looking to take on more responsibilities.

P&F
A busier year with a doubling of hours (20hrs) over 8 meetings, plus the setting up of an additional 7 working parties:

- 5 ambitiously titled Task and Finish groups are formed as a result of a "Strategy Away Day":
- Acquisition of Community Assets,
- Traffic & Pedestrian Issues,
- Community Safety,
- FTC Partnerships, and
- Litter & Recycling. It was not clear if any ever met;

- The main excitement is Twinning, with the adoption of a Polish town bringing the number of Twinned towns to three. With this there is a change from the previously more distanced approach.

The Council and the Twinning Association combine into a shared organisation to pursue business, cultural and education links rather than the purely social, all celebrated with an annual Civic Reception. European funding is thought possible and a promise of *"no financial implications"* for the town's taxpayers.

- The Town Clerk is sent to negotiate, UK Mayors do not have the spending/decision making powers of their continental cousins a situation which always rankles. 20 people travel to Poland from the town. What happened is unminuted and tangible benefits to Frome elusive. Frome's turn to host the delegates from all 3 towns will be in 2011 and the cost guessed at £35,000;

- The Town office move grows apace but a move to the Cheese & Grain is now rejected in favour of something new in the Saxonvale retail development site as part of a Section106 agreement – just off the town centre, it is predicted it will be built within 5 or 10 or so years' time. After disappearing into closed session the office move re-emerges with a Working Party and a brief, but the inclusion of a Mayoral Parlour in the proposed new Town Hall, the subject of a named vote, is rejected. Now the Council, which has always held the lease of "The Tower" – the rear of the Cheese & Grain, looks at its conversion. Instead two architects are appointed to redesign the present Palmer Street office layout;

- Another swathe of policies are adopted and green issues are to the fore with paper and energy use in the office questioned. A "Green Conference" of seminars on sustainability for local businesses is organised via a working party - it takes 9 months;

- July brought surprises as the Frome Ratepayers Alliance - which voices a complaint to the Auditor, refuses to meet Councillors to discuss the challenged accounts. A rattled Council decides to hold a full explanation at an open day on the accounts and an internal inquiry once the external auditor has finished his investigations. The Council is anxious to know how it can protect itself from multiple and disturbing queries. Nothing takes place.

Full Council
Over 7 meetings of about 12 hours, presentations are the mainstay: from Vision 4 Frome, the Youth Council, and District staff on Planning and climate change. Followed by:

- Meetings are now "the thing": the monthly" Meet the Mayor" in the town centre starts as has the monthly secret meetings of the party leaders with the Town Clerk;

- Two possible take-overs are discussed: Shopmobility - which lends mobility scooters to town shoppers and the Tourist Information Centre both of which have had funding cuts;

- There is agreement to have a "youth engagement" item on every agenda, but nothing happens;

- Car parking charges are thought so serious they are discussed at Full Council. The District's proposed annual rise always causes rage and is a perennial problem with the arguments well-rehearsed. District needs the income from Frome, the biggest provider. The town shops say trade will be undermined and motorists point to free parking in nearby towns. The Council wants a strong letter of protest sent; it asks the Councillor who is on the 4 man District Committee setting the charges to write it;

- Allotments, the Town Clerk states, *"there is no duty to provide allotments to everyone."*

R&P
Responsible for most of the town's obvious spending it met for about 7 hours over 5 meetings:

- Views will be sought on a new skateboard park and Rodden Meadow will be surveyed for wildlife. Hedge cutting is outsourced and town trees surveyed;
- The Tennis Club suggests the Council builds new tennis courts and a car park on the Mary Bailey Playing Field – the Council declines;
- A Tea Room in Victoria Park is agreed and is going on apace;
- Some budget area spends are unexpectedly listed;
- Frome in Bloom hands over their regeneration grant to the Town Council.

Planning
Apart from commenting on applications, "A" Frame boards, blocked drains and obscured traffic signs dominated the public forum:

- "A" frames in Stony Street and Cheap Street are reported as blocking the highway in the April 2008. County is asked for help but complaints rumble on all year without resolution. Indeed in Cheap Street 18 "A" frames, 13 tables with 43 chairs and 5 hanging basket poles crowd the short narrow mediaeval path with its picturesque shops divided by a shallow central rill. Small children and dogs frequently enjoy a dunking. This is the premier shopping street of the town, although no-one eradicates the splotches of pigeon poo edging the pavement of each shop front;
- An application for Listed Building status for the remaining cast iron Cockey street lamps is compiled until it is later discovered (2011) that many are clever copies putting Listing on hold;
- Councillors are cross that the town has not been consulted by County or District on the Bailey Bridge demolition following the damming structural survey the previous year and the withdrawal of money for a replacement. A strong case for a replacement is gathered by the same Councillors wearing their District Council hats and made at East Mendip Partnership meetings where funding for a replacement footbridge is hinted at;
- New town entry signs, these are now termed "celebratory" perhaps because each has a new flower bed. County and District agree to part-fund and there are hopes the town's businesses will contribute.

April 2009- 2010

There was now a change in tone as the Council hits its stride. Confidence mounts, minutes become more perfunctory - some are missing from the archive. There were big projects in the offing as P&F draws more of the power and decision making to itself. The national General Election was on the horizon, with the town election the following year. The police join Full Council; it was unclear why. Frome's only Independent Councillor resigned in frustration.

P&F
Possibly 8 meetings totaling around 16 hours:

- Tour of Britain cycle race - hosting the start is costed at c £10,000, and hopes are, as always, to get sponsorship from businesses, or license fees from street traders;

- The Cost of External Auditor's investigation concludes with a bill of £2,200. The Auditor suggests Earmarked Reserves are planned with a time scale attached;
- A temporary sub-committee of 4 Councillors goes to France for a Twinning meeting to make policy and financial decisions about Polish Twinning. Twinning supports the Youth Ambassador Scheme, (sponsoring two youngsters to go to the next Twinning event). Applying for European Union funding is suggested;
- Office relocation options are updated to members only, and a developer will be contacted, again more mystery locations are looked at;
- Château Gontier Walk transfer goes ahead although the Council is uncertain what land is included and asks for a map. More unnamed acquisitions are discussed including a mystery service acquisition!
- At last the Cheese & Grain lease will be signed - it wasn't.

Full Council

6 meetings totaling around 10 hours, fewer presentations now, just a couple of charities outlining what they do, Mendip explained how it will rejuvenate the Charter Market - nothing happens:

- Jan 2010, this is the final attempt to save the Bailey Bridge, the chief enthusiast explains Frome will have the first listed Bailey Bridge in the country which he will restore himself. The funding for the new pedestrian bridge is still not explained. The town offers up to £50,000, with British Telecom Open Reach contributing £60,000 and Mendip c£150,000 - equivalent to the cuts in voluntary organisation grants of this year. The named vote shows 12 in favour, 1 against with 2 abstentions;
- However, not everyone is happy for the Council to sign up to the campaign to cut carbon emissions by 10%, 7 voted for, 1 against but there are 6 abstentions. More successful is the 5 minute Extraordinary Meeting held to give the Freedom of the Town to Jenson Button, 11 are in favour and only one abstains;
- The Power of Well-Being is adopted as an adjunct to Quality Status allowing unfettered spending which not all Councillors are happy with, 7 voted for, 3 against with 2 abstentions.

R&P

Most discussion focuses on Victoria Park and the adjacent Playing Field. This is where the majority of the tangible benefits of the town's money is seen and the staff based. Decisions were made over 8 hours in 5 meetings. The minutes have improved and there was now an "action line". However, the vague resolutions usually resolved to consider doing something at some point in the future:

- However, the Tea kiosk/café is completed and leased out, the skate park finished, Rabka rock garden planned as is the tennis courts refurbishment. The Bowls club lease is signed and the Cheese & Grain "Tower" is found to be structurally sound. £30,000, of spending is allotted to Rodden Meadow with £16,000 suggested to Château Gontier walk.
- Zion Path a narrow winding tree–lined tarmac path and a Somerset County Council responsibility with its own annual budget line of £1,000 was informally adopted in 1993. Now triumphantly it belongs to the town with the Council putting their name to it at the Land Registry ending a baffling decades long "dispute". Or has it, as later the Council is unsure. So perhaps it still belongs to the County or the District.

Planning

Planning has also caught the change in the air, and the tone of Planning applications comments changes, although still not included in the archived minutes, from a jaunty, "approve – subject to neighbours or the tree officer," to a more pretentious, "proceed to a decision." In general only one or two lines of comment were ever made, if for "approval" then it was – "proceed to a decision." Or alternatively "leave decision to the Planning officer," if for "refusal," the building was commonly described as "out of character" or "detrimental to the street scene", leaving, for those who would like to rectify the problem, little to go on.

- The local sub-group of Sustainable Frome gives a presentation proposing the completion of the Great Elm to Frome Cycle path; they offer a web link to garner support.
- Planning is developing a Masterplan and Design Guide and transfers nearly £11.000 from Street Furniture to this new Budget heading hitting opposition. Two of the 4 Councillors present vote against but the Chairman's casting vote means the transfer goes ahead. Not forgiven by the next meeting Planning's annual Budget is also rejected this time by three Councillors abstaining. But the motion is carried because it was proposed and seconded by the same cabal of Councillors.
- There is a proposed visit by architect students from the University of Notre Dame, Indiana who propose to use Frome as a case study offering solutions and a Masterplan to the towns problems - later cancelled as the world financial crisis bites.

April 2010- 2011

Triumph, as the sitting Liberal Democrat MP was returned in the May 2010 General Election winning this very marginal constituency against an unpopular Conservative candidate with a non-existent campaign, a Labour party which was just joining in and the United Kingdom Independence Party (UKIP) which continued to successfully nibble away at the Conservative vote locally. All was set fair for victory at Town and District elections in May 2011. So a busily ambitious year was ahead to bring ideas to fruition. However, much was discussed in private and cryptically minuted. There were also complaints that minutes were slow to be available on-line, some do not appear. With the Town Council elections (May 2011) looming the final meetings were full of praise for staff and a general sense of bonhomie.

P&F

- Office relocation (don't know where) returns with a detailed investigation of the lease needed, particularly with a view to extending the unknown building, boreholes are requested.
- Acquisitions top the agenda, lists are made including car parks, unknown assets bid for and two grassy open spaces and a footpath successfully acquired. There are further requests to Mendip to see what else can be bought but nothing is noted.
- Another working party, this time on the Council's tourist & information service.
- Cheese & Grain (C&G) lease is signed at last. But, by September there is a change of heart.

Arguments came to a head in October when the wording of a contentious resolution is e-mailed round by the new interim Town Clerk (the Town is between Town Clerks) to the 4 Committee Councillors after the Committee meeting in an attempt to get agreement. The shock decision is to withdraw all funding which will mean the Council will take the C&G under its control as the charity will no longer be able to trade. The decision is expected to be ratified at Full Council, further discussions are in secret.

- £3,000 is put aside for grit bins as the cold weather hits.
- The Town's savings (£600,000) now earn 1.2% interest.
- The CCTV minutes are received from Mendip – a first.
- The new Town Clerk and a Chamber of Commerce representative visit a Trade Fair in Murrhardt but time has run out so we do not know what happens.
- The Partner desk donated to the town long ago (though not on the list of assets) is to be sold.

Full Council

- There are 5 new grant aided Outside Bodies for Councillors to join.
- A big effort is made to sort out car parking. The townspeople determinedly parked on residential streets to avoid paying charges, leaving the car parks half empty - ideas mooted are: employers providing free permits to park in a named car park, a low cost voucher scheme for residents, or the Town could consider buying car parks from Mendip and set its own rate, perhaps free.
- Budget for after the coming local election is set. With £105,658 taken from Reserves to balance it.
- The now deeply controversial Cheese & Grain has a new Working Party by the end of January, made up of 2 Councillors who are its main detractors and a Councillor who is retiring at the May local election.
- Council's Library Information Centre opens.
- The Magistrates Court is definitely closing. The Mayor will lobby MP and Mendip in one last final effort to keep it open.
- It is a very relaxed, confident Council which meets in March for the final time before the May election (other than Planning). Animosities forgotten as Councillors make thank-you speeches to each another for their achievements, time, and commitment in working together, sharing concerns over illnesses.
- Wootton Basset's new title of "Royal" prompts a letter of congratulations to be sent.
- The Recruitment Panel appoints a new Town Clerk and a named vote of the 13 Councillors present records they are all in agreement, but not why a named vote is thought necessary.
- The Town Crier's contract is to be renewed on a rolling basis, not sure why he needs one as he self-funds in any case.
- The interims Town Clerk's contract is discussed. And the meeting resolves to agree to an action it had previously agreed to the previous October, although what is not recorded. However, this is the first time a publicly excluded discussion has been minuted in the main minutes.

R&P

- Lots about flowers, with sponsors sought – indeed many local business have their names printed on sticky labels and attached to floral tubs around the town only for them to be quickly covered by the verdant growth of the plants.

Floral displays for the four towns Twinning summer get-together are discussed and an £800 windfall from Mendip in Bloom is received.

- The search for new allotment sites is abandoned. It will be down to Planning to persuade developers to provide them. More staff to be taken on, but hanging basket watering is to be out- sourced.
- FROGS, Frome Open Spaces charity plans to apply for £50,000 of Lottery funding to put play equipment on the newly acquired town land at Welshmill.
- The Tennis Club again requests the Council builds extra tennis courts with car parking in the Park, and again the Council declines.
- Rotary, with local youngsters under the auspices of "Prospects" and the Friends of the River Frome helps out with river clearing work and planting wildflowers and crocuses.
- The local Forest School gives a presentation. It wants to use Town land to introduce youngsters to playing outdoors. The Council agrees.
- The Slipps Section106 agreement money (£58,900, the amount changes with every telling) is received by Mendip. Spending suggestions are now needed as well as suggestions on how to consult the public.
- Shock as FROGS Lottery application will not be pursued when the Council's agreement to contribute £8,000 is queried. The Meeting decides it will have its own 2 year plan putting £958 into repairs. Confusion over which of the newly acquired land at Welshmill and the footpath into town is now owned by the Council.
- A 45 minute, late afternoon Extraordinary meeting of 3 Councillors make a raft of decisions. A tractor will be purchased, the outsourced flower watering quote tops £15,950 and will come back in-house along with the grass mowing. The meeting agrees the Somerset Wildlife Trust will act as consultants.
- Mendip confirm the Slipps Section106 agreement money. £59,450 will be spent in the Mary Bailey Playing Field but the "trim trail" equipment from the new hospital Section106 agreement goes to the Park putting green. (Is the Park getting too full of equipment?)
- FROGS Lottery application succeeds, continuing to the second stage.
- A Beech tree is felled, the press release to the newspaper asks for "arty" suggestions. None comes forward.

Planning

- A Colliers Way Cycle Route Working Party is set up; a web page link opened to gather public support for the completion of this 2-3 mile section of Sustrans Route 24.
- A new Standing Committee is proposed to cover Economic Development, Tourism and Twinning with Planning as a sub-committee and it is rumoured a new post of town centre manager.
- The Public Forum revives the "A" (advertising) frame controversy in another year long debate. And we are told, in Cheap Street (18 "A" frames, 13 tables and 43 chairs, 5 hanging basket posts along a 100 yard stretch of a narrow pedestrian shopping street- not forgetting the central stream) "they" (the obstructions) do not fit "the criteria" but the chairs are probably "in breach." Police towards the year end state, an obstruction occurs when a double buggy cannot get by and agree to talk to shop owners - nothing changes. Later again, the Committee decide, in a clever sideways move, to ask Somerset County Council if it can license "A" frames.

Dogs fouling and overgrown hedges are another constant as is a street light on 24 hours a day for months and a wood pile by the church unmoved for 6 months.

- The Committee is enthused by a presentation which suggests putting false fronts on empty shops, making, it is claimed, an area more desirable, encouraging people to stop and visit and new businesses to establish. The idea is enthusiastically sent to Full Council who it is felt would be happy to pay the £3,000 needed.
- The Design Statement surfaces with a 2nd Draft - it is a rehash of Mendip's evidence for the District wide plan and the Vision4Frome surveys put together by one enthusiastic Councillor. Consultants will now be engaged to produce a design guide for public consultation - neatly missing the point that it should be an area by area discussion by townspeople of how they see and what they want for the town. Mendip has already hired consultants to do a design guide for the town's conservation area to prevent design mishaps.
- With the unexpected cold, snowy, winter weather, Frome's steep streets are treacherously icy. The Committee's newly bought bright canary yellow grit bins are placed around the town for motorists to use and to be an anathema to all future photographers, the weather promptly improves and the ice and snow disappears.

Sub Committees 2007- 2011

Grants
Frome, in common with most Parishes, grant aids a range of voluntary organisations, from sporting to social groups from buildings to equipment. Generally there is a specific project but there is also help for new groups to set up. All have to directly benefit the townspeople of Frome referencing the Council's Strategic Plan. They may only receive a proportion of their request. Each successful group should report back on how the grant was used but not all do. These were not published.

The 2007-08 annual round of one off grants gave 32 organisations £25,150 (see Chapter 10). Sums ranged from the smallest - £200, for a digital camera to help publicise a social group to £3,000 to the Frome Youth Council for a Youth Café. The 10 organisations holding 3 year funding agreements gained £43,500 (see Chapter 10).

In 2008-09 the amount given to one off grants dropped to £20,100 covering 32 organisations 12 were from last year. The smallest was £50, funding a summer outing for an older person's social club and the largest at £4,000 to Frome Youth Council for a Café and to run its own grant aid scheme funding youth groups. The 10 organisations holding 3 year funding agreements gained £43,500.

2009-10 many funding agreements finished, only 4 organisations now held 3 year funding agreements gaining £20,000. However, 3 totaling £17,500 continued under the annual small grants banner. The small grants, £23,530 went to 16 organisations, was dominated by sports and children's play schemes, with the largest at £3,582 going to Frome Town Ladies Football Club; and the smallest at £150 to Frome Society for Disabled Artists for art materials.

In 2010-11 £53.837 is granted in total. The funding agreements have finished but most apply anyway under the annual one-off grant scheme. Of the 28 successful applications, the smallest for £150 went to Home in Frome to record memories in a town wide oral history project, the largest, £7,500 went to Young People Frome to pay for a co-ordinator.

Harry's Hydro (a new state of the art hydrotherapy centre for children and adults) outlook was precarious when after 10 years of fund raising (it had raised £300,000) the school whose site the centre would share withdrew its long term support. The town stepped in with a promise of £80,000 over 10 years.

There was an unexpected windfall when the town's antique partner desk raised £6,501 at auction. P&F will decide what to do with money on 2nd March - they don't; perhaps it went to Grants?

The Christmas Spectacular
A Sunday afternoon of entertainment in the Market Yard Car Park (an area of dark puddles) in the run up to Christmas with reindeer, Santa, carol singing, music, a brass band, an "ice" rink, food stalls, fairground rides and the Christmas Lights switch on followed by a fireworks finale. Initially a Committee with 2 Councillors (unusual as best practice is 3) plus unusually, 5 non-Councillors providing input from the schools, Chamber of Commerce, Tourist Information Centre, and the nearby shopping precinct management company.
Committee numbers rocketed by the end of the electoral cycle to 18 including three Council staff. It held about 6 meetings a year totaling around 9 hours. The Committee also organised the Mayor's Christmas card competition and chose the leasing arrangements for the Christmas Lights.

Ambitious at the beginning with a substantial budget of around £35,000 most of which paid for the Christmas Lights, it was keen to buy in innovative entertainments in what was hoped would be the forerunner of a series of Council organised events. The minutes patchily charted progress: the high cost of the "ice rink" which initially charged £2 a head, was free to townspeople in its final year - courtesy of the Mayor, the doubts and concerns raised that the nearby street craft fayre took trade away from the Spectacular, attempts to have a teenage "Chill-out zone," the huge number of police and stewards (around 50) employed, and the eventual recognition that the Committee should scale back and rely on local organisations who would happily run things for free.

Sponsorship never took off although the Chamber of Commerce collected about £500-700 each year towards the cost of the Lights and Rotary uneasily contributed £50 to the Christmas tree. Whether it was ethical for a Council with such a huge overall Budget to take money from a charity was not discussed by the Committee. In the end a newly invigorated Chamber seized back the event: the name would be changed back to Extravaganza, the Christmas tree would also be back in the Market Place without a forlorn shrouding of crash barriers, and the connection between late evening shopping and a fun celebration returned.

Personnel
Primarily looked after staffing issues, produced policies and protocols e.g. maternity leave, bullying, pay etc. with outside expertise bought in on issues such as recruitment. It held 4 meetings totaling less than 6 hours in its first year but only an occasional one in later years when recruitment was necessary. Most notably the Council restructured its staff following the "Clerk's visionary recommendations" changing job titles and introducing new ones such as Mayor's Secretary and replacing the title Town Clerk by Chief Executive Officer in order, it noted, to reflect the status and the nature of the job.
The Planning administrator was expected to gain a Planning qualification.

There were congratulations in 2009 as a swathe of staff achieved extra qualifications but R&P's request to buy in a project manager to oversee the Park Lottery bid was refused.

Civic Affairs

Says a lot about how the Council viewed itself holding 6 or 7 meetings a year totaling about 8 hours. The Mayors Civic Service was reinstated, a church service for the Council and around 90 invited dignitaries from the surrounding towns followed by a stately procession to a cream tea to the music of the local Cadet Band. There is much debate on the wording of the invite, who should welcome the guests and who should walk with whom and even whether to have a red carpet.

The Mayors Spring Charity Fair was started, to help small local charities fundraise, each were given a trestle table in the Cheese and Grain. The annual Mayors Charity Dinner organised by the town office sold tickets to around 50 or so invited dignitaries many being fellow Mayors from the surrounding towns to fundraise for the Mayors chosen Frome charities (usually 2). Invitations were later extended to the townspeople as numbers needed a boost. Around £1,000 to £2,000 was raised annually.

The Committee decided to reward each Mayor with a Badge as a token of appreciation and included all past Mayors in a grand presentation ceremony. but again it decided against becoming a robed Council. A Junior Mayor is briefly discussed but thought inappropriate.

The Civic Community Awards, for townspeople nominated by colleagues and friends for their outstanding contribution to the life of the town was revived, with the winners receiving a paperweight and a framed certificate. All the local papers quickly copied and overshadowed the Council's award with larger more exciting schemes of their own voted on by their readers.

Frome born Jenson Button's racing championship win was celebrated with a scroll and a grand ceremony in the Market Yard car park watched by hundreds including national and local newspapers and television. A plaque was ordered for the new, yet to be built, Jenson Button Bridge.

The Mayors Christmas Card competition for under 9's was organised. The winning drawing was used on the 200 or so cards posted annually sponsorship was sought from businesses and a Mayors Middle School competition was agreed – but details unknown.

Curiously, the success of a Frome County Councillor in bringing the staging of the one of the 2010 Tour of Britain cycle race starts to Frome is not mentioned; despite the fact the Council hosted the cycle teams breakfasts and persuaded businesses and churches to open early to serve breakfasts to sight-seers. Whilst the promised windfall for businesses had not happened, the Council answering criticism in the local newspapers was hopeful that a beneficial effect would be accumulative, with time.

THE BLUE HOUSE FROME

24 - INVOLVEMENT - Being There

Having a go yourself

Frome has been traditionally fought over by the Conservatives - plodding and a touch unexciting, Labour - pursuing 19th century values and the Liberal Democrats - flexible, determined, media savvy and organised after their political makeover in the late 1980's.

Election procedures

Parish Councils in England and Community Councils in Wales share for the most part the same electoral procedures as the principal authorities of England and Wales: the District and County Councils, Metropolitan Borough Councils, Unitary Councils, and Welsh Unitary Councils.

Everyone who stands for election does so because they *"want to make a difference."* Often egged on by friends they are determined to reverse the mistakes of others, support neglected areas and causes, square unfairness, and bring about fundamental even radical change, or otherwise be a steadying and profound influence against rash and unwise decisions. If they belong to a group there is the importance of promoting shared values whilst being part of a wider political stage where perhaps an individual's influence could be heard beyond the confines of their own Parish. The Government which is very keen to encourage people to vote does not promote standing for election quite so enthusiastically. There has been much talk of lowering the voting age to 16 (to be tried in Scotland first) adding just under 2 million potential voters. It is hoped by voting on issues affecting their futures there will be greater participation in later life.

How to get Elected

Local elections are generally held on the first Thursday in May to elect or re-elect Councillors for all the electoral Wards of a Parish Council and could include sections of the principal authorities: which for County Councils are electoral divisions, and for Unitary/District are electoral Wards. Electoral divisions are combined to create parliamentary constituencies which in turn elect a Member of Parliament (MP) to the House of Commons.

...Frome Watch...

UK Youth Parliament

600 youngsters aged between 11 and 18 are elected and meet annually (since 2011) to give a voice to young people's concerns and opinions. It was set up in 1999 by Andrew Row MP, Kate Parish (youth worker) and the NSPPCC. Somerset has 4 constituencies with a Member and Deputy Member in each, meeting monthly to develop an action plan. Mendip's 14 year old Youth Parliament Member had a weekly column in Frome's local newspaper.

Each local authority has its own four-year cycle of elections run by the Acting Returning Officers with an Elections officer in charge of the day to day running providing information and nomination papers for all local authority elections. The Parish Clerk may distribute nomination papers to potential candidates at Parish Council level. The Acting Returning Officer hires the buildings which become Polling Stations, providing the 2 or 3 staff for each one as well as staff for the Count – often Council employees or retirees. The costs can be passed on to each Parish.

...Frome Watch...

Who is in charge?

Frome's Acting Returning Officer is Mendip's Chief Executive (the Electoral Registration Officer). The Returning Officer in Somerset is the High Sheriff.

Candidates can stand for the Parish, District/Unitary and the County Council singly or in any combination. Elected Councillors normally stay in office for the full four year term and can stand for re-election at its end. However, if a Councillor resigns, or dies, a by-election (for that Ward only) may be held to fill the vacancy.

Councillors are described by Government as democratically accountable (that is to say they were voted in) to the residents of their Ward but with an overriding duty to the whole community including those who did not vote for them. All Councillors sign a Code of Conduct and a complete the Register of Interests (at Parish, District, County and Unitary level) and with it comes the expectation of high standards of behaviour. Each principal authorities Standards Committee trains and advises on the Code.

Who can stand

With no formal qualifications needed, anyone can stand as a candidate if eligible on the day nominated and on Polling Day by being:

- at least 18 years of age and;
- a British citizen, a citizen of a member state of the European Union or a Commonwealth citizen.

Plus comply with one of the following in the local authority area in which they wish to stand:

- named on the Electoral Register and remaining registered for the term of office or,
- living in the authority area for the whole of the previous 12 months and in case of a Parish Council within 4.8 kilometres or,
- occupying as an owner or tenant (paying rent) any land or premises during the whole of the 12 months before the nomination day or,
- as the main or only place of work during the last 12 months.

...Frome Watch...

Costs

Frome's 2007 Town elections cost an unexpected £12,000. Twice what was budgeted for to the disbelief of Councillors. It topped Council meeting after Council meeting until a couple of years of intermittent wrangling with Mendip reduced the bill to £9,000.

However, the nearby new Unitary authority of Wiltshire decided not to charge any of its Parishes for elections (2009) in order, it said, to promote democracy. As an average, Mendip reckoned each Polling Station cost about £1,300 to run.

Someone **cannot** stand for election if:

- in the 5 years before Polling Day they have been imprisoned for, or on a suspended sentence of 3 months or more or;
- subject to a Bankruptcy Restriction Order or have made a composition or interim order with creditors or;
- employed by the local authority or as an employee of a connected organisation - there is quite an extensive and complex list or;
- previously disqualified, this includes corruption and illegal election practices.

Becoming a Candidate

A notice announcing the forthcoming election is posted in the usual public places: the library, Council offices, community notice boards and in the local newspapers. This triggers a strict timetable, giving nominees about a week to get the nomination papers sent to the Elections officer before the deadline. Delivery by hand is recommended to ensure the deadline is not missed. This is followed by about 3 to 4 weeks of intense election campaigning before Polling Day.

How many Parishes can you stand for?

Across the border in Wiltshire one dedicated Councillor serves on four Parish Councils - perhaps a record and as a Unitary Councillor.

Two electors must sign a Parish or Town Council candidate's nomination papers and 10 if a candidate stands for a principal authority such as a District Council. The electors must live in the Ward and be registered for local government elections; their electoral registration numbers are noted on the nomination forms. No candidate may stand in more than one Ward within the same electoral area but candidates can stand in more than one Parish.

Registering a Political Party

Candidates can register their own political party. All that is needed is a completed application form, a copy of the party's constitution, a draft financial scheme and a £150 (2011) fee. 4 weeks should be allowed for the Electoral Commission to process the application. Registering as a Minor Political Party protects the name and emblem. The party's details can be amended later to enable it to stand elsewhere.

Nomination papers can be inspected by the public up until Polling Day, if a candidate is found guilty of supplying false information, one year's imprisonment, a fine or both can be imposed. Candidates must also sign a Declaration of Consent. This written and witnessed consent lists all the grounds on which the candidate is qualified to stand including a declaration that the candidate is "*not disqualified*" from standing.

Candidates are listed alphabetically on ballot papers and it is said that names at beginning of the ballot, such as Aaron Aardvark, get more votes than candidates towards the end of the alphabet. Nicknames or the shortened versions of first or last names can be used such as "Bob" for Robert making a favourite candidate easier to spot.

If there are two vacancies in a Ward and two candidates their election is uncontested and automatic, no vote is taken.

If there is a vacancy any 10 electors can request an election to fill it – this is little used.

Political Parties

No one needs to belong to a political party or have a political preference to stand for election, anyone can stand as an Independent and those who do may not necessarily agree with each other. In more recent years candidates standing on local single issues such as hospital closures have been particularly successful. Candidates representing a registered political party and authorised by its nominating officer can use the party name or one of the twelve registered descriptions and the party emblem on their ballot paper.

Those not standing for a party can use the description "independent", or use up to six words or no description at all but cannot use an emblem.

Political parties can give their candidates help, advice, co-ordinate the campaign, or provide financial help via their constituency associations e.g. for election leaflets, posters and rosettes during the campaign. Candidates may need to be in party membership for a set time before nomination is allowed. Parties can be desperate for candidates but membership is still not a guarantee of nomination indeed two of Frome's Councillors found themselves forced to stand as Independents as their term came to an end in the May 2011 elections.

The main political parties keep to their own traditionally distinctive colours: Conservatives - blue, Labour - red and Liberal Democrats - yellow, and will brand all their campaign literature accordingly including rosettes.

...Frome Watch...
New Independents
Frome was part of a local surge towards Independent Councillors, Midsomer Norton whose Councillors had been re-elected unopposed for the previous eight years this time found the 11 seats contested by individual Independents. Each making the most imaginative use of the six words available to them on their ballot paper: "A fresh Start," "Listening to You," "Prosperity through Commerce," or simply "Local Citizen," or as a description: "Retired Civil Servant," Community Candidate," "Farmer," to brilliant electoral success.

In the nearby village of Peasedown-St-John all 17 Councillors were elected standing as a community group "Peasedown First" a newly created minor party.

Councillors can and do swap allegiances once elected changing to a different political party or becoming an Independent, this does not result in another election. However, it can upset the balance of power in a Council, more notably at principal council level where it is the assumption and practice that the biggest political grouping should control or lead the decision making process. A Councillor's decision to change party is politically embarrassing; causing much distrust and perhaps leading to a re-shuffling of Councillors on Committees even a loss of pay for some who were previously chairing or portfolio holders. Consequently creating deeply held resentments which lasts years.

Election Agents
Parish Council candidates do not have election agents. Candidates in principal authority elections as well as Parish elections can be their own agent but more usually use someone from within their political party or group. An agent organises: the writing, printing and delivery of election literature, leaflets or newsletters; Organising: public meetings and the canvassing of the local electorate by volunteers before Polling Day, the tellers on Polling Day and goes to the Count; oversees all the financial aspects of an election, from spending to collecting donations. It is only the agent who can legally pay the election expenses however, the candidate is responsible for any malpractice.

Candidates can also choose their own observers (the polling and counting agents) to watch that everything done is above board.

The Campaign - Getting Support

A campaign starts with the candidate declaring they are standing, perhaps by making a statement to the press, putting up posters, holding meetings, or getting their political party to organise events. It is tricky deciding when to start, no-one wants to peak too early and no-one wants to be left behind, the electorate are quick to grumble, so consequently there is about 3 weeks of intense activity when doormats are deluged with leaflets and unexpected visitors.

...Frome Watch...

What did they do?

40 people put themselves forward for the 17 seats in the 2011 Parish elections across the 6 Wards. In Frome Park, 9 candidates stood for 3 seats. A contrast to the 2007 election where 3 of the 6 Wards were uncontested and 8 seats therefore filled by political party appointees. Even so for many candidates campaigning was limited to getting their personal leaflets delivered, a few posters up and a photo with a personal profile in the local newspaper – these said very little and nothing was promised. Canvassing was minimal although one Mendip District candidate, Frome's youngest at 19, saw his first priority to sort out dog poo – a Frome perennial, adding he had delivered to every house in his Ward some 1,800. He won a seat beating all his fellow candidates with an outstanding 743 votes (on a 43% turnout).

Overall Liberal Democrats delivered the most, some 5 pieces of literature, indeed householders complained of being woken at 5am by their dogs barking, only to look out of their windows to see the retreating figures of early morning leafleters delivering the final flyer on the morning of Election Day - the belief is the more pieces of literature that are sent out the better the result. But considering what was at stake: the possible overall control at Mendip District, retaining even extending control in the town, real engagement was small. The new Independents for Frome had a weekend stall in town – encouraging townspeople to register to vote, a website, a Twitter and a Facebook page as did the Liberal Democrats, no-one held public meetings.

Many Town Council candidates also hoped for election at Mendip, perhaps explaining why so little attention was paid to Frome?

Unusually, a prospective Frome Parish and District Councillor was also prospective candidate for a Ward in the nearby Unitary Authority of Bath and North East Somerset some 13 miles away; whilst he failed, he did raise the Liberal Democrat vote by 10% on a surprising 57% turnout.

Each candidate gets a free copy of the Register of Electors (to be kept confidential) including electors using postal or proxy voting, this helps with organising the leafleting and canvassing of the Ward. The Elections Officer has a list of free available meeting rooms such as halls or schools for which there is only a nominal charge for heating and lighting.

The Election Leaflet

The election leaflet is the heart of the campaign and many have expanded into newsletters, delivered to every home in the candidate's Ward often written to a basic template containing at the very least: brief biographical details of the candidate, including a photograph plus any aspirations or promises of actions which will be taken if elected; perhaps a list of what they personally contributed to past Parish successes: or more frequently a list of the failures and failings of the other candidates, sometimes rounding up with a summary of beliefs, before finishing with an exhortation to vote and a large **X**.

Party newsletters distributed at same time often only obliquely refer to the candidates to avoid being part of the candidates costs. An Independent candidate without a party template to follow can be freer to express their views. A good leaflet has a double purpose, the reverse side can be used as a poster with the name of the candidate emblazoned on it ready to be placed in supporting householders windows.

There are offences to be avoided including making defamatory or abusive statements, or false statements about a candidate's character or conduct, with a possible £5,000 fine, the loss of voting rights for 3 years and a ban from standing for an elected office. In case of a complaint or query about content, all election literature such as posters, placards, newsletters, leaflets, including websites and ipodcasts carry the names and addresses of the person on whose behalf it is published, the printer and the organiser of the literature.

Breaches again can incur a £5,000 fine. This is in addition to the general civil and criminal law relating to any published material.

Pitcombe Poster
Police conducted house to house enquiries through the South Somerset hamlet of Pitcombe to catch the person who had drawn a Hitler-style moustache on to a Tory campaign poster on the village noticeboard, but while the police were worried the poster might cause, "harassment, alarm or distress," the villagers thought it an extraordinary waste of police time and taxpayers money.

Equally serious is persuading a voter to vote or not to vote by:
- bribery - such as giving money, gifts or a job;
- treating - giving food, drink or entertainment; and
- undue influence - such as threats of violence or damage or hindering or preventing a voter from voting.

Local newspapers may run stories up to an election or give a list and short biography of each of the candidates. While the allocation of broadcast time on radio and television is prescribed in legislation, the way newspapers give their views on political issues is not. Newspapers may take whatever view they like and may include as much or as little coverage as they decide. The inclusion of a candidate in a newspaper article does not count towards election expenses, although paying for an advertisement in a newspaper does.

...Frome Watch...
What did they say? - election leaflets.
Surprisingly with a new "party" of Independent candidates (IfF) in the town wanting to win Town Council seats the 3 traditional parties largely ignored it concentrating solely on winning the Mendip Distinct Council elections taking place at the same time as the Parish elections. Whilst all voiced pledges and priorities town issues were barely mentioned. In many ways elections are still very private affairs; with the usually unspoken politically personal battles emerging. It was a rare opportunity for Frome to see what was thought behind closed doors.

With the 3 traditional parties giving the town only the barest mention, reliance on a vote placed on the District ballot paper carrying over to the town ballot paper was heavy.
No mention was made of town successes or the main areas of contention: the expensive Christmas lights and with it the sad saga of the Christmas tree, the Tourist Information integration, the Cheese & Grain debacle or the completed or any other proposed land purchases.

Successful national events such as the cycling Tour of Britain, or even the new bridge failed to be mentioned.

Only the buying of grit bins was triumphantly waved – a Liberal Democrat dominated Town Council initiative, ignoring so much that could have been said or challenged. No one felt the need to explain the near £1 million of budgeted expenditure every year.

Candidates under the Conservative (Tory) banner, with fuzzy photographs, stuck to random generalities to take a stand on issues as litter, traffic, employment, the control of development, and green spaces using triumphs from the distant past to illustrate success certainly not giving the impression of a confident ruling party which was about to have a landslide victory at District level.

Labour retro in red and yellow and with the best photos led a lack lustre campaign. Choosing a simplistic approach, concentrating on generalised national issues: the Tory led Coalition cuts, broken national Liberal Democrat promises and with a stout defence of the National Health Service (NHS), seemingly trying to re-run the 2010 General Election None of its 3 candidates were successful.

The Liberal Democrats were particularly jubilant hoping a recent Ward by-election result at Mendip would translate into a 10 Councillor majority (Mendip District was precariously balanced, with Conservatives in control with 24 Councillors against the Liberal Democrats 23).

They produced a raft of chatty and increasingly clichéd newssheets, leaflets and "personal" letters, and a survey - the Liberal Democrats always do a survey, mostly devoted to resentful criticism of the Conservative's County and Mendip administration. Picking this time on the Special Expenses Rate and labelling it a stealth tax – it pays for maintenance of the cemetery and the town's play areas (£7.51 per D band household in Frome 2011). There were column inches given to listing national Liberal Democrats successes (as part of the Tory led Coalition Government. This was underplayed at one point making it very clear that, "that sort of thing" (a Coalition) would not happen locally. Frome was reduced to a one line reminder to vote.

The Candidates' own choice of issues ranged around now familiar themes: parking, green spaces, development, libraries and the NHS. The Liberal Democrats secret weapon was the sitting MP's smiling endorsement of each candidate, perhaps hoping to bring out the vote that took the party to national "victory" in only the previous year.

Help from inside the party machine for the traditional parties can be patchy each area has its constituency party organisation geared to national politics and help, general administrative support or monies may not seamlessly swing into action. There is not the strong steer on policies or issues that might be expected giving local meaning to a national organisation and as they would have us believe their fundamental grassroots. There is a very much "just get on with it attitude." This general lack of a positive stance gets mired in local political resentments, the embarrassment of being in the Coalition or re-runs of 19th century politics, ideology drowning out any doubts candidates may have about what they were standing for.

Perhaps they really hope no one reads the literature. Most in any case is written in election-speak everyone promises: *"to work hard…,"* *"provide what the community wants…,"* *"safeguard green spaces…,"* *"support local businesses…,"* *"partnership working…,"* *"work to provide facilities…,"* *"fight for the views of young people."*

With so little detail it will be about turning aspirations or it could be argued empty phrases into workable polices. With the parties, sounding similar and vague no-one would be able to accuse anyone of breaking promises. It will be, as always, a question of faith.

IfF was staggeringly different, fresher, straightforward, up-beat (even the leaflets were in black and white) not bound up in political clichés; they caught the need for change promising to be boldly interventionist abandoning the dithering of the past, perhaps a product of the split allegiances of the town's District/Town Councillors. Earnest and hype-free, the lengthier on-line biographies backed their leaflets thumbnail sketches giving a sense of real people not manufactured party apparatchiks. The leaflets emphasised: the need for pride in the town divorced from party politics, for a Council working for its town and open to new ideas and illustrated by 17 independent candidates coming together to support one another - no one thought it would last.

Perhaps IfF's main tenet and appeal was its Frome focus, unlike the other parties it's candidates did not stand for Mendip District (which was voted for on the same day) creating an inherent likeability, emphasising an impartiality with an ability to scrutinise the higher tiers of local government from a moral high ground.

Each of the half dozen broad principles included a list of areas which would be tackled:
- Strengthening the community, its groups, organisations and businesses : by auditing their needs, giving them a voice, talking and taking note, especially of the young and the town's businesses;
- A cleaner, greener town: regaining control of street cleaning, a safer Market Place for pedestrians and all users, more trees to be planted, allotments to be provided, air quality and the river and its banks improved. Tapping into the green economy;
- Listening to the townspeople: providing more informal opportunities for the townspeople's views to be heard, getting local businesses to help run Council affairs, supporting business and community enterprises, making evidence based decisions, using the new powers given under the Localism Act, creating a "can do " culture;
- Keeping Frome unique: By planning for better urban design, with fewer cars, more open space and getting more decisions made in Frome. Writing a Neighbourhood Development Plan endorsed by a referendum;
- Putting a sustainable future at the heart of policies: Improving and regaining control of the twice weekly markets, lobbying to improve transport links including the "Missing Link" cycle path, supporting local energy generation;
- Promoting arts and culture: funding the Cheese & Grain, sharing resources and creating networks, encouraging local businesses to fund the arts, looking at the future of the town's library.

It was enough. They would be heroes.

Volunteers are essential and this is where belonging to a political party comes into its own. Party members on the local list can be asked to deliver leaflets, put up and take down posters, act as tellers at Polling Stations, ferry voters to the Polling Station and walk the streets door knocking canvassing for votes.

Canvassers go door to door during the weeks up to an election, an unpaid thankless task particularly if it rains, asking for support for their candidate or party. Many who answer their front doors regard this with suspicion and won't say, others feel it is a good opportunity to argue about the shortcomings of the Government, the Council, Councillors, their neighbours and the youth of today.

Canvassers hope to discover who their supporters are and will cross reference these results with the electoral registration numbers taken from voters outside the Polling Station by the tellers. If the hoped for supporter has not turned up at the Polling Station, this is known because the voters electoral number has not been noted, a volunteer is sent round to remind the voter that there is still time to vote and perhaps offer a lift.

This can be vital when an election can be won or lost by a few votes which is likely to be the case in Parish elections. Whilst canvassers may offer a lift to the Polling Station they cannot ask or insist the voter votes for their candidate. If a voter admits to being a supporter they will be asked to have a poster in the front window or garden, these spring up gaudily before an election and disappear just as suddenly afterwards (within ten days).

The tellers sit outside Polling Stations collecting electoral numbers; they are not allowed to ask voters how they will vote or be intimidating, and voters do not need to speak to them. It can be very convivial and many tellers will swap numbers when there is a rush on so none are missed. It is best to dress warmly and hope that there is a chair to sit on. With the increase in postal voting this role is becoming less crucial. Candidates waylaying voters for a chat, groups of campaigners, parked cars covered in posters, the use of loudspeakers or any poster too close to the Polling Station can be seen as intimidation and the Polling Station's presiding officer will decide what is OK and may ask for things to be moved.

Election Spending and Donations
Deposits (needed at national elections) are not needed in local authority elections. However, the limit each candidate can spend on getting elected is based on the number of electors in a Ward. In 2008 it was £600 plus 5 pence, per local government elector. With joint candidatures for a Ward the amount is reduced, so with two candidates for two vacancies the amount allowed is reduced by a quarter etc.

...Frome Watch...
Frome expenses
May 2011 Parish election expenses were perhaps surprisingly modest. With the majority of expenditure on election leaflets. The Conservatives declared between £0 and £120 each. Labour who only fielded 3 candidates out of a possible 17 spent around £114 each. The Liberal Democrats around £30 each reflecting the campaign's Mendip focus where the expenses claimed were higher. The new IfF party's shared spending averaged out at around £76 each. An ex-Liberal Democrat Councillor now standing as an Independent and therefore funding himself still only spent £226 on leaflets and delivery.

Anything a candidate uses to get elected from the date they become a candidate whether it was incurred before, during or after the election counts as an election expense. Only the candidate, or their Agent at principal authority level, can authorise the expenditure. Election expenses can be money spent on: advertising; unsolicited material addressed to electors and includes design, printing and distribution; transport such as petrol and car hire costs; public meetings such as venue hire; staff or election agent salaries; accommodation and administration costs such as property, perhaps renting an office; goods, such as stationery; services and facilities such as phones. It is best practice to collect all invoices and receipts for all payments (over £10 in value at Parish level and £20 at principal authority level) to corroborate the expenses. Where candidates share expenses the cost is split accordingly.

Bills must be paid promptly after the results are announced, 21 days if a Parish or Community Council election or 28 days for a principal authority.

Donations

Money comes in many forms from: supporters, bequests, the constituency association, sponsorship, free advertising, discounted goods such as leaflets, free use of offices or hire car and even cash in blank envelopes. All donations over £50 are listed, except volunteer time or a loan of a car, home or computer, with the donors' full names and addresses with 30 days to check that they are acceptable and on the "permissible list" which includes UK electors and UK based organisations.

All candidates whether elected or not send in an election expenses return (they can be prosecuted for not doing so) to the Returning Officer which details all donations and all spending within 28 days of the Parish election result, these are not reimbursed and can be inspected for up to 1 year for Parish and 2 years for general elections.

The Poll and Count

Voters have between 7am and 10pm on Polling Day to go to the Polling Station, usually a public building: a school, community hall, or church, to put their cross against the name or names on the list of candidates they want to be their Councillors. Handing in their polling card, or giving their name and address to be ticked off on the Electoral Register and given a ballot paper in return. This is taken to a flimsy wooden booth and using a pencil on a string to put a cross or crosses against an often dauntingly long list of candidates hoping to be Councillors before pushing it through the slot of the ballot box in front of the Polling Clerk. The ballot paper is numbered on the back against the electoral registration list so in theory a voter could be traced.

Candidates can appoint polling agents to verify the voting processes and procedures are correct before the Poll is opened, indeed candidates can visit any Polling Station in the Ward in which they are standing and this is often a welcome encouragement for the tellers sitting outside noting down the electoral registration numbers from voters as they arrive.

The Count begins after close of the Poll, the culmination of several frantic and intense weeks of campaigning. The relief is tempered with an increased anxiety of what if nobody voted or only in embarrassingly small numbers. The ballot boxes and any handed in postal ballots are taken in sealed boxes to the Count. This generally takes place in a centrally placed hall or school where long rows of tables are set out with counting agents ranged along the sides. When the ballot box is opened the numbers of papers inside should tally with what is expected if there is a variation the Acting Returning Officer will decide if the discrepancy is important. The ballot papers are sorted into bundles by candidate and counted to see which candidate has won. Some count painfully slowly stopping occasionally to recheck for heart stopping moments, others super-fast making it difficult to believe they could be accurate as the ballot papers are bundled into 100's to make re-checking easier.

Candidates can invite family, friends or supporters to watch the Count with them, through the often long hours helping to avoid looking at the successes of the other candidates and agonise over the results as the bundles of ballot papers are slowly added to.

The Acting Returning Officer may delay the Count till the next day in difficult geographic areas, but there is still an intense enthusiasm for counting through the night – many do not start until the small hours and trying to be first with the result even at a Parish level.

Mendip was proudly the first with the result of the national referendum on the proposed new Alternative Vote voting system in 2011 which was concurrent with the Parish elections. There are strict rules regarding secrecy and if breached there is a £5,000 fine or a 6 months prison sentence.

As the popularity of postal votes has increased, the resulting large numbers are opened before Polling Day at "special openings" which can be observed as can the Count.

...Frome Watch...

Frome Riots

Fierce fighting occurred over three days when Frome, now a Parliamentary Borough, elected its first MP in 1832 under the new Reform Act. Thomas Sheppard for the reform group – the Radicals and Sir Thomas Champneys for the Tories were bitter enemies. Both sides arrived at the hustings in the town centre and were duly nominated, and seconded as candidates. Each made a speech, although Sheppard's was drowned out by Champneys raucous supporters. Both sides were there in force with several hundred men a piece - Champneys men armed with bludgeons and cudgels. Fighting broke out and was so fierce - one of Sheppard's supporters was killed; the magistrates swore in Special Constables who were then set upon by the mob so a troop of Dragoons were summoned from nearby Trowbridge to be on hand. Voting was in public not by secret ballot and was held over four days. By day two Sheppard had polled over half the vote, this so incensed Champneys supporters they attacked the George and the Crown Inns in the Market Place where Sheppard's supporters were sheltering. The Riot Act was read and the Special Constables were ordered to fire, wounding the leading rioters. By the end of the day the Dragoons re-entered the town and restored order. Champney resigned, 100 had voted for him. Sheppard was duly elected with 163 votes. He won 3 subsequent elections. Many had been injured; both Inns and houses throughout the town were wrecked including a draper's house in the Market Place which was completely demolished. The Reform Act had revolutionised voting giving around 14% of the adult male population a vote although it was still based on land ownership.

The postal ballot papers and their voting statements are checked not counted and at least 20% of the total will have a personal identifier verification check.

The candidates can watch or appoint counting agents, who oversee the process, watching at least one of the counting assistants (who actually count each ballot paper checking for spoiled or doubtful papers. Traditionally these were bank tellers who were both quick and accurate) and can observe the opening of the postal ballot papers. The agents ensure secrecy is maintained and the Count is accurate, and orderly, pointing out doubtful papers and defending those marked for their own candidates which have been objected to. They are not allowed to handle the ballot papers. There are always spoiled ballot papers at an election, many are left blank perhaps in protest, some are just scrawled across, and on some the cross can look uncertain or badly placed. These can be negotiated over and added to a candidate's total perhaps making the difference between winning and loosing. Candidates with the highest number of votes win, until all the Parish seats are used up, so many may become Councillors on very few votes indeed.

The candidates, the election agents or the Returning Officer can ask for a recount, there is no limit to the number. If there is a tie, the winner is decided by the drawing of lots whoever wins is given an extra vote and is elected.
The Returning Officer declares the winner and states the number of votes.

Later he will publish the names of the candidates, the number of votes cast for each and the number of rejected ballot papers. The ballot papers are kept for 6 months before being destroyed.

After the Election

After the celebrations the winning candidates are appointed as Councillors on the 4th day after the election. Signing a declaration of Acceptance of Office, otherwise a new by-election must be held. This is a simple document where Councillors declare *"to duly and faithfully fulfil their duties to the best of their judgement and ability."* A declaration agreeing to abide by the Code of Conduct is signed. A Register of Interests is also completed for themselves and, since the Localism Act (2011), their partners within a month of the election. Interests on the Register are declared at the start of Council meetings, although they are not checked. Parish Registers can be inspected at principal Councils' offices and on their websites and on the Parish website, if there is one.

And finally, all election spending is listed and backed up by receipts or invoices and all donations received and offered are listed with the name and address of the donors whether the candidate is elected or not. These are kept and can be inspected for up to 1 year for Parish elections (2 years for general elections), although very few do.

Objections

Election results can be challenged by an election petition presented by four electors or another candidate on grounds of corruption, illegal practices or using the fact that the successful candidate was actually disqualified. This is generally done within 21 days of the election and a petition lodged with the High Court for an initial fee of £450, however, total costs can run into £1,000s.

Polling Stations should be an easy distance from voters' homes. Parish Councils and voters can suggest re-siting to their principal Councils who must review their ease of use regularly under the Representation of the People Act 1983.

...Frome Watch...
The story of IfF

In 2011 the unexpected happens. Started in response to the Town Council's high-handed actions over the running of the Cheese & Grain, the Independents for Frome (IfF) field 10 of their 17 candidates to success in the May Parish elections.

The disbelief that followed the Council's Cheese & Grain ultimatum, stirred a small group to call a public meeting. Not even certain anyone would turn up the resulting packed meeting, above the Lamb pub, rapidly voiced a desire to shun national party politics asking for Councillors who would be: Frome centred, making open, fair and evidence-based decisions.

The 7 founders outlined 6 principles for all candidates to agree to:
* Independence - no party politicking,
* Integrity – transparency and openness,
* A "can do" approach,
* Developing a sustainable way of working – looking at the Council's role,
* Fairness - respect for local democracy,
* Cleaner and greener – by developing alliances.

Numerous volunteers stepped forward to help. For the first time the whole range of social media was used: Facebook, Twitter, You-Tube, a dedicated website on which candidates talked about themselves and their beliefs, and an unexpected novelty, a flash mob.

The town's evening Sainsbury's shopping was interrupted when one or two shoppers suddenly stopped then started to sing the Jimmy Cliff classic, "You Can Get It If You Really Want." Joined by 70 odd other shoppers singing to the end of the song before continuing with their shopping. Organised to raise awareness of voter registration for the forth coming May election. It was a You-Tube success. Indeed they were the only party encouraging voter registration holding a stall every Saturday handing out voter registration forms. They caught the mood of the moment in a slogan-" IfF not now when?"

Letters in the press were not so complimentary, is it: an alliance, a group, a party, is it "old Labour" in disguise, is it possible to have a coalition of Independents, rumours spread: the Mayor would be abolished, there would be no chief executive, no Xmas lights, what about the Christmas tree, they have no costed policies, they won't know what to do, how can the "Iffy" party possibly work.

How to be a Voter

Voters are something of a problem for politicians. If voters vote at all it is the older age groups who bother. Folklore says Tory voters are the most guaranteed to vote whilst Labour voters are most easily put off by the weather. Government has put some thought into popularising voting with a jolly website and by encouraging postal voting despite the hazards of fraud and vote stealing. Students for instance can end up with two votes often being registered at their parental home address and at their university address. The lowering of the voting age to 16, it is suggested, would help stop the steady decline in election turnout. Polling Day is traditionally a Thursday from a time when workers were paid weekly on a Friday so could vote before spending their wages in the public houses. A move to weekend voting is regularly suggested as more in keeping with modern life styles and certainly most Polling Stations have a rush of voters before work and after work with queues forming. Lengthy queues at the days end in the 2010 General Election meant many voters were denied their opportunity to vote as the Polling Stations closed.

Who can vote

All those who are:
- 18 years of age or over on Polling Day but can be registered when aged 16.
- Resident in the UK.
- A British citizen living abroad for parliamentary elections but not local elections.
- British citizens, qualifying Commonwealth, or Irish Republic citizens in all elections.
- EU citizens in local elections but not parliamentary.
- Not subject to any legal incapacity to vote.

All the above will need to be registered with their District or Unitary Council, either by filling in the annual canvass form which is sent to every household or by "rolling registration" filling in a form at any time. There are two registers the full version which contains everyone's details or the edited version which you can choose to be on and is sold to companies for marketing.

Once registered, a voter votes in person, by post or by proxy.

In Person
- A polling card is sent a week or two before the election, giving details of when and where to vote, it should be reasonably close by.

- On Polling Day, the allotted Polling Station (Polling Places in Scotland) is open from 7am to 10pm and is generally a public building, such as a local school or hall although in more rural areas pubs are used.
- On arrival the Presiding Officer or his clerks (they stay there the whole 15 hours) will ask voters on arrival their name and address or use the proffered polling card to help tick off the names on their check-list to avoid duplicate voting. The ballot paper is stamped to validate it and numbered to combat fraud, this could be theoretically traced back to the voter. Ballot papers are destroyed six months after the election.
- The ballot paper lists candidates alphabetically and includes the political party name; shorn of all detail it can be tricky to remember who is who. If there are several elections at the same time a different coloured paper is used for each set of candidates.
- Voting is in one of the flimsy wooden screened booths ensuring secrecy.
- A cross is put in the box next to the name of the person or persons you want to vote for by using the pencil provided. Papers which are badly marked, scribbled on, defaced or with rude comments written on them or left blank will not be counted.
- The ballot paper is folded so others cannot see the choices made and posted into the ballot box.

...Frome Watch...

Frome local election turnouts	
2009. County Council Election	32-39%
2011. Mendip District Council and Frome Town Council	c43%
2011. postal ballots	c63%

By Post

- A voter can register as an elector and request a new postal vote up to 11 working days before the poll. There is no need to give a reason. For replacement of lost or spoilt postal votes the deadline is 5pm on Polling Day.
- A ballot paper will normally be sent out about a week before Polling Day.

By Proxy

A voter can appoint someone else to cast their vote on their behalf if there is a valid reason, sudden illness or being unable to get to the Polling Station or abroad during the election such as in the armed services. If incapacity or illness is sudden a proxy vote for medical reasons can be applied for until 5pm on Polling Day.

Boundaries

...Frome Watch...

General Elections - turnouts for the Somerton and Frome Constituency	
1992	c83%
2005	c69%
2010	74% nationally it is c65%

The Constituency has been consistently higher than the national average.

Boundaries for Parliamentary constituencies, County electoral divisions, District Wards and Parish boundaries do not necessarily coincide leading to a situation of baffling complexity, but are organised so each Councillor has roughly an equal number of electors.

Polling Stations should be reasonably easy to get to - tricky in very rural areas, and where there is an identifiable community.

Reviewed every 8 to 12 years to take account of shifts in population, changes can be politically disastrous altering the political bias of a Council. In the case of District Ward boundaries a Boundary Commission review asks the District Council, its Parish Councils, local political parties, Councillors and the general public, - if they know about it - there should be a brief announcement in the local newspapers for ideas and suggestions. Reviews take around 18 months.

...Frome Watch....

Somerton and Frome

Somerton and Frome is one of 650 parliamentary constituencies (May 2010), a review started in 2012 primarily to balance the population growth of urban areas and reduce the number of constituencies overall.

Somerset County has 58 electoral divisions of which Frome has 3: Frome North, Frome South, and Frome Selwood - which includes a part the surrounding rural Parishes.

The 5 District Councils of Somerset are in turn divided into electoral Wards. In Mendip there are 34 covering the 62 Parishes. Many Parishes combine with a neighbour, the largest Parishes – the towns, have several Wards.

The Problem

Frome Wards were previously like slices of a cake stretching from the fields at the edge of town and meeting in the middle at the Market Place. Their names taken from the original hamlets which grew into the town: Badcox, Keyford, Welshmill, Fromefield and on the outskirts Berkley Down.

Shifting populations had at the end of the 1999 review redefined the Ward boundaries, losing Badcox Ward but gaining Park, Each Ward contributing two District Councillors making 10 of the District's total of 46.

The June 2005 review tackled the unequal growth in the populations of Welshmill and Keyford. The Boundary Commission suggested an extensive rejigging of Ward boundaries as well as an extra Frome District Councillor. The Liberal Democrat dominated Town and District Councils and the local Liberal Democrats Party rejected the idea of an extra Councillor. However, their proposal to keep to 10 Councillors would have combined parts of Frome with the rural areas of other Parishes.

The same 2005 review also looked at the six town Wards: Berkley Down, Fromefield, Keyford, Welshmill each returned 4 Parish Councillors with Park East and Park West returning 2 each, giving a Town Council of 20. The Commission was somewhat surprised at a proposal to decrease the number of Councillors by 3 to 17 a move supported by the District Council, the Liberal Democrats Group on the Council, Somerton and Frome Liberal Democrats and the Frome branch of the Liberal Democrats (often the same people). The Commission wanted to keep 20 Councillors. The sitting MP's only comment was a request for his constituency boundaries to be unchanged, something which was not going to be proposed until 2011. The Town Council had not commented.

The Result

The Commission stuck to its proposal for an additional Frome District Councillor and rejigged the boundaries of all the Wards to create six irregularly shaped District Wards with the addition of Frome West and therefore an enlarged District Council of 47.

Aiming to reduce the projected number of electors per Councillor from 1,860 to 1,821 by 2009.

The Town Council with its Liberal Democrat majority were prodded into responding and agreed it did want a reduced Town Council. It was only on the basis of this final comment the Commission took the extraordinary step of agreeing. It was the only Parish to request such a change. No reasons were given but with such strong Liberal Democrat backing it must be assumed there was a strong party political reason. In previous elections the now missing Councillors were likely to have been from opposing parties, the change bringing about the final destruction of the remnants of the town's Labour Party strongholds, lessening the chance of any opposition and enabling a clean sweep to be made and held by the Liberal Democrats.

Ward names were changed along Liberal Democrat suggestions making a further break with the past: Welshmill becomes Market, Fromefield becomes College and the newer Park West becomes Oakfield. The Parish Wards of: Berkley Down, College, Keyford, Park, and Market are now represented by 3 Councillors and Oakfield by 2.

This was not without its problems as in the May 2007 elections Parish Councillors were also elected to the District Council and County (10 of them), severely stretching resources as the Liberal Democrats became the controlling party in the Town, the District and the County. This put a strain on the number of Parish meetings arranged with the additional risk of them being unquorate and having to be cancelled. At the same time the budget and staffing levels were increased dramatically to take advantage of the hoped for change from a County to a Unitary authority, increasing the pressures on decision making. For a growing town there was less representation and fewer Councillors whose concerns were completely Frome focused, as Councillors' juggled Parish, District and County roles. By comparison Frome's sister parliamentary constituency town of Somerton has 15 Councillors for a population a fifth of Frome's size.

Datafile

Local Government Boundary Commission for England, www. lgbce.org.uk
Boundary Commission for England, www.boundarycommissionforengland.org.uk
About my vote, www,aboutmyvote.co.uk
Uk Polling Report, www.ukpollingreport.co.uk
Directgov,www.directgov.co.uk
Do Politics, www.do-politics.org.uk
UK Political Info, www,ukpolitivalinfo.uk
Midsomer Norton Journal, www,mnrjournal.co.uk

25 - THE KNOWN UNKNOWNS

Tales of Mystery and Suspense

6 Frome Short Stories: Tourism, Land Purchases, The Bailey Bridge, The Cheese and Grain, Twinning, Shopping, Shops and Supermarkets.

There have been six main topics dominating discussion within the town down the years but it was only during 2007-11 that events crystallised. By now an increasingly confident and self-assured Town Council, having seen off a weak challenge by the external auditor, sensed its own omnipotence, but ever benevolent it was ambitious to create a legacy. In the mix there was national government, Mendip and Somerset Councils, Councillors, developers, and lastly the townspeople's views - perhaps too easily pushed aside.

These events however left the barest trace in the minute archives. Why so little discussion took place or such secretiveness developed without formal resolutions being made is not clear. Perhaps the total domination of one political grouping made discussion seem superfluous, or the large number of Councillors serving on principal Councils as well as the Town blurred a line with the town just a side-show. But this does not explain why Councillors outside the ruling group did not challenge or raise queries or why the Town Clerk allowed the custom to develop. The choices made would have a real and lasting influence on the town and would resonate for years to come, colouring its outlook, and locking it into spending commitments not only for now, but long into the future.

What of the public, change had begun, the "new kids on the block" or "blow-ins" as the locals began to call them were beginning to take the reins. Supremely confident, capable, articulate, media savvy, unapologetic, and well-connected, with a sense of infallibility and, perhaps their main strength, no doctrine to follow. Many had lived in Frome 5 even 10 years and they would now step forward (20 years had previously been thought to be the minimum) to take the reins displacing the now old guard made up of in the main of retiring teachers and social workers anxious, hesitant with their uncertainties of belief who had seen themselves as the town's protectors over the years and would now feel pushed aside.

The chronicles that follow were pieced together by talking to those concerned, reading sketchy reports in the press and from the discussions and decisions noted elsewhere making it is possible, to a degree, to draw together, something of what happened.

1. Tourism

Frome, lacking the pretty charm of Wells, the mystery of Glastonbury or the designer shopping of Street, is only given a glancing reference in Somerset County web promotions (2011) with only the monthly farmers markets highlighted – the illustrative photograph was of another town. Mendip District had queried County's strangely clichéd yet minimalist approach and considered withdrawing its contribution of money wanting something more robust and more Mendip targeted and fitting for the modern holiday-maker but let itself be persuaded against its better judgement to continue financing. Over the years the national broadsheet Sunday newspapers have happily and regularly listed Frome as either a "hot spot" or most recently one of the "coolest places in the United Kingdom" to live (6th apparently).

Citing its popularity with the number of celebrities living or visiting locally and the town's summer markets, all of which keeps house prices buoyant.

In the past previous national coverage only extended to the crushing of the Christmas lights by the Mayor, tabloid coverage of a couple caught "inflagrante delicto" on the Lamb Inn roundabout on a Sunday morning and in the late 1990's the filming of the television series "Drovers Gold" which transformed the streets into the 18th century with cattle running loose through the town. More recent triumphs have been the listing of Frome on the nightly national weather maps.

The town crier adds a welcome touch of colour. Dressed in a heavy scarlet coat, a frilly white shirt and a black tricorn hat, he rings a hand-bell and reads announcements from a scroll adding a sense of occasion to the opening of events. Self-funding, he also organises a national town crier's competition in Frome and takes part in competitions across the country with some success.

With only 20 hotel/B&B beds in the town (there are none listed on the Somerset tourism website) it is a tricky destination for anything more than a day visitor though self-catering (in a 16 km/10 mile radius) is a buoyant 600 beds. Mendip Lodge the town's only coach-party friendly hotel set in grounds with fabulous views closed in 2006 with Planning permission for housing. Mendip, too easily persuaded it was not a viable hotel, with the then newly built Frome Flyer on the bypass some two miles away cited as overwhelming competition. A previous attempt for housing in 1998 had failed.

Originally the site of a manor house, The White House, as it was originally known, was an elegant building surrounded by gardens hosting many of the town's "better" weddings and was the place to be seen. Built in the 1900's it became home to the 5th Dorset Regiment in World War II. Later an Italian prisoner of war camp, with its inmates helping on neighbouring farms - many stayed on after the war to make their homes locally. Later, in the 1960's it became the Mendip Travel Lodge, bringing something new, daring, with an unexpected level of American modernity and sophistication to the town. Once closed and after 3 arson attacks it was demolished, the site remains empty (2012).

Whilst town centre shopping is now seen as strongly "artisanal" – small shops on hilly streets epitomising a more sociable and people orientated shopping, this is very recent. With many of the independent businesses supporting themselves with an online presence, indeed the town won a Google award for the fastest growth in online selling in the Westcountry. The shops themselves are seen as a tourist plus. For the rest there is a rich melange of arts, music and alternative therapies to enjoy amongst a chaos of old buildings.

The Tourist Information Centre (TIC) had provided help and advice to tourist and residents alike in its restored wool drying tower home for about 10 years – it had previously been in a portacabin in the Market Yard Car Park. So it was a surprise when newspaper headlines baldly announced that the Town Council was set to run it.

Funding had been cut by Mendip District Council in 2009 when the surge in enthusiastic free bus pass usage by older people across the District left it with a budgetary shortfall combined with a slowdown in its Planning application revenue and reduced central government funding (15% in 2010 alone).

The TIC struggled on eventually going to Frome Town Council for help, instead of presumably, a hoped for increased grant the Town Council decided to absorb it. Creating a "One Stop Shop" providing a Town Council and tourist information service - something that the Quality Council scheme was very keen to promote. In any case the Town already funded a town guide.

Tour of Britain Cycle Race

"Showcases Somerset and Devon as great places to cycle," paid for by Somerset County Council in a 5 year agreement (£775,000). The economic benefits are explained in varying reports and in varying £millions: £5 or £6 million per County, or perhaps £6 million shared between the two Counties or again £10 million depending on the commentator, with between 100,000 to 250,000 spectators guessed at. However, it is not enough to continue the sponsorship as the County faces financial cuts and £350 million of debt.

The 23 volunteers were summarily dismissed to the shock of the town and years of friendly knowledgeable service disappeared although the four employed staff were retained. However, this was short lived as the Council would not agree a new lease for the TIC's Round Tower home at the Black Swan Arts Centre so moved to the Library next door, adjacent to the District Council's own information point.

The TIC had funded itself with grants from Mendip (£19,000) and Frome (£8,000) Councils, modestly boosted by sales and commission it earned from ticket sales and accommodation enquiries providing an income between £13,000 and £20,000 annually. But with the Town intervention the planned cost of the service was budgeted to rise to £80,000.

All 5 TIC's in the District's market towns had lost funding and the District was not unsympathetic employing consultants to advise on a strategy. Their report concluded the 5 should co-operate more, combining staff and resources missing the point that each TIC was a separate not for profit company and each town a good 10 miles apart. However, each imaginatively solved their own financial problems in various ways: Shepton Mallet introduced a monthly raffle; Glastonbury offered visitor tours led by the town crier and its garden as a wedding venue, Street produced a calendar and Glastonbury and Street together produced an annual guide book to sell; Wells decided to close as it souvenir sales had collapsed and moved the service to the Wells Museum. Luckily Mendip changed its plans and did provide some funding - £10,000 for each TIC.

The move to the Library was a success, footfall rising from 20,000 to 200,000.

With a hoped for tourism triumph a Frome County Councillor brought the start of a West Country Race Stage of the 2010 Tour of Britain cycle race to Frome. The culmination of a spectacular couple of days of cycling events and the beginnings of the annual Cobble Wobble, a race for all ages, with participants in fancy dress, cycling up the cobbled and the steepest of the town's shopping streets – Catherine Hill (there had been an annual on-foot sprint in the 1990s).

The Council hosted the Tour's cycle team's breakfasts and persuaded businesses and churches to open early to serve breakfasts to sight-seers. Cheering crowds packed behind crash barriers and sponsorship banners, flag waving school children lined the route and the normally sleepy Thursday half-day closing day was overwhelmed.

Experimental groups of youngsters and more self-conscience middle-aged men dashed by trying out the route on their bicycles first.

On a gloriously sunny September day the Mayor raises the start flag at 10.15 and the competitors are over the river bridge and beginning the steep climb out of the town centre. Whizzing by in seconds followed by a long cavalcade of back-up crews, team coaches, police outriders and film crews, all of whom are enthusiastically waved. Half an hour later the crash barriers are whisked away and the town is quiet and empty again.

Letters to the papers complained that the promised windfall had not happened, and there are anecdotes of many breakfast providers being out of pocket. The Council countered, explaining carefully, that the hoped for effect would be accumulative, over time. As always and despite often quite heroic attempts tourism is still largely illusory.

The Alcove Garden -"Events dear boy, events"

What is a Funicular Railway
A funicular, also known as an inclined plane or cliff railway, is a cable railway in which a cable attached to a pair of tram-like vehicles on rails moves them up and down a steep slope; the ascending and descending vehicles counterbalance each other. Some are built using water tanks under the floor of each car which are filled or emptied until just sufficient imbalance is achieved to allow movement. This is then controlled by a brakeman. The smallest funicular in the world is the Fisherman's Walk Cliff Railway in Bournemouth, at a length of 128 feet (39 m).

A funicular railway *"would be the making of Frome"* and was greeted enthusiastically by District Councillors, local traders and with Frome scepticism by everyone else.

The small white-washed Co-op supermarket had suffered a lingering death and was demolished; a 62 bed nursing home would be erected to the astonishment of the town, dividing Town Councillor opinion. Part of the land was the Alcove Garden, also known as Thomas Bunn Garden, in the grounds of Thomas Bunn's Monmouth House home. A 19th Century Frome philanthropist, who instigated many architectural, and road improvements but remains today relatively unknown. His garden, he describes in his diary, *"is full of scent, flowers and fruit"* and he had intended gifting much of his property to the town but wrote a complicated 85 page will (he was a solicitor) so difficult to interpret it was eventually ignored.

The Frome Funicular
- 20 passengers at a time
- 200 passengers an hour
- 10 trips an hour
- 1 minute travel time
- Water driven
- Length 60 metres or about 200ft
- Capital cost £302,000 part of a £1 million restoration project which included 2 later 3 listed buildings
- £16,900 was the annual estimated running costs

This by now (1997) the heavily tree'd Garden was neglected, although it had been a tennis lawn as late as 1886. A pocket park was suggested (very much in vogue, indeed plans were drawn up by Mendip District redesignating much its own land- odd bits of grassy areas, in the town into a scattering of pocket parks) to provide a much needed peaceful town centre retreat. Adding a funicular railway would, it was argued, regenerate the town and bring in tourism particularly the new "green" tourism. Many were sceptical even Town Councillors suggested it was a Trojan horse to get the nursing home through the Planning process commenting it would be too massive as well as in the wrong place.

Plans were drawn up and the railway with its souvenir selling kiosk designed, 15p a ride had been guessed at, and passenger numbers carefully calculated for it to break even. The journey starting by Thomas Bunn's Monmouth House taking passengers up the cliff like garden over a high stone wall into the cemetery of the United Reformed Church. Here passengers would alight to continue shopping from the top of Frome's Catherine Hill, once the main shopping street of the town. Bypassing the steep windy climb which many thought was a hindrance to trade and indeed its many shops were in need of rejuvenation and a lick of paint. A Millennium Lottery bid, which included restoring Monmouth House and the neighbouring stables and coach house, was made for this *"brilliant and visionary"* scheme but it was turned down as not distinctive enough.

Later a new bid was made this time to the Heritage Lottery Fund again to build the Railway, restore the Alcove Garden including an additional listed building, the United Reformed Church Sunday School, a circular building of great charm, at the setting down point. To create a café serving cream teas to exhausted shoppers. This too was rejected.

The selling off of the land piecemeal left the Garden in limbo; Mendip District had demanded as part of the nursing home Planning permission a park for the town via a footpath link (this took some 7 years to complete) which is now padlocked and chained. It was the eventual new owners (2003) of Monmouth House who promised the townspeople access on at least 20 days a year, (a common enough agreement but generally, as access is rarely achieved, a very poor deal for the public). In taking on the task of restoration an earlier garden was discovered dating back to the beginning of the 1700s. It is thought in celebration of the Duke of Marlborough's continental victories and so the gardens were re-named Bastion Gardens. This now small garden of sculptured banks nestles against the warm limestones of the cemetery wall, with white picket fencing, yew hedging and roses, the lawn dominated by a large stone pond. Completed in 2010 there are extensive views over Frome and the rear of the very large nursing home. Access though is rare and intermittent, but the Garden can still be peaked at, on tip toes, over the top of the cemetery wall where the landing stage for the railway would have been.

This and certainly the Rook Lane Chapel conversion are arguably the only successful examples of "gains" via the Planning system where the townspeople have had any visible benefit.

2. Land Purchases - give me land lots of land

Ownership has been important for the town's sense of itself, still stung by the losses resulting from the 1970's Government reorganisation; generations of Councillors have absorbed the sense of injustice that has trickled down with the years.

Frome, after reorganisation, was reduced to owning a few allotment sites scattered throughout the town on odd scraps of land plus its one park and playing field until riverside Rodden Meadow was added in the 1990's. Most of the town's play areas and open spaces are owned and maintained by Mendip District for which the townspeople pay a Special Expenses Rate as part of the Council Tax.

Rodden Meadow, home to the nationally rare Corky-fruited Dropwort, is a favourite with dog walkers. It had been left to its own devices for years and the views of the river and places to fish had become overgrown because Mendip District awkwardly retained ownership of the river banks (until recently). A year-long wildlife and habitat survey by the Somerset Wildlife Trust concluded, brambles should be cleared, hedges trimmed back and fences mended. A team of 10 volunteers from the "Friends of the River Frome" – a practical charity, spearheading river improvements and co-ordinating landowners has planted trees, litter picked and fundraised, providing signs and seating in the Meadow. The "Friends" were recently spotted in high visibility jackets helped by groups of local youngsters planting 1,000 wildflowers paid for by a Government Grassroots grant scheme complimenting the 60 trees planted as a memorial by the Lyn Young Trust (1998). With the neighbouring Millennium Green, (the initiative of one Labour Councillor) a hillside of trees, sculpture and paths, completed in the year 2000 - part of a national scheme of 250 Greens and part of a green river corridor running through the centre of the town.

Frome had for many years budgeted for Zion Path (a County Council responsibility) a short, narrow, dark, overgrown footpath squeezed between the United Reformed Church and a fine 18th century merchants house. The generous annual £1,000 budget went annually unspent. Amazingly until 1985 this footpath was part of the route of a proposed inner relief road dating from the 1965 Town Plan (a simple document which was later formalised into the more complex District wide Local Development Framework and later again renamed as the Local Plan). It would have cut a dramatic swathe of demolition through the historic heartland of the town, looking fine on a plan with pleasing sweeping curves which included two improbable river crossings. Today, it is perhaps baffling that the town still continued to budget improbably large sums for the Path's up-keep.

Land Bought in August 2010	
Château Gontier Walk	£1 pound
Welshmill	£7,500
Weylands	£11,000

In 1990 the Local Health Authority bought from the town and built on the Victoria Park plant nursery, an additional small Hospital. Now after the main Hospital's, closure and the Health Centre finally moving, the whole site is awaiting redevelopment. Traditionally Councils have first refusal on land sold to a public body either to have it returned or to re-purchase it. But in this instance the Council will benefit from 50% of the value from any land sale. Councillors have been advised to not take this into consideration when looking at the Planning issues of the site, currently as a possible Steiner Free school (2011).

Increasing land ownership had become a Town Council priority (during the 20007-11 electoral cycle) but it was not until the end of the electoral four years that anything had been achieved.

Then in quick succession Château Gontier Walk, a riverside path recently revamped by District was acquired and replanted yet again; followed by the Welshmill Adventure Playground. Part of the leat to one of Frome's many long demolished mills. It was a pioneering play area funded by Frome Round Table in 1971 in celebration of their 21st anniversary. At one time containing a decommissioned quarry shunting engine beloved of small boys though uselessly big to play on, it adjoined an old orchard and a pleasant woodland river path into town. A group dedicated to Frome's open spaces FROGS made a bold move to revamp the Welshmill Play area and applied for and got Big Lottery funding of around £50,000 to provide seating, a bike track, a woodland play and fitness area including commissioned sculpture. Weylands also fell into ownership, a boggy (formally part of the river bed), grassy riverside kick-about area and a surprising choice.

Mendip District Council has over the years sold off odd parcels of land hitting the headlines in 2006 as horrified residents viewed the prospect of housing on what was considered green open play space. Details are sparse and in general these sell offs were poorly advertised but modestly priced.

Car Parking Charges

Car park charges (under the Road Traffic Regulation Act (1984)) should reflect the cost of their administration not the aspirations of their Councils to raise revenue. Any fortuitous surpluses are expected to fund off-street parking and transport services aimed at preventing and relieving congestion.

Requests to Mendip (2013) for a breakdown into the cost of running Frome car parks (these were lost to Mendip in the local government reorganisation of the 1970s) revealed some startling facts:

- Annual income for all car parks £400,000,
- Most of which funds Mendip's central services
- 80% of the running costs are non-domestic rates.
- The 360 space Market Yard car park:
- used £16,000 of stationery over 3 years,
- has an annual income of £230.155,
- with annual direct costs of £41,261 including rates.

Car parking, always an issue to raise hackles, provides Mendip with much needed income with the only concession to free parking reluctantly made to Frome for a couple of weeks before Christmas and then after 3.00 o'clock in the afternoon. Free parking at the crowded edge of town stores contrasts somewhat bitterly with near empty town centre car parks. An earlier Councillor campaign to save the free car parking in the neighbourhood shopping area of Badcox with battalions of Liberal Democrat Councillors (two were part of the working party setting the charges) and their supporters looking grim faced and waving placards resulted in a limited concession from Mendip, 5 free one hour parking spaces.

A more robust strategy was sought. The 12 spaces next to Boyle Cross in the Market Place, could be transferred to town administration and set aside for disabled parking although the Wednesday and Saturday Charter Market would remain, and the space would continue to stage Festival and Christmas events. The Badcox car park (22 spaces) would be included in these negotiations.

Mendip though queried the Town's intended usage and in any case wanted a lump sum and compensation for the loss of revenue (£3,000 a space was suggested). Whether parking would be free, the gold standard, is unclear. But with this dragging of feet it had all been left too late to be completed by the May 2011 elections.

The Cheese and Grain (C&G) had plans with the parking to its side illustrated in ambitious architect's plans showed landscaping, an outdoor café and the suggested relocation of the 12th Century Charter Market stalls. This would also be in line with the Town Council's plan to absorb the C&G back into its care as, it was suggested, a conference and wedding venue.

Whilst these acquisitions raised the spectre of Double Taxation an accusation which led to the external auditor making a cursory additional inspection a few years earlier no questions appear to have been asked so perhaps the townspeople would pay twice.

3. The Bailey Bridge – a bridge too far

Spanning the river since 1986 and replacing an earlier bridge it provided a single lane second exit to the Market Yard car park and was part of a circuit beloved of boy racers who spent the evenings perfecting their handbrake turns and playing the car equivalent of "chicken." With no maintenance the wooden deck, which gave such a satisfying rattle as cars passed over it, began to rot and was closed to traffic in December 2007, pedestrians continuing to happily use it.

Bailey Bridges

Donald Bailey was knighted in 1946 for his design of a light, strong, easily assembled, versatile, low cost, modular system, steel bridge. It proved to be one of the greatest inventions of WWII becoming the standard military bridge from 1941. The standard parts meant manufacture could be spread across the country in a large number of factories. Rapid assembly "in the field" provided an "instant" bridge capable of taking heavy loads. 2,000 were used across Europe hastening the end of the war. They are still manufactured and used around the world today.

Owned by Mendip District Council the decision of what to do with it rested with the District, drawing in the East Mendip Community Partnership (EMCP), with its strong contingent of Frome Councillors but causing little discussion at Town Council even though local bridge enthusiasts lobbied strongly and tried to raise interest.

It was not the only river crossing. A footbridge 50 paces away, a new steel replacement for the Millennium (estimated at £80,000 and rising to £120,000), built to a design no one liked – many remarked it would be more suitable for a prison, but still with an interesting, but slight bounce of its early years. Townspeople wondered at the sense of spending vast sums of money duplicating it. Much hinged on Mendip's decision making Cabinet and its priorities.

Initially a replacement was earmarked but reports made in August 2008 gave this a low priority. Mendip with their bridge consultants (the designer of the new bridge) had decided repair was unworkable particularly as it exceeded the budget of £114,000 Luckily EMCP had already agreed in the previous November that a vehicular crossing, which the townspeople preferred, was unnecessary.

Jenson Button Bridge Contributions:
Frome TC say they gave £50,000
Whereas Mendip say it was in fact £68,500
Mendip District Council itself contributed £120,000
British Telecom contributed £90,000

By September 2008 demolition was now actively considered at a cost of £15,000 as the cost of replacement had risen sharply to £150,000 whilst the cost to make it adoptable by County, it was suggested, would easily top £1 million. Bridge enthusiasts wanted it repaired but EMCP were told by English Heritage that this variant of the original classic Bailey Bridge design, although interesting, was not historically significant. A snap survey by Mendip of 157 people discovered they wanted a pedestrian bridge.

As County confirmed the structure unsafe in March 2009 designs for a foot and cycleway bridge were underway at a now estimated cost of £200,000 with British Telecom, whose cables it was belatedly discovered ran beneath the bridge, contributing a hoped for substantial amount with perhaps something from Frome Town Council £10,000 was mooted although the final sum was never discussed or noted.

The local enthusiasts stressed the Bridge could and should be repaired and asked to be given the Bridge and the original earmarked £15,000 for repairs. Although Mendip is asked to look into the practicalities nothing is reported. EMCP's attitude hardened as it requests repair or replacement but is warned if Mendip's ruling Cabinet do not budget for it, the Bridge will be demolished.

Heralded as a *"clear District Council investment into Frome, a desire to give the public an opportunity to say how best to spend their money,"* and this, *"really empowers people to make decisions about their local area."* Townspeople looked at the four designs offered at the September 2009 EMCP meeting (unrecorded) although a preference for a timber walking surface by both public and Town and District Councillors was noted. The resulting gravelly tarmac surface is regularly swept and large dark puddles form with every rain. The bridge sides, it was suggested, could have removable panels which could be replaced by specially commissioned artworks at a later date *"to meet the requirements and aspirations of the users"* something of a sop to the artistic pretensions of the town.

By October a very grand cable stayed suspension bridge with an improbable spike and rust effect colouring is chosen. Some say over-engineered and a second emergency exit to the car park lost. Mendip District Council's quarterly news magazine describes it as a *"desperately needed replacement to the Bailey Bridge"* although the town's mood and furious letters to the local newspapers belied this view. It is signed off by two Frome Town/District Councillors, and undiscussed at Town Council *"an appropriate asset to the social and physical fabric of the town."* In nearby Bradford-on-Avon the same bridge design by the same designer was put to a town referendum and rejected.

Local campaigners applied to get the Bailey Bridge Listed Grade II and their local consultant says the Bridge is structurally sound but English Heritage considers it not of special architectural interest in a national context and the Listing fails (October 2009); a later appeal fails, partly because the Bridge had been demolished.

Funding Cuts

Mendip District Council in 2009 and 2010 along with most local authorities attempted to make budgetary savings, and the easiest to make were the cuts to grant funding of outside organisations. The £150,000 Mendip wide cuts deeply affected Frome arts. The Bridge, perhaps something of a luxury, was kept.

October 2010 with the budget now standing at £279,000 the Bridge is dismantled and the rotten wooden decking and corroded stringers scrapped. The remainder is given to the Wiltshire and Berkshire Canal Trust to build a farm crossing across the canal at nearby Semington, its history to be commemorated in an interpretation board.

With a plaque naming the new bridge, Jenson Button Bridge, it opens without fuss - there is no official opening. The Freedom of the Town, given in honour of his Formula One Championship win, is celebrated in great excitement with Jenson (he was born and went to school in Frome) visiting many of the towns schools, and in some style with a lunch with Councillors and to vast crowds, (the speeches sadly silent as the public address system failed) as television and press filled the Market Yard Car Park. It was to coincide with the new Bridge opening but by then the celebration was long forgotten.

Bradford-on-Avon - Wiltshire

The riverside woollen mills in Bradford-on-Avon had lain empty and increasingly derelict over some 20 years since their closure as a tyre factory. Schemes had come and gone before the final successful scheme for homes and a second river crossing - a footbridge was approved.

The town sponsored cable-stay design with a massive "rusty spike" and cable anchors, the same design as the Frome bridge, would span the 26 metre river with a diagonal 36 metre length bridge. With a small contribution (£65,000) from the developer for the foundations the town planned to raise the remainder from grants and donors –there would be no rise in Council Tax.

Bradford Bridge Concern queried the design, its impact and financing and at a public meeting got agreement to hold a Parish Poll with the question:
"The Town Council's footbridge, estimated at £850,000, should be put on hold until local people have been presented with an acceptable design that does not impose a financial burden on the town."

Long queues formed on a pleasant sunny evening with a successful 25% turnout - this would have been more if the poll had not closed before many had voted. With 1,356 in favour and 561 against, the poll cost just £3,000. The Town Council now consults with the town groups and reviews the designs. The town's Preservation Trust and Bradford Bridge Concern come up with a slim profiled, low cost beam bridge, opponents pointed to its poor wearing surface and risk of wobble when walked on. A year on into discussions and the town decides to keep with its cable-stay bridge anyway so another town meeting and another Poll is in the offing with a new question:

"If there is a new footbridge, do you prefer the Unity 3 beam bridge to the Town Council's cable-stayed bridge?"

Instead a posted paper survey is chosen asking: should a bridge be built? There is a 61% response from the town and 57 % say no. By October 2011 the idea is scrapped.

4. The Cheese & Grain (C&G)

What started as a rumour, easily dismissed by most people, soon blew up into an extraordinary confrontation between town and Councillors.

Public Loan Board

The Cheese & Grain Loan
- £215,000 in 1998-2022 at 6%
- £150,000 in 2002-2026 at 5.5%
- £200,000 in 2002-2027 at 5.125%
- £55,000 in 2003 -2027 at 4.9%

Total £620.000
Around £46,000 is repaid annually

The Cheese & Grain had been the hub of the agricultural life of the town backing on to the railway track so cattle, grain and notably cheese from the surrounding farms could be railed in, bought and sold taking advantage of the growing Victorian economy.

The 1874 Market building modest in design, used the pale local limestone with arched Venetian style windows edged in the new red brick, also brought in by rail. It overlooked rows of cattle and sheep pens and the auction ring. When not a market it was used for, theatricals and major town events, later munitions during the World War I and II and later again manufacturing of kitchen units and finally storage, most worryingly of car tyres, when it was under the ownership of Mendip District Council in the 1990s.

Cheese & Grain Statistics
- Grant £35,000 annually
- Annual footfall 110,000
- 80,000 attend markets
- 17,000 attend concerts
- 3 markets and 2 bingo sessions/week
- 50 music events a year many with an international reputation
- plus lots of community, schools, charity and family events
- the Hall adds an estimated £280,000 to the local economy
- market traders alone add £11,000 in parking fees
- the hall meets 75% of its running costs
- the hall holds 850 people standing and is the largest venue in the area.
- there is a close Partnership with Frome Festival it is its largest venue and also provides the box office
- Shortlisted as Music Venue of the year by Music Week 2011

The townspeople had long since been moved to a nearby black-boarded wooden Market Hall for auctions, jumble sales - now professionalised into 7 charity shops in town, exhibitions, parties, concerts, clubs, flea and craft markets and the highly esteemed Women's Institute markets. It was dusty, smelling of dry wood and creosote, draughty and in winter freezing.

In the late 1990's an ambitious Labour Council planned to take back the 1874 Market building.

Planning to turn it once more into a community space transferring all the wooden Market Hall's activities into an improved space with a café, bar and toilets with a hope that any profits would finance Town Council spending and provide a home for advice charities, tourist information and Council offices.

After much wrangling, Mendip District Council still hoping its own town centre backed supermarket development might take place - when the building would be demolished, eventually granted the town a lease but no land around it making usage difficult. But with a bit of borrowing the C&G opened in 1998. Spartan inside, though teams of keen Councillors helped with the refurbishment painting the concrete floor and with plain brick walls. It was as many of the comedy acts commented, playing to a new evening audience sitting muffled in overcoats on uncomfortable plastic bucket seats, an aircraft hanger of a building, where they had just pushed the aircraft to one side.

The difficulties of running a hall soon became apparent, as the old users horrified at a huge hike in rental costs coupled with an entry fee to the newly established markets launched a campaign of outrage, after some discussion, the Town Council backed down. However, the transfer of activities faltered. With endless Committee meetings making agonizingly slow decisions running costs over income mounted to over £60,000 a year. Unexpected complaints about noise, from nearby new to the area homeowners, closed it for two years from 2001. Whilst another loan was taken out for sound insulation and a new mezzanine floor (the Town Council has since considered and rejected the mezzanine twice as offices - it remains empty (2012)).

The Council decided to lease the main hall to the Cheese & Grain Trust, a charity in 2003 when it opened again, leaving the Council with the building loans and the rear "tower" which had never been developed. Taking on the Council's remaining debt (around £30,000) and with an annual grant of £35,000 the hall was affordable for the markets, local clubs, charities and groups that had used the old wooden Market Hall. The Council gave itself 6 free days a year and the Trustees forged ahead building a business as a community hall. A 30 year lease was eventually settled by May 2010 giving the Trustees the opportunity to apply for Lottery and other funding to redesign and develop areas of the building under a new 5 year business plan.

By July there was a sudden and unexpected turn round as the Council considered withdrawing all funding under secret agenda items and had started negotiations with Mendip to buy the building's freehold and the surrounding car parking. This blew up in the October when a dispute arose between the 5 Councillors of the Policy & Finance (P&F) Committee over the wording of a resolution to end funding and return the running of the building to the Council again incorporating the Town Council offices. The wording was settled the next day by a round of frantic e-mails.

Despite a last minute change of venue November's Full Council meeting was packed with townspeople facing an unexpectedly large number of Councillors who had come to be part of a group photo announcing the Council's success on becoming a Quality Council. The Public Forum rang with impassioned speeches from the floor, to be met with silent, stony faced Councillors and an early attempt to curtail the public forum met with bafflement. The Cheese & Grain was almost the last thing on the agenda as the meeting ground slowly towards the discussion.

At last a PowerPoint presentation by the Chairman of P&F outlined the C&G failings.

The lack of value, citing the national spending cuts for the necessity to save money (although Parish Councils, independent from Government are unaffected).

The Council needed to regain control, explaining the town had invested over £1 million since 1998 and therefore the present situation was unsustainable. It briefly suggested tapered funding and a lump sum to employ a consultant to research extra funding. Whilst it would withdraw funding it was up to the Trustees to decide whether to hand the lease back to the Council. A nearby example of a community hall in Dorset incorporating a theatre, concert hall, medical centre, room hire, Town Council offices and a Co-op food store which Councillors had visited was shown as what the Council thought was possible. Although barracked by the audience, the Chairman kept going concluding the building was not fit for purpose. It was too dependent, turning what had been given as an example of magnificent support for a much appreciated local organisation into an unfair burden on the taxpayers of Frome.

The sense of outrage was palpable. No one could quite believe what was said. Many left in disgust and chance conversations outside the meeting resulted in a new political grouping being born - Independents for Frome (IfF).

It was obvious the Cheese & Grain Trustees were left with little choice as it could not trade with financial uncertainty. Indeed the Council's actions had already prevented it from pursuing contracts and there was the need to protect staff jobs (20) in the long term, it was *a gun to the head."*

As the presentation wound its way to a formal resolution it was at this point, the meeting Chairman pointed out a vote could not be taken as members had not had sufficient notification or any background papers on the proposal. The Interim Town Clerk argued that the PowerPoint presentation would suffice as that was written down. After a heated exchange an extra meeting was proposed two days before Christmas, the townspeople left in uproar.

The letters pages of the newspapers, which had settled into quiet rounds of tales of lost kittens and thank-yous from charitable events, and the streets of the town were alive with opinion and questions. Why the change of heart by the Council, why no public consultation, why did the Council not seem to know what the hall did, where were the Councils ideas and business plan, why had the Council's observer on the Board of Trustees not liaised between the two, why so near to an election, what if the incoming Council had little interest in the hall, why put the Trustees into such an invidious position; wouldn't it cost more in wages - it's a small amount against the Council wage bill of £350,000, didn't the Council know the Trustees could apply for funds not available to it; why do they want to close it down; why don't they use the empty semi-derelict three storied "tower" at the back of the Hall if they want Council offices; doesn't the Council normally give two years notice when it plans to end an organisations funding; was it just empire building; how unexpected when local authorities elsewhere are looking for experienced, enthusiastic people to take on services; what was really behind it and wasn't it all a bit odd.

Membership of the Cheese & Grain soared as support piled in, with even the objecting Councillors joining.

The Council's supporters for change accused the Trustees of pandering to ageing hippies; stressing the Council was right to raise the concerns of whole town; the Hall was a sponge and would probably want another £1 million spent on it; the Council only wanted to make it even better and achieve more; and in any case the Trustees should have planned for this eventuality.

In the interim the Cheese & Grain held its Annual General meeting, the Town Council sent its PowerPoint presentation and script by way of explanation but no Councillors.

On a treacherous, icy, freezing night two days before Christmas the townspeople again faced the Town Council in a hope of influencing its presumed decision to withdraw funding. One after another the townspeople, C&G Trustees (architects plans showed the exterior of the building with a new market stalls area, an outdoor café, trees and a park) and staff, gave considered, well thought out and conciliatory reasons why the Cheese & Grain's funding should continue, or asked questions (unanswered). Councillors again sat in stony blank-faced silence staring straight ahead, unblinking (their rules of engagement it transpired did not allow for a reply). Only one Councillor broke ranks to table an amendment for a partnership approach, there was no support. The resolution to end funding stood, with no discussion, no debate.

By way of reply the lead Councillor waved her written report and explained: the Trustees' plan had lacked imagination to secure the halls financial future, the Council was being emotionally blackmailed into continuing support. The building was not fit for purpose and funding was unsustainable; it had become a private club where a minority had pursued the dream of a fantastic music venue - which it wasn't. The Councils own Quality Council award showed it had sound financial management capabilities and it had agreed sound policies.

Taking control would mean the Hall would be more community orientated, with the Council managing and promoting the building other groups would be able to use it. And couldn't the Trustees replace the grant easily, perhaps selling t-shirts and badges or charging an entrance fee to the markets - this had been tried at the hall's very beginnings with disastrous and unforgiven consequences.

However, although stung by accusations of a lack of vision the Council could still not offer a business plan or budget but would do so if the C&G agreed to hand the lease back. All it would offer was a monthly grant, saying it, *"had been subject to an unfair torrent of abuse which it would not tolerate."*

The resolution was passed without discussion by nine Councillors with one abstention. The Hall would get its grant in monthly payments for a year then no more, but its Lottery plans were scuppered. The cost and time in preparation lost, it was slow strangulation rather than instant death.

Now both parties would have fresh talks and March brought news headlines declaring a new bright future, as Councillors, Trustees and staff brainstorm for money making ideas, many echoing the Trustees plans and the Council's ambitions. An arcade built on the exterior to house a new café and bar, a new covered market, and, town rumours said, a conference and weddings venue topping the list. The next step would be a public consultation. But time had run out and the May town elections loomed.

5. Twinning

Twinning started in earnest with the idealistic post World War II spirit of reconciliation to heal the divisions of conflict and seek support for the rebuilding of Europe. The Frome Twinning Association sees itself very much in this light.

Beginning in 1975 with Château Gontier on a wave of optimism which coincided with the Labour Government's referendum which gave overwhelming support to Britain remaining in the, then named, European Community after years of wrangling and vetoing by the French (Britain was finally accepted in 1973). The then named Twinning Committee was an arm of Frome Town Council and was generously financed being the main budgetary item for decades. Murrhardt in Germany was added in 1983.

Indeed, of the 2,000 formal Twinning arrangements nationally half are with France and just under a quarter with Germany. Some Twinning has been imaginative, Swindon across the border in Wiltshire twinned with Walt Disney World in Florida and Wincanton 12 miles away to the south had previously twinned with Ankh-Morpork a fictional city in Terry Prachett's novels. Frome itself "twinned" with the BBC magazine programme "The One Show" after a townswoman won a poetry competition and was visited by helicopter by the programme's presenters.

Nationally, with the recent spending crisis Councils are reviewing their involvement arguing it has made no difference to their economy and concluded only a dozen or so people ever benefited. Twinning's supporters countered with accusations of insularity and wilful ignorance of the outside world.

Over the years, Frome clubs and societies from cycling to choirs have visited fellow enthusiasts on the continent. The volunteer Fire Brigade was first invited by Château-Gontier's Fire Brigade in 1975 and still exchange each year. Enthusiasts have suggested other towns; the "Frome is a Wonderful Place" promotional campaign and organisation, set up by the manager of the town centre George Hotel, hoped to forge an alliance with Drogheda in Ireland, Drogheda's Mayor visiting several times to have talks with the Town Council who were not keen. Earlier In the mid-1980's Frome had Twinned with a Romanian village sending clothing and textiles. Indeed even Mendip District Council Twinned with Belarus for a brief period in its first few years without communist rule, helping set up the new state's bureaucracies!

Schools over the years have organised their own student and teachers exchanges: Selwood Middle School with a village on Lake Victoria in Uganda. Currently both Middle Schools: Oakfield, and Selwood and the Frome Community College are twinned with Ghana. St Louis was involved in the European Union Cormenius scheme linking schools, sharing projects, and exchanging teachers and pupils. North Hill House has shared projects with partners in Belgium, Italy and Germany preparing youngsters for adulthood and work.

Perhaps most impressive is the The Reg Gilbert International Youth Friendship Trust (GIFT) administered by the Rotary Clubs of Frome. GIFT part funds bursaries (£500) for under 25 year olds, generally gap year students or post graduates wanting educational front-line experience. Some 300 have undertaken project work with communities (some 52 countries from Ghana to Peru) in the underdeveloped world. Set-up as a result of over-subscription in fund-raising for a Frome college student visit to Papua New Guinea in 1982 when it was hoped students would return the visit to the UK.

Perhaps the most unexpected is the European Community of Stones amphitheatre built in 1991. The 2.5 metres (about 8-9 feet) high monoliths were generously donated by the 12 European quarrying communities which were in the European Union at the time. Craned in on top of a semi-circle amphitheatre of grassy terraced banks, it is now the place of summer concerts and plays.

An accidental explosion and fire in one of the nuclear reactors in Chernobyl in the Ukraine (1986) released large quantities of radioactive particles into the atmosphere, blowing over much of Western USSR and Europe including Belarus. A Nunney based group (1992), offered a month long break with local families in Nunney, Frome and its surrounding villages to a dozen or so children and their interpreters from the village of Bolotyna Belarus. Locals taking the opportunity for a reciprocal visit. Funded by events such as concerts or auctions the charity provided new clothes, shoes and medicines making additional trips to the village with supplies. It was hoped the fresh air, food and exercise would boost the children's health against cancers and other diseases strengthening, for up to two years, immune systems weakened by the radiation.

Certainly when Frome's Twinning Committee (later Association) started, foreign travel was exotic and beyond most pockets - particularly as spending money that could be taken abroad was limited to £25 in the 1960s. In Europe the Cold War was at its height, a week's beach holiday in sunny high-rise Benidorm was still in its infancy and Interrail (begun in 1972) had just started providing cheap rail travel to the whole of Europe for 100,000s of British under 21 year olds. However, in the interim, attitudes to travel, studying and working abroad have changed by-passing Twinning's formal arrangements. Indeed the surprising number of schools forced to close because of teachers, pupils and families stranded abroad by the Icelandic Eyjafjallajökull volcanic eruption in Easter 2010 demonstrated the everydayness of foreign travel. No longer does the famous 1929 Times newspaper headline "Fog in Channel, Continent Isolated" which epitomised British insularity ring true. However, Twinning between Parishes and at least one European Union town remains a much heralded constant, funded at least in part by the local electorate.

In 1977 the Queen's Silver Jubilee was celebrated by the "Frome Review" – a one-off magazine, spotlighting Twinning, indeed the Committee's Chairman wrote an enthusiastic article about his trip to newly Twinned Château-Gontier. Directions were carefully given with a very large map. Food, readers were advised, was expensive so a selection of tinned meats and other necessities including a camping gas cooking stove was suggested. The four day trip for four cost £140.00 (around £1,000 today) and included the ferry and 2 night's hotel accommodation. Twinning's heyday was the early 1980's when the town's musicians, choirs and occasional school sports teams travelled on exchanges.

Resentment at Twinning has rumbled on for years no one quite understanding why the Parish should subsidise a social club seen as elitist and a "bit of jolly" for Councillors. The Twinning Association countered that membership is open to the whole town and with it the opportunity to make a new friend and it is the townspeople who are at fault for not taking advantage of what is on offer. The Associations members (around 25) themselves have formed strong friendships staying with the same families over the ensuing years. The benefit to the wider community is negligible.

A swathe of past Mayors (2011) stung by recent criticisms wrote to the local paper, again emphasising the endless possible economic and creative opportunities Twinning could provide for the town's businesses particularly its creative sector and for its schools. Certainly the European Union offers a selection of funding streams. Frome's Twinned towns have undoubtedly been very successful in obtaining annual European grant funding to underwrite the cost of their visits.

To mark these affiliations portions of the town has been renamed as a tribute and a mark of friendship to the Twinned town. Ribbons have been cut at: Château-Gontier Walk - a footpath beside the river after its £4,600 revamp by Mendip District Council later sold to the town for a £1; Murrhardt Gardens – a strip of grass and trees opposite North Hill House - the towns old Council offices; and a very modest raised bed of rock and gravel – the Rabka Zdroj Rock Garden in a discreet corner of Victoria Park.

Each year is marked with a Civic long weekend in July which each of the four towns take turns in hosting, although there are occasional visits and business meetings in between for Councillors and the Town Clerk. The Mayor of each town with their entourages, the Twinning Association and invited guests enjoy a 3 day itinerary of eating and entertainment.

Usually gifts are presented to the Mayors of each town to further commemorate the visits, to date Frome has given and received approximately 70 items sadly unrecorded which are tucked away somewhere unseen, and not as could be expected proudly displayed as symbols of Twinning's importance and its proud links. The Town Council office has only a few odds and ends: heavy plaques of the coat of arms of both the French and German towns, very large pieces of pottery, an assortment of guide books, two impressively huge fossilised tree cross sections from Germany, and an eclectic choice from Poland, such as a child might give a difficult to please maiden aunt: two large copper roses, a giant green crayon, slippers, a traditional hat – small size, and a wooden weather house. Frome in turn has, over the years, given books and pictures of itself, local pottery and glassware as well as welcome packs of pens, badges and guidebooks.

2011 was Frome's first opportunity to host the quadripartite with 118 guests expected including a Polish folk dancing troupe. Too many for the 68 volunteer hosts whose numbers have dwindled over the years so much so accommodation was sought in nearby Bath. The folk dancers visited several local schools and there were also church services and local sight-seeing for the guests. A roped off area of the Park housed a huge marquee for the Civic Reception of local food for Councillors and the Twinning party from where much laughter and music could be heard. The townspeople uninvited could only look on. The Citizens for Europe fund provided around 15,800 euros (about £13,300) a third going to the twin towns to subsidise their travel, supplemented by roughly a further £8,000.

Parish funding has become the norm, (more recently essential when applying for European funding) varied over the years but settling around £3,000 sometimes including Councillors and other of the town's representative's expenses, supplementing the very reasonable membership rate of £5.00.

The Mayor and Deputy Mayor have had honorary membership in order to participate in the formal side of Twinning such as signing the Charters of Friendship and so have had their expenses paid (hospitality supplied should be declared as part of the Declaration of Interests but no-one bothers). The Mayor after the amalgamation between Council and the Association became President of the Association.

Twinning Objectives

The town's own Twinning objectives now echoed the European ideal. The advantages of international partnership were defined as learning, cooperation and understanding becoming part of the town's 4 new corporate aims:

- Promoting Twinning, trade and learning the way other nations work;
- Bringing in Twinning tourists;
- Encouraging peace and friendship between diverse cultures fostering openness and fairness;
- Appreciating Twinned cultures to improve the quality of the townspeople's lives.

A lot to achieve over a long weekend.

Change had come in 2005 when Murrhardt and Château Gontier decided to extend Twinning to Eastern Europe initially choosing 6 towns in Poland with Councillors and the Association visiting the final two contenders Zabkowice Slaskie and Rabka-Zdroj. Rabka was chosen in May 2008 and the alliance sealed with a first visit in 2009. Originally the Association wanted the Polish link to be a partnership with its lower level of commitment however; Frome's Councillors were more ambitious.

This would be a major new initiative to promote international economic partnership through Twinning. Councillors enthusiastically explained the opportunities for businesses winning economic development, and regeneration benefits and a strong impact on tourism in the town. With high hopes of tapping into European funding the Council acknowledged this new phase would demand more open involvement with the town with specific European objectives in mind rather than the purely social element.

The previously casual arrangements were changed to a formal agreement (2009) with the Association maintaining its social links and the Town supplying administration and a website. A chimaera in which the Council gained control but the Association was still a separate organisation. Against the increasingly common practice of creating Charitable Trusts or Community Interest Companies which separates good intentions from the vagaries of politics, by providing clear distinctions, with a measure of independence and transparent oversight.

Meanwhile the new Twin town Rabka successfully gained funding (9,000 euros around £8,000 in 2008) for themed networking entitled "Four Countries – One Europe" which suggested schools, local artists and language students would like to take part in exchanges. Two Youth Ambassadors went from Frome.

By 2011 little had been achieved, the town's new Independents coalition Council noted the town had had no benefit from what was *"a significant expense."* Indeed the most the town sees are photographs of congratulatory handshakes of the various Mayors. It is difficult to see what realistic objectives such a split organisation could achieve especially with no real mechanism to propose, assess or monitor.

The Mayor at joint meetings is hindered by an inability to make decisions without reference to the whole Council - European Mayors can make policy and funding decisions as needed.

Murrhardt however, was applying for European funding, themed "Thinking European – Acting Local" to finance a five day festival in July 2013. The initial cost to the town would be £8,000 with a European grant applied for of 150,000 euros (around £120,000) dependent on all four towns taking part. Frome not wanting to let the others down and as always having little time for a considered decision or discover what the tangible benefits were, indeed the Council was worried about the cost, staff time and resources but the decision had to be made immediately. A rough cultural itinerary had been mapped out with a focus, as always, on children and particularly teachers with an added heavy emphasis on folk dancing. Unexpectedly Frome demurred.

Frome's Twin Towns:

Château Gontier (Population c11,000)
150 miles south of Cherbourg. In the valley of the navigable River Mayenne. With historic buildings many half-timbered. Notably Les Ursulines Convent is now a cultural centre. The town famed for its floral displays is a good holiday centre. It is an important farming centre holding the largest veal market in Europe weekly. There are arts festivals, a festival to the patron saint of firemen, pony trotting races as well as the usual team games including water sports.

Murrhardt (Population c14,000)
On the thickly wooded slopes of the river Mur near Stuttgart on the remains of a Roman fort - The Limes an UNESCO site. Nearby Waldsee Lake is a centre for boating, walking, camping and in winter cross country skiing. A town of timbered buildings many with unique gilded signboards. There are festivals in the arts, a carnival and a Christmas market.

Rabka-Zdroj (Population c13,000)
On a confluence of a river near Krakow, its Patron Saint is St Nicholas. Originally famous for its salt works this mountain Spa town is Poland's main spa centre for children, In summer it hosts folk events, with camping and hiking and in winter skiing, ice skating, tobogganing and sleigh rides.

Europe for Citizens Funding
The European Union, now consisting of 27 countries, set up a Europe for Citizens funding programme. The general objectives have a strong European flavour and aimed to bring Europe closer to all its citizens and involve as many as possible in the construction of an integrated Europe:
by providing opportunities to take part in and work together to form a closer Europe and develop a sense of citizenship of the European Union;
- to develop a European identity based on common European values;
- to develop a sense of ownership of the European Union amongst its citizens;
- to create understanding and tolerance between European citizens whilst keeping and encouraging cultural diversity.

Grants have been available since 1989, with 215 Euro millions set aside for projects between 2007 – 2013 under four specific funding areas or Actions.

It is Action 1, Active Citizens for Europe which is designed specifically to develop town – twinning with an emphasis on involving large numbers of people from all backgrounds, rather than just nominated representatives. There were specific European orientated criteria, and the programmes of activities must clearly state the community involvement at all stages and have the benefits detailed. Projects were expected to have a measurably high quality, relevance, and impact, with expected achievements and follow– up coupled with wide publicity and transparency of undertaking.

Measure One covered:
1.1. Town twinning meetings, (grants from 2,500 to 22,000 Euros) for one meeting a year with at least 25 invited representatives from two countries. Aiming to: reinforce European integration, develop a sense of belonging by learning about European culture, history, and common values with discussion of views, issues and experiences set against a European background. Active participation from a large part of the local community in the planning and subsequent activities was expected;
1.2. Inter-town networking under a set theme, issue or subject, (funding from 10,000 to 150,000 Euros). For 3 events planned within 24 months with at least 30 invited representatives from 4 countries. To create cooperation on European issues and policies of common interest with a defined target group. The projects were expected to be the basis for future initiatives.

Grants were calculated using a flat-rate/ day /person (if the United Kingdom is organising: in Measure 1.1. 21.98 Euros, in Measure 1.2. 53.82 Euros (Jan 2009)), and contributes towards the organisational costs of the host town (accommodation, meals, local transport, meeting rooms, etc.), and the travel expenses of the invited delegations. Costs did not have to be accounted for or justified.

Measure Two covered:
2.1 For ambitious projects on single issues which crossed national boundaries involving 5 countries, with at least 200 ordinary people consulted. This bottom-up approach ran over a 12 month period. The "citizen's panel" made recommendations feeding into the policy process at a European level. There were grants available for up to 60% of costs for projects costing between 100,000 to 250,000 Euros;
2.2 Supported measures to improve the quality of projects under 2.1 such as training or events which developed, promoted, revitalised town twinning, sharing experience and best practice. Support was funded up to 80% of costs from 30,000 to 100,000 Euros.

An alternative version of Twinning - using the British Council's Active Citizens funded scheme ran for a year (2011). Co-sponsored and co-hosted by Vision4Frome with the community volunteer training and development charity VISTA. A travel exchange between Latvian and Serbian volunteers, the 4 representatives from Frome voluntary groups looking at issues in common. 6 Frome groups received a modest sum of £100 each to further their projects. There are 21 Active Citizens groups in the UK.

6. Shopping, Shops and Supermarkets
There are 90,000 supermarkets and convenience stores in the country (2012)

Frome like many towns has had its run in with supermarkets which has left it feeling slightly mangled by the encounter.

As far back as anyone can remember Frome like everyone in the country shopped in the myriad of small shops immortalised in sepia toned photographs with their proud shopkeepers posing stiffly outside.

That was the problem, with more stuff to buy, bigger; squarer, less curiously shaped shops were needed. In the 1960's an ambitious modernising Urban District Council planned an inner relief road and a reshaping of the town centre Market Place, by demolishing most of it and building arcades of shops at right angles to the present-day main road.

Instead by the mid 1970's two new modern precincts had sprung up indifferent to their surroundings. The Westway, which ignored it's pretty river bank location creating an enclosed canyon, winning a Royal Institute of Architects prize (1979) and decades later given a "Georgian makeover" and The Kingsway, a short parade of shops which marooned two clothiers' mansions in a sea of tarmac and paving. There was no attempt to reflect local architecture and even after this length of time both sit awkwardly within the town. However, four new supermarkets did open and rumours abounded that the ultimate prize Marks and Spencer wanted to come to Frome (that would show nearby Trowbridge) but was prevented by a Frome style "mafia." True or not it has become part of the folklore of the town and is still given as the reason for the town's slide into a slumbering retail decline as *"it would have been the making of Frome."*

The mid 1970's also brought a change in national shopping habits: part-time jobs for women burgeoned, particularly in local councils, credit and mortgage rules eased. With more money came more cars and with a bigger choice of goods to buy, customers ventured further afield to shop. In Frome, the library moved from the main but hilly shopping street of Catherine Hill to the Westway precinct and the retirement of a generation of shopkeepers meant empty, awkwardly small shops particularly on steep Catherine Hill.

By the late 1980's an opportunist Mendip District Council sought again to solve all problems by encouraging the building of a supermarket on the town's main and only sizable car park cum cattle market, the Market Yard - which it had inherited from the Frome Urban District Council. An early attempt in 1985 to demolish and build on the Cheese & Grain site met with fierce opposition. Coaches were hired and packed with Frome protestors who descended on Mendip's Planning Board (although supplicants were only allowed to speak in 1995) and the idea was shelved. However, Mendip eventually forced out the cattle and produce auction markets (the lease had also ended) by March 1991 to nearby Standerwick taking many of the town's market stalls with it. This is still seen by many as the pivotal point which sealed the town's fate and ended a "golden age."

It is here on Wednesdays against the background of the auctioneers' hammers, the lowing of cattle and the metal clang of gates; cows and sheep are bought and sold, furniture and bric-a-brac auctioned, vegetables, flowers and eggs from local gardens bid for. The market stalls have grown in number selling country things such as wellies and waxed jackets as well as food and hardware as farmers and their families cogitate about the price of livestock and the latest government legislation. A day out can be rounded off by a substantial roast dinner and a pint of local ale, and it is the last place an "old" Frome can still be found.

In the Market Yard several developers (4 plus the newly formed Frome Town Trust (FTT) - put forward schemes. FTT was quickly dropped by Mendip. Then responding to accusations of hastiness backtracked, reconsidered, before dropping it again).

The varying schemes moved the car parking to another emptying town centre industrial site and included a terraced Mediterranean style river bank to be funded by a supermarket anchor store. The proposed loss of 10 car parking spaces was hotly debated.

Frome - a Study

The Study (1987) ambitiously funded by the Town Council essentially critiques the draft Local Plan (which set out targets for the local economy, housing and leisure facilities) but aimed to reflect local views and put forward concrete suggestions focusing on the town centre. Both the Plan and the Study highlight issues which remain current today indeed there must be a library of consultations, surveys, plans and studies added to over the years commissioned by either the Town or Mendip.

As is the way of these things a group, the Future For Frome (FFF), formed in response to the Local Plan and the Town Council started a Frome Town Plan Advisory Committee. The FFF mutated into the Civic Society becoming the Independent Liaison Committee who in turn left the recording and circulating of information to the Advisory Committee!

A constant through time has been the fear of an over dominate supermarket, this time in the Market Yard, together with the fears of Frome becoming merely a dormitory town. Not helped by Mendip which will, over the decade which is to follow, allow the sell-off of most of the town's employment land for housing, taking investment and jobs from the town, whilst its own analysis continues to deplore the majority of townspeople working outside the town. Retail "leakage" (people shopping in other towns) is also generally condemned but how to solve it is as always unclear.

The Study made bold suggestions:
- The present employment sites should be nurtured, with the Cattle Market moved to the town edge rather than miles away;
- A Town Scheme to conserve and repair the older buildings removing the overall air of neglect, faded paint work, trailing wires and street clutter is strongly endorsed. Over the next decade with government funding and money from County, Mendip and the Town variously named schemes provide building owners with 50% of funding with grants to do just that.
- The new bypass (to be built the following year) was confidently expected to ease Market Place traffic congestion; re-routing the dozens of quarry lorries daily away from the town centre also helped by the Cattle Market's move.
- Innovative multi-storey car parks at Rook Lane and in the Market Yard – accessed by a bridge over the railway, and
- A meadow on the Saxonvale side of the river to create a new town centre park to energise the town.

The main focus is to be the Market Yard with shops, music, fountains, trees, riverside walks, bars, and restaurants with a Town Trust to oversee the development with any profits ploughed back into the town.

Frome Town Trust

Set up in 1987 with an intended initial two year life span to implement a report the Town Council itself had commissioned. Composed of 3 Town, 2 Mendip District, and 1 County Councillor with 5 townspeople from a business background. Looking at development in the Market Yard, Garsdale and the Kingsway Precinct. The Trust planned to employ a town centre manager to gather financial support and negotiate with Mendip and County. It ceased in 1992.

The Frome Town Trust (FTT) formed to take these ideas forward rapidly gaining a 500 strong membership and raising £27,000 in donations. Innovative it set up a parallel Development Company and waded into the supermarket debate producing an architect's sketch layout for the Market Yard, what was by now a £14.6 million project.

There were 11 starters and 4 in the final line up for the public exhibition for town comments, FTT whilst not exhibiting still considered itself in the running.

But there were problems Mendip did not own the Market Hall (today's Cheese and Grain) and there was unexpected hostility from the Hall owner towards FTT. The narrow street into the Market Yard is awkward and the proposed road bridge across the railway had not been thought through. There were fears British Rail will apply Cambridge Rules (they could ask for 1/3rd of the whole site value) leaving it was felt little for the Market Hall owner. Now with an economic downturn the figures do not stack up. FTT's 2 financial backers withdraw but the Trust, although abandoning its own plans, is pleased to get an advisory role with Mendip over the development and looking at the two final schemes chosen criticises them on design, materials and overbearing unsympathetic car parking. Interest drains away and nothing happens.

For Frome, supermarkets were very much like busses not one but 5 more alternative schemes across the town were tabled, including the town centre industrial Saxonvale although initially successful, could not get a Section106 agreement settled, and so failed, the nearby commercial Garsdale area was also refused – it is now housing (2012).

Meanwhile the focus had moved to the edge of town. The Marston Trading Estate first built in the 1970's for the new industries and start-ups which would grow to stand alongside Frome's then still flourishing traditional industries became the ideal spot for a new idea - an edge of town superstore. Sainsbury's got there first. The national fight for market share between the major supermarkets had created intense competition and on the opposite side of town, at Wallbridge, a green field site bordered by a stream and the River Frome was suggested for another edge of town superstore this time Safeway and to complete the hat trick a supermarket was proposed on the Frome Showfield. The obvious argument was that trade would be drawn from the town centre although embarrassingly Mendip's own Planning framework demonstrated the Showfield to be an ideal contender.

However, Mendip protecting its own scheme in the Market Yard, deftly refused all three and all three appealed, Sainsbury and Safeway were allowed but the Showfield was dismissed. Mendip's own plans melted away as a new national financial crisis hit and funding dried up. Sainsbury built quickly and opened in 1993 providing a very modest Section106 agreement of £24,000 to enhance the town centre in compensation with assurances that this was a one off.

Other national retailers soon followed it creating a town edge trading centre with cafés, restaurants around a conference centre.

In 2005 Sainsbury asked for a 40% increase in size, building a giant white cube, in order to remain viable, it said, adding a café, pharmacy and clothing. This would be a one off. Another Section106 agreement was offered this time £40,000 and the deal was done.

The opposition to the riverside supermarket had grown spearheaded by Frome's District Councillors. Safeway had hit a snag; Mendip would not accept its flood prevention scheme (estimated at £2 million) because it had not included the nearby main road. The site amongst low lying traditionally flooding fields was a problem compounded by the mediaeval packhorse bridge throttling the flow. Although predictions gave an annual 1 in 5 chance of a flood, a succession of harsh winters ensured extensive floods and dramatic pictures of stranded vehicles. Councillors were determined to try and stop the build. With Safeway's agents in receivership it was the administrators who took Mendip back to court, but with a poorly argued case Mendip lost and eventually the flood prevention scheme was approved. The administrators laid the base for the petrol station to keep the Planning permission alive, stopped work and Safeway faded away.

A new supermarket hoved into view, rumours were rife settling on, new to the area Asda, the town was increasingly horrified when it was rumoured Asda had been bought by American Wal-Mart whose reputation for low pay, a poor environmental record and the damaging effect on small towns became known. "The Heart of Frome" group formed to counter any development of this riverside site over the town centre, Garsdale was suggested as Asda revised the previous plans. "The Heart of Frome" raised a petition delivering it to the Prime Minister (Tony Blair) at 10 Downing Street asking for support for the town centre site. The Somerset Standard ran a "Shop Local Shop Frome" campaign giving away free plastic shopping bags – before newer campaigns grew up to ban their usage.

Mendip said the permission had lapsed and local Councillors determined this time to win went back to the courts who ruled that starting to build the petrol station was enough and the Appeal in the High Court was lost. Mendip's legal costs including employing a top barrister ((Christopher Katowski) had rocketed to around £250,000 severely stretching its finances to breaking point. Asda opened in 2005 some 17 years after a supermarket was first promoted by the landowners.

There was a growing realisation in the town that any objections made in future would never again be taken too seriously by Mendip, and a culture of wariness, in both Councillors and Mendip crept into all dealings with controversial applications. The Inspectors and the High Court appeal decision become part of local Planning folklore tempering every Planning decision and every Planning objection since. Seen as a lesson for the unwary, a cautionary tale for new Councillors and cynicism in local people when, *"local decisions are snatched from local people."*

Frome's traditional industries which had reliably provided employment were coming to an end either bought out by foreign companies or just those from another part of the country. After the usual reassurances, the often renamed new companies continued for a short time, gradually reducing staff followed by sudden closure. Most of this industrial land became housing partly in response to the 1997 Government's drive to build on Brownfield sites and Mendip District not wanting to preserve the underpinning industrial and commercial base to the town's economy.

Resulting in the now, much criticised situation, of 50% of the town's workforce working outside the town.

Saxonvale, an industrial area in the town centre, whose staff in past times poured out of the factories as the lunch time whistle sounded to do a quick bit of shopping, was by 2005 largely closed, leaving just the steady heavy clunk of Notts Industries' metal presses echoing across the town (punching out specialist parts for the car industry) and the abattoir (which enterprisingly sold sausages and packs of meat for a time). With, a large chunk of the factories empty and the remaining, of what had been working factories, bought by the government development agency SWRDA (South West Regional Development Agency) - which promised great things (until it to was abolished) but left them abandoned, effectively sterilising the whole site. The opportunity for new industries to root and develop naturally into future new employers was lost. Only wholesale redevelopment was now on the cards.

The Saxonvale Planning Brief (2005) was consulted on, researched, and funded by Regional Development Agency. It was hailed as pioneering and an example of best practice. The result was a map of the site and an accompanying description, *"a mixed use, high density scheme including housing, retail accommodation, employment and open spaces."* Much, as always, was made of the design to be in keeping with local traditions: the height of buildings, street patterns and traditional materials - which in Frome's case was rapidly becoming render, followed by brick. There would be larger shops, offices, restaurants, a hotel and art galleries with workshops in an "Artisans Quartier", similar in many ways to what the town already offered, with new leafy urban squares with perhaps a community building – new Town Council offices? And a long forgotten stream cum ditch turned into a tree lined boulevard with the conversion of one of the town's remaining empty mills (it later burnt down in 2010) into a new home for the nearby adult training centre (FETE). A town centre supermarket was not thought necessary with the building of a new edge of town Asda.

Expectations were raised amongst the townspeople which have been grimly held on to and amongst the landowners who have been hoping the high land values first suggested would be achieved as the Brief has, over time, become increasingly difficult to fulfil.

Oddly enough Marks and Spencer unexpectedly arrived to replace the defunct town centre Safeway and latterly one of the town's two Somerfield stores – poor margins were later sited for both eventual Somerfield closures; the town held it's breathe for the briefest second, but the magic had gone.

A Planning application was launched by one of the Saxonvale landowners who held an agreement to negotiate with only one of the other land holdings. Unusually, all five of the site owners had not come to a formal agreement which would help them share the value of the redeveloped site based on the land area they owned. There were a couple of crowded public consultations hosted by the East Mendip Partnership (EMP) and a poorly attended one by the Town Council whom Mendip had forgotten to consult.

The Council were in broad agreement with the Civic Society analysis in any case (there was something of a working party with a Frome Councillor on it but it never reported to the town, and EMP grumbled it had not been included in the discussions).

The public meetings threw up well thought out comments and eventually a scaled model of the site (costing £7,000) highlighted that *"a seamlessly extension to the town's centre,"* had not been created. No windy mediaeval streets or terraced 18th century industrial housing but an odd mix of extremely high buildings, crammed housing over underground car parking, and awkward roads. By 2011 permission was granted, but only if the details of the sesssion106 could be thrashed out (it remains today undecided), and the agreement to negotiate with the single landowner also ran out. Now there was a new developer on the block.

Who said it would be Tesco nobody knows, but a 40,000 square foot supermarket became a given as the new developer faced a hostile public audience at the start of another long haul to put together a new Planning application. A supermarket was needed now to provide the anchor and pay up front for some of the road improvements which would be needed in the surrounding area. But at this size it would expect to sell: gifts and toys, CD's, homeware, electronics, etc competing with the other two edge of town supermarkets and threatening an estimated 30 independent shops in the town.

3 packed public meetings listened to the importance of beginning a campaign and rallying support beforehand: using social media: twitter, blogs and Facebook. There was added support from Frome TV's internet posts and a local TV celebrity. The organisers, Keep Frome Local/Saxonvale Concern paced out the 40,000 square foot of the proposed store in the local park to give an idea of its size. Produced a manifesto outlining the issues for Frome and other small towns when faced with the behemoth of the supermarkets and was regularly referenced in a national broadsheet newspaper courtesy of a local journalist.

Everyone was reminded of Shepton Mallet – Frome's sister town, whose High Street struggled and steadily emptied as it fell foul to a new Tesco sitting on the towns previously main industrial employment site at the top of the town. Even now this supermarket has re-jigged its site to increase its sales area and added a café leaving little if anything the town's traditional High Street offers that it does not duplicate.

The supermarket opposition was not universal, seen by some as incomer values, *"few Somerset accents heard"* in what had become increasingly seen as an anti-supermarket debate, foisted onto the rest of the town. Councillors suggesting, *"the less vocal indigenous population has waited for more than 20 years for more shops."*

Frome, ever a socially minded and politically active town regularly took to the streets. Saturdays had long been the day not only to bump into acquaintances and friends but for the setting up of stalls raising awareness, garnering support, signing petitions, selling raffle tickets for local and national causes, or mustering strategically placed supporters with their collecting tins. This of late had more or less come to a stop as a generation of activists faded away and shopping habits changed.

A 1991 Mendip shopping survey had shown 77% of groceries bought in Frome and since then the town's supermarket floor space had grown 10 fold to 185,000 sq feet (2010). Probably making it one of the highest sales floor space per person in the country (an estimated 3.5 square foot of sales area/person net floor space). This does not count the 7 neighbourhood shopping centres each with its convenience store, a hairdresser and very often a take-away.

Supermarket supporters suggested choice was important and needed; the town has 6 major supermarkets and floor space had increased by two thirds in the last 15 years, detractors argued small shops would benefit and the local economy energised. Town centre supermarkets have not necessarily fared well in the past, as Safeway and the two Somerfields closures showed - put down to poor, marginal trading, one Councillor commenting *"those people (shoppers) were lost to the town centre."* However, others still think it is worth the adventure as Iceland occupies the old Woolworth store, the local Radstock Co-operative Society has taken a Westway precinct unit (2011), a new Co-op has been suggested for Badcox, and a new home store has opened by the railway station – a supermarket by another name which went unremarked and unchallenged. Later in a bold pre-emptive move, whilst the Saxonvale wrangling continues, Asda plan (2012) a 40% increase in floor space (it overtrades by 30% in Frome, making it one of the most successful stores in the country).

A new group formed "Frome For All" (FFA), rapidly gaining 300 members which welcomed a central supermarket, echoing the "Heart of Frome," campaign a decade or so earlier, reasoning it would attract new High Street brand stores and provide jobs. Shoppers would be drawn into the town and not tempted to the edge of town stores or neighbouring towns such as Trowbridge - which had gained and then lost its Marks and Spencer store in the interim. Car journeys, in a now carbon conscience world, FFA suggested would decrease, although there was a counter suggestion that a new Tesco would attract Tesco tourism shoppers despite the fact there are 4 within a 16Km/10 mile radius. The group were challenged on the increase in traffic into an already difficult to access site with the consequent rise in air pollution; the town centre in its river bottom already has high levels of nitrous oxide from car exhausts.

Clone or Ghost Town
- Clone Towns: High Street dominated by chain stores and supermarkets. Every town takes on the same bland look and offers identical products. The diverse and independent shops close. Shopping and towns become less sociable, less employment, money not kept in local circulation i.e. small local businesses buying from and employing each other.
- Ghost Towns: High Street abandoned. Boarded up shops, vandalism and graffiti.

Pedestrianisation would save the town centre. It had been mooted in the late 1990s and County had come forward with a brave plan to rid the town centre of traffic allowing just buses into the Market Place and oddly car transporters because the bridges on the new bypass were too low and they could not fit underneath. Questions were asked: could the market stalls still set up, what about emergency vehicle routes - they had always raced through the town centre, what about the taxis, disabled parking, or shop deliveries – most do not have any rear delivery access, what, the townspeople said, if we just want to use the bank cash points, and anyway, it would not work in Frome.

Disagreement chipped away at County's plans. After much wrangling the plans and the budget were watered down. The now £150,000 was mostly spent on re-paving the now widened pavements in the same material they had been previously paved in; the camber of the road was forgotten so a large ever-deepening puddle steadily grew on one side of the Market Place with every rain.

The opportunity to re-route the traffic was avoided, and lost forever as County sells off a key piece of land and Mendip approves housing, on a industrial site, over the only other possible exit route. The bus stops were fought over, so today two buses, going in opposite directions, but arriving together, can halt traffic in both directions for hundreds of yards. Pedestrians still adroitly dap between passing cars in a Frome version of "shared space." It was a solution that pleased no-one.

But, the town does take the opportunity to try the 1997 Labour Government's enthusiasm for cosmopolitan European shopping sophistication. In deep shade, on dusty windswept corners and steep precipitous pavement edges, small tables appear, sometimes unexpectedly balanced on a brick against the slope of the hill. Here (the incomers?) townspeople enjoy Frome's continental urban café culture, well wrapped-up in heavy coats sitting in exposed self–conscience nonchalance, clutching warming cups of coffee or casually flicking open newspapers (The Observer or The Guardian). No cheerily striped umbrellas or banks of raised planters of brightly coloured geraniums to rendezvous, relax behind or secretly people watch.

The last few years have brought a wave of a new type of metropolitan coloniser (joining a clutch of media and music celebrities living locally) and with them the introduction of new words such as artisanal - tricky to say with a Somerset accent, new concepts - designer-maker and upcycling and new ideas - mis-matched china and cup-cakes in the newer cafés and on innovative market stalls. Subtly changing the culture giving the town a shiny Sunday supplement feel underlined with the sale of white truffle oil in the now renamed Badox "village" just beyond the newly named and branded "old quartier" of "St Catherine's" (2012). The colonisers settle in the larger houses especially in the nearby smaller villages, modernising, adding electric gates and CCTV. But still restless they push on after a couple of years, ever westwards, to a new rural idyll.

Frome's previous cosmopolitan past ended in 1992 with the final trip of last French onion seller seen in Frome, Monsieur Jean Claude Le Breton, in a traditional French beret and stripy jumper. He travelled over every year in May with 70 strings of onions to sell at £5 a string. Carrying on his father's tradition of using a British bike as he said French bikes collapsed under the weight.

Fears for Frome shops have swung between two scenarios, a Clone town or a Ghost town as shops have struggled, the specialist independents opening and closing a little too frequently on Catherine Hill in particular. The Hill has only of late attracted a critical mass of small specialist shops: boutiques, interior designers, jewellers, potters, bric-a-brac, retro, vintage, cafés, flowers, gifts and an unexpectedly practical hardware shop, after years of a marginal existence. A generation of shopkeepers (grocers, bakers, photographers, butchers, clothing, stationers and green-grocers), who had shared the habits, beliefs, schooling, pass-times and daily life with their customers had retired. It is this perhaps sentimental view of a shopping "golden age" that the supermarket protesters hope to save. A large number of the town's shops are part of large national retail chains most, including the small independents, have adopted the self-service model and minimum contact with customers.

There has also been a shift, amongst the smaller shops in the town, towards an artisanal flavour encouraged by the summer Sunday stall market on the Hill, (following on from the now defunct September Catherine Hill Mediaeval Fayre).

Exciting and buzzing, it felt "right" and what a market town should be. Stallholders lining both sides of narrow Catherine Hill. Until recently the only shops to open in the town centre were estate agents, charities and weirdly, greeting card shops – perhaps their sudden decline and a switch to hairdressers and cafés shows Frome is *"up and coming."*

In the interim and in the countryside, the rise of the local farmshop with their promise of integrity and local provenance in food, brilliant cafés, pleasing gift shops and bijou garden centres have a rusticated authenticity that attract enviable crowds, beginning a new concept in shopping that the tired High Street lacks.

Meanwhile with Terramond's permission (August 2010) subject to a Section106 agreement on highways, open space and a footbridge across the river (this would need the agreement of the other Saxonvale landowners) and the supposed "Tesco application" now quiet. By the end of 2011 stalemate had been safely reached, a Frome tradition, which seems likely to prevail.

The Government belatedly concerned at the loss of shops in the High Street acts (Deloittes report (2011) says 40% will be closed in 5 years as online shopping grows). Appointing a retail television guru whose successful television series focussed on the plight of High Street shops and their poor management skills, to research, report and recommend. Action was immediate £1.2 million (2011) was put up to fund 12 Portas Pilot rejuvenation schemes to trial the report's ideas. 371 Town Teams put together videos as part of their bid. Frome was not one of the successful towns. It would go it alone.

Datafile
GIFT Trust, www.giftfriendshiptrust.com
Active citizens, www.activecitizens.britishcouncil.org
The Saxonvale Manifesto, www.saxonvalesupermarket.blogspot.com
European Funding, www.welcomeeurope.com or www.ec.europa.eu
Frome For All, www.facebook.com/frome4all

The epilogue

By the end of the electoral cycle 2007-2011 and through into 2012 and 2013 the Parish landscape had dramatically changed. The Parishes are now encouraged indeed challenged to be bolder and spending is now unlimited on projects or ideas, on whatever is wanted. The test nominally, to bring benefit to at least a section of the Parish community (The Power of Competence). Many see this "localism" as a call to arms.

Overall, whilst there are rules there is no enforcement, no ombudsman for the public to complain to, the external auditor merely reprimands in a perhaps terse exchange of letters, the District or Unitary authority's monitoring officers only have the power to advise and not compel and in any case there are no punitive sanctions – the ability to surcharge, that is, reclaim money misspent from Councillors or authority employees was abolished in 2000, some Councillors had in the past been bankrupted. Transparency and with it its bedfellow accountability with the detailed disclosure regimes now demanded are largely ignored, public consultation is as ever piecemeal and seemingly difficult to achieve or the result of asking groups who have a vested interest in, and thankfully know the correct answer.

The Coalition Government has thrown down a challenge to stem a tide of complaints of unfairness, lack of money and lack of understanding, *"we know what our Parish needs."* The Parishes are, as they always had been, on their own but this time armed with the new spiritual force of "localism" and this time, if they co-operate with their sister authorities and armed with a selection of new and newish funding regimes, they could be audacious.

ROOK LANE CHAPEL BATH STREET FROME

26 – TOWN WALK

The sights in a morning

Start with a late breakfast in one of the cafés and pubs in and around the Market Place in the town centre. At the Boyle Cross (1) and with the George Hotel (2) to your left take a moment to wander up Cheap Street (3) a narrow path with independent shops and a charming central stream fed from a fountain which still pours from under the churchyard of St John's Church (4). Double back to the Cross and head north towards the river passing the 18th century almshouse, The Blue House (5) on its island, taking a moment to look at its intriguing sculptures. The bridge crossing the river Frome has, unusually, shops along one side. Head to the Museum (6) an extraordinary triangular building taking time to pop in and look at its exhibitions on local history (March to November).

At the top of the hill to your left are Murrhardt Gardens (7), a narrow strip of grass and trees whilst to the right is North Hill House (8) a fine Georgian Mansion and the final home of Frome Urban District Council. Take a moment to cross the road through the public car park to the Millennium Green (9) to sit and admire the views across the river valley with Rodden Meadow (10) below. Retrace your steps, recross the main road and bear left down a slip road to the Market Yard Car Park (11). In front is the Black Swan Arts Centre (12) with craft workshops and across the car park is the Cheese and Grain (13) don't miss its regular stall markets, the revamped café or perhaps book a concert ticket.

At the river's edge follow the water's flow under the railway bridge and along the new Riverside Walk (14) to the weir and Welshmill Park (15) with its very popular cycle track. At the main road a quick excursion along the footpath opposite, still following the river, will bring you to the marshy field of Low Water (16) edged by a housing estate. Retrace your steps to the main road walk over the river bridge to the Welshmill Allotments (17). Ducking under the railway bridge keep heading left till the river is again reached and the Cheese and Grain glimpsed through the trees. Pieces of machinery – the Singers Artefacts (18), are all that remain of the Singers Factory on which the housing estate is built. The riverside path leads to the new Jenson Button Bridge (19) and a few steps further on to Château Gontier Walk (20). Pause on a bench or grassy bank to look at the names of Frome's French and German twinned towns immortalised in rubberised paint. Across the river is the Library with Frome's Tourist Information point (21).

But head into the Westway Precinct (22) crossing it and heading to the Zion Path (23) on the right-hand side of the Care Home. Quickly up this gloomy footpath and left past the United Reformed Church, noting that Thomas Bunn's Alcove Garden (24) lies behind the churchyard wall whilst in front was the proposed dropping off point for the Funicular Railway (25). A few steps more and you are on Catherine Hill (26), to your right is the Valentine Lamp (27), but check out the amazing range of independent shops as you saunter down the cobbled road, branching right onto the high pavement of Paul Street and into Palmer Street passing the shop windows of the present day Town Council Offices (28).

At the end of the road on the right-hand corner were the offices of the Frome Union (29).

Take a moment to cross the busy road to St John's Church passing the charming St John's Cottage **(30)** previous offices of the Town Council. Retracing your steps it's up the hill past the magnificent Rook Lane Chapel **(31)** popping in to see an art exhibition or book a concert.

Right at the pub roundabout and along to the Memorial Theatre **(32)** to perhaps book a show. Opposite are the splendid "renaissance" Public Offices **(33)** crowned by Alderman Flatman's clock where the first Town Council had rooms (the Frome Union, the Frome Local Board and the Frome Urban District Council had previously had rooms here). To the side is one of a pair of pillars which was to be the start of Thomas Bunn's, crescent of fine town houses – Golden Knoll. It is a short walk up Park Road past the empty Victoria Hospital **(34)** to the Mary Bailey Playing Field **(35)** and the children's playground with skateboard and cycle ramps, the narrow footpath decorated with a mural leads to Victoria Park **(36)**. A diagonal stroll across the Park ends at the Rabka Rock Garden **(37)** in honour of the town's Polish third twinned town.

Round off the morning with a coffee and a snack in the Park café, or take a picnic, or indulge in a game of tennis, boule, bowls or putting.

THE END

Frome Town Walk - the sights in a morning

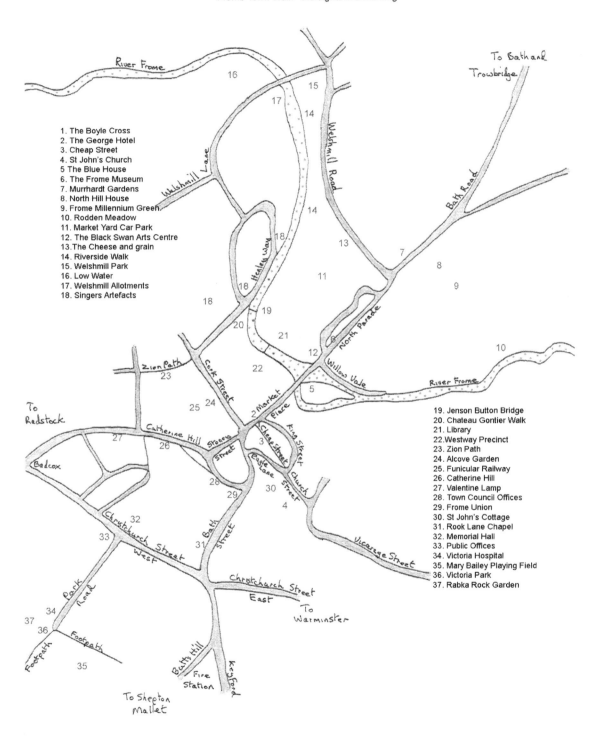

1. The Boyle Cross
2. The George Hotel
3. Cheap Street
4. St John's Church
5 The Blue House
6. The Frome Museum
7. Murrhardt Gardens
8. North Hill House
9. Frome Millennium Green
10. Rodden Meadow
11. Market Yard Car Park
12. The Black Swan Arts Centre
13.The Cheese and grain
14. Riverside Walk
15. Welshmill Park
16. Low Water
17. Welshmill Allotments
18. Singers Artefacts

19. Jenson Button Bridge
20. Chateau Gontier Walk
21. Library
22.Westway Precinct
23. Zion Path
24. Alcove Garden
25. Funicular Railway
26. Catherine Hill
27. Valentine Lamp
28. Town Council Offices
29. Frome Union
30. St John's Cottage
31. Rook Lane Chapel
32. Memorial Hall
33. Public Offices
34. Victoria Hospital
35. Mary Bailey Playing Field
36. Victoria Park
37. Rabka Rock Garden

Index

General Reserves 194,196,198,199,205, 211
Heritage Lottery Fund 207,319
Income 193-95,198
Internal Audit 202
Loans 204
Making the Decisions 231
Matters Arising 226
Mayor & Deputy 28,32,33,34,55,57,58,71, 72,85,235,244
Minutes 223-25,272
Office for National Statistics 220
Outside Body(ies) 32,55,63-88
Parish Council Audits 199
Parish Meetings 23,28,186-87,249,280
Parish Publication Scheme 29,199,208, 216,260,280-2
Personal and Prejudicial Interests 40,41
Parish Forum 209,220
Parish Poll 30,117,187-90,
Petition 134,171,225,242-3,251-55
Planning Principles 166,248
Points of Order 232
Power of Competence 32,117,165,194, 210,233,236,244,249,275,343
Power of Well-Being 86,165,193-4,210, 233,235-36,249,261,291,
Precept 79,194-7 203,205, 206-7
Predetermination 244
Proactive Councillor 29
Prohibition Order 200
Public /Open Forum 29, 52,53,91,136,225
Public Interest Report 25,200
Quality Parish and Town Council Scheme 27,217,239-41,243,269,270,280,317
Regeneration 95
Register of Interests 41-3,240,268,300, 310
Remembrance Sunday 33
Reports 226,234,277,285
Reserves 195,199,202,207,209
Revenue Expenditure 194
Review 252
Roll Call 225
Seven Principles of Public Life 39,43
Special Rate Precept 59
Special Expenses Rate 80,197,305,320
Standards Boards/Committee 39,41,43, 44,233,235,244
Standing Committee 55,294
Standing / Financial Orders 53,55,216, 226,283
Statements of the Accounts 203
Street Cleaning 206
Street Lighting 206
Surveys 239
Sustainable Development 242,244
The Agenda 223-4
The Discussion 230
The Meeting 224,229,272
The Opening 229
The Paperwork 223
The Third Sector 241
Value for Money 193,199,200,207
Volunteering 69
Voting 231
Wednesbury Unreasonableness 237,249
What do Parish Councillors Think 88

Council People :
Apprentices 218
Chief Executive Officer 92,137,219,275, 296
Conservation Officer 143
Consultants 218
Elections Officer 291,301,303
Parish Clerk 203,207,215-7,220-1,227
Parish Lengthsman 218
Planning Officer 127,149
Presiding Officer 311
Responsible Finance Officer 203,215,220, 227
Returning Officer/Acting Returning Officer 189,299,300,308
Town Centre Manager 219,220-1
Ward Councillor 128,131,170
Youth Ambassador Scheme 290

History:
Assembly Rooms 20,100,108
Board of Guardians 18,19
Boards of Health 19
Bussman Cooper 176
Butler & Tanner 66,93
Catherine Hill Mediaeval Fayre 342
Charter Markets 17,32,93,291,321,322
Coat of Arms 34,37,271,331
Cockey Lamps 140,159,189,278,290
Coloroll/Elworthy Park 100,178
Community Charge 196
Cottage Hospital 19,106
County Records Office 223
Domesday 17
Emigration 106
Feather Factory 101
Frome is a Wonderful Place 329
Frome Literary & Scientific Institution 67,106
Frome Market Company 20,65
Frome Riots 309
Frome Rural District Council 19,21
Frome Town Trust 335,336
Frome Urban District Council 19,20,125 59,65,100,101,125,335,345,346
Frome Water Works 19,100,101
Funicular Railway 318-9,345
Fussell Iron Works 66
Golden Knoll 204,346
Gypsy Lane Flying Ground 21-2
Hungerfords 271
Justices of the Peace 18
Market Hall 20,65,325,326,337
Mendip Lodge Hotel 91,316
Memorial Hall 20,22
Napoleonic Wars 18
Notts Industries 339
Officers of the Vestry 17,52
Parish/Poor Rate 18,52,107,123
Parish Vestry 17
Poll Tax 93,196
Poor Law Commissioner's Report (1834) 123
Poor Law Union 18,19
Public Offices 18,19,21,346
Rural Sanitary Authorities 123
Singers 80,176,177,178,345
Society of the Friends of the Poor 123
St Aldhlem 11,271
Task Force 91
Thorpe Report (1969) 124

Quarter Sessions 18
Victoria (Swimming) Baths 19,20,106
Victoria Hospital 85,102,346
Walwin Gemtleman's Outfitters 22
Warmer Frome Scheme 107,205,206

Local authority areas:
Bath & North East Somerset 47,253,257, 260,303
Dorset South 26
Electoral Wards: Frome North Frome South 32,313
Frome Wards: Keyford, College, Berkley Down, Fromefield, Park, Oakfield, Market, Welshmill 78,87,91,112,145,255,303,313, 314,
Lambeth Council 148
Liverpool Council 148
Mendip 8,13,16
Sedgemoor 13,16,81
Selwood (Frome)19,32
Somerset 8,13,16
Somerton and Frome13,22,26,27,48,49,259,260,312, 313
South Somerset 13,25,47,176,259,267, 304
Swindon South 27
Taunton Deane 13,16,81
Wansdyke 21
West Somerset 13,16,81
Wilts Unitary Authority 45,47,262,300

Members of Parliament:
Members of Parliament Allowances 47
Parliamentary Allowances 48
Winding –up Allowances 49
Resettlement Grant 49
Member of Parliament 135,214
Independent Parliamentary Standards Authority 214

Money:
Car Parking Charges 321
Charities 104,105
Community Interest Company 94,103,104, 254
Conservation Area Grants 205-6
Consumer Price Index 214
County Councillor's Community Budget 96,98
County Councillor's Local Initiative Budget 96,98
Defined Benefit Scheme 213
Defined contribution Scheme 213
East Mendip Community Partnership Budget 94
Europe for Citizens Funding 333
Frome Area Regeneration Fund/Programme 87,94,100
Heritage Lottery Fund 207,319
Local Government Pension Scheme 213
Retail Price Index 214
Mendip Road Safety Improvement Programme 96
Millennium Lottery 319
Parish Remuneration Panel 45
Public Works Loan Board 22, 65,204,209
Somerset Aggregate Levy Fund 60,81,99
Somerset Community Chest 96,98

Towns and Villages:

Made in the USA
Charleston, SC
12 June 2015